FODOR'S BED & BREAKFASTS AND COUNTRY INNS

D0838735

The Pacific Northwest's Best Bed & Breakfasts

2nd Edition

Delightful Places to Stay and Great Things to Do When You Get There

Fodor's Travel Publications, Inc.
New York • Toronto • London • Sydney • Auckland

The Pacific Northwest's Best Bed & Breakfasts

Editors: Robert I. C. Fisher, Jillian L. Magalaner, Anastasia Mills
Contributors: Robert Blake, Susan English, Tom Gauntt, Jeff Kuechle, Dawn Lawson, Melissa Rivers, Greg Smiley
Creative Director: Fabrizio La Rocca
Cartographer: David Lindroth
Illustrators: Alida Beck, Karl Tanner
Cover Design: Guido Caroti
Cover Photograph: Eberhard Brunner/Photographers/Aspen

Special Sales

Contributors

Susan English, who lives in Spokane, Washington, contributed to the chapters on central and eastern Oregon and Spokane and environs. She also updated the Spokane and environs, Cascade Mountains, and The Palouse chapters. Editor of the entertainment and travel sections of Spokane's daily newspaper, the *Spokesman-Review,* Ms. English has published numerous articles on the Northwest in guidebooks and magazines.

Tom Gauntt, who wrote the chapter on central and eastern Oregon and wrote and revised the north Oregon coast and Columbia River Gorge and Mt. Hood chapters, lives in Portland, Oregon. He is managing editor of Portland's *Business Journal* and has written for *Emmy, Ford Times, Advertising Age,* and *Omni.*

Jeff Kuechle, who lives in Portland, Oregon, wrote and revised the chapters on Portland and the Oregon wine country and updated the Olympic Peninsula and Seattle and environs chapters. He is a frequent contributor to Fodor's publications, and his work has also appeared in *Advertising Age, Ford Times,* and *Emmy.* He recently completed his first novel, *Sholto the Slayer.*

Melissa Rivers lives near Portland, Oregon, and wrote and revised the Willamette Valley, southern Oregon, south Oregon coast, and the four British Columbia chapters; she also updated the chapters on Washington's Whidbey Island, San Juan Islands, and Whatcom and Skagit counties. She has contributed to many travel guides, including the *Wall Street Journal Guide to Business Travel: Pacific Rim* and *Hidden Pacific Northwest.*

Greg Smiley revised the chapters on central and eastern Oregon and Washington's Columbia River and Long Beach Peninsula. He lives in Grants Pass, Oregon, where he is a reporter for the *Daily Courier* covering city government and business issues.

Loralee Wenger, who wrote seven of the nine Washington chapters, lives in Seattle. She has written for *Glamour* and *Parade* and for the *Washington Post, San Francisco Examiner,* and other newspapers. She contributed to Fodor's *Pacific North Coast* and *USA* guides.

Maria Zacharias lives in Spokane and wrote the Spokane and environs chapter. Formerly with ABC News and Time-Life Books, she has a Spokane-based editing and consulting business.

Contents

Foreword

While every care has been taken to ensure the accuracy of the information in this guide, the passage of time will always bring change, and, consequently, the publisher cannot accept responsibility for errors that may occur.

All prices and listings are based on information available to us at press time. Details may change, however, and the prudent traveler will avoid inconvenience by calling ahead.

Fodor's wants to hear about your travel experiences, both pleasant and unpleasant. When an inn or B&B fails to live up to its billing, let us know and we will investigate the complaint and revise our entries where the facts warrant it.

Send your letters to the editors of Fodor's Travel Publications, 201 East 50th Street, New York, NY 10022.

Introduction

You'll find bed-and-breakfasts in big houses with turrets and little houses with decks, in mansions by the water and cabins in the forest, not to mention structures of many sizes and shapes in between. B&Bs are run by people who were once lawyers and writers, homemakers and artists, nurses and architects, singers and businesspeople. Some B&Bs are just a room or two in a hospitable local's home; others are more like small inns. So there's an element of serendipity to every B&B stay.

But while that's part of the pleasure of the experience, it's also an excellent reason to plan your travels with a good B&B guide. The one you hold in your hands serves the purpose neatly.

To create it, we've handpicked a team of professional writers who are also confirmed B&B lovers: people who adore the many manifestations of the Victorian era; who go wild over wicker and brass beds, four-posters and fireplaces; and who know a well-run operation when they see it and are only too eager to communicate their knowledge to you. We've instructed them to inspect the premises and check out every corner of the premier inns and B&Bs in the areas they cover, and to report critically on only the best in every price range.

They've returned from their travels with comprehensive reports on the pleasure of B&B travel, which may well become your pleasure as you read their reviews in the pages that follow. These are establishments that promise a unique experience, a distinctive sense of time and place. All are destinations in themselves, not just spots to rest your head at night, but an integral part of a weekend escape. You'll learn what's good, what's bad, and what could be better; what our writers liked and what you might not like.

Fodor's reviewers also tell you what's up in the area and what you should and shouldn't miss—everything from historic sites and parks to antiques shops, boutiques, and the area's niftiest restaurants and nightspots. We also include names, addresses, and phone numbers of B&B reservation services, just in case you're inspired to seek out additional properties on your own. Reviews are organized by state or province and then by area.

In the italicized service information that ends every review, a double room is for two people, regardless of the size or type of its beds. Unless otherwise noted, rooms don't have phones or TVs. Note that even the most stunning homes, farmhouses and mansions alike, may not have a private bathroom in each room. Rates are for two, excluding tax, in the high season and include breakfast unless otherwise noted; ask about special packages and midweek or off-season discounts. What we call a restaurant serves meals other than breakfast and is usually open to the general public.

Where applicable, we note seasonal and other restrictions. Although we abhor discrimination, we have conveyed information about innkeepers' restrictive practices so that you will be aware of the prevailing attitudes. Such discriminatory practices are most often applied to parents who are traveling with small children and who may not, in any case, feel comfortable having their offspring toddle amid breakable bric-a-brac and near precipitous stairways.

When traveling the B&B way, always call ahead; and if you have mobility problems or are traveling with children, if you prefer a private bath or a certain type of bed, or if you have specific dietary needs or any other concerns, discuss them with the innkeeper. At the same time, if you're traveling to an inn because of a specific feature, make sure that it will be available when you get there and not closed for renovation. The same goes if you're making a detour to take advantage of specific sights or attractions.

It's a sad commentary on other B&B guides today that we feel obliged to tell you that our writers did, in fact, visit every property in person, and that it is they, not the innkeepers, who wrote the reviews. No one paid a fee or promised to sell or promote the book in order to be included in it. (In fact, one of the most challenging parts of the work of a Fodor's writer is to persuade innkeepers and B&B owners that he or she wants nothing more than a tour of the premises and the answers to a few questions!) Fodor's has no stake in anything but the truth. If a room is dark, with peeling wallpaper, we don't call it quaint or atmospheric—we call it run-down, and then steer you to a more appealing section of the property.

So trust us, the way you'd trust a knowledgeable, well-traveled friend. Let us hear from you about your travels, whether you found that the B&Bs you visited surpassed their descriptions or the other way around. And have a wonderful trip!

Karen Cure
Editorial Director

The Pacific Northwest

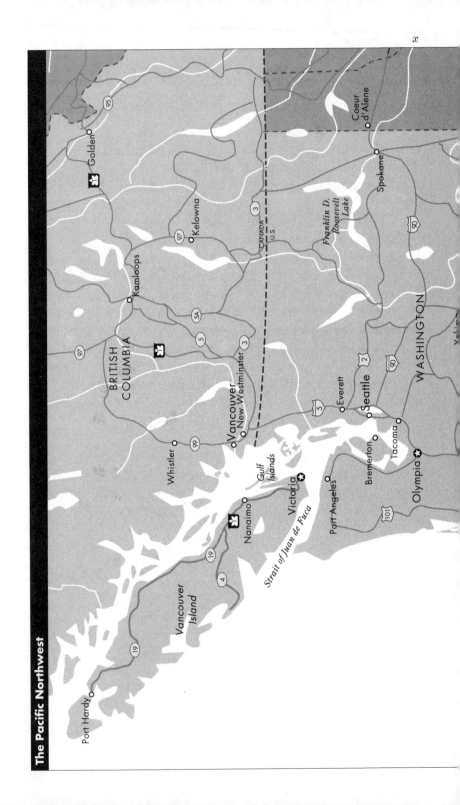

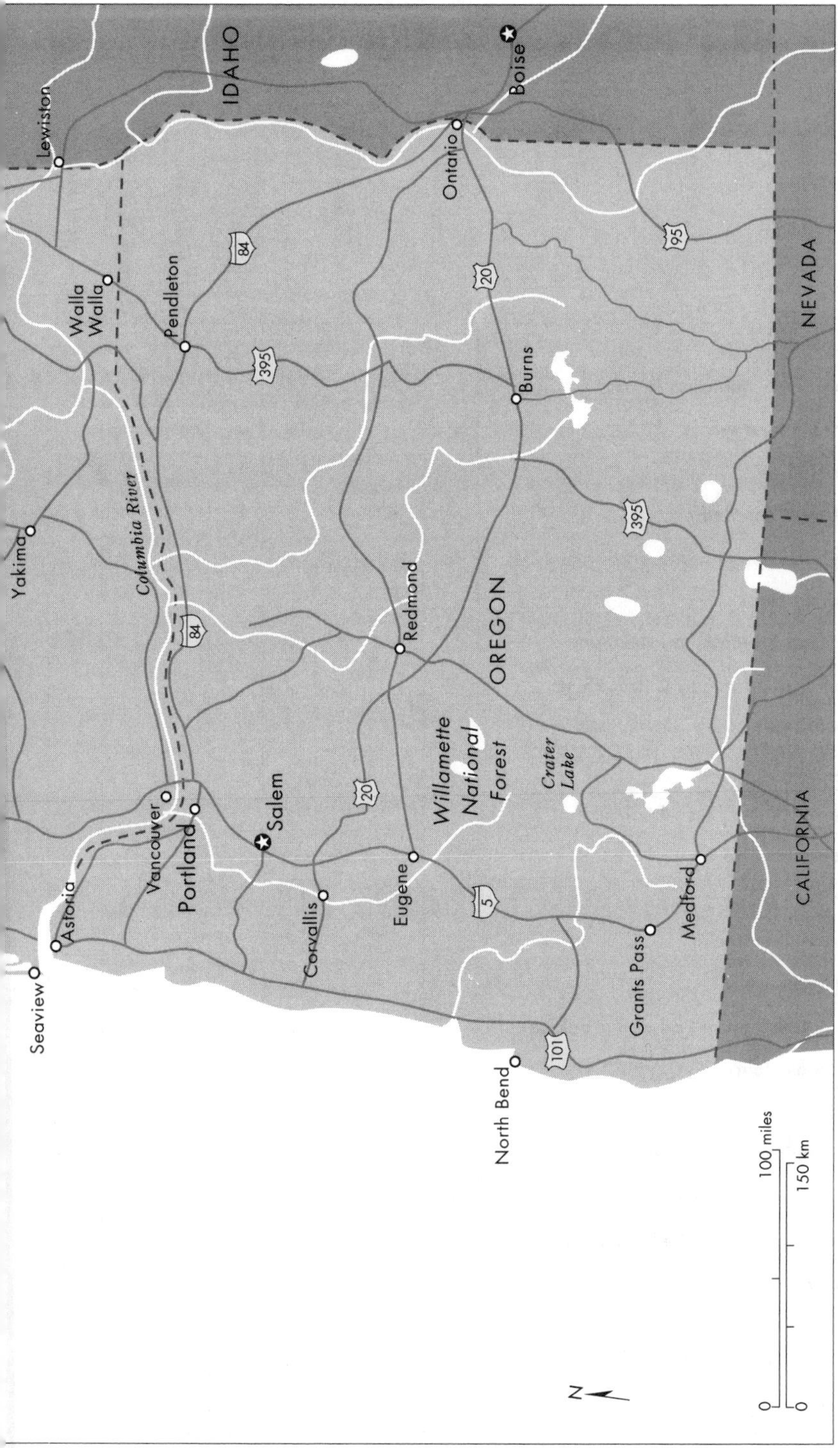

Seaview
Astoria
Vancouver
Portland
Salem
Corvallis
Eugene
Grants Pass
Medford
North Bend

OREGON

Willamette
National
Forest

Crater
Lake

CALIFORNIA

NEVADA

IDAHO

Lewiston
Walla Walla
Pendleton
Yakima
Ontario
Boise
Burns
Redmond

Columbia River

101
5
20
84
395
395
95
20
84

100 miles
150 km

N

Special Features at a Glance

Name of Property	Accessible to Guests with Disabilities	Antiques	On the Water	Good Value	Car Not Necessary	Full Meal Service	Historic Building	Romantic Hideaway	
OREGON									
Anderson's Boarding House		✓	✓		✓		✓		
Arden Forest Inn	✓			✓	✓				
Astoria Inn				✓			✓	✓	
Auberge des Fleurs		✓					✓		
Bayberry Inn Bed and Breakfast				✓		✓			
Beckley House		✓					✓		
Bed and Breakfast by the River			✓	✓					
Birch Leaf Farm Bed & Breakfast		✓	✓	✓			✓		
Bridal Veil Lodge		✓		✓			✓	✓	
Chamberlin House		✓							
Chandlers Bed, Bread & Trail Inn				✓					
Channel House			✓					✓	
Chanticleer Inn		✓			✓			✓	
Chetco River Inn			✓	✓		✓			
Chriswood Inn				✓					
Clear Creek Farm Bed and Breakfast				✓				✓	
Clemens House		✓		✓					
Cliff House		✓	✓				✓	✓	
The Clinkerbrick House		✓		✓	✓				
Columbia Gorge Hotel	✓	✓	✓			✓	✓	✓	
Columbia River Inn Bed and Breakfast		✓					✓		
Coos Bay Manor		✓		✓			✓		
Country Willows Bed and Breakfast Inn			✓	✓				✓	
Duckworth		✓		✓					
Elliott House		✓		✓			✓	✓	

Luxurious	Pets Allowed	No Smoking Indoors	Good Place for Families	Beach Nearby	Cross-Country Ski Trails	Golf Within 5 Miles	Fitness Facilities	Near Wineries	Good Biking Terrain	Skiing	Tennis	Swimming on Premises	Conference Facilities	Hiking Nearby
		✓	✓	✓		✓			✓					✓
		✓	✓			✓		✓	✓					✓
		✓				✓			✓					✓
✓		✓			✓	✓		✓		✓			✓	✓
		✓				✓			✓	✓				✓
		✓				✓			✓					✓
		✓	✓		✓				✓					✓
		✓	✓		✓				✓	✓				✓
		✓	✓											
		✓												✓
		✓	✓		✓				✓	✓				✓
				✓		✓			✓					✓
✓		✓		✓					✓	✓			✓	✓
		✓	✓	✓	✓								✓	
		✓				✓			✓				✓	
		✓	✓		✓				✓	✓				✓
		✓				✓		✓	✓					✓
✓		✓		✓		✓			✓					
		✓	✓			✓			✓					
✓	✓	✓				✓			✓				✓	✓
		✓	✓		✓	✓			✓					✓
	✓	✓							✓					✓
		✓				✓						✓	✓	✓
		✓				✓		✓	✓					✓
✓		✓				✓			✓					✓

Special Features at a Glance

Name of Property	Accessible to Guests with Disabilities	Antiques	On the Water	Good Value	Car Not Necessary	Full Meal Service	Historic Building	Romantic Hideaway	
Farewell Bend Bed & Breakfast								✓	
Floras Lake House by the Sea	✓		✓					✓	
Flying M Ranch			✓			✓			
Franklin St. Station		✓					✓		
Frenchglen Hotel				✓		✓	✓		
General Hooker's B&B							✓	✓	
The Georgian House		✓		✓					
Gilbert Inn		✓		✓			✓	✓	
Grandview Bed & Breakfast				✓			✓		
Hackett House				✓					
Hanson Country Inn		✓		✓			✓	✓	
Heather House Bed and Breakfast		✓		✓					
Heron Haus		✓			✓		✓	✓	
The Highlands		✓		✓					
Home by the Sea			✓	✓					
Hood River Hotel	✓					✓	✓		
House of Hunter		✓		✓					
Hudson House		✓		✓			✓		
Inn at Manzanita								✓	
Jacksonville Inn		✓				✓	✓	✓	
The Johnson House	✓	✓	✓						
K.C.'s Mansion By-the-Sea		✓	✓	✓			✓	✓	
Kelty Estate				✓			✓		
Lakecliff Estate Bed & Breakfast		✓	✓	✓			✓	✓	
Lara House		✓						✓	
The Lighthouse			✓						

Luxurious	Pets Allowed	No Smoking Indoors	Good Place for Families	Beach Nearby	Cross-Country Ski Trails	Golf Within 5 Miles	Fitness Facilities	Near Wineries	Good Biking Terrain	Skiing	Tennis	Swimming on Premises	Conference Facilities	Hiking Nearby
		✓	✓		✓	✓			✓	✓				✓
		✓	✓	✓					✓					
	✓	✓	✓		✓			✓	✓		✓	✓	✓	✓
		✓	✓			✓			✓					✓
		✓							✓					✓
		✓		✓		✓	✓		✓					
		✓				✓			✓					
✓		✓		✓		✓			✓				✓	✓
		✓	✓			✓			✓					✓
		✓	✓			✓				✓			✓	✓
		✓	✓			✓		✓						✓
		✓		✓		✓			✓					
✓		✓				✓			✓			✓		✓
		✓		✓										✓
		✓		✓					✓					✓
		✓				✓				✓			✓	✓
		✓				✓		✓						✓
✓			✓	✓					✓					✓
		✓	✓			✓			✓					✓
	✓	✓						✓				✓	✓	
		✓		✓	✓	✓			✓					✓
✓		✓				✓			✓					✓
		✓				✓		✓	✓					
✓		✓						✓						✓
		✓	✓				✓		✓	✓				✓
		✓	✓	✓		✓			✓					✓

Special Features at a Glance

Name of Property	Accessible to Guests with Disabilities	Antiques	On the Water	Good Value	Car Not Necessary	Full Meal Service	Historic Building	Romantic Hideaway
The Lion and the Rose		✓			✓		✓	✓
MacMaster House					✓		✓	✓
Main Street Bed & Breakfast				✓				
Mattey House		✓					✓	✓
McGillivray's Log Home Bed and Breakfast	✓							
McMenamin's Edgefield	✓					✓	✓	✓
Morical House		✓			✓			
Mountain Shadows Bed & Breakfast				✓				✓
Mt. Ashland Inn								
Odell Lake Lodge & Resort	✓		✓			✓		✓
Old Stage Inn	✓	✓						✓
Old Welches Inn		✓	✓	✓			✓	✓
Orchard View Inn	✓	✓						
The Oval Door Bed and Breakfast		✓		✓	✓			
Paradise-by-the-Sea Bed & Breakfast		✓	✓	✓				✓
The Partridge Farm		✓		✓			✓	✓
Pine Valley Lodge and Halfway Supper Club		✓		✓		✓		
Portland Guest House		✓		✓	✓			✓
Portland's White House		✓			✓		✓	✓
River Banks Inn				✓				
RiverPlace Hotel	✓		✓		✓	✓		✓
River's Reach Bed and Breakfast	✓							
Romeo Inn	✓							
Sandlake Country Inn	✓	✓					✓	✓
Sea Quest		✓	✓					✓
Sea Star Guest House			✓			✓		✓

Luxurious	Pets Allowed	No Smoking Indoors	Good Place for Families	Beach Nearby	Cross-Country Ski Trails	Golf Within 5 Miles	Fitness Facilities	Near Wineries	Good Biking Terrain	Skiing	Tennis	Swimming on Premises	Conference Facilities	Hiking Nearby
✓		✓	✓			✓		✓	✓					✓
		✓				✓			✓					✓
		✓						✓	✓					
✓		✓				✓		✓	✓					
		✓						✓	✓					
		✓	✓	✓		✓			✓				✓	✓
		✓				✓		✓	✓					✓
	✓	✓	✓		✓	✓			✓	✓				✓
		✓	✓		✓				✓	✓			✓	✓
	✓			✓	✓	✓			✓	✓		✓		✓
✓		✓							✓				✓	✓
	✓	✓	✓		✓	✓			✓	✓				✓
		✓			✓			✓	✓					✓
		✓	✓						✓					✓
		✓	✓	✓		✓								✓
✓	✓	✓						✓	✓					
	✓	✓			✓				✓					✓
✓		✓				✓	✓		✓			✓		
✓		✓	✓			✓			✓				✓	
		✓						✓						✓
✓				✓		✓	✓		✓				✓	
	✓	✓	✓			✓			✓			✓		✓
		✓				✓		✓	✓			✓		
✓		✓		✓		✓			✓					✓
		✓		✓					✓				✓	
		✓		✓					✓					

Special Features at a Glance

Name of Property	Accessible to Guests with Disabilities	Antiques	On the Water	Good Value	Car Not Necessary	Full Meal Service	Historic Building	Romantic Hideaway
Shaniko Hotel				✓		✓	✓	
Sonka's Sheep Station Inn		✓						
Springbrook Hazelnut Farm		✓					✓	✓
Stange Manor	✓	✓					✓	
State House								
State Street Bed & Breakfast				✓				
Steamboat Inn	✓		✓			✓		✓
Steiger Haus		✓		✓				
Sylvia Beach Hotel	✓	✓	✓	✓		✓	✓	✓
Touvelle House		✓			✓		✓	
Tu Tu Tun Lodge	✓		✓			✓		✓
Westfir Lodge		✓		✓		✓	✓	
Whiskey Creek Bed & Breakfast	✓	✓	✓	✓			✓	
Williams House		✓		✓			✓	
Willowbrook Inn Bed and Breakfast								
The Winchester Country Inn		✓				✓	✓	
Wolf Creek Tavern		✓				✓	✓	
Woods House					✓			
Youngberg Hill Farm	✓					✓		✓
Ziggurat			✓	✓				✓
WASHINGTON (including Idaho)								
Albatross				✓	✓			
Alexander's Country Inn	✓	✓				✓	✓	✓
All Seasons River Inn Bed & Breakfast		✓	✓					✓
Anchorage Inn				✓				

Luxurious	Pets Allowed	No Smoking Indoors	Good Place for Families	Beach Nearby	Cross-Country Ski Trails	Golf Within 5 Miles	Fitness Facilities	Near Wineries	Good Biking Terrain	Skiing	Tennis	Swimming on Premises	Conference Facilities	Hiking Nearby
		✓	✓											
		✓	✓					✓	✓					✓
✓		✓				✓		✓	✓		✓	✓	✓	
			✓		✓	✓			✓	✓				✓
		✓	✓					✓						
	✓	✓				✓								✓
	✓	✓	✓						✓			✓	✓	✓
		✓	✓			✓		✓	✓				✓	
		✓		✓		✓			✓				✓	✓
		✓			✓	✓		✓	✓	✓			✓	✓
			✓	✓		✓						✓	✓	✓
		✓			✓	✓			✓	✓				
	✓	✓	✓	✓					✓					✓
		✓	✓			✓			✓					✓
			✓		✓	✓			✓			✓		
		✓	✓			✓		✓	✓				✓	
	✓	✓											✓	
		✓	✓			✓		✓	✓					✓
✓		✓	✓			✓		✓	✓			✓	✓	✓
✓		✓			✓				✓					✓
	✓	✓	✓	✓					✓					✓
		✓			✓					✓				✓
✓		✓			✓	✓			✓	✓		✓		✓
		✓			✓				✓		✓			✓

Special Features at a Glance

Name of Property	Accessible to Guests with Disabilities	Antiques	On the Water	Good Value	Car Not Necessary	Full Meal Service	Historic Building	Romantic Hideaway
Anderson Creek Lodge	✓							
Anderson House		✓		✓			✓	
Ann Starrett Mansion		✓					✓	✓
Bacon Mansion/Broadway Guest House		✓					✓	✓
Blackwell House		✓			✓		✓	
Blair House		✓					✓	
Bombay House		✓					✓	✓
Boreas Bed and Breakfast			✓	✓				✓
Captain Whidbey Inn		✓	✓				✓	
Cashmere Country Inn		✓					✓	✓
The Chambered Nautilus		✓					✓	✓
The Channel House		✓		✓			✓	✓
Chez Nous							✓	✓
Clark House on Hayden Lake	✓		✓				✓	✓
Cliff House and Sea Cliff Cottage			✓					✓
Coast Watch Bed & Breakfast			✓					✓
Colonel Crockett Farm		✓	✓				✓	✓
Country Cottage of Langley		✓						✓
Country Keeper Bed & Breakfast Inn		✓	✓					✓
Cricket on the Hearth Bed & Breakfast Inn				✓				
Deer Harbor Inn				✓			✓	✓
Domaine Madeleine			✓					✓
Downey House	✓	✓					✓	✓
The Duffy House	✓	✓	✓					
Eagles Nest Inn	✓							✓
Edenwild Inn	✓	✓			✓			✓

Luxurious	Pets Allowed	No Smoking Indoors	Good Place for Families	Beach Nearby	Cross-Country Ski Trails	Golf Within 5 Miles	Fitness Facilities	Near Wineries	Good Biking Terrain	Skiing	Tennis	Swimming on Premises	Conference Facilities	Hiking Nearby
		✓	✓						✓				✓	✓
		✓				✓			✓					✓
✓		✓		✓		✓			✓		✓			
✓		✓	✓											
				✓		✓								✓
		✓	✓			✓			✓			✓		
		✓		✓		✓			✓		✓		✓	
		✓	✓	✓		✓			✓					✓
				✓					✓		✓		✓	
		✓			✓				✓	✓		✓		✓
		✓		✓		✓			✓					
✓		✓		✓		✓			✓					
		✓	✓		✓	✓	✓		✓	✓		✓		✓
✓		✓	✓	✓		✓							✓	✓
✓		✓		✓				✓	✓					
		✓		✓		✓			✓					✓
		✓		✓				✓	✓					✓
✓		✓		✓		✓			✓					
		✓							✓					
		✓		✓		✓								✓
		✓		✓		✓			✓					✓
✓		✓		✓					✓					✓
✓		✓							✓					
		✓		✓		✓			✓					
		✓		✓		✓			✓					✓
✓		✓	✓	✓		✓			✓					✓

Special Features at a Glance

Name of Property	Accessible to Guests with Disabilities	Antiques	On the Water	Good Value	Car Not Necessary	Full Meal Service	Historic Building	Romantic Hideaway
Flying L Ranch								
Fort Casey Inn	✓	✓		✓			✓	✓
Fotheringham House		✓					✓	✓
Gallery Bed & Breakfast at Little Cape Horn			✓					✓
Gaslight Inn		✓			✓		✓	✓
Green Gables Inn		✓					✓	✓
Gregory's McFarland House		✓					✓	✓
Guest House Cottages		✓	✓					✓
Gumm's Bed & Breakfast		✓					✓	
Hasty Pudding House		✓		✓				
Heather House		✓						
Heritage House	✓	✓					✓	✓
Heron Inn		✓						✓
Hillside House		✓		✓	✓			✓
Home by the Sea Bed & Breakfast and Cottages		✓	✓					✓
Hotel Planter							✓	
Hous Rohrbach Pensione								
Inn at Ilwaco		✓					✓	✓
Inn at Langley	✓		✓					✓
The Inn at the Market	✓		✓		✓	✓		✓
Inn at Penn Cove		✓					✓	
Inn at Swifts Bay		✓		✓	✓			✓
Inn at White Salmon		✓					✓	
James House		✓					✓	✓
Kangaroo House		✓					✓	
Kola House Bed & Breakfast				✓			✓	

Luxurious	Pets Allowed	No Smoking Indoors	Good Place for Families	Beach Nearby	Cross-Country Ski Trails	Golf Within 5 Miles	Fitness Facilities	Near Wineries	Good Biking Terrain	Skiing	Tennis	Swimming on Premises	Conference Facilities	Hiking Nearby
	✓	✓	✓		✓				✓					✓
		✓	✓	✓					✓				✓	✓
		✓				✓					✓			
	✓	✓	✓	✓					✓					
✓		✓				✓			✓			✓		
✓		✓				✓		✓	✓	✓				
✓		✓		✓		✓			✓					✓
		✓	✓	✓			✓	✓	✓			✓		
		✓	✓	✓		✓			✓					✓
		✓	✓	✓		✓			✓					
		✓				✓			✓					✓
✓		✓		✓		✓			✓		✓			
		✓				✓			✓					
		✓		✓		✓			✓					
	✓	✓	✓	✓		✓			✓					✓
		✓		✓		✓			✓					
		✓	✓		✓	✓			✓	✓		✓		✓
		✓				✓			✓					✓
✓		✓		✓		✓			✓				✓	✓
✓						✓	✓				✓		✓	
		✓	✓	✓										
✓		✓		✓		✓			✓					✓
	✓		✓			✓			✓					✓
✓		✓		✓		✓			✓		✓			
		✓		✓		✓			✓					
			✓	✓		✓		✓	✓					✓

Special Features at a Glance

Name of Property	Accessible to Guests with Disabilities	Antiques	On the Water	Good Value	Car Not Necessary	Full Meal Service	Historic Building	Romantic Hideaway
La Conner Channel Lodge	✓		✓					✓
Lake Crescent Lodge	✓	✓	✓			✓	✓	✓
Lake Quinault Lodge		✓	✓			✓	✓	✓
Land's End		✓	✓					✓
Lizzie's Victorian Bed & Breakfast		✓					✓	✓
Log Castle Bed & Breakfast		✓	✓					✓
Lone Lake Cottage and Breakfast			✓					✓
Love's Victorian Bed and Breakfast		✓						✓
MacKaye Harbor Inn		✓	✓				✓	
Majestic Hotel	✓	✓				✓	✓	✓
The Manor Farm Inn		✓				✓	✓	✓
Maple Valley Bed & Breakfast		✓						✓
Marianna Stoltz House				✓			✓	
Mariella Inn & Cottages		✓	✓		✓		✓	✓
Mazama Country Inn	✓					✓		
Mio Amore Pensione		✓	✓			✓	✓	✓
Moby Dick Hotel and Oyster Farm							✓	
The Moon and Sixpence		✓					✓	✓
Moore House Bed & Breakfast		✓					✓	✓
Mountain Home Lodge		✓				✓		✓
Mountain Meadows Inn		✓					✓	✓
M. V. Challenger			✓		✓			✓
My Parents' Estate							✓	
Old Consulate Inn		✓					✓	✓
Old Honey Farm Country Inn	✓							✓
Old Trout Inn			✓	✓	✓			✓

Luxurious	Pets Allowed	No Smoking Indoors	Good Place for Families	Beach Nearby	Cross-Country Ski Trails	Golf Within 5 Miles	Fitness Facilities	Near Wineries	Good Biking Terrain	Skiing	Tennis	Swimming on Premises	Conference Facilities	Hiking Nearby
✓		✓	✓	✓		✓			✓					
	✓		✓	✓	✓							✓		✓
		✓	✓	✓				✓	✓		✓	✓	✓	✓
✓		✓	✓			✓			✓					✓
		✓	✓			✓	✓		✓		✓			
		✓	✓			✓			✓					✓
		✓	✓						✓		✓			
	✓	✓			✓				✓					✓
		✓	✓						✓					
✓			✓	✓		✓			✓					✓
				✓					✓		✓			
		✓	✓			✓	✓		✓	✓				✓
		✓												
		✓	✓	✓		✓			✓			✓	✓	
		✓	✓	✓	✓				✓	✓				✓
	✓	✓				✓			✓	✓				✓
		✓	✓		✓				✓					✓
		✓				✓			✓					
		✓	✓		✓	✓			✓	✓				✓
		✓			✓	✓			✓	✓	✓	✓		✓
		✓				✓			✓	✓		✓		✓
		✓			✓	✓			✓					
		✓			✓	✓	✓		✓	✓				✓
✓		✓		✓		✓			✓			✓		✓
		✓	✓		✓	✓			✓	✓				✓
		✓		✓		✓			✓					

Special Features at a Glance

Name of Property	Accessible to Guests with Disabilities	Antiques	On the Water	Good Value	Car Not Necessary	Full Meal Service	Historic Building	Romantic Hideaway
Olympic Lights		✓		✓			✓	✓
Orcas Hotel		✓	✓		✓	✓	✓	✓
Orchard Hill Inn				✓				
The Portico		✓					✓	
The Purple House Bed and Breakfast		✓				✓	✓	
The Quimper Inn	✓	✓					✓	✓
Ravenscroft Inn		✓						✓
Ridgeway House		✓						
Roberta's Bed & Breakfast		✓			✓		✓	
Run of the River Inn			✓					✓
Salisbury House		✓					✓	✓
Salish Lodge	✓	✓	✓			✓	✓	✓
Sand Dollar Inn								
San Juan Inn		✓					✓	
Scandinavian Gardens Inn	✓			✓				✓
Schnauzer Crossing	✓		✓					✓
Shelburne Inn	✓	✓			✓	✓	✓	✓
Shumway Mansion		✓			✓		✓	✓
Silver Bay Lodging		✓	✓					✓
Sorrento Hotel	✓	✓			✓	✓	✓	✓
Sou'wester Lodge				✓			✓	✓
Spring Bay Inn			✓					✓
States Inn	✓							
Stone Creek Inn		✓					✓	✓
Sun Mountain Lodge	✓					✓		
Tudor Inn		✓					✓	✓

Luxurious	Pets Allowed	No Smoking Indoors	Good Place for Families	Beach Nearby	Cross-Country Ski Trails	Golf Within 5 Miles	Fitness Facilities	Near Wineries	Good Biking Terrain	Skiing	Tennis	Swimming on Premises	Conference Facilities	Hiking Nearby
		✓		✓		✓			✓					
✓		✓		✓		✓			✓				✓	
		✓			✓	✓			✓					✓
		✓				✓			✓					
✓	✓	✓			✓	✓		✓	✓	✓		✓		✓
✓		✓		✓		✓			✓		✓			
✓		✓		✓		✓	✓		✓		✓		✓	
		✓				✓			✓					
		✓				✓			✓		✓			
✓		✓			✓	✓			✓	✓				✓
✓		✓				✓			✓					
✓					✓	✓	✓		✓	✓			✓	✓
		✓		✓										✓
		✓				✓			✓					
✓		✓				✓		✓	✓					✓
✓	✓	✓				✓			✓					✓
		✓			✓	✓			✓					✓
✓		✓			✓	✓	✓		✓			✓		✓
✓		✓			✓				✓			✓		✓
✓						✓	✓					✓	✓	
	✓	✓	✓	✓		✓			✓					✓
		✓	✓	✓	✓				✓			✓		✓
		✓			✓				✓					✓
		✓				✓		✓	✓	✓				
				✓	✓	✓	✓		✓	✓	✓	✓	✓	✓
		✓			✓	✓	✓		✓	✓	✓			✓

Special Features at a Glance

Name of Property	Accessible to Guests with Disabilities	Antiques	On the Water	Good Value	Car Not Necessary	Full Meal Service	Historic Building	Romantic Hideaway	
Turtleback Farm Inn	✓	✓		✓			✓	✓	
Villa Heidelberg		✓		✓	✓		✓	✓	
Warwick Inn		✓			✓		✓	✓	
Waverly Place		✓		✓	✓		✓		
Wharfside Bed & Breakfast			✓		✓			✓	
Whidbey Inn		✓	✓						
White Swan Guest House		✓					✓	✓	
BRITISH COLUMBIA									
Abigail's		✓						✓	
The Aerie		✓				✓		✓	
April Point Lodge and Fishing Resort	✓		✓			✓			
Beach House Bed & Breakfast			✓					✓	
The Beaconsfield		✓					✓		
The Bedford	✓				✓	✓	✓	✓	
Borthwick Country Manor		✓		✓					
Carberry Gardens		✓		✓					
Carney's Cottage Bed and Breakfast				✓		✓			
Chalet Luise					✓				
Chesterman's Beach Bed and Breakfast			✓					✓	
Cliffside Inn			✓						
Corbett House									
Durlacher Hof	✓				✓			✓	
Edelweiss Pension					✓				
English Bay Inn		✓						✓	
Fernhill Lodge		✓						✓	

Luxurious	Pets Allowed	No Smoking Indoors	Good Place for Families	Beach Nearby	Cross-Country Ski Trails	Golf Within 5 Miles	Fitness Facilities	Near Wineries	Good Biking Terrain	Skiing	Tennis	Swimming on Premises	Conference Facilities	Hiking Nearby
		✓		✓		✓			✓					
		✓		✓		✓			✓		✓			
		✓		✓		✓								✓
		✓												
	✓	✓	✓	✓		✓			✓					
		✓	✓	✓					✓					✓
	✓	✓							✓					
✓				✓		✓			✓					
✓						✓	✓		✓		✓	✓	✓	✓
	✓		✓	✓		✓	✓		✓			✓	✓	✓
		✓		✓		✓			✓			✓		
✓		✓		✓		✓								
			✓	✓		✓							✓	
		✓	✓	✓		✓			✓					
		✓		✓		✓			✓					
		✓	✓		✓	✓			✓	✓				✓
		✓			✓	✓			✓	✓				✓
	✓	✓	✓	✓		✓			✓					✓
		✓		✓		✓			✓					✓
		✓				✓			✓					✓
		✓			✓	✓			✓	✓			✓	✓
		✓	✓		✓	✓			✓	✓				✓
✓		✓	✓	✓					✓					✓
		✓		✓					✓					✓

Special Features at a Glance

Name of Property	Accessible to Guests with Disabilities	Antiques	On the Water	Good Value	Car Not Necessary	Full Meal Service	Historic Building	Romantic Hideaway
Greystone Manor		✓		✓			✓	
Hastings House		✓	✓			✓		✓
Haterleigh Heritage House		✓			✓		✓	
Holland House Inn	✓				✓			
Joan Brown's Bed and Breakfast	✓	✓		✓			✓	✓
Johnson House		✓		✓				✓
Laburnum Cottage	✓	✓						✓
Lacarno Beach Bed & Breakfast			✓	✓				
Le Chamois	✓				✓	✓		✓
Malahat Farm Guest House		✓					✓	
Mulberry Manor		✓					✓	✓
Oak Bay Beach Hotel		✓	✓			✓		✓
Ocean Wilderness	✓	✓	✓			✓		✓
Oceanwood Country Inn		✓	✓			✓		✓
Old Farmhouse Bed and Breakfast					✓		✓	✓
Penny Farthing		✓		✓				
Pine Lodge Farm		✓		✓				
Prior House		✓					✓	
Sky Valley Place								✓
Sooke Harbour House	✓	✓	✓			✓		✓
Suitl Lodge			✓					
Swans	✓				✓	✓	✓	
Tsa-Kwa-Luten Lodge	✓		✓			✓		✓
Wedgewood Manor		✓					✓	✓
West End Guest House					✓		✓	✓
Weston Lake Inn								

Luxurious	Pets Allowed	No Smoking Indoors	Good Place for Families	Beach Nearby	Cross-Country Ski Trails	Golf Within 5 Miles	Fitness Facilities	Near Wineries	Good Biking Terrain	Skiing	Tennis	Swimming on Premises	Conference Facilities	Hiking Nearby
		✓		✓					✓					✓
✓				✓		✓			✓				✓	✓
		✓	✓	✓		✓			✓					
		✓		✓		✓			✓					
✓		✓		✓		✓			✓					
		✓				✓								
✓	✓	✓	✓	✓		✓			✓					✓
		✓		✓		✓			✓					✓
✓			✓		✓	✓	✓		✓	✓		✓	✓	✓
		✓		✓					✓					✓
✓		✓				✓			✓					✓
			✓	✓		✓			✓					✓
✓	✓	✓		✓					✓					✓
✓				✓					✓				✓	✓
		✓				✓			✓					
		✓	✓	✓		✓			✓					✓
		✓				✓			✓					✓
✓		✓	✓			✓			✓					
		✓				✓			✓			✓		
✓	✓	✓	✓	✓		✓			✓				✓	✓
		✓	✓	✓		✓			✓			✓		✓
			✓	✓		✓							✓	
			✓	✓		✓	✓		✓				✓	✓
✓	✓	✓		✓	✓				✓					✓
✓		✓		✓					✓					✓
		✓		✓		✓			✓					✓

Special Features at a Glance

Name of Property	Accessible to Guests with Disabilities	Antiques	On the Water	Good Value	Car Not Necessary	Full Meal Service	Historic Building	Romantic Hideaway	
Willow Point Lodge		✓					✓	✓	
Woodstone Country Inn	✓	✓							
Yellow Point Lodge	✓		✓	✓		✓		✓	

	Luxurious	Pets Allowed	No Smoking Indoors	Good Place for Families	Beach Nearby	Cross-Country Ski Trails	Golf Within 5 Miles	Fitness Facilities	Near Wineries	Good Biking Terrain	Skiing	Tennis	Swimming on Premises	Conference Facilities	Hiking Nearby
	✓		✓	✓	✓	✓				✓	✓			✓	✓
			✓				✓			✓					
				✓	✓					✓		✓	✓	✓	✓

Oregon

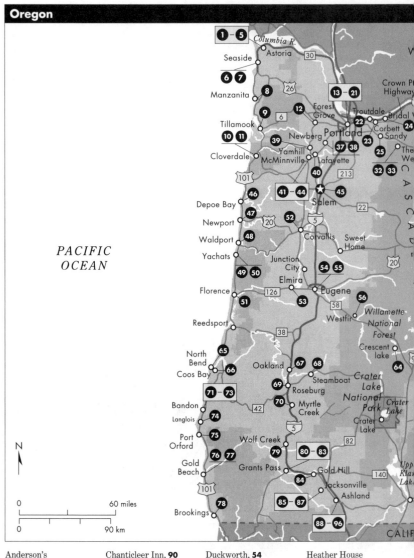

Oregon

PACIFIC
OCEAN

N

| 0 | | 60 miles |
| 0 | | 90 km |

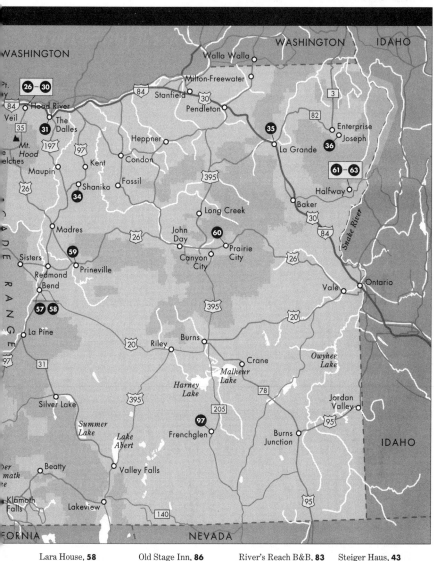

South Coast

Thanks to the foresight of the state legislature, Oregon's nearly 300-mile coastline is preserved for "free and uninterrupted use" by the public, preventing commercial corruption of its awe-inspiring beauty. Only the mighty Pacific has changed its profile, leaving it looking as untamed and natural as it did a hundred years ago. The southern part of the coast—from points south of Newport down to Brookings on the Oregon-California border—is a kaleidoscopic landscape of rugged offshore monoliths, sweeping dunes, towering cliffs, and quiet coves dotted with bayfront communities and an extensive network of state parks connected by Highway 101, often said to be the most scenic highway in the United States.

Winter is the time for storm- and whale-watching here; spring is cool and breezy enough for kite festivals; summer brings sunny beach days; and autumn is dependably warm and calm, perfect for viewing blazing fall foliage. Photographers will have a field day with the many old-fashioned-looking (though automated) lighthouses that dot the coast, including Heceta Head Lighthouse (Devil's Elbow State Park north of Florence), Coquille River Lighthouse (Bullards Beach in Bandon), Umpqua River Lighthouse (south of Winchester Bay), Yaquina Bay Lighthouse (south of Newport), and Cape Blanco Lighthouse (north of Port Orford), Oregon's tallest. Also picture-perfect are the offshore seal rookeries, favorite sea lion sunning spots, rocky bird hatcheries, and numerous tidal pools. Avid bicyclers probably won't mind the many steep hills and cliff-hugging passes of the well-marked Oregon Coast Bike Trail, parallel to Highway 101 and running from Astoria in the north all the way to Brookings. They'll certainly appreciate the special campgrounds in Bullards Beach, Cape Arago, Cape Blanco, Samuel Boardman, Harris Beach, Humbug Mountain, William Tugman, and Umpqua River state parks.

As in the north coast, the economy concentrates on fishing, shipping, and lumber, though tourism continues to grow in importance. Small coastal towns such as Bandon, cranberry capital of Oregon, and Gold Beach have blossomed into resort communities, with year-round activities and festivals to entertain visitors.

The tiny burg of Yachats has acquired a reputation that's disproportionate to its size, offering a microcosm of all the coastal pleasures: bed-and-breakfasts, excellent restaurants, deserted beaches, surf-pounded crags, and fishing and crabbing. It is also one of the few places in the world where the silver smelts come inland, celebrated by a community smelt fry each July.

Just past Heceta Head, Highway 101 jogs inland, and as you head south, you'll notice that the headlands and cliffs give way to endless beaches and rolling dunes. Nearby is Florence, a popular destination for both tourists and retirees and the gateway to the Oregon Dunes National Recreation Area. The picturesque waterfront Old Town has restaurants, antiques stores, fish markets, and other wet-weather diversions. The largest metropolitan area on the Oregon coast, Coos Bay is the world's largest lumber shipping port. But the glory days of the timber industry are over, and Coos Bay has begun to look in other directions, such as tourism—the Golden and Silver Falls State Park is close by—for economic prosperity.

Starting at Gold Beach, where the Rogue River, renowned among anglers, meets the ocean, is Oregon's banana belt. From here to Brookings, mild California-like temperatures encourage a blossoming trade in lilies and daffodils, and you'll even see a few palm trees. Brookings is equally famous as a commercial and sportfishing port of the incredibly clear, startlingly turquoise-blue Chetco River, and it is even more highly esteemed among lovers of fishing and the wilderness than is the Rogue.

Places to Go, Sights to See

Cape Perpetua. The lookout at the summit of this basalt cape, 3 miles south of Yachats, is the highest point along the Oregon coast, affording a panoramic view of the dramatic shoreline. Forestry service naturalists lead summer hikes along trails from the visitor center, on the east side of the highway, to quiet, sandy coves and fascinating tide pools. During winter storms and high tide, water shoots up at the rear of the steadily worn chasm known as Devil's Churn, just before the entry to the Cape loop drive.

Darlingtonia Botanical Wayside (Mercer Lake Rd.). Immediately east of Highway 101, 6 miles north of Florence, a paved half-mile trail with interpretive signs leads through clumps of rare, carnivorous, insect-catching cobra lilies (*Darlingtonia californica*), so named because they look like spotted cobras ready to strike. The park is most attractive in May, when the lilies are in bloom.

Mt. Emily. This mountain northeast of Brookings was the only spot in the continental United States to be attacked from the air during World War II. According to local accounts, a single Japanese pilot using a small plane assembled aboard a submarine offshore dropped an incendiary bomb here in 1942. (You can get to the Bomb Site Trail via forestry service road 1205.) Decades later the pilot presented his sword to the town as a gesture of goodwill; it is displayed at the Brookings city hall. Recently the Japanese contributed $2,000 to the town library to promote intercultural understanding.

Oregon Dunes National Recreation Area (tel. 503/271–3611). Stretching between Florence and North Bend are 32,000 acres of shifting sand dunes, said to be the largest oceanside dunes in the world. This enormous park encompasses beaches, trails, campgrounds, lakes, marshes, and forested areas. Even though forestry service regulations require mufflers on all vehicles, the screeching of dune buggies, four-wheel-drives, and other all-terrain vehicles careening through the dunes can be overwhelming in some areas. The quietest spot from which to see the dunes is the Dunes Overlook, off Highway 101 about 30 miles north of Coos Bay.

Redwood Nature Trail. This mile-long hiking trail on the north bank of the Chetco River in Brookings takes you along paths shaded by an immense canopy of giant redwoods ranging in age from 300 to 800 years.

Rogue River Tours. You might see bald eagles fishing for salmon, ospreys perched atop high trees, or black bears and deer roaming the banks of the Rogue on the half- and full-day wilderness trips offered by *Jerry's Rogue Jets* (tel. 503/247–4571 or 800/451–3645) or *Mail Boat Hydro-jets* (tel. 503/247–7033 or 800/458–3511), both of which leave from Gold Beach.

Sea Gulch (east side of Hwy. 101 in Seal Rock, tel. 503/563–2727) is a full-size ghost town inhabited by more than 300 fancifully carved wood figures. Ray Kowalski, a master of chain-saw carving—a peculiar Oregon art form—wields his Stihl chain saw with virtuosity to create his cowboys, Indians, hillbillies, trolls, gnomes, and other mythical figures. Visitors can watch him work in his adjoining studio.

Sea Lion Caves (91560 Hwy. 101, Florence, tel. 503/547–3111). During the fall and winter months, hundreds of wild Steller sea lions gather in the warm amphitheater of this huge, multihued sea cavern, 208 feet below the highway and about a mile south of Heceta Head. Visitors ride an elevator down to the floor of the cavern, near sea level, to watch from above the antics of the fuzzy pups and their parents. In spring and early summer, the sea lions move to the rocky sun-warmed ledges of the rookery outside the cave.

Shore Acres Arboretum and State Park (Cape Arago Hwy., Charleston, tel. 503/888–3732). Once the summer estate of a powerful Coos Bay lumber baron, all that remains of Shore Acres, 15 miles south of Coos Bay just outside Charleston, are the grounds, which include a Japanese garden and lily pond, rose garden, and formal box-hedged gardens of azaleas, rhododendrons, and flowering annuals and perennials, modeled after those at Versailles. The glass-enclosed gazebo on the sea cliff is a warm and protected spot for whale-watching.

South Slough National Estuarine Research Reserve (Seven Devils Rd., tel. 503/888–5558). Bobcats, raccoons, bears, bald eagles, cormorants, and great blue herons are only a few of the species living in the varied ecosystems (tidal flats, salt marshes, open channels, and uplands) of this 4,000-acre reserve 4 miles south of Charleston. More than 300 species of birds have been sighted here. South Slough, the first estuary reserve in the nation, has well-marked nature trails, guided walks, and an informative interpretive center.

Strawberry Hill. A few miles north of Yachats on Highway 101 is one of the best spots along the Oregon coast from which to view harbor seals at rest on small rocky islands just offshore, and peer at the starfish, anemones, and sea urchins living in the tide pools and exposed at low tide.

Beaches

Virtually the entire coastline of Oregon is a clean, quiet white-sand beach, publicly owned and accessible to all. A word of caution: The Pacific off the Oregon coast is 45°–55° F year-round, temperatures that can be described as brisk at best and numbing at worst. Tides and undertows are strong, and swimming is not advised. When fishing from the rocks, always watch for sneaker or rogue waves, and never play on logs near the water—they roll into the surf without warning and have cost numerous lives over the years. Above all, watch children closely while they play in or near the ocean.

Everyone has a favorite beach, but Bandon's **Face Rock Beach** is justly renowned as perhaps the state's loveliest for walking, while the beach at **Sunset Bay State Park** on Cape Arago, with its protective reefs and encircling cliffs, is probably the safest for swimming. Nearby, **Oregon Dunes National Recreation Area** adds extra cachet to Florence's beaches. Fossils, clams, mussels, and other aeons-old marine creatures, easily dug from soft sandstone cliffs, make **Beverly Beach State Park** (5 mi north of Newport) a favorite with young beachcombers.

Restaurants

Bandon Boatworks (tel. 503/347–2111) on the jetty offers outstanding ocean views, heaping buckets of steamer clams, delectably sweet cranberry bread, and passable Mexican specialties. Creative vegetarian and Mediterranean fare emphasizing organically grown produce and herbs is the focus at the **Sea Star Bistro** (tel. 503/347–9632) in Bandon's Old Town, which also operates a small youth hostel and a romantic, wharf-front guest house. Poor service mars the dining experience at the much-touted **La Serre** (tel. 503/547–3420) in Yachats; clam puffs in fluffy phyllo pastry are front-runners on the seafood, soup, and salad menu. A better option for fine Continental fare is the **Sweetwater Inn** (tel.

503/563–5664) in Waldport. **Mo's,** a favorite local chain with a well-deserved reputation for outstanding clam chowder and seafood, also serves chicken, salads, and sandwiches. All six Mo's (Florence, Cannon Beach, Lincoln City, Otter Rock, and two in Newport) are clearly marked on blue state highway signs along Highway 101. **Yuzen** (tel. 503/563–4766) in Seal Rock (near Waldport) is overpriced and understaffed, but it offers the only authentic Japanese cuisine on the south coast.

Tourist Information

Bandon Chamber of Commerce (350 E. 2nd St., Box 1515, Bandon, OR 97411, tel. 503/347–9616); **Bay Area Chamber of Commerce** (50 E. Central, Box 210, Coos Bay, OR 97420, tel. 503/269–0215 or 800/824–8486); **Brookings-Harbor Chamber of Commerce** (Lower Harbor Rd., Box 940, Brookings, OR 97415, tel. 503/469–3181); **Gold Beach Chamber of Commerce** (1225 S. Ellensburg Ave., No. 3, Gold Beach, OR 97444, tel. 503/247–7526 or 800/525–2334); **Oregon Coast Association** (Box 87, Depoe Bay, OR 97341, tel. 503/768–5371); **Port Orford Chamber of Commerce** (Box 637, Port Orford, OR 97465, tel. 503/332–8055); **Waldport Chamber of Commerce** (620 N.W. Spring St., Box 669, Waldport, OR 97394, tel. 503/563–2133); **Yachats Area Chamber of Commerce** (441 Hwy. 101, Box 174, Yachats, OR 97498, tel. 503/547–3530).

Reservation Services

Bed & Breakfast Reservations—Oregon (2321 N.E. 28th Ave., Portland, OR 97212, tel. 503/287–4704); **Northwest Bed and Breakfast** (610 S.W. Broadway, Suite 606, Portland, OR 97205, tel. 503/243–7616).

Chetco River Inn

By the time you reach the Chetco River Inn, 17 slow miles inland from Brookings along a twisting, single-lane forest service road that runs beside the Chetco River, you'll feel that you have left the busy world far behind. The large, cedar-sided, contemporary inn was designed over the phone by owner Sandra Brugger and the architect, who has never actually visited the property! While it fits well into the rugged surroundings, the inn is thoroughly modern rather than rustic.

Broad covered porches, cross-ventilation windows, and deep-green marble floors keep the inn cool during those occasional hot days of summer, when guests can usually be seen lounging in shaded hammocks, casting a fishing line (the Chetco is just outside the front door), or bobbing in the river in inner tubes. During the evenings, everyone gathers to talk in the airy, vaulted-ceiling common room furnished with Oriental carpets, leather couch, caned captain's chairs, and Chippendale dining ensemble. A collection of wreaths adorns the walls of the open kitchen at the end of the room.

Upstairs are tall shelves of books and games on the banistered landing leading to the guest rooms. A fishing motif dominates the River View Room, with cedar-paneled ceiling, red-and-black plaid bedspread, wicker furnishings, and a collection of antique creel baskets and duck decoys. The other rooms, which look out on the lush trees surrounding the house, are slightly larger, furnished with Oriental rugs, eclectic antiques, and reproduction brass and iron bedsteads. All rooms have vanity areas and robes. An overflow room that opens onto a private bath can be used by families or friends of guests.

Your best bet for dining is to enjoy Sandra's five-course dinners, which are available by advance notice. Featuring fresh local ingredients, the menu might include smoked salmon pâté, orange-carrot soup with Grand Marnier, grilled game hen, and homemade ice cream.

Address: *21202 High Prairie Rd., Brookings, OR 97415, radio tel. 503/469–8128 or 800/327–2688.*
Accommodations: *4 double rooms with baths.*
Amenities: *Lunch and dinner available; badminton, darts, horseshoes, swimming holes, nature trails, deep-sea charters or fishing guides by arrangement, fishing packages.*
Rates: *$85; full breakfast, afternoon refreshments. MC, V.*
Restrictions: *No smoking indoors, no pets; closed Thanksgiving and Christmas–New Year's Day.*

Cliff House

This large, 1930s gable-on-hip-roofed house, perched on Yaquina John Point in the coastal town of Waldport, is perhaps the closest you'll come on the Oregon coast to the Smithsonian's attic, with pieces by Steuben, Lalique, Tiffany, Dresden, and Rosenthal among the amazing abundance of objects here. Elaborate lead-glass chandeliers contrast—not unpleasantly—with knotty pine and cedar paneling, modern skylights, and an enormous river-stone fireplace. Window seats on the banistered, wraparound landing above the living room provide a cozy spot for sitting and taking in the sights, both inside and out. The setting is spectacular, a green headland jutting into the sea, with endless white beaches, shore pines, cliffs, and green surf.

Each of the four guest rooms reflects the romantic whims of owners Gabrielle Duvall and D. J. Novgrod. In the bedrooms, guests will find potbellied wood-burning stoves; a profusion of fresh-cut flowers; trays of sherry and chocolates; fluffy down comforters; and mounds of pillows on brass, sleigh, or four-poster rice beds. The Bridal Suite, with a positively royal 15th-century French gilt and ice-blue velvet Louis XV bedroom set, and mirrored bathroom with two-person shower and whirlpool tub overlooking the ocean, is by far the most opulent chamber. Terry robes and thongs are supplied for the short trip from your room to the large hot tub on the broad back deck overlooking the ocean and the Alsea Bay and bridge.

A run on the beach below or a vigorous game of croquet is a good way to work off the large morning meal, an elegant affair served at the black lacquer table on fine china with silver or gold flatware and plenty of fresh flowers. Gabby is happy to arrange a variety of romantic interludes—including catered dinners, sunset horseback rides, or champagne limousine drives into the nearby mountains.

Address: *Yaquina John Point, Adahi Rd., Box 436, Waldport, OR 97394, tel. 503/563–2506.*
Accommodations: *4 double rooms with baths, 1 2-bedroom housekeeping cottage.*
Amenities: *Cable TV with VCR and individual heat controls in rooms, wood-burning stoves in some rooms, Jacuzzi in suite, catered meals and masseuse available; hot tub on deck, aviary, rental bicycles.*
Rates: *$95–$125, suite $225; full breakfast. Rental Cottage $125; no breakfast. MC, V.*
Restrictions: *No smoking indoors, no pets; 2-night minimum on weekends, 3-night minimum on holidays; limited service Nov.–Mar.*

The Johnson House

ntering Ron and Jayne Fraese's simple Italianate Victorian in Old Town Florence—the house celebrated its centennial in 1992—guests pass into a different era, accompanied by the sounds of Jack Benny, Fred Allen, and Fibber McGee and Molly emanating from a 1930s Philco radio in the living room. Antique sepia photographs and political cartoons adorn the walls, and vintage hats hang from the entryway coat tree. Furnishings throughout the house date from the 1890s to the mid-1930s, and include marble-top tables and dressers, Queen Anne– and Chippendale-style chairs, walnut armoires, cast-iron beds, and a sprinkling of ornate Victorian pieces. In the bedrooms are lace curtains, crocheted doilies, and eyelet-lace-trimmed percale duvet covers on goose-down comforters and pillows. Sadly, the old hardwood floors have been covered over in industrial-brown paint. The best room in the house isn't actually in the house but in the tiny garden cottage, with a claw-foot tub in the sunny bedroom. Although the porch with wicker rockers is billed as private, you'll probably find yourself sharing it with a pair of lazing kittens.

Jayne's green thumb is evident in the celebrated delightful gardens surrounding the cottage, producing the fresh herbs, fruits, and edible flowers that garnish her breakfasts.

The Johnson House is a five-minute walk from ocean beaches and only a block from the quaint antiques shops, crafts boutiques, and eateries on the bay dock. A bowl of chowder at Mo's on the dock will do for a casual meal, but for a more refined atmosphere, head to the Windward Inn Restaurant (3757 Hwy. 101 N, tel. 503/997–8243), a few miles to the north; top choices include broiled scallops, mounds of steamer clams, fragrant veal in Madeira sauce, and a sumptuous chocolate-mocha toffee torte. Also nearby are the Sea Lion Caves, Oregon Dunes National Recreation Area, and the strange carnivorous lilies at the Darlingtonia Botanical Wayside.

For those who want to reside smack on the ocean, the Fraeses have a romantic vacation rental 9 miles north on Highway 101. Moonset, an octagonal cedar cabin for two, sits on a high meadow with a spectacular view of the coastline.

Address: *216 Maple St., Florence, OR 97439, tel. and fax 503/997–8000.*
Accommodations: *2 double rooms with baths, 3 doubles share 2 baths, 1 cottage suite.*
Amenities: *Individual heat controls in rooms; croquet and boccie ball.*
Rates: *$75–$105; full breakfast. MC, V.*
Restrictions: *No smoking indoors, no pets; limited service Jan.*

Sea Quest

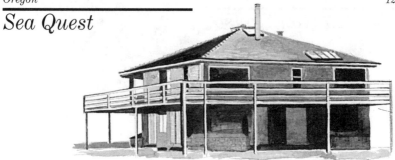

When Elaine Ireland and George Rozsa bought this contemporary cedar-shingle-and-glass home on a low coastal bluff outside Yachats, they remodeled it to create a romantic seaside retreat. They installed five guest rooms, a lounge, and a rounded entry on the ground floor, as well as a huge suite (which they occupy but will occasionally give up to honeymooners) and a roomy kitchen open to the main living area on the second floor. A round driveway was also added to the property, but otherwise the grounds were left in their natural state.

Elaine describes the decor as "eclectic, early garage sale," but her treasure trove of fine antique furniture and accent pieces would be the envy of any antiques hound. A pair of wooden skis and a weathered snowshoe hang over the driftwood mantel of the massive fireplace, competing for attention with the intriguing geodes, coral, and polished stones used as accents in the brickwork.

Wall colors coordinate with valances, bed linens, and mounds of pillows on queen-size beds in the guest rooms, each equipped with ocean-view Jacuzzi. Room 2, with twig furnishings and dried flower arrangements, and Room 4, with a telescope and book-filled secretary desk, are particularly popular, but a private entrance also makes Room 1 an appealing choice.

The hosts are friendly and cheerful. Their L-shaped kitchen island becomes a buffet each morning, filled with platters of seasonal fruit, fresh baked goods, hot entrées such as sautéed apples and sausages, fluffy quiches, and a large bowl of Elaine's homemade granola. Guests can dine out on the deck or at smartly set tables in the great room, protected from ocean breezes.

Both the deck and the large picture windows inside the house are excellent vantage points from which to experience one of this inn's special attractions: It's not at all surprising to see whales pass by fairly close to shore during their twice-yearly migrations between Baja California and Alaska.

Address: *95354 Hwy. 101, Yachats, OR 97498, tel. and fax 503/547-3782.*
Accommodations: *5 double rooms with baths.*
Amenities: *Guest lounge with phone and wet bar.*
Rates: *$105–$120, suite $245; full breakfast, evening snacks and beverages. D, MC, V.*
Restrictions: *No smoking, no pets; 2-night minimum on weekends, 3-night minimum on holidays.*

Tu Tu Tun Lodge

Fine-dining options in the tiny coastal town of Gold Beach are few, but follow the Rogue River 7 miles inland and your culinary prayers will be answered at Tu Tu Tun (pronounced "too too tin") Lodge. Owners Dirk and Laurie Van Zante, an exceptionally friendly young couple, preside over cocktails and hors d'oeuvres as guests relax on the piazza, enjoying the breathtakingly beautiful river scenery. Then it's on to a multicourse, fixed-price dinner that often features barbecued Chinook salmon or prime rib accompanied by a superior selection of wines. During the busy high season (May–October), there are only four spaces at the table for nonguests at breakfast and dinner (lunch is for guests only), so reservations are highly recommended.

Tu Tu Tun, named after the peaceful tribe of riverbank-dwelling Indians, is an ideal retreat. Surrounded by an abundance of wildlife dwelling in the old-growth timber and the rugged river, you'll quickly get back in touch with nature. In the evenings, guests often sit near the big stone fireplace in the modern, open-beam cedar inn watching for the pair of bald eagles that fly down over the river at sunset. At "O'dark hundred" (the Van Zantes' expression for daybreak), avid anglers are down at the dock raring to tackle the Rogue's mighty steelhead and salmon.

The two-story wing of riverside guest rooms is motel-like in structure only.

Named after favorite fishing holes on the Rogue River, each room features individual artwork and appointments; some have fireplaces, other have outdoor soaking tubs, but all have wonderful river views from a balcony or patio and thoughtful touches such as fine toiletries and fresh flowers. The cedar-lined, two-bedroom River House shares the great view and is equipped with a kitchen, as are the spacious suites in the main lodge and the charming, three-bedroom Garden House next to the orchard.

Address: *96550 N. Bank Rogue, Gold Beach, OR 97444, tel. 503/247–6664, fax 503/247–0672.*
Accommodations: *16 double rooms with baths, 2 housekeeping suites, 1 2-bedroom housekeeping unit, 1 3-bedroom housekeeping unit.*
Amenities: *Restaurant, full service bar, fireplace or soaking tub in several rooms, conference facilities; lap pool, 4-hole pitch-and-putt, horseshoe court, jet-boat tour pickup from dock, guided fishing.*
Rates: *$120–$225; breakfast extra. MC, V.*
Restrictions: *No pets July–Aug.; main lodge and restaurant closed last Sun. in Oct.–last Fri. in Apr.*

Ziggurat

L ike some fanciful dream of ancient Babylon, Ziggurat rises out of the tidal grasslands of the Siuslaw River. Seven miles south of Yachats, this terraced, step-pyramid-shaped inn, hand-built with native salt-silvered cedar siding, is without question the most unusual member of Oregon's B&B fraternity. Owner Mary Lou Cavendish soon realized that the interest the pyramid generated would bring a steady stream of visitors and that she and partner Irving Tebor had more than enough room to share, so she opened her amazing home as a bed-and-breakfast after construction was completed in 1987. (A cottage on the property in the shape of a tetrahedron is in the planning stages.)

Inside, an eclectic collection of original artwork—from Indonesian *wayang* puppets to Buddhist paintings from Nepal—and specially commissioned wooden furniture complement the house's sleek, ultramodern lines, stainless-steel trim, black carpeting, slate-like tiles, smooth white walls, and tinted triangular windows. On the ground floor, a narrow solarium surrounds two guest suites that share a living room/library, complete with microwave, sink, and refrigerator. The East Room has a modern canopy bed in elm and a sauna in the bathroom. The West Room has a 27-foot-long glass wall and a glass-block shower in the slate-tiled bathroom. A library nook, living room with grand piano and wood-burning stove, and dining room, kitchen, and bathroom with steam

shower share space on the second floor. Forty feet up and tucked under the eaves of the pyramid is another guest room, with two balconies and parallelogram windows overlooking the ocean and the arched bridge that spans the Yachats River. Guests residing here have exclusive use of the steam shower two floors below.

A brisk walk to the beach below the house is a good follow-up to the large breakfast served on one of the two glass-enclosed sun porches. Ziggurat is within easy reach of the area's many coastal pleasures, including Cape Perpetua, Sea Lion Caves, Strawberry Hill Wayside, and the boutiques and restaurants of tiny Yachats. Those interested in shells should make a stop at the Sea Rose Gift Shop (95478 Hwy. 101, Yachats, tel. 503/547–3005) to see the displays of rare, exotic, and common shells from around the world.

Address: *95330 Hwy. 101, Yachats, OR 97498, tel. 503/547–3925.*
Accommodations: *1 double room with detached bath, 2 suites.*
Amenities: *Library, grand piano.*
Rates: *$95–$110; full breakfast. No credit cards.*
Restrictions: *No smoking indoors, no pets; 2-night minimum on holidays.*

Coos Bay Manor

This 15-room Colonial Revival manor house, built in 1912 and listed on the National Register of Historic Places, is now a charming bed-and-breakfast, thanks to the efforts of transplanted Californian and former banker Patricia Williams. Visitors enter through a formal English garden and imposing, wisteria-draped portico to find such original features as glowing hardwood floors and painted wainscoting, and a tasteful mixture of antiques and period reproductions (although the red-and-gold flocked wallpaper is reminiscent of a Victorian bordello). The star of the living room is an 1870 Weber box baby grand piano with ornate lions' heads adorning the legs.

The guest rooms are theme oriented, such as the frilly Victorian Room, with lace-canopy bed; the Cattle Baron's Room, with antique roping saddle and bearskin wall hangings; and the Colonial Room, with velvet curtains and four-poster beds. The wharf and waterfront walking paths are only two blocks away; other sights of interest nearby include Shore Acres Arboretum and the South Slough Estuary.

Address: *955 S. 5th St., Coos Bay, OR 97420, tel. 503/269-1224.*
Accommodations: *1 double room with bath, 4 doubles share 2 baths.*
Amenities: *Robes and coffeemaker in rooms, well-mannered pets welcome; bicycles.*
Rates: *$60–$70; extended Continental breakfast. MC, V.*
Restrictions: *Smoking outside only.*

Floras Lake House by the Sea

When the property overlooking Floras Lake, a small body of fresh water only a few feet from the ocean, went up for sale, Will Brady and his wife, Liz, decided that a bed-and-breakfast would be the perfect extension for the windsurfing school they had established here. Even those who don't windsurf will enjoy the natural setting and the contemporary (1991) board-and-batten cedar home.

The interior is light and airy, with picture windows, exposed beams, and classic furnishings. While the contemporary couches and wood stove in the great room are inviting, guests more often spend their time outside on the decks, in the garden, or roaming the beach.

One of the two larger guest rooms has an Early American atmosphere, while the other is more feminine, with wildflower wallpaper, lace curtains, and white wicker furniture, but both offer fireplaces. Nautical and garden themes dominate in the two smaller rooms.

Address: *92870 Boice Cope Rd., Langlois, OR 97450, tel. and fax 503/348-2573.*
Accommodations: *4 double rooms with baths.*
Amenities: *Guest phone; windsurfing classes and equipment, boats and bicycles.*
Rates: *$95–$130; extended Continental breakfast. D, MC, V.*
Restrictions: *No smoking indoors, no pets; closed late Nov.–mid-Feb.*

Heather House Bed and Breakfast

Each spring and summer, mounds of heather surround Bob and Katy Cooper's 1947 Craftsman, perched on a hill overlooking the coast at Gold Beach. It's not Brigadoon, but Katy's Scottish accent and customs might almost convince you that it is. Precisely at 4 each afternoon, out comes the tea with finger sandwiches, little tarts, scones, and shortbread.

Each of the guest rooms has a different look: blue-and-green plaids and kilted soldier dolls in the Tartan Room; lace-trimmed rose-print bed linens and curtains and graceful, authentic Queen Anne pieces in the Victorian Room; and geisha doll and samurai helmet on the shiny black alcove dresser in the Oriental Room.

Jet-boat tours on the Rogue are just minutes away from Heather House, as is fun and funky Honeybear Campground (34161 Ophir, Gold Beach, OR 97444, tel. 503/247–2765), where an oompah band and lederhosen-clad waiters liven up the German buffet. Reservations are a must for this weekends-only diner.

Address: *190 11th St., Gold Beach, OR 97444, tel. 503/247–2074.*
Accommodations: *2 double rooms with baths, 2 doubles share 1 bath.*
Rates: *$55–$70; full breakfast, afternoon refreshments. MC, V.*
Restrictions: *No smoking indoors, no pets; closed Oct.–Mar.*

The Highlands

By the time you reach this delightful bed-and-breakfast— 1½ miles up an old logging road and into the mountains overlooking Haines Inlet and a grassy meadow of grazing cattle in the valley far below— you'll know how it got its name. Hovering high above the fog and cool winds of the coast, Marilyn and Jim Dow's contemporary cedar-and-glass home is immediately welcoming and comfortable.

Guests have the run of the entire lower level, which includes a huge den with enormous picture windows for valley gazing. Tole objets d'art, antique dolls, a delicately stitched whole-cloth quilt, and other family heirlooms give the decor a homey, country feel. The furnishings include wicker, country-pine antiques, and tasseled canopy pencil-post or cast-iron beds covered with floral or Battenberg lace–trimmed bed linens. Breakfast, served on the upstairs deck above colorful terraced gardens, might feature fresh eggs from the Dows' flock of free-range chickens.

Address: *608 Ridge Rd., North Bend, OR 97459, tel. 503/756–0300.*
Accommodations: *2 double rooms with baths.*
Amenities: *Telephone and individual heat controls in rooms, whirlpool tub in 1 bathroom, hot tub spa in 1 bathroom, fully equipped kitchen available.*
Rates: *$65–$75; full breakfast. MC, V.*
Restrictions: *No smoking indoors, no pets; limited service Dec.–Apr.*

Home by the Sea

This quirky little B&B on a headland above Battle Rock Park in Port Orford enjoys a most spectacular view of the south Oregon coast. Built by owners Alan and Brenda Mitchell in 1985, the three-story shingled house is decorated with stained-glass hangings and Brenda's handmade quilts (all for sale). The mix-and-match Americana furnishings are comfortable and low-key; the rare myrtlewood bedsteads in both ocean-view bedrooms were specially commissioned. Bathrooms are cramped, but tidy and functional; a washer and dryer (which are available for guests' use) take up space in one bathroom.

Breakfast is served either in the lower-level solarium, which offers a conversation-stopping ocean view, or on the porch. This is a prime spot for watching whales (October–May), winter storms, and birds; the Oregon Islands National Wildlife Refuge is just offshore. The Wooden Nickel (Hwy. 101, Port Orford, tel. 503/332–5201), a nearby myrtlewood factory with weekday tours, is a good spot for picking up souvenirs of the area.

Address: *444 Jackson, Box 606-F, Port Orford, OR 97465, tel. 503/332–2855.*
Accommodations: *2 double rooms with baths.*
Amenities: *Cable TV in rooms.*
Rates: *$70–$75; full breakfast. MC, V.*
Restrictions: *No smoking, no pets; 2-night minimum on summer weekends.*

The Lighthouse

This 1980 contemporary cedar in Bandon is named for its view of the Coquille River Lighthouse across the estuary. Wide windows in the large sunken living room and a porch off the raised dining room take advantage of the view. The simple, eclectic furnishings throughout—from Art Deco to contemporary—are brightened by painted rainbow supergraphics on the walls, colorful Guatemalan masks, whimsical prints, family photos, huge plants, and battered, neon-colored fishnet floats hanging from the ceiling. Vivacious Linda Sisson, who performs with the local theater group, and her husband Bruce, a contractor and former Frisbee champion, no longer live on the property and have hired a resident manager, Julia, to run the inn. The Lighthouse is a great spot from which to watch the timber-rattling storms that draw tourists to the coast in winter; the Bandon Storm Watchers (Box 1693, Bandon, OR 97411) can provide information on storm-watching, whale-watching, and tide-pool exploring in Bandon.

Address: *650 Jetty Rd., Box 24, Bandon, OR 97411, tel. 503/347–9316.*
Accommodations: *4 double rooms with baths.*
Amenities: *Whirlpool tub, fireplace, and TV in 1 room, cable TV and wood-burning stove in common area.*
Rates: *$75–$100; Continental breakfast. MC, V.*
Restrictions: *No smoking, no pets; closed July 4.*

Paradise-by-the-Sea Bed & Breakfast

If ocean views are your weakness, this new B&B is for you. Many of the picture windows of this two-story ranch house look out onto the white waters that form a backdrop for Cats and Kittens—a rock formation just offshore—and, on the right nights, moon-splashed ocean panoramas.

Beyond white iron gates, visitors enter a garden with an Oriental feel—all fir trees, pebble paths, and shrubs. Indoors, the living room is decorated with Victorian sofas and a glass cabinet that survived the 1906 San Francisco earthquake. There are two guest rooms: The Angel Room honors artist Frederick Beck (a former owner of the house), whose images of angels adorn the walls, while Lyn's Room has abundant planters and flowers.

On special request, manager Julia Prince can whip up her cranberry-bread French toast. Then guests can visit the nearby Bandon Beach Riding Stables to take a scenic ride along the shore.

Address: *3795 Beach Loop, Bandon, OR 97411, tel. 503/347–3956.*
Accommodations: *2 double rooms with private baths.*
Amenities: *Whirlpool tub in 1 room, wet bar in 1 room, cable TV in both rooms, kitchen privileges for light cooking.*
Rates: *$55–$115; Continental-plus breakfast. AE, MC, V.*
Restrictions: *No smoking, no pets.*

Sea Star Guest House

The Sea Star Guest House, which overlooks a small marina, is ideally located in Bandon's Old Town. This two-story cedar cottage has some motel-like aspects: There are no common areas for guests, and the rooms open out to the exterior. However, this could be considered a plus for those seeking privacy, and the place is far from faceless and generic. Shades of mauve and blue figure prominently in the sophisticated contemporary decor of the four guest rooms. Cramped bathrooms are a minor drawback.

The two second-floor units offer the best views. The larger of the two accommodations has a loft bedroom, while a skylight over the pine four-poster in the smaller one allows for stargazing.

You won't spend much time chatting with owners Monica and Dave Jennings, who are usually busy working in the Sea Star Bistro at the back of the property. Breakfast, included in the tariff, is served in the bistro; overnight guests can choose from anything on the menu (*huevos rancheros*, snapper hash, three-cheese or prawn omelets, and more) or opt for one of the daily specials.

Address: *375 Second St., Bandon, OR 97411, tel. 503/347–9632.*
Accommodations: *2 double rooms with baths, 2 housekeeping suites.*
Amenities: *Cable TV in rooms; restaurant.*
Rates: *$60–$95; full breakfast. AE, MC, V.*
Restrictions: *No smoking, no pets.*

Southern Oregon
Including Ashland

Protected by the Klamath and Siskiyou mountain ranges from the extreme weather patterns of the Pacific Ocean, southern Oregon—from points south of Roseburg, past Ashland, to the Oregon/California border—enjoys a much warmer, drier climate than the Willamette Valley to the north and the coastline to the west. As in the valley, the economy centers on farming and ranching, with an additional boost from tourists, lured by the area's many historic sites, natural attractions, and cultural events.

With more than its fair share of national parks and challenging rivers, southern Oregon is a paradise for outdoors enthusiasts. At the Mt. Ashland Ski Area there are plenty of cross-country and downhill courses (four lifts and 23 runs at 1,150 vertical feet) to keep skiers busy from Thanksgiving through April. There are also cross-country trails in the heights around Crater Lake and snowmobile trails around Diamond Lake. The Pacific Crest National Scenic Trail and the Siskiyou National Forest offer the best hiking and camping in the region. Water adventurers turn to the Klamath or Rogue rivers for recreation.

The Rogue, one of Oregon's most scenic rivers, bores through the verdant Siskiyou National Forest and the coastal mountains, rushing full force to meet the ocean. It is a favorite for jet-boat and rafting tours out of Grants Pass, an old stagecoach stop along the Portland–San Francisco route named in 1865 to honor Grant's capture of Vicksburg. Approximately 20 miles north of Grants Pass off busy Interstate 5 is Wolf Creek, another vintage way station, and Golden, an entertaining gold-mining ghost town 3 miles farther east, up Coyote Creek. When gold was discovered in 1851 in Jacksonville, just southeast of Grants Pass, a wave of saloons, gambling houses, and brothels opened to coax the shiny dust from the hordes of miners; today it remains a good *example of a Gold Rush boomtown, with more than 75 historic buildings, many dating from the late 19th century.*

Southeast on Highway 99 and one of the state's chief tourist destinations, Ashland is home to the renowned Oregon Shakespeare Festival, "festival" being somewhat of a misnomer, since it runs for nine months out of the year. Its immense popularity has provided fertile ground for a flourishing arts community and profusion of boutiques, galleries, taverns, fine restaurants, and exceptional bed-and-breakfasts.

Places to Go, Sights to See

Actors Theater (101 Talent Ave., Talent, OR 97540, tel. 503/535–5250 or 503/779–4010). Audiences cheer on the hero, hiss at the villain, and sing along at the Gay Nineties–style revue staged here on weekend evenings from June to September.

Butte Creek Mill (402 Royal North Ave., tel. 503/826–3531). This historic mill on the banks of the Little Butte Creek at Eagle Point has been in operation since 1872. Visitors can watch enormous French-quarried millstones hard at work making flour. Next door to the mill is an old-fashioned country store selling a variety of fresh-ground grains and bulk spices, teas, granolas, and raw honey.

Crater Lake National Park (Box 7, Crater Lake, OR 97604, tel. 503/594–2211). Crystal-clear blue waters fill this caldera at the crest of the Cascade Range, formed 6,800 years ago when Mt. Mazama decapitated itself in a volcanic explosion. You can drive, bicycle, or hike the 33-mile rim road. Boat tours leaving from Cleetwood Cove, on the lake's north side, go to Wizard Island, a miniature cinder cone protruding above the surface. A lodge offers summer accommodations, but the cabins at Diamond Lake Resort (Diamond Lake, OR 97731, tel. 503/793–3333) just north of Crater Lake are a better option.

Golden Ghost Town (3482 Coyote Creek Rd., Wolf Creek, tel. 503/866–2685). Golden is a partially restored, century-old gold-mining town with a general store, post office, blacksmith shop, schoolhouse, and church. Fake wooden gravestones planted next to the church were left behind after the shooting of a 1972 episode of the TV series "Gunsmoke." Guided tours, complete with spicy stories from the Old West, are free; call first to schedule tour times.

Jacksonville. This 1850s Gold Rush town, on the National Register of Historic Places, has dozens of historic homes and buildings, a fascinating cemetery, a schoolhouse, several saloons, and numerous shops and antiques stores. The *Jacksonville Museum* (206 N. 5th St., tel. 503/773–6536), in the old Jackson County Courthouse, houses an intriguing collection of Gold Rush–era artifacts and outlines the rich local history. Jacksonville is also home to the popular *Peter Britt Festival* (Peter Britt Gardens, tel. 503/773–6077 or 800/88–BRITT), a weekly series of outdoor concerts and theater lasting from late June to early September that features classical music, jazz, bluegrass, and folk music and dance.

Klamath Basin National Wildlife Refuge (1800 Miller Island Rd. W, Klamath Falls, tel. 503/883–5734). There are many viewing sites around this protected 80,000-acre habitat of marshland and shallow lakes, home to a wide variety of birds and waterfowl. Visitors can observe hundreds of bald eagles that nest here over the winter or watch the endless legions of ducks and geese fly over during spring and fall migrations.

Oregon Caves National Monument (on Hwy. 46, 50 mi southwest of Grants Pass, tel. 503/592–2100). Known as the Marble Halls of Oregon, Oregon Caves National Monument, high in the Siskiyou Mountains, entrances visitors with prehistoric limestone and marble formations. Dress warmly and wear sturdy shoes for the chilly, mildly strenuous 75-minute, half-mile subterranean tour. The rustic *Oregon Caves Chateau* (Box 128, Cave Junction, OR 97523, tel. 503/592–3400) offers food and lodging at the monument from June through September.

Oregon Shakespeare Festival (15 S. Pioneer St., Box 158, Ashland, OR 97520, tel. 503/482–4331). A Tony Award–winning repertory company presents 11 different Shakespearean, classic, and contemporary plays on three different stages during a season that stretches from February through October. The informative "Festival Tour," often led by company members, goes behind the scenes of the festival's three theaters, including the Elizabethan, a re-creation of Shakespeare's Fortune Theatre that operates only from June to October. The tour also visits the Shakespeare Festival Exhibit Center, exploring the festival's history in costumes, props, set designs, and photographs. In the Fantasy Gallery, visitors can don elaborate robes, gowns, and crowns and pose for pictures on an Elizabethan throne. *The Feast of Will*, held in early June in the lovely neighboring Lithia Park—designed by the man who was responsible for San Francisco's Golden Gate Park—kicks off the lively summer season. Lectures, concerts, play readings, and other events are part of the festival activities; some are free, others are ticketed (call for schedule of events and admissions).

Pacific Northwest Museum of Natural History (155 Walker Ave., Ashland, tel. 503/488–1084). This museum, opened in the summer of 1994, has captivating exhibits covering the diverse ecosystems of the Pacific Northwest, from lush coastal waterways and estuaries to rain forests, alpine wilderness, and high desert. There's a lava tube to explore, native animals to watch, and a variety of interactive computer exhibits to help visitors learn about the use of natural resources and the effects our choices have on the natural world.

River Rafting. Wet-knuckle enthusiasts flock to the challenging Rogue River, near the California border. Many parts of the river flow through true wilderness, with no road access. Deer, bears, eagles, and other wild creatures are abundant here. Outfitters based in Grants Pass and nearby Merlin include *Hellgate Excursions* (953 S.E. 7th St., tel. 503/479–7204 or 800/648–4874), *Orange Torpedo Trips* (209 Merlin Rd., tel. 503/479–5061), and *Rogue Wilderness, Inc.* (325 Galice Rd., tel. 503/479–9554 or 800/336–1647).

Wineries and Breweries. Top wineries in the region include *Bridgeview Vineyards* (4210 Holland Loop Rd., Cave Junction, tel. 503/592–4688), which also offers B&B–style accommodations; *Valley View Vineyard* (1000 Upper Applegate

Rd., tel. 503/899–8468) just south of Jacksonville in Ruch; and *Weisinger's* (3150 Siskiyou Blvd., tel. 503/488–5989 or 800/551–WINE) in Ashland. The *Rogue Brewery and Public House* (31 Water St., tel. 503/488–5061), a small brewery in Ashland, is also worth a visit.

Restaurants

Just as southern Oregon has an abundance of B&Bs, so, too, is there an ample crop of restaurants to choose from, with many concentrated in Ashland. **Chateaulin** (tel. 503/482–2264), in Ashland, serves fine French cuisine in charming ivy-and-brickwork surroundings; after-theater crowds come here for the extensive wine list and light café fare. You can enjoy Texas-style barbecued steaks, ribs, and chicken from May through September on the creekside deck of the **Back Porch Barbecue** (tel. 503/482–4131), and fine Italian fare at the new **Cucina Biazzi** (tel. 503/488–3739). Just north of Ashland in Talent, the **Arbor House** (tel. 503/535–6817) features an eclectic international menu that includes jambalaya, curries, braised lamb, charbroiled steaks, and seafood. **New Sammy's Bistro** (tel. 503/535–2779), also in Talent, is a pricey, reservations-only diner offering trendy Oregon cuisine that's strictly organic. The **McCulley House Inn** (tel. 503/899–1942) serves nouvelle Californian cuisine and is the current favorite in Jacksonville. Best bets in Grants Pass are **Matsukaze** (tel. 503/479–2961), for reasonably priced Japanese fare, and **Legrand's** (tel. 503/471–1554), for French, Italian, and Continental dishes. A bit farther north, **Buzz's Blue Heron** (tel. 503/479–6604) in Merlin features steaks and burgers as well as Cajun, Italian, and Oriental specialties and local dinner-theater productions.

Tourist Information

Ashland Chamber of Commerce (110 E. Main St., Box 1360, Ashland, OR 97520, tel. 503/482–3486); **Grants Pass Visitor and Convention Bureau** (1501 N.E. 6th St., Box 1787, Grants Pass, OR 97526, tel. 503/476–5510 or 800/547–5927); **Jacksonville Chamber of Commerce** (185 N. Oregon St., Box 33, Jacksonville, OR 97530, tel. 503/899–8118); **Medford Visitors and Convention Bureau** (304 S. Central Ave., Medford, OR 97501, tel. 503/779–4847 or 800/448–4856).

Reservation Services

Ashland's B&B Clearinghouse (Box 1376, Ashland, OR 97520, tel. 503/488–0338); **Ashland's B&B Reservation Network** (Box 1051, Ashland, OR 97520, tel. 503/482–BEDS or 800/944–0329); **Bed and Breakfast Reservations—Oregon** (2321 N.E. 28th Ave., Portland, OR 97212, tel. 503/287–4704); **Country Host Registry** (901 N.W. Chadwick La., Myrtle Creek, OR 97457, tel. 503/863–5168).

Chanticleer Inn

Named after a strutting rooster in Chaucer's *Canterbury Tales*, Chanticleer has good reason to crow. This trilevel 1920 Craftsman built into a hill is surrounded by cheerful gardens and a long river-rock porch. Unfortunately, the inn lost its comfortable home-away-from-home ambience with a change in ownership in 1993, but it's still tidy and extremely well-run. New owner Pebby Kuan and her staff continue to pay attention to detail—including a stuffed cookie jar and a selection of teas and coffees left out for guests—a major factor in the previous owners' success.

The country French decor seems fresh and new (reproduction pieces are, however, interspersed with antiques), from the thick carpets and soft-colored paint and paper on the walls to the shiny Pierre Deux fabrics covering the cushions and pressed white percale-and-lace pillowcases and duvets on the beds. Carved pine armoires function as closets, and fluffy down comforters cover antique brass and wrought-iron beds in the various guest chambers. Scripts of the current Oregon Shakespeare Festival plays are stacked on the bureaus. Other special touches include fresh flowers, sewing baskets, turndown service, alarm clocks, telephones, and individual climate control. The only negative among a long list of positives is the rocket-engine sound made by the exhaust fans in the bathrooms.

Italian roast coffees, vegetable latkes topped with apple sauce or sour cream, cheese blintzes, British banger sausages, and lemon-strawberry cake with crème fraîche are among the gourmet breakfast specialties. The inn is just four blocks from the festival theaters and the countless boutiques and shops of downtown Ashland. Dining options, including the Winchester Country Inn (35 S. 2nd St., tel. 503/488–1113) and Primavera (241 Hargadine St., tel. 503/488–1994), both strong contenders in the Ashland dining scene, are also close at hand.

Address: *120 Gresham St., Ashland, OR 97520, tel. 503/482–1919.*
Accommodations: *6 double rooms with baths.*
Amenities: *Phone and individual climate control in rooms, wood-burning stove in living room, stocked refrigerator in kitchen.*
Rates: *$115–$155; full breakfast, evening refreshments. MC, V.*
Restrictions: *No smoking indoors, no pets; 2-night minimum on weekends Feb.–Oct.*

Clemens House

A few blocks from the city center of Grants Pass in a quiet residential neighborhood, the Clemens House is a 1905 Craftsman surrounded by enormous camellias, rhododendrons, and a bushy holly tree. Lovingly restored by Gerry and Maureen Clark, it's listed on the National Register of Historic Places and is a favorite stop on the local historic walking tour.

The sunken living room features dark fir paneling, a large fireplace, an Oregon white oak floor, wing chairs, a Duncan Phyfe table, and other period antiques. Nearby are an inviting sunporch furnished in white wicker and a dining room with a polished walnut table, set each morning with fine stemware, silver, and china.

Americana dominates here: Family heirlooms include a framed, hand-stitched sampler and an old Singer sewing machine, and a white iron-and-brass bed occupies the smaller of the two second-floor guest rooms. The Camellia Suite, in shades of mauve with camellia-patterned wallpaper and trim, is roomier and more elegant, but it lacks an in-suite bath. It features broad, padded window seats, Oriental-style carpets on hardwood floors, and fine reproduction furniture (lyre-back chairs, tea tables, bureau bookcase, plump love seat, and oval ottoman) in the bedrooms and sitting room. A brick fireplace, lace curtains, and taffeta bedspread lend romance.

The popular, 800-square-foot Penthouse Suite, tucked under the rafters, has sunny dormers and slanted ceilings. A blue carpet and salmon easy chairs echo the colors in the Waverly floral wallpaper and the bedspread and window swags. There are built-in shelves full of books and shells, a small kitchen, and a private bathroom with pink, 1950s-style fixtures.

Herb-fried potatoes, scrambled cream-cheese eggs, oven-baked apples, and sliced peaches in honey-vanilla crème are typical of the morning repast Maureen serves her guests. On cool mornings you might find her cooking pancakes on the handsome antique wood stove in the kitchen. After-breakfast options include rafting on the Rogue River, antiques hunting in nearby boutiques, taking in a play during the Shakespeare Festival in Ashland, or exploring the restored gold-mining town of Jacksonville.

Address: *612 N.W. 3rd St., Grants Pass, OR 97526, tel. 503/476–5564 or 800/344–2820.*
Accommodations: *1 double room with bath, 1 2-bedroom suite, 1 housekeeping suite.*
Amenities: *Air-conditioning, bedside truffles.*
Rates: *$60–$70; full breakfast, evening refreshments. MC, V.*
Restrictions: *No smoking indoors, no pets.*

Jacksonville Inn

Gold flecks still sparkle in the mortar of the locally made bricks and quarried sandstone used to construct this two-story building in 1863. On the main street of Jacksonville, this historic building has served as a general store, bank, hardware store, office complex, and furniture repair shop. Purchased in 1976 by Jerry and Linda Evans, it is now an inn and dinner house, with a well-deserved reputation for the best wining and dining around.

Of the eight guest rooms on the top floor, the best and largest is the Peter Britt room, with a whirlpool tub, canopy bed, antique desk, and comfy wing chairs. All the rooms have wood trim salvaged from buildings of the same period, and frontier American antiques including bedsteads, dressers, and chairs. Telephones, minifridges, and TVs hidden away in specially constructed armoires that match the period furnishings are standard features. Tall brass-and-oak bedsteads have been lengthened to accommodate queen-size mattresses. Seven of the rooms have been redecorated and now feature cheerful floral wallpapers and linens, upgraded bathroom fixtures, and double-pane windows.

For breakfast, guests choose from a gourmet menu; entrées might include a chef's choice omelet, spinach and mushroom *gâteau* in Mornay sauce (scrambled eggs with cream cheese and sherry in a puff-pastry cup), or brioche French toast with maple butter and cinnamon sugar, preceded by fresh-squeezed orange juice and a fruit platter. The dining room is open to inn guests and the general public for breakfast, lunch, dinner, and Sunday brunch. There's also a quiet bar/lounge and a bistro in the basement that features a lighter and less formal menu.

The newest offering in the inn's growing retinue is a large, one-room woodframe cottage two blocks away. With a canopy pencil-post bed across from a marble fireplace, wet bar, stocked kitchenette, and whirlpool tub and sauna shower in the spacious bathroom, it is a romantic little hideaway. Ashland and its Oregon Shakespeare Festival activities are about 20 minutes away by car.

Address: *175 E. California St., Box 359, Jacksonville, OR 97530, tel. 503/899–1900 or 800/321–9344, fax 503/899–1373.*
Accommodations: *8 double rooms with baths, 1 housekeeping cottage.*
Amenities: *Air-conditioning, phone, and TV in rooms; whirlpool tub, steam shower, and fireplace in cottage; restaurant, lounge, wine shop, conference facilities, dining patio; bikes available.*
Rates: *$80–$125, housekeeping cottage $175; full breakfast. AE, D, DC, MC, V.*
Restrictions: *No smoking.*

Old Stage Inn

On a quiet country lane a mile or so north of Jacksonville, in the heart of southern Oregon's Gold Rush territory, stands an immaculate white 1857 Greek Revival farmhouse that was up for sale in 1994. Present owners Hugh and Carla Jones, an amiable, devoutly religious couple who truly believe that "guests who come as strangers should leave as friends" have done an admirable job of refurbishing and decorating this bed-and-breakfast. The inn's elegant decor is the work of Carla, an interior decorator by profession. Eastlake, Rococo Revival, and other period furnishings are surrounded by thick Oriental carpets, polished wood floors, rich brocade swag curtains, and vibrant wallpapers.

Eleven-foot-high ceilings; broad, lace-curtained windows; and plenty of square footage give the bedrooms a spacious, airy feel, complemented by Carla's sense of style. A plump bunny pillow sits on a large four-poster rice bed with silk-ivy-entwined canopy in one room. In another room, doors were removed and antique lamps added, turning a shallow pegboard closet into an interesting alcove framing the carved oak headboard of a lace-covered bed. Victorian-style floral wallpaper above penny-tile wainscoting, a Queen Anne reproduction velvet armchair next to the double shower, and a brocade step stool leading to the raised whirlpool bath surrounded by candelabras help make you forget that this is a shared bathroom.

A charming cottage with seating alcove offers more privacy and is completely accessible to wheelchair users.

Carla's breakfasts are magnificent presentations, with fresh flowers and ivy decorating the table. The meal starts with a variety of homemade tea breads and a fruit dish such as poached pears in raspberry puree or baked Alaska grapefruit, followed by an entrée of orange-pecan pancakes or smoked turkey in cream sauce on whole wheat and wild rice waffles. During the summer, guests enjoy sipping lemonade on the side porch as they watch Canada geese in a nearby pond, or taking part in croquet on the side lawn. All-terrain bicycles are available for outings to the Britt Music Festival or for a tour of historic Jacksonville.

Address: *883 Old Stage Rd., Box 579, Jacksonville, OR 97530, tel. 503/899–1776 or 800/US–STAGE, fax 503/899–1776.*
Accommodations: *2 double rooms with baths, 2 doubles share 1 bath.*
Amenities: *Air-conditioning; fireplace in 2 rooms; bicycles and coach rides available.*
Rates: *$90–$110; full breakfast, afternoon refreshments. MC, V.*
Restrictions: *No smoking indoors, no pets; 2-night minimum on weekends June–Aug. and on holidays.*

The Winchester Country Inn

O f the many Victorian bed-and-breakfasts in Ashland, this 1886 Queen Anne is the only one with a restaurant, and it's the closest to the Shakespeare Festival theaters as well. Painstakingly renovated by Michael and Laurie Gibbs during the early 1980s and listed on the National Register of Historic Places, the Winchester has established a reputation as one of the finer dining spots in Ashland. Open to the public for dinner and Sunday brunch, it offers a seasonal menu plus favorites such as French Vietnamese *teng dah* beef (broiled fillet marinated in a lemon-peppercorn sauce) and duck with orange sauce. The outstanding food makes up for the fact that the small guest sitting room just beyond the gift shop is almost entirely overshadowed by the restaurant.

The decor of the guest chambers maintains the period style of the house without the Victorian clutter. A mixture of American Colonial reproductions and antiques, as well as Rococo Revival and Eastlake reproductions, including tall mirrored wardrobes and brass-and-iron or heavy, carved wooden bedsteads, add distinction, while contemporary cushioned chairs and wall-to-wall carpeting lend comfort. A hand-painted porcelain sink set into an antique dresser serves as a vanity in the bedroom; scented salts in the attached bathroom make for a luxurious soak in the deep claw-foot tub. A crystal decanter of sherry and sinfully rich truffles on a tray on the dresser make a late-night snack irresistible.

Favorite rooms include the Sylvan Room, in sunny shades of peach, and the creamy blue Garden Room, both of which have delightful bay sitting areas overlooking the terraced gardens. The Sunset Room has its own balcony view of the treetops of downtown Ashland. Rooms at the basement level have garden patios or small decks as compensation. A private cottage with two beautiful luxury suites was added in 1993, and the Victorian and its carriage house next door were purchased, gutted, and completely redone in 1994, adding four more suites and five double rooms (one which is accessible to wheelchair users) to Winchester's growing retinue.

During winter and spring, the Gibbses offer a variety of special packages, from murder-mystery weekends to a popular Dickens Christmas Festival tie-in.

Address: *35 S. 2nd St., Ashland, OR 97520, tel. 503/488–1113 or 800/972–4991.*
Accommodations: *12 double rooms with baths, 6 suites.*
Amenities: *Air-conditioning, phone in rooms; some suites with fireplaces, whirlpool tubs, TV, VCR, and stereo; restaurant, sitting room.*
Rates: *$89–$125, suites $115–$160; full breakfast. MC, V.*
Restrictions: *No smoking, no pets.*

Arden Forest Inn

This early-20th-century cross-gabled farmhouse sits on a small plot of land in Ashland's historic district, within walking distance of the Festival theaters but removed from noisy downtown.

Its eclectically decorated interior reflects the interests of owners Audrey Sochor, an artist, and her husband, Art, a retired English teacher and an active theater buff. Contemporary furnishings in the common rooms include rattan and director's chairs and glass-top tables with stacks of art books as pedestals. Bleached fir floors, whitewashed walls, abundant windows, and track lighting form a bright showcase for the Sochors' folk art collection, Audrey's paintings and textiles, and Art's impressive library. A dearth of fragile collectibles and antiques makes this bed-and-breakfast a good choice for families. It is also the only inn in Ashland that is completely accessible to guests with wheelchairs.

The Sochors' low-fat, low-calorie vegetarian breakfasts featuring fruit platters, cobblers, crepes, and fresh popovers are very satisfying.

Address: *261 W. Hersey St., Ashland, OR 97520, tel. 503/488–1496.*
Accommodations: *4 double rooms with baths, 1 2-bedroom suite.*
Amenities: *Air-conditioning; horseshoe court.*
Rates: *$78–$85; Continental breakfast. AE, MC, V.*
Restrictions: *No smoking, no pets.*

Bayberry Inn Bed and Breakfast

The entire first floor of this white-trimmed, gray clapboard 1925 Craftsman on Ashland's Main Street has been taken over by the Fireside Dining Room. The restaurant, well regarded among locals for its innovative Continental cuisine, is a nuisance for guests seeking privacy and peace (guests walk through the restaurant to get to their rooms, which are directly above the dining room).

Innkeepers/restaurateurs Marilyn Brittsan Evans and Cheryl Lynn Colwell selected an English country decor for the interior. Deep green carpeting, mauve floral wallpaper, and a green marble fireplace give the dining room a touch of formality. The cozy Sheffield Room upstairs features dark floral swagged draperies, candlestick lamps, and graceful Louis XV–style chairs and other French reproductions. Two other second-floor rooms are bright and spacious, with broad window seats beneath wide, lace-swathed dormer windows.

Guests have the opportunity to sample Marilyn's cuisine at her memorable morning repasts, served in the dining room off the kitchen or on the sunny back deck.

Address: *438 N. Main St., Ashland, OR 97520, tel. 503/488–1252.*
Accommodations: *3 double rooms with baths.*
Amenities: *Air-conditioning, dinner available by reservation.*
Rates: *$60–$95; full breakfast, afternoon refreshments. MC, V.*
Restrictions: *No smoking, no pets.*

Chriswood Inn

In Grants Pass, the midpoint of the Rogue River, a Union Jack hangs opposite the American flag at the door of this 1927 English Tudor. George and Jeanne Woods spent six months touring B&Bs in Scotland prior to opening their British-style inn near Old Town. The inn's decor leans toward the casual but refined, with a mixture of antiques, reproductions, and contemporary furnishings, and a sprinkling of fine prints the couple kept from their days as gallery owners.

The surprisingly large bedrooms, equipped with sinks, are country quaint, with Jeanne's handcrafted floppy-ear, fabric bunnies and mice poised on beds and bookshelves, garlands or baskets of dried flowers on walls and tables, and cheerful quilts and comforters on sturdy brass beds.

Victorian Rococo wicker chairs placed around small tables in spacious sitting areas invite repose.

In keeping with English tradition, a downstairs pub-like game room is replete with card table, dartboard, and a bumper pool table.

Address: *220 N.W. "A" St., Grants Pass, OR 97526, tel. 503/474–9733 or 800/457–9733.*
Accommodations: *3 double rooms share 2 baths.*
Amenities: *Air-conditioning, vanity sinks, cable TV, and robes in rooms; meeting room.*
Rates: *$55–$70; full breakfast. No credit cards.*
Restrictions: *No smoking indoors, no pets.*

Country Willows Bed and Breakfast Inn

Two miles south of downtown Ashland, this blue clapboard 1896 farmhouse sits on 5 acres with willow trees and a brook, overlooking the Cascade and Siskiyou mountains. Guests enjoy nestling into willow furniture on the two-tiered front porch to soak in the scenery and the antics of all the creatures (ducks, geese, goats, horses, and rabbits) that live on the property.

The guest rooms are appointed with period reproductions and modern pieces, individual air-conditioning, and small private baths. Skylights, a stone fireplace, a two-person oak-framed tub, and a large brass bed in the main room of the new Sunrise Suite in the renovated barn make it a romantic guest room. There is a potbellied wood-burning stove and a kitchenette

in the little cottage just beyond the hot tub and heated swimming pool.

Gracious hosts Dan Durant and David Newton, formerly frequent guests of the inn, became the proud new owners in late 1993.

Address: *1313 Clay St., Ashland, OR 97520, tel. 503/488–1590.*
Accommodations: *4 double rooms with baths, 2 housekeeping suites, 1 2-bedroom housekeeping cottage.*
Amenities: *Air-conditioning and robes in rooms; VCR, video library, gift shop, swimming pool, hot tub.*
Rates: *$85–$150; full breakfast, evening refreshments. MC, V.*
Restrictions: *No smoking indoors, no pets; 2-night minimum on weekends Feb.–Oct.*

Morical House

Peter and Patricia Dahl have a charming 1880s Victorian farmhouse—for sale in 1994—surrounded by 1½ acres of trees, tall shrubs, and cheery flower gardens. Not readily visible from the road, it's on the primary drive into town, only a mile from the theaters and plaza.

Inside, period antiques and family heirlooms fit well with the original red fir floors, leaded- and stained-glass windows, and elaborate woodwork of the wide entry staircase, paneling, and moldings. The guest rooms offer antique bedsteads and dressers, balloon valances over double-sashed windows, and little reading lamps on bedside tables. The attic room is a favorite because of its garden views and distance from the traffic noise in the front of the house.

Generous breakfasts of fresh seasonal fruits, homemade baked goods, and smoothies to accompany the main course are served in the dining room or out on the cheery sun porch.

Address: *668 N. Main St., Ashland, OR 97520, tel. 503/482–2254.*
Accommodations: *5 double rooms with baths.*
Amenities: *Air-conditioning; putting green, badminton, croquet.*
Rates: *$95–$120; full breakfast, afternoon refreshments. MC, V.*
Restrictions: *No smoking inside, no pets; 2-night minimum on weekends Mar.–Oct.*

Mt. Ashland Inn

It's just not possible to get closer to the cross-country and downhill skiing on Mt. Ashland or the hiking on the Pacific Crest Trail than the Mt. Ashland Inn, a contemporary cedar-log chalet designed by Jerry and Elaine Shanafelt. A crackling fire in the large stone fireplace in the living room provides a welcome hearth for all who enter this cozy mountain retreat 16 miles south of Ashland in the cool heights of the Siskiyou Mountains. The Shanafelts' attention to decorative detail can be glimpsed throughout the inn, from Jerry's stained-glass entryway panels, handmade cedar dining table and Windsor chairs, and high relief carving on the guest room doors, to Elaine's hand-stitched quilts and selection of quality Eastlake pieces. The gigantic McGloughlin Suite, with windows on three sides overlooking the various peaks surrounding the lodge, has the best view, but the Sky Lakes Suite, with a small waterfall cascading beside a two-person whirlpool tub, is the most romantic. This fine inn was on the market in 1994.

Address: *505 Mt. Ashland Rd., Box 944, Ashland, OR 97520, tel. 503/482–8707.*
Accommodations: *3 double rooms with baths, 2 suites.*
Amenities: *Wet bar, refrigerator, and whirlpool tub in 1 room; ski storage room, TV, VCR, and wet bar in conference room.*
Rates: *$80–$90, suites $100–$130; full breakfast. MC, V.*
Restrictions: *No smoking indoors, no pets; 2-night minimum on weekends June–Sept. and holidays.*

River Banks Inn

This lodge-style house on the banks of the Rogue River 15 winding miles outside Grants Pass is a cross-cultural fantasy, starting with the Navaho "sweat lodge" and Zen meditation room. Then it's on to the main house, with its skylighted and plant-filled Garden Room, where you can soak in a sunken whirlpool tub; and to the Casablanca Room, with its carved Peruvian bed frame and nightstand and Afghan and Kurdish rugs.

What sounds funky comes off as fun, especially in the genial company of owner Myrtle Franklin, who put the inn on the market in 1994. More than anything, the River Banks Inn carries reminders of different phases of Myrtle's life: The pillow- and fur-covered stone ledge couch in the living room and the massage room are carryovers from her days as a therapist at the Esalen Institute in Big Sur; the Steinway piano a reflection of her past as a musician; and the restaurant-style kitchen a throwback to her stint as a chef.

Address: *8401 Riverbanks Rd., Grants Pass, OR 97527, tel. 503/479–1118.*
Accommodations: *3 double rooms with baths, 2 suites.*
Amenities: *Phone in rooms, cable TV and VCR in 3 rooms, whirlpool tub in 1 room; steam room, children's playhouse.*
Rates: *$75–$150; full breakfast. MC, V.*
Restrictions: *No smoking indoors, no pets.*

River's Reach Bed and Breakfast

A year-long tour of bed-and-breakfasts in the United States, followed by a stint managing a lodge on Lake Tahoe, were part of Russ Reichert's preparation for opening this Grants Pass B&B in 1991.

Once you're inside the compound, the peaceful surroundings will make you forget that the city is so close by. Both children and adults love the ponds, rambling trails up rolling hillsides, paddocks of horses and llamas, turkeys, cows, and dogs.

Inside the 1986 ranch house, a freestanding brick fireplace and large, hung panels of leaded and stained glass add distinction to the living room. Art prints overshadow the simple but comfortable furnishings in the guest rooms. A large country breakfast features the fresh eggs, sausage, and produce of this self-sustaining ranch.

Address: *4025 Williams Hwy., Grants Pass, OR 97527, tel. 503/474–4411.*
Accommodations: *2 double rooms share bath, 1 suite, 1 housekeeping suite.*
Amenities: *Air-conditioning, wood-burning stove in 1 room, TV in 2 rooms, VCRs available, whirlpool tub in shared bath; pets of all sizes welcome (stables available).*
Rates: *$60–$115; full breakfast, evening refreshments. No credit cards.*
Restrictions: *No smoking indoors.*

Romeo Inn

Margaret and Bruce Halverson's sprawling 1930s Cape Cod features family heirlooms that blend well with the contemporary decor. An L-shaped living room has a large fireplace and a sliding door opening onto the patio pool area and garden.

Amish quilts stand out in the functionally furnished guest rooms, several of which have private entrances and fireplaces. Canterbury features a modern oak four-poster, while Coventry is more traditional, with an antique rocker and commode that have been in the family for generations. The Stratford Suite above the detached garage enjoys a view of a pastoral valley to the south from the double whirlpool tub.

The Halversons have a repertoire of 40 to 50 breakfast entrées, offering something sweet one morning, something savory the next.

Address: *295 Idaho St., Ashland, OR 97520, tel. 503/488–0884 or 800/915–8899, fax 503/488–0817.*
Accommodations: *4 double rooms with baths, 1 suite, 1 housekeeping suite.*
Amenities: *Air-conditioning, phone in rooms, piano, library, swimming pool, hot tub.*
Rates: *$115–$140, suites $160–$175; full breakfast, all-day refreshments, bedtime truffles. MC, V.*
Restrictions: *No smoking, no pets; 2-night minimum June–Oct. and weekends Mar.–Oct.*

Sonka's Sheep Station Inn

After enjoying numerous sojourns on farms in New Zealand, Evelyn and Louis Sonka decided to open their own ranch and share the experience with others. Their Folk Victorian–style farmhouse sits on a 400-acre working sheep ranch in a cloud-shrouded valley 18 miles south of Roseburg.

The sheep motif is everywhere: in artwork, etched glass, wallpaper, and even trim. Furnishings consist of traditional-style pieces and oak spoolwork antiques. Guest rooms boast patchwork quilts and color-coordinated dust ruffles on iron-and-brass beds. The remodeled bunkhouse holds three double rooms and a full kitchen.

Guests are welcome to join in on the early morning herding; the less active can watch Louis's border collies chase the sheep around the field later in the day. Pots of steaming coffee and hot muffins greet guests in the kitchen each morning.

Address: *901 N.W. Chadwick La., Myrtle Creek, OR 97457, tel. 503/863–5168.*
Accommodations: *2 double rooms share bath, 1 triple housekeeping suite.*
Amenities: *Satellite TV; nature paths.*
Rates: *$50–$60, suite $130; full breakfast. No credit cards.*
Restrictions: *No smoking indoors, no pets; closed 2 weeks at Christmas.*

Touvelle House

This carefully restored 1916 Crafts-man, with its broad covered porches and shingle exterior, is on a peaceful street next to a historic cemetery, just two blocks from the sights, shopping, and dining of down-town Jacksonville. The quick humor and "welcome-home-y'all" attitude of own-ers Dennis and Carolee Casey make this inn a true charmer, as do the strik-ing architectural features of the house: 14-foot box-beam ceilings in the mas-sive living room, shelf-lined walls in the library, and numerous built-ins, includ-ing a beautiful hutch in the dining room.

Favorite rooms are Prairie West, with wicker-and-pine furniture, claw-foot tub, holster, bridles, bear traps, and period photographs, and Granny's Attic, tucked under the gables. All guest rooms have modern bathrooms.

Guests frequently play card games or charades; Callie, the calico house cat, is equally happy to entertain. Outside are gardens and a small orchard, and a hot tub and swimming pool. Breakfast spe-cialties include Greek soufflés, tar-ragon-egg croissants with mushroom sauce, and waffles with pear pecan sauce.

Address: *455 N. Oregon St., Box 1891, Jacksonville, OR 97530, tel. and fax 503/899–8938.*
Accommodations: *3 double rooms with baths, 2 suites.*
Amenities: *Swimming pool, hot tub, bikes; cable TV in library.*
Rates: *$90–$95, suites $95–$145; full breakfast. No credit cards.*
Restrictions: *No smoking indoors, no pets.*

Willowbrook Inn Bed and Breakfast

Gold Hill, a small farming com-munity on the banks of the Rogue River, enjoys a slower pace than the neighboring towns of Grants Pass and Medford, and nowhere is that lifestyle more evident than at the Willowbrook Inn. Guests can sip lemonade while they relax in sturdy willow-branch chairs or in a ham-mock on the front porch, watching the birds flit among the old trees in the yard.

The interior of this 1905 Dutch Colo-nial–style farmhouse echoes the coun-try charm of its setting, with a spinning wheel, bow-back Windsor armchairs, parson's bench, and Colonial reproduc-tions. A peek into the kitchen offers evidence that Tom and Joann Hoeber formerly ran a gourmet cookware shop. Guest rooms have coordinated floral wallpaper, curtains, and bed covers, and step-up four-poster beds.

After a robust breakfast of sage-sausage pie and other dishes seasoned with spices from the Hoebers' massive herb garden, guests can enjoy rafting and fishing on the Rogue River or make the half-hour drive to Ashland.

Address: *628 Foots Creek Rd., Gold Hill, OR 97525, tel. 503/582–0075.*
Accommodations: *2 double rooms with baths, 1 suite.*
Amenities: *Air-conditioning; outdoor swimming pool, hot tub.*
Rates: *$60, suite $70; full breakfast. MC, V.*
Restrictions: *No smoking indoors, no pets.*

Wolf Creek Tavern

This handsome Classical Revival inn, in the tiny town of Wolf Creek, is a nostalgic example of a postal town hostelry in the late 19th century.

The Victoriana-filled ladies' parlor and saloonlike men's tap room have fireplaces. The tiny Jack London Room is kept as a showroom, with tattered quilt on the short, narrow beam bed and a candle on the rough-hewn desk table, typical furnishings found in lodgings of the period. The master chamber, the oldest and largest of the guest rooms, is furnished with simple 19th-century folk antiques. The rooms in the south wing are much smaller, with patinated brass beds and oak or mahogany dressers.

The concessionaires currently running the historic tavern for the Oregon State Parks and Recreation Division have many management kinks to work through; service is not what it should be, though the period costume–clad staff does try.

Address: *100 Front St., Box 97, Wolf Creek, OR 97497, tel. 503/866-2474.*
Accommodations: *8 double rooms with baths.*
Amenities: *Restaurant, gift shop, air-conditioning, conference room.*
Rates: *$55–$75; Continental breakfast extra. D, MC, V.*
Restrictions: *small pets only; closed 2 weeks in Jan.*

Woods House

Named for one of the founding families of Ashland, this 1908 Craftsman rests on noisy Main Street in the historic district, just blocks from the festival theaters. Lace curtains, dried flower arrangements, reproduction Early American pieces, and polished fir floors and staircase furnish this rose-scented home now owned by Françoise and Lester Roddy.

Also decorated in Victorian style, the guest rooms are appointed with antique bedsteads (some with lace canopies), floral comforters, lace curtains and doilies, pastel watercolors, and a profusion of preserved roses. Behind the house, the lovely English garden, which has a grape arbor, 110 rosebushes, and several interesting sculptures, is a good spot to unwind.

Meals served at the large oak dining table, set with fine china and crystal, might start with Françoise's delicious chocolate-orange or almond-poppy seed scones, followed by such main dishes as sautéed leeks with poached eggs in wine and caviar sauce or cheese blintzes in raspberry sauce.

Address: *333 N. Main St., Ashland, OR 97520, tel. 503/488-1598 or 800/435-8260, fax 503/482-7912.*
Accommodations: *6 double rooms with baths.*
Amenities: *Air-conditioning.*
Rates: *$90–$110; full breakfast, afternoon refreshments. MC, V.*
Restrictions: *No smoking indoors, no pets; 2-night minimum June–Oct.*

Willamette Valley
Including Eugene

Cradled between the Cascade Mountain range to the east and the Coast Range and Pacific Ocean to the west is the serene green expanse of land known as the Willamette Valley. Cloud-shrouded craggy bluffs and sheep-dotted, pastoral meadows line I–5 and Highways 99W and 99E, the major arteries through this lush north–south corridor. Historic stagecoach stops and gold-mining boomtowns, culture-rich college towns, and small farming communities dot the valley between Salem, Oregon's state capital in the north, and Roseburg in the south. For the most part, industry here revolves around what the fertile land and mild climate provides: rich, moist soil for hundreds of thriving farms, orchards, and nurseries; rolling meadows of pastureland for ranching; and stands of timber for the logging trade. During harvest season, highways and byways are lined with roadside stands overflowing with colorful fresh fruits and vegetables, nuts, jams, and flowers. Vineyards abound as well, producing mainly such cool-climate varietals as Pinot Noir, chardonnay, and Riesling.

Many of Oregon's rivers and streams—including the Deschutes, McKenzie, North Umpqua, and Willamette rivers—cut through this valley, providing thrilling rapids rafting and outstanding fishing for steelhead, sockeye, trout, and bass. About a dozen of Oregon's remaining 54 covered bridges, dating from the turn of the century, are scattered throughout the Willamette Valley.

Colleges and universities in the valley—including Oregon State University in Corvallis and the University of Oregon in Eugene—provide academic and cultural life to the entire region. With its own ballet, opera, symphony, and theater companies, Eugene, Oregon's second-largest metropolitan area, is host to the valley's strongest arts programs.

Places to Go, Sights to See

Albany. There are three distinct historic districts in this vintage Victorian town, each with numerous commercial and residential buildings representing scores of architectural styles and periods. Albany is also a good jumping-off point for the covered-bridge circuit through Eugene and Cottage Grove.

Cottage Grove. "Tour the Golden Past," a pamphlet available at the ranger station on Row River Road, is a good guide to the abandoned mines, historical buildings, and covered bridges (six in this area) of this nostalgic Gold Rush boomtown. The rangers can also direct you to public gold-panning areas. The Bohemian Mining Days festival in July celebrates Cottage Grove's mining tradition.

Covered Bridges. There are dozens of covered bridges in the Willamette Valley, most of which are clustered in and around Cottage Grove and in Linn County. Contact the Albany Convention and Visitors Commission (*see* Tourist Information, *below*) for a touring map. The Covered Bridge Society of Oregon (Box 1804, Newport, OR 97365, tel. 503/265–2934) can also provide historical information.

Euphoria Chocolate Company (6 W. 17th Ave., tel. 503/343–9223). This little company a few blocks south of the heart of downtown Eugene makes some of the best-loved chocolate in Oregon.

Finley National Wildlife Refuge (26208 Finley Refuge Rd., Corvallis, tel. 503/757–7236). This refuge is a bird-watcher's paradise, with large fields of grasses and grains that attract Canada geese, grouse, pheasants, quail, wood ducks, and other varieties of birds. The refuge is also home to numerous deer.

Hult Center for the Performing Arts (One Eugene Center, Eugene, tel. 503/687–5000). This world-class arts complex in Eugene is an airy structure of glass and native wood, containing two of the most acoustically perfect theaters on the West Coast. It hosts everything from heavy-metal concerts to classical ballets and is the home of Eugene's symphony, ballet, and opera companies. It is also the site of the renowned two-week Oregon Bach Festival that takes place in June and July.

Museums. The top museums in the valley include the *University of Oregon Museum of Art* (1430 Johnson La., Eugene, tel. 503/346–3027), best known for its Oriental collection; the *Horner Museum* (Gill Coliseum, Oregon State University, Corvallis, tel. 503/737–2951), featuring artifacts from Oregon's natural and cultural history; and *Wistec* (2300 Centennial Blvd., Eugene, tel. 503/687–3619), a science and technology museum.

Oakland. The citizens of this small community on the old stage line between San Francisco and Portland have done a lot to restore their 19th-century pioneer town, which is on the National Register of Historic Places. Blocks of refurbished buildings representing styles dating from 1860 include several saloons, the gristmill, livery stable, general mercantile, opera house, icehouse/butcher shop, and pioneer post office, once the distribution center for the West Coast.

Saturday Market (8th and Oak Sts.). This bustling art, craft, and food market in Eugene attracts big crowds each Saturday from April through December, when farmers sell fresh produce and flowers, chefs create ethnic fare, and entertainers perform in the streets.

Wineries. There are nearly two dozen wineries in the valley, offering tours, tastings, and gorgeous scenery. The Oregon Winegrowers' Association (1200 N.W. Front Ave., Suite 400, Portland, OR 97209, tel. 503/228–8403) can provide information and brochures on the region's wineries.

Restaurants

Chef Rolph Schmidt's **Chanterelle** (tel. 503/484–4065) in Eugene offers hearty French and other European cuisines and delicious pastries in intimate surroundings. Other top restaurants in Eugene include **Ambrosia** (tel. 503/342–4141) for Italian cuisine and **Willie's on Seventh** (tel. 503/485–0601) for Continental fare. **Tolly's** (tel. 503/459–3796), a combination soda fountain/wine library/restaurant/antiques shop/art gallery in Oakland, offers the best dining in town, with bistro fare, standard American favorites, and a dash of Scandinavian cuisine. The authentic spätzle, schnitzel, and sausages make **Teske's Germania Restaurant** (tel. 503/672–5401) a favorite in Roseburg.

Tourist Information

Albany Convention and Visitors Commission (300 2nd Ave. SW, Box 965, Albany, OR 97321, tel. 503/928–0911 or 800/526–2256); **Corvallis Convention and Visitors Bureau** (420 N.W. 2nd St., Corvallis, OR 97330, tel. 503/757–1544 or 800/334–8118); **Cottage Grove Chamber of Commerce** (710 Row River Rd., Box 587, Cottage Grove, OR 97424, tel. 503/942–2411); **Eugene–Springfield Visitors Bureau** (305 W. 7th Ave., Box 10286, Eugene, OR 97440, tel. 503/484–5307 or 800/547–5445); **Roseburg Visitors and Convention Bureau** (410 S.E. Spruce, Box 1262, Roseburg, OR 97470, tel. 503/672–9731 or 800/444–9584).

Reservation Services

Bed and Breakfast Innkeepers (711 W. 11th Ave., Eugene, OR 97202, tel. 503/345–7799); **Bed and Breakfast Reservations—Oregon** (2321 N.E. 28th Ave., Portland, OR 97212, tel. 503/287–4704); **Country Host Registry** (901 N.W. Chadwick La., Myrtle Creek, OR 97457, tel. 503/863–5168); **Northwest Bed and Breakfast** (610 S.W. Broadway, Suite 606, Portland, OR 97205, tel. 503/243–7616).

Hanson Country Inn

In 1928 Jeff Hanson built this rotund Dutch Colonial on a high knoll overlooking the rolling Willamette Valley as the headquarters for his prospering poultry-breeding ranch. Here, in the egg house opposite the main house, he developed his world-famous strain of White Leghorn chickens. After Hanson died, the house stood empty for 13 years. In 1987 it was purchased by Patricia Covey, a friendly Californian looking for escape from the Bay area, who had seen Corvallis listed in *Best Cities to Live in in America*. With plenty of polish and elbow grease, Patricia was able to restore the original grandeur of the house's unique features, including the carefully laid honeycomb tile work in the bathrooms and the intricately carved spindle room divider and sweeping spindle staircase, both made of New Zealand gumwood carved by local craftsmen.

A baby grand piano, 1920s American furniture, assorted sculptures, and a selection of Patricia's own paintings bring understated elegance to the great living room with its massive central fireplace. Sun pours through tall windowpanes, brightening the cozy reading nook where a plump easy chair sits beside floor-to-ceiling bookcases. The sunporch, with sparkling stained-glass windows and casual rattan furniture, looks onto a terraced garden with a stone fountain and a white vine arbor.

The suite, in shades of peach and sea-foam green, has a lovingly polished four-poster bed, an attached sitting room, and a private veranda overlooking a gentle slope to the valley below. The largest double room, a favorite of wedding couples because of its romantic box-canopy bed, has a sitting alcove and windows on three of its sides—providing views of the valley, the terraced garden, and the quiet pasture behind the house. All rooms are appointed with 1920s American furniture and soft bed linens imported from England. A two-bedroom cottage with hardwood floors, iron bedsteads, and down comforters was added in 1993; families will appreciate the greater space and privacy.

Guests can get acquainted with resident cats, chickens, and sheep, explore the unrestored egg house, or take walks in the gardens and orchards on the 5-acre grounds. Wine tasting at nearby vineyards or a visit to the University of Oregon's Horner Museum are other entertainment possibilities.

Address: *795 S.W. Hanson St., Corvallis, OR 97333, tel. 503/752–2919.*
Accommodations: *1 double room with bath, 2 doubles share 1 bath, 1 suite, 1 2-bedroom housekeeping cottage.*
Amenities: *Phone and cable TV in 2 rooms.*
Rates: *$55–$65, cottage $125; full breakfast. AE, D, DC, MC, V.*
Restrictions: *No smoking indoors, no pets.*

Odell Lake Lodge & Resort

The Pacific Crest Trail passes right by this mountain resort in the Cascade Mountains at Willamette Pass. The two-story wood-frame building, made of contemporary rustic lumber, has a broad front porch from which guests can watch the marina activities or keep an eye on the waterfowl dipping into an adjacent stream for stone flies. In winter, visitors can sink into comfy overstuffed chairs by the fireplace in the modest library/living room off the lodge entryway.

Boating and fishing are popular on this deep-water, high-elevation lake that's too cold for swimming, even in summer. Fishers pull in record-setting Mackinaw lake trout, rainbow trout, and kokanee; it's possible to catch trout from the dock. In the Deschutes National Forest and adjacent to the Diamond Peak Wilderness, the resort is also a mecca for hikers and mountain bikers; Crater Lake National Park, 55 miles south, and the Lava River Cave and Lava Cast Forest, 52 miles north, are easy day trips. In the winter, Willamette Pass offers downhill skiing; there are also plenty of cross-country trails around the resort.

If you're staying in the lodge, the lakeside rooms on the second floor are your best bet. Room 3, a knotty pine–paneled corner accommodation with views of the lake and the stream, is especially cozy. (Take Room 4 only under duress—the bed consumes nearly all of the space, and views are of the parking lot out back.) Similarly, the few additional dollars required to get one of the lakeside cabins are well spent. All are clean and offer wood stoves as well as bedding and kitchen equipment (cabins 1–3 have microwaves but no ovens, however). The much smaller second-tier cabins have tiny windows that look out only on adjacent cabins, the road, and parking areas. Of all of the cabins, the newly rebuilt No. 10, a rustic, pine-paneled room with large windows and a deck, is the best.

The lake-view restaurant is well worth a drive up the mountain pass. In addition to standards such as pasta, steak, and chicken, the menu includes such specials as fillet of coho salmon with raspberry butter.

Address: *Box 72, Crescent Lake, OR 97425, tel. 503/433–2540.*
Accommodations: *7 double rooms with baths, 12 housekeeping cabins.*
Amenities: *Wheelchair-accessible cabins; marina with dock moorage and boat rentals; mountain bike, cross-country ski, and snowshoe rentals; volleyball court; restaurant.*
Rates: *$38–$50, cabins $55–$185; no breakfast. D, MC, V.*
Restrictions: *Pets in cabins only; 2-night minimum weekends and July–Aug., 3-night minimum on holidays.*

The Oval Door Bed and Breakfast

This 2½-story, pitch-roofed house with a wraparound porch was built in 1990 but matches the surrounding homes from the '20s and '30s in this centrally located, older neighborhood in Eugene near the University of Oregon and the Hult Center for the Performing Arts. A whimsical purple door hints at the unconventional things to come.

Inside, a collection of modern art by Pacific Northwest artists is a counterpoint to centuries-old antiques and comfortable, modern American furniture. The dining room has an 1860 Eastlake walnut dining table and floral prints filling one wall; another wall has glass doors that open onto a broad wraparound porch with cushioned chairs and a swing for resting beneath the rustling leaves of the shade trees.

Guest rooms are furnished with a mixture of contemporary and antique pieces; an open steamer trunk that serves as a dresser in one room is especially striking. Extra touches include Perrier and water glasses on doily-covered trays, fresh and dried flower arrangements, candles and books of poetry, a choice of pillows (down, poly, or orthopedic), thick terry robes, and a selection of current paperbacks that guests are free to take when they leave. The cozy, two-person whirlpool tub room is adorned with candles, flower arrangements, mirrors, a stereo, and a selection of scented bath salts and oils. The heated towel rack is a rare joy to find in the United States.

Hostess Judith McLane dropped out of the California corporate fast lane to run the inn. She uses a large tile set on the dining room buffet as a blackboard to announce the breakfast menu of the day; her specialties include Popeye's Morning (creamed spinach) and Idaho Sunrise (a twice-baked potato stuffed with a poached egg).

Address: *988 Lawrence St., Eugene, OR 97401, tel. 503/683–3160, fax 503/485–5339.*
Accommodations: *4 double rooms with baths.*
Amenities: *Whirlpool tub, phones, ceiling fans, and individual heat control in rooms; airport and train station pickup, bicycles.*
Rates: *$65–$83; full breakfast. MC, V.*
Restrictions: *No smoking inside, no pets.*

Steamboat Inn

Deep in the Umpqua National Forest, 38 winding miles east of Roseburg, this 1855 river-rock and pine lodge sits alongside the luminous blue North Umpqua River. Fisher folk from around the globe come here to test their skills against the elusive steelhead and trout. Owners Jim and Sharon Van Loan were themselves frequent visitors and worked as members of the inn's summer crew for three years before buying it in 1975.

While its fishing tradition is still much in evidence—rehabilitated fly-tying cabinets serving as the reception desk and an unobtrusive fly shop—the Steamboat has seen a shift toward a more refined country inn. The rough edges of this fishing camp have been delicately hewn down with coordinated pastel bedding, draperies, and carpets, as well as thoughtful decorative touches of dried flowers, botanical prints, and hand-quilted comforters in the refurbished riverside cabins. Knotty pine paneling and rustic Americana furnishings in the guest rooms echo the decor of the main lodge.

Recent additions to the property include two detached suites along the river and five roomy, lofted chalets a half mile up the road. A king-size bed in the master bedroom, twin beds in the loft, a fireplace in the living room, deep-soaking tub in the roomy bathroom, and a kitchenette stocked with dishes and cookware make the chalets perfect for families or small groups.

The riverside suites offer intimate seclusion, with large wood-burning fireplaces, two-person Japanese-style soaking tubs, and large private decks looking onto the river.

The Steamboat's famous candlelit "fisherman's dinner" might include Northwest wines, salad spiced with roasted local nuts or garden-fresh herbs, fresh bread, a vegetable dish, and roasted lamb or fresh spring salmon steamed, poached, or grilled. Wine-tasting dinners are available on winter weekends.

Nonfishing activities in the area include backpacking and hiking on the trails of the surrounding Umpqua National Forest, soaking in swimming holes, picking wildflowers, or making a day trip to cross-country ski at Diamond Lake or to admire the breathtaking, crystal-blue waters of Crater Lake.

Address: *Steamboat, OR 97447, tel. and fax 503/498–2411.*
Accommodations: *8 cabins with baths, 5 2-bedroom housekeeping cottages, 2 suites.*
Amenities: *Full meal service, air-conditioning in lodge, meeting room, large library/conference room, small pets allowed for extra fee.*
Rates: *$85–$125, suites $195; breakfast extra. MC, V.*
Restrictions: *No smoking indoors; closed Jan.–Feb.*

Westfir Lodge

Anchoring the tiny community of Westfir, just west of the crest of the Cascade Mountains, Westfir Lodge was long the hub of activity in the town, which boasted a population of several thousand in its heyday a half-century ago. However, you can't tell by looking at the two-story clapboard Arts and Crafts–style building that it was formerly the main office of the Westfir Lumber Company.

Gerry Chamberlain and Ken Symons, who bought the building in 1990 after a search across six states for a suitable place to open a B&B, added bathrooms to the building and converted the offices, which ring the first floor, into bedrooms. Over the years, four additional guest rooms were added on the second floor. The large central space became a living area, kitchen, and formal dining room. Antiques—some family heirlooms, others procured in Southeast Asia, and some purchased at local estate auctions—as well as heavy formal drapes on the windows create a kitschy English country ambience in the public spaces.

The 10-foot ceilings almost make the accommodations seem spacious. Two adjoining bedrooms on the north side of the lodge have views of the woodpile, trees, and a neighbor's home, and are quieter than those on the east side, which face a road traveled by logging trucks that often leave town before daylight; in addition, the many logging trains that whistle past Westfir can be heard from here. However, the Willamette River is just across the road from the lodge, and if you're a sound sleeper, the river views and larger room size are inducements to opt for the accommodations on the east side of the building.

Full English breakfasts are offered here, a result of the fact that Ken hails from Australia. He gets English bangers at a butcher shop in Portland, three hours to the north, and serves the traditional British sausage with fried potatoes, eggs, and a broiled half-tomato topped with cheese, mushrooms, and bits of vegetables. Accompaniments include scones, other English breakfast breads, and Australian biscuits, as well as fresh fruit. Guests can eat on the patio looking out at pink hedge roses, daisies, poppies, and varied annuals; the garden also offers a view of the recently renovated, 180-foot-long Office Bridge, the longest covered bridge in Oregon.

Address: *47365 1st St., Westfir, OR 97492, tel. 503/782–3103.*
Accommodations: *5 double rooms with baths, 2 double rooms share 1 bath.*
Amenities: *Wood-burning stove in living room, reception facilities; nearby kennel for pets.*
Rates: *$65; full breakfast. No credit cards.*
Restrictions: *No smoking inside, no pets.*

Beckley House

The entire town of Oakland is on the National Register of Historic Places, and this clapboard Italianate Victorian fits right in. The large, bright living room features diamond-paned windows, oak floors, whitewashed walls, and high ceilings. Dark cedar wainscoting, shiny wall sconces, and a large central fireplace give a formal feel to the dining room. Oil paintings and intricately carved wardrobes and bedsteads fill the roomy second-floor guest rooms. The radiantly sunny suite, a converted sunporch, has a white iron bed topped with a canopy-like drapery and a colorful quilt.

Sally Wheaton, an interior decorator, and her husband, Floyd, retired from the sheet-metal business, left California and bought Beckley House during the summer of 1991. However, the property was on the market in 1994, so ownership may change.

A complimentary breakfast is served two blocks away at Tolly's, the combination soda fountain/restaurant/wine library/art gallery/antiques shop that has long been a treasured Oakland fixture.

Address: *338 S.E. 2nd St., Oakland, OR 97462, tel. 503/459–9320.*
Accommodations: *2 double rooms share 1 bath, 1 suite.*
Amenities: *Horse and carriage rides available.*
Rates: *$65–$85; full breakfast. No credit cards.*
Restrictions: *No pets.*

Duckworth

Peggy and Fred Ward left a frenetic life in San Diego for quieter Eugene, where they bought a 1926 garden cottage with some Tudor features just blocks from the university. Duckworth is furnished with English antiques and collectibles of all kinds—clocks, china, hatboxes, jewelry—that complement the original hardwood floors as well as the striking stained-glass windows added during renovations.

The two front bedrooms with queen-size beds are cheerful, but the most popular is the English Garden Room with private bath, English Victorian comforter, and a broad window seat overlooking garden paths that wind through billowing trees, flowering shrubs, and a swing out back.

A handsome sideboard that survived San Francisco's 1906 earthquake stands out in the garden-side dining room where breakfast is served family style. Afterward you might relax in the twig rocker in the sweetly scented sitting room or strike up a ditty on the player piano in the living room.

Address: *987 E. 19th Ave., Eugene, OR 97403, tel. 503/686–2451 or 800/713–2461.*
Accommodations: *1 double room with bath, 2 doubles share 1 bath.*
Amenities: *TV with VCR in all rooms, phone in 1 room; video library, games, player piano, bicycles.*
Rates: *$75–$85; full breakfast, afternoon snacks. No credit cards.*
Restrictions: *No smoking indoors, no pets.*

House of Hunter

A path of roses beside two giant tulip trees leads to the bright red door of this somewhat stern-looking Italianate Victorian overlooking downtown Roseburg. Walt Hunter and his wife, Jean, have done an admirable job of restoring the house they bought in 1989.

The interior is mostly formal, especially in the front dining room, where massive cabinets display fine family china and cut glass. The living room, furnished with early 20th-century American chairs and couches, is less stiff and more inviting. Second-floor guest rooms have small vanities, tall armoires, frilly curtains, ruffled bedspreads, fringed lamp shades, and lacy pillows that Jean created.

Each morning trays of steaming coffee and freshly baked breads and muffins await early risers, followed by a large full breakfast. A back porch looks out onto Walt's developing English flower garden.

Address: *813 S.E. Kane, Roseburg, OR 97470, tel. 503/672–2335.*
Accommodations: *2 double rooms with baths, 2 doubles with basins share 1 bath, 1 2-bedroom suite.*
Amenities: *Air-conditioning, laundry room, VCR library, TV and VCR in guest living room.*
Rates: *$50–$75; full breakfast. MC, V.*
Restrictions: *No smoking indoors, no pets.*

McGillivray's Log Home Bed and Breakfast

W hether it's the cozy feeling of being surrounded by wood, or owner Evelyn McGillivray's congeniality, this bed-and-breakfast is welcoming and homey.

From the split-log staircase to the colorful stained-glass windows on the second-floor landing, the McGillivrays did it all themselves. Rough strips of wood frame old photos of loggers hard at work, appropriate in this structure of pine, fir, oak, chinquapin (an Oregon hardwood), and other woods. Ruffled curtains; quilted pillows and bedspreads; and hand-hewn wood-slab headboards, bedside tables, and dressers add to the rustic atmosphere.

Breakfast is an event. Evelyn stands before her antique wood-burning stove preparing fresh coffee, bacon-wrapped eggs, and buttermilk pancakes; other culinary trimmings might include fresh-squeezed juice, baked fruit, hazelnut-honey butter, and maple or choke-cherry syrup.

Address: *88680 Evers Rd., Elmira, OR 97437, tel. 503/935–3564.*
Accommodations: *2 double rooms with baths.*
Amenities: *Air-conditioning.*
Rates: *$60–$70; full breakfast. MC, V.*
Restrictions: *No smoking indoors, no pets.*

Wine Country
Including Salem

Years ago, researchers at Oregon State University concluded that the soils and climate of the Willamette Valley were unsuitable for the cultivation of fine varietal wine grapes. Fortunately for oenophiles everywhere, they were much mistaken. Oregon's first vineyards took root during the early 1960s. Caressed by moisture-laden breezes off the Pacific and coddled by Oregon's long, warm summers and crisp autumns, cool-climate varietals such as Pinot Noir, Riesling, and chardonnay soon proved the academics wrong.

The vintages of 1983 and 1985 put the stamp of greatness on Oregon's Pinot Noir, as wines from the Yamhill and Willamette valleys won numerous gold medals in blind tastings against the best from California and France. Perhaps afflicted with Pinot envy, Burgundy's Drouhin family bought 180 acres here in 1987; they released their first bottling in 1991.

If you've been to California's famous Napa and Sonoma wine districts, you'll have an idea of what the Oregon wine country is not. The state's 100-plus bonded wineries have about 7,000 acres under cultivation, compared with California's 800 wineries and 700,000 acres of vineyards. Oregon's wineries tend to be small, personal, and family run. In fact, if you make a disparaging remark about the Riesling while you're in the tasting room, you may find yourself answering to the owner, who, it just so happens, is pouring out the samples.

Oregon's wine country lacks the maturity and sumptuous splendor of California's—as well as its pretensions. Its wineries are scattered from the Columbia River gorge, just across the river from Washington, all the way south to Ashland, near the California border. But the greatest concentration—more than 60 in all—is found within an hour's drive of Portland, dotting the hills as far south as Salem. Geographically, the wine country occupies a wet, temperate trough between the Coast Range to the west and the Cascades to the east. The landscape is a beguiling one—green and rugged, rich with soothing picture-postcard views that invite picnicking.

The small towns along the way—Forest Grove, McMinnville, Yamhill, Dundee—retain their rural charm. If that means they have yet to succumb to rampant commercialism, it also means you may have to hunt a bit for the best available food, lodging, and other amenities. Oregon's wine country is a quiet district, heavy on bucolic serenity but lightly endowed with sites of noteworthy historical significance, national parks, or other tourist attractions. Napa Valley it's not, but Oregon's wine country makes a fine side trip from Portland—and it's an even better destination for two to three days of quiet R&R.

Places to Go, Sights to See

Bush House (600 Mission St. SE, tel. 503/363–4174), just south of Salem's downtown district in the 105-acre Bush's Pasture Park, is a creaky, gaslit Italianate mansion from 1878 with 10 marble fireplaces. (Next door is the Bush Barn Art Center, a gallery selling works by Northwest artists.) A few blocks away, the fanciful 1894 *Deepwood Estate* (1116 Mission St. SE, tel. 503/363–1825) is in better taste. Built in the Queen Anne style, the estate is noteworthy for its splendid interior woodwork, original stained glass, and formal English-style garden.

The **Lafayette Schoolhouse Antique Mall** (Hwy. 99W, between Newberg and McMinnville, tel. 503/864–2720), a large, freshly restored 1910 schoolhouse, houses Oregon's largest permanent antiques show. It's filled with a vast assortment of collectibles and antiquities—from toys to clothing to furniture, china, glass, silver, and Native American artifacts.

McMinnville is the largest (population 16,000) and most sophisticated of Oregon's wine-country towns. Its central location, excellent restaurants and shops, and collection of top-notch B&Bs make it the headquarters of choice for most wine-country tourers. Founded in 1849, *Linfield College* (tel. 503/472–4121), an oasis of brick and ivy in the midst of McMinnville's farmers' market bustle, hosts Oregon's International Pinot Noir Celebration, which attracts a who's who of international wine makers each July.

When it opens in late 1996, McMinnville's *Evergreen Airventure Museum* (on Three-Mile Lane east of downtown McMinnville, tel. 503/768–5038) will be a spectacular new addition to the wine district's roster of attractions. You won't be amazed by its more than 30 rare antique aircraft, many restored to flying condition, including a B-17G, a Ford Trimotor, a P-40, a P-51, a Corsair, and a Spitfire—that is, not after you've caught sight of Howard Hughes' Spruce Goose, the largest airplane ever to fly. When it goes on view, this monument in aviation history will attract visitors from far and wide.

Mission Mill Village and Thomas Kay Woolen Mill Museum (1313 Mill St. SE, tel. 503/585–7012) in Salem offers visitors a vivid glimpse of a late-19th-century woolen mill, complete with waterwheels and mill stream. Teasel gigging and napper flock bins are just two of the processes and machines on display at the museum complex. Everything still works; it looks as if the workers have merely stepped away for a lunch break. The *Marion Museum of History* displays a fine collection of pioneer and Calipooya Indian artifacts. The spare simplicity of the *Jason Lee House, John D. Boone Home,* and the *Methodist Parsonage,* also part of the village, offer a glimpse of domestic life in the wilds of pioneer Oregon.

Newberg, a graceful old pioneer town in a broad bend in the Willamette River half an hour southwest of Portland, is also worth a visit. One of the oldest and most significant of the town's original structures is the *Hoover-Minthorn House* (115 S. River St., tel. 503/538–6629), the boyhood home of President Herbert Hoover. Built in 1881, the beautifully preserved frame house includes many original furnishings and features, as well as the woodshed that no doubt played a formative role in shaping young "Bertie" Hoover's character.

The **Oregon Wine and Food Festival** (Oregon State Fair and Exposition Center, 2330 17th St. NE, Salem, OR 97310, tel. 503/378–3247) is held each January at the State Fairgrounds in Salem. Dozens of Oregon's top wineries bring their current releases, and wine lovers can taste to their heart's content for a modest fee. For the resilient of palate, it's an excellent opportunity to compare wines, styles, and vintages.

Salem, Oregon's state capital, is on the 45th parallel about 45 miles south of Portland, precisely halfway between the North Pole and the equator. Even if you have no political ambitions, make time for a visit to the *Capitol* complex (900 Court St., tel. 503/378–4423). The view of the city, the Willamette Valley, and the mountains from its 140-foot-high dome is impressive; there are surprisingly good murals and sculptures inspired by the state's history; and when the legislature is in session, you can observe Oregon's political movers and shakers in action. Tours of the rotunda, the House and Senate chambers, and the governor's office leave from the information counter under the dome. Just across State Street are the tradition-steeped brick buildings and immaculate grounds of *Willamette University* (tel. 503/370–6303), the oldest college in the West. Founded in 1842, Willamette has long been a mecca for aspiring politicians. The tall, prim Waller Hall, built in 1841, is one of the five oldest buildings in the Pacific Northwest. The university hosts theatrical and musical performances, athletic events, guest lectures, and art exhibitions year-round.

Wine Touring, by car or bicycle, is obviously the star attraction here. First pick up a copy of *Discover Oregon Wineries,* a free guide available at visitor information centers and at most places where Oregon wines are sold (it's also available from the Oregon Winegrowers' Association, 1200 N.W. Front St., Portland, OR 97209, tel. 503/228–8403). The guide is an invaluable companion, with maps to each winery, opening hours, and suggested itineraries.

Day tourers can begin anywhere, but if you're planning a more extended exploration of the wine country, you should choose a base of operations central to the area you intend to explore. McMinnville has the best concentration of restaurants and bed-and-breakfasts. Salem to the south and Forest Grove to the north also make good headquarters.

Opening hours vary widely. The tasting rooms of some wineries are open daily year-round; others are either open only on weekends or closed for lengthy periods during the winter. Some of the state's best wineries, such as Adams, Adelsheim, Cameron, and Eyrie, have no tasting rooms and are open to the public only on special occasions such as Thanksgiving weekend (call the individual wineries for details).

The etiquette of Oregon wine tasting is simple. You select a winery and present yourself at its tasting room. The attendant provides glasses and offers samples of the wines available for tasting that day. There is seldom a charge for tasting, though an exception may be made for particularly rare bottlings. Feel free to try any or all of the available wines; swishing and spitting are allowed, and you're not compelled to buy anything.

Many of the establishments command hilltop views and maintain picnic areas for visitors' use. McMinnville and Hillsboro offer the greatest variety of delis and specialty food shops. During the summer and fall, the wine country's many roadside produce stands yield luscious strawberries, raspberries, marionberries, pears, nectarines, peaches, plums, apples, kiwis, and other local fruits.

Choosing Oregon's top wineries is as subjective as choosing its top wines. It's fair to say that *Adelsheim Vineyard* in Newberg (22150 N.E. Quarter Mile La., tel. 503/538–3652), *Cameron Winery* in Dundee (8200 Worden Hill Rd., tel. 503/538–0336), *Eyrie Vineyards* in McMinnville (935 E. 10th St., tel. 503/472–6315), *Knudsen-Erath Winery* in Dundee (Worden Hill Rd., tel. 503/538–3318), *Ponzi Vineyards* near Beaverton (Vandermost Rd., off Scholl's Ferry Rd., tel. 503/628–1227), *Shafer Vineyard Cellars* in Forest Grove (Hwy. 8, tel. 503/357–6604), and *Tualatin Vineyards* in Forest Grove (Seavy Rd., tel. 503/357–5005) are among the state's oldest and most consistently esteemed operations. *Chateau Benoit* in Carlton (6580 N.E. Mineral Springs Rd., off Hwy. 99W, tel. 503/864–2991), *Elk Cove Vineyards* in Gaston (27751 N.W. Olson Rd., tel. 503/985–7760), *Laurel Ridge Winery* in Forest Grove (David Hill Rd., from Hwy. 8, tel. 503/359–5436), *Rex Hill Vineyards* in Newberg (30835 N. Hwy. 99W, tel. 503/538–0666), and *Yamhill Valley Vineyards* in McMinnville (16250 S.W. Oldsville Rd., off Hwy. 18, tel. 503/843–3100) have some of the most beautiful winery views and picnic grounds in the area.

Restaurants

The wine country's culinary star is undoubtedly **Nick's Italian Cafe** (tel. 503/434–4471) in McMinnville. A favorite of tourists and local winemakers alike, Nick's serves up spirited northern Italian home cooking in modest surroundings. The five-course, fixed-price menu changes nightly to reflect the region's exquisite seasonal produce. Don't overlook the extensive wine list of Oregon's vintages. **Roger's** (tel. 503/472–0917) is a McMinnville family favorite that emphasizes reasonably priced fresh seafood. The restaurant has a pleasant streamside location, and there's patio dining during the summer. **Lavender's Blue, A Tea Room** (tel. 503/472–4594), in McMinnville, serves up an impeccably English high tea, great homemade desserts, light lunches, and dinners. Tiny Dundee, between Newberg and McMinnville on Hwy. 99W, now boasts not one but two outstanding eateries. **The Red Hills Cafe** (tel. 503/538–8224) offers lovely and imaginative dinners featuring local seafood, game, mushrooms and garden-fresh herbs. **Tina's** (tel. 503/538–8880) roams the far corners of the globe for its culinary inspirations, and features impeccably prepared risottos, grilled fish and meat, and dishes from Pacific Rim regions. The **Inn at Orchard Heights** (tel. 503/378–1780), across the river from downtown Salem, is a handsome hilltop restaurant filled with the soothing sounds of rippling water and classical music. The European owner/chef puts a richly sauced Continental spin on fine local beef, seafood, and game. Salem's **Thompson Brewery & Public House** (tel. 503/363–7286) is a fun, casual outpost of the Portland-based restaurant and pub chain. It serves wonderfully eclectic and inexpensive cuisine, preferably washed down with local "microbrews."

Tourist Information

McMinnville Chamber of Commerce (417 N. Adams St., McMinnville, OR 97128, tel. 503/472–6196); **The Oregon Wine Center** (1200 N.W. Front Ave., Portland, OR 97209, tel. 503/228–8336); **Portland/Oregon Visitors Association** (26 S.W. Salmon St., Portland, OR 97204–3299, tel. 503/275–9750); **Salem Convention & Visitor Center** (Mission Mill Village, 1313 Mill St. SE, Salem, OR 97301, tel. 503/581–4325).

Reservation Services

Bed & Breakfast Reservations—Oregon (2321 N.E. 28th Ave., Portland, OR 97212, tel. 503/287–4704); **Northwest Bed and Breakfast** (610 S.W. Broadway, Portland, OR 97205, tel. 503/243–7616).

Flying M Ranch

The mysterious red "M" signs begin in downtown Yamhill—a somnolent town of 700 or so in the very press of the wine country—and continue west for 10 miles into the Chehalem Valley, in the rugged foothills of the Coast Range. Following them alertly will bring you to the 625-acre Flying M Ranch, perched above the Yamhill River.

The centerpiece of this rough-and-ready, Wild West–flavored amalgam of motel, campground, dude ranch, timber camp, and working ranch is the great log lodge, decorated in a style best described as Paul Bunyan Eclectic and featuring a bar carved from a single, 6-ton tree trunk. On weekends, this is *the* happening place; the adjoining restaurant serves thick steaks and prime rib, and there are even a few fish dishes on the menu now. Sensitive souls may notice the accusing eyes of dozens of taxidermied trophies watching while they eat.

Guests have a choice of eight secluded cabins and 28 motel units. (Ask about special packages: The Retreat package includes dinner for two with wine, wine and fruit in the room, a full breakfast, and horseback riding.) The motel is modern and clean, but lacks personality. (All the beds, however, do have log frames.) The cabins, a better choice, are equipped with kitchens, living rooms, wood-burning stoves, and decks overlooking the river. All are spacious, and evoke a rustic, log-cabin charm. The cozy Honeymoon Cabin has a huge stone-and-brick fireplace and a double whirlpool tub. The recently renovated Wortman Cabin sleeps four and has the newest furnishings.

Be sure to book ahead for a longtime Flying M specialty, the Steak Fry Ride. Participants ride a hay wagon to the ranch's secluded creekside elk camp for a barbecued steak dinner with all the trimmings, including a crooning cowboy. The more adventuresome can ride horses from the ranch's stables, one of the Flying M's many countrified amenities. There are horseshoe pits, a big swimming hole, good fly-fishing, even a family of domesticated but ill-tempered buffalo (please, no petting). As if this weren't enough, the wineries are a half-hour drive away over backcountry gravel roads. Be sure to make it back by dusk, because finding the Flying M in the dark could be a real challenge.

Address: *23029 N.W. Flying M Rd., Yamhill, OR 97148, tel. 503/662–3222, fax 503/662–3202.*
Accommodations: *28 double rooms with baths, 6 housekeeping cabin suites, 2 2-bedroom housekeeping cabin suites.*
Amenities: *Restaurant, bar, radios in cabins, TV in 2 cabins, live entertainment, meeting and catering facilities; campsites, fishing, hiking trails, horseback riding, horseshoe pits, swimming hole, tennis court.*
Rates: *$60–$70, cabins $75–$200; breakfast extra. AE, D, DC, MC, V.*
Restrictions: *Closed Dec. 24–25.*

Mattey House

Mattey House is a sprawling Queen Anne mansion nestled behind its own little vineyard a few miles north of McMinnville. Its tasteful, distinctively western Victorian ambience and its experienced hosts make Mattey House the area's most consummate B&B.

The house itself was built in 1892 by Joseph Mattey, a prosperous local butcher and cattle rancher. Jack and Denise Seed, originally from England, bought it in 1993 and have lavished considerable time and expense on the guest rooms, public areas, and grounds.

To wine-country visitors tuckered out by a long day's slurping, Mattey House is an oasis of welcoming warmth. Entering the living room, which is framed by Ionic columns and fretwork, you'll find a beckoning fire in the old carved-wood-and-marble hearth, soothing classical music on the CD player, wallpaper reproducing a William Morris pattern, and a cheerful mix of period furnishings and more informal modern pieces, such as deep, comfy couches and wicker tables. There's a porch swing overlooking the vineyard and 10 acres of largely unlandscaped grounds for those in a strolling mood.

Upstairs are the four guest rooms, all named for locally grown varieties of grapes. The Chardonnay Room, with its tall windows and crisp white decor, is bright and sunny; so is the Blanc de Blancs Room, with its pearlescent, off-white tones, white wicker, antique brass bed, and soothingly pastoral artwork. Chardonnay has a connecting door to the burgundy-hued Pinot Noir Room; for an added fee it's possible to reserve them as a two-couple suite. These three rooms share two baths. The Riesling Room, with an antique pine dresser and a 6-foot-long claw-foot tub, is the only room with a private bath. (Note the wine-glycerine soaps in all the bathrooms and the homemade quilts on all the beds.)

The Seeds fortify their guests well before launching them on a morning's wine touring. Breakfast features fresh local fruit—perhaps a baked apple or peach in raspberry sauce—followed by fresh-baked scones and the house specialty, a Spanish-style frittata. At the end of their tour, guests are rewarded with hors d'oeuvres and one last cheering glass of the Oregonian grape.

Address: *10221 N.E. Mattey La., McMinnville, OR 97128, tel. 503/434–5058.*
Accommodations: *1 double room with bath, 3 doubles share 2 baths.*
Amenities: *Robe and clock in rooms.*
Rates: *$65–$75; full breakfast, afternoon refreshments. MC, V.*
Restrictions: *No smoking, no pets.*

Steiger Haus

Zsa Zsa Gabor slapped here," proclaims the plaque in Steiger Haus's hallway, covered with hundreds of pictures of guests. Well, actually it says "slept." These little mementos aren't just there for show; they're an illustration of the genuine affection innkeepers Lynn and Doris Steiger feel for their guests. After a weekend at Steiger Haus, you feel like family.

On a quiet residential street near downtown McMinnville, the modern, cedar-sided structure was built in 1984 as a B&B. Linfield College, the site of Oregon's annual International Pinot Noir Celebration, is just across the creek at the back of the property.

Steiger Haus is a warm, fuzzy sort of place, thanks largely to Doris Steiger's fondness for sheep, wool, spinning, and weaving. Many of the inn's colorful rugs and place mats were woven by Doris in her cedar-walled solarium/ studio.

The inn's public areas have a country-contemporary charm. On the main level are an open kitchen with breakfast bar, brick fireplace, an antique deacon's bench, and oak dining suite with Windsor-style chairs built by an Oregon craftsman. There are comfortable, modern TV rooms upstairs and downstairs. In summer and fall, most of the action shifts outdoors to the inn's four decks and parklike, oak-shaded grounds.

Steiger Haus's five guest rooms are cool and contemporary, enlivened with woolly artwork, bright florals, fresh paint, and sunlight. (Two of them can be linked to form a suite.) Handmade Amish quilts and hand-woven coverlets in many of the rooms provide a warming touch. The downstairs room, which opens onto one of the decks, has a brick fireplace, a small, cozy sitting area, and a pretty private bath. The Treetop Room upstairs features a handmade oak bed with curved head- and footboards of turned spindles, tall windows, and a late-Victorian Wakefield wicker-and-oak desk. It also boasts a huge skylighted bath. An adjacent room is equipped with two single beds, goose-down comforters, and a bent-willow settee. An old grape-harvesting bin forms the base of a table in another guest room.

Breakfast, served at the guest's convenience, is a hearty affair; Lynn says that he's constantly giving out recipes for their oatmeal-granola hotcakes.

Address: *360 Wilson St., McMinnville, OR 97128, tel. 503/472–0821 or 503/472–0238.*
Accommodations: *5 double rooms with baths.*
Amenities: *Fireplace in 1 room, cable TV and VCR available, phone on each floor, conference room.*
Rates: *$65–$90; full breakfast. MC, V.*
Restrictions: *No smoking indoors, no pets.*

Youngberg Hill Farm

Like ghostly twilight sentinels, the deer come down to greet guests at Youngberg Hill Farm. They have free run of this 700-acre estate, high in the hills west of McMinnville. Well, nearly free run—guests must remember to close the gate of the deer fence that surrounds the house itself and its 10 acres of young Pinot Noir vines, a favorite midnight snack for these graceful stags. During the fall the deer are more wary, because innkeeper Norm Barnett and his wife, Eve, are keen hunters.

Norm and Eve built the inn from scratch in 1988, a monster-size replica of a classic American farmhouse commanding breathtaking views over mountain and valley from atop a steep-sided hill. Early spring evenings at Youngberg Hill, a working farm, means dozens of tiny white-faced lambs wobbling through the lush pastureland on knobby knees.

Youngberg Hill is a comfortable place that has now acquired a proper, lived-in warmth. The common areas are spacious, modern, and high-ceilinged, with Victorian belly-band molding and bull's-eye corners. The furnishings are largely golden oak period reproductions; the sitting room's deep sofa and settee, upholstered in an unusual grapevine-patterned chintz, are a welcoming touch, as are the suede-covered armchairs and wood-burning stove. Big windows make the most of the hilltop estate's romantic views. The five guest rooms are small to medium in size; furnished with golden oak and Victorian Cottage reproductions, they have a cozy modern ambience.

Breakfast is Eve's province. Her Austrian-influenced specialties—rich, puffy *Kaiserschwarm* served with warm marionberry syrup and smoked pork chops are typical fare—linger on the palate well into the afternoon. Among the inn's special attractions are a nicely stocked, reasonably priced wine cellar and special hunters' weekends in the fall.

Address: *10660 Youngberg Hill Rd., McMinnville, OR 97128, tel. 503/472–2727.*
Accommodations: *5 double rooms with baths.*
Amenities: *Air-conditioning in rooms, fireplace in 2 rooms, cable TV in common area, wine available, meeting facilities, hiking trails, hunting, swimming hole.*
Rates: *$110; fall hunting packages (including 3 meals) $100 per person per day; full breakfast. D, MC, V.*
Restrictions: *Smoking on porch only, no pets; 3-night minimum for hunting package.*

Kelty Estate

This simple white-clapboard farmhouse, built in 1872, is on busy Highway 99 between Newberg and McMinnville, directly across the street from the Lafayette Schoolhouse Antique Mall.

New owners Ron Ross, a former facilities manager, and his wife, JoAnn, a nurse, spent most of 1990 renovating the estate. The Rosses' hard work is reflected in the house's handsome living areas. Sunlight from tall windows gleams on newly refinished oak floors and tasteful wine-colored patterned rugs; an elegant border of green and blue paisley circles the freshly painted walls.

The two upstairs guest rooms have received similar care. Paint, carpets, and furnishings are all new, and there's an austere, contemporary emphasis on brass and velour. White lace curtains add an old-fashioned note. Both rooms have queen-size beds, hardwood floors, and private baths. If possible, reserve the room at the back of the house; the front room, overlooking Highway 99, is a little noisier. Guests have their choice of Continental or full farmhouse breakfast.

Address: *675 Hwy. 99W, Lafayette, OR 97127, tel. 503/864–3740.*
Accommodations: *2 double rooms with baths.*
Amenities: *Cable TV in living room.*
Rates: *$55–$65; full breakfast. No credit cards.*
Restrictions: *No smoking, no pets.*

Main Street Bed & Breakfast

The first inn in this part of the wine country, Main Street Bed & Breakfast is in Forest Grove, 25 miles west of Portland and hard by such highly regarded wineries as Tualatin, Shafer, and Ponzi.

The B&B occupies a 1913 Craftsman bungalow that has a stone foundation, cross-gabled roof, and a wide front porch with glider. The corner lot, in a quiet residential neighborhood, is filled with flowers and trees. Inside, innkeeper Marie Mather has decorated with a mix of contemporary furnishings and her various collections: owls, kaleidoscopes, and old handmade aprons. Though modern, the carpets, couches, and baths are softened with old-fashioned touches—a lace tablecloth here, a claw-foot tub there.

The two upstairs guest rooms are a little fussy, decorated in florals and lace, with dried flowers and stuffed or painted tole geese in profusion. There's an extra room that, when available, can be used for children. The full breakfasts are hearty, not arty: Rhubarb crisp, smoked pork chops, and fried potatoes are some of Marie's standbys.

Address: *1803 Main St., Forest Grove, OR 97116, tel. 503/357–9812.*
Accommodations: *2 double rooms share 1 bath.*
Amenities: *Phone in rooms.*
Rates: *$50–$55; full breakfast, afternoon refreshments. MC, V.*
Restrictions: *Smoking on porch only, no pets; 2-night minimum on weekends.*

Orchard View Inn

I n 1990, Wayne and Marie Schatter escaped the southern California rat race to run Orchard View Inn. Southern California seems a world away from the long, sunlight-warmed deck of this octagonal redwood house, 1,000 feet up in the Chehalem Mountains west of McMinnville. Birdcalls, the rustle of wind through the evergreen canopy overhead, and the music of water cascading from pool to pool down the hill are the only sounds.

Inside, the inn mixes contemporary vaulted ceilings and velour-upholstered couches with beautiful Chinese antiques. Guest rooms are smallish, modern, and simply furnished. The Antique Room displays a framed collection of Marie's family heirlooms: 19th-century lace gloves, purses, fans, a silver cane handle that belonged to

her mother. The lower-level Studio Room has a private entrance and bath; a tasteful mixed-tweed carpet is complemented by a series of gorgeous vintage 1930s Chinese prints on the wall.

Address: *16540 N.W. Orchard View Rd., McMinnville, OR 97128, tel. 503/472–0165.*
Accommodations: *2 double rooms with baths, 2 doubles share 1 bath.*
Amenities: *Kitchen and laundry room available; hammock.*
Rates: *$65–$70; full breakfast. MC, V.*
Restrictions: *No smoking indoors, no pets; 3-night minimum during Pinot Noir Celebration.*

The Partridge Farm

T he wine country's newest B&B sits on a 5-acre farm just west of the Rex Hill winery, surrounded by raised-bed vegetable gardens, lush orchards, and a finely landscaped perennial border.

This yellow, 1920-vintage classic American farmhouse is run like a small European guest house by innkeeper Agnes Laube, a former New Yorker, and, fittingly, the decor is accented with antiques from Germany and France. For those who think there is no greater luxury than a cozy bed and a good novel, the Partridge features a well-stocked library. TV and VCR options are also available.

Three of the guest rooms share a single bath, although two have in-room sinks—so things can get a little hectic

around morning shower time. The best room has its own bath, plus a sitting room with a handsome dark-wood armoire and overstuffed chairs.

Breakfasts, as might be expected, are farmhouse-hearty and filling, featuring in-season fruits and berries from the grounds, as well as local eggs, sausage, and bacon. The warm blueberry muffins are an especially appreciated eat-treat.

Address: *4300 E. Portland Rd., Newberg, OR 97132, tel. 503/538–2050.*
Accommodations: *3 double rooms share 1 bath, 1 suite.*
Rates: *$55–$80; full breakfast. MC, V.*
Restrictions: *No smoking, pets boarded at nearby kennel.*

Springbrook Hazelnut Farm

Chuck and Ellen McClure have owned this quiet, 60-acre hazelnut farm, with its lovely Craftsman-style farmhouse—listed in the National Register of Historic Places—for almost 30 years. The sense of place is evident, from the bucolic nut-tree stand out front to the fine collection of Northwest contemporary art on view inside.

The entry hall alone is magazine-worthy (and, indeed, has been featured in several national layouts): an expanse of high-beamed ceilings and hand-screened French wallpaper in shades of yellow leads through the house to the flower-filled rear garden. An enormous fireplace of brick and carved wood welcomes guests during the chillier months. Guest room furnishings are farmhouse-comfortable.

After the morning meal—served on antique Wedgwood china—guests craving post-breakfast exercise can take their choice: a private tennis court, swimming pool, or a stroll through the inn's orderly orchard of hazelnut trees.

Address: *30295 N. Hwy. 99W, Newberg, OR 97132, tel. 503/538–4606 or 800/793–8528.*
Accommodations: *4 double rooms share 2 baths; carriage-house with private bath and kitchen.*
Amenities: *Tennis-court, swimming-pool, trout-pond.*
Rates: *$90; carriage house $125. No credit cards.*
Restrictions: *Children by arrangement; no pets, no smoking indoors. Carriage house open year-round; main inn closed Nov.-Mar.*

State House

The only licensed B&B in Salem, State House is on busy State Street in an older residential neighborhood. The best thing about this 1920s Craftsman is the gazebo and hot tub in the landscaped backyard. Drawbacks include a diminutive gravel parking area and the continuous din of traffic just outside.

Guest rooms on the second floor are simply furnished with mix-and-match contemporary pieces; the largest has a sitting area and a kitchenette, and the smaller two share a bath down the hall. The third-floor penthouse suite is equipped with small kitchenette, TV, stereo, and king-size waterbed. There are also two more private suites in the garden bungalow. Owners Mike Winsett and Judy Unselman, longtime residents of Salem, are happy to point the way to Bush Park, the capitol building, and other local sites of interest.

Address: *2146 State St., Salem, OR 97301, tel. 503/588–1340 or 800/800–6712.*
Accommodations: *2 double rooms share 1 bath, 3 housekeeping suites, 1 2-bedroom housekeeping suite.*
Amenities: *Phone in all rooms, TV in suites, air-conditioning in house, cable TV in common room; hot tub.*
Rates: *$45–$65 in main house, breakfast included; $60–$70 in bungalow, breakfast extra. D, MC, V.*
Restrictions: *No smoking indoors, no pets; 2-night minimum during university graduation in May.*

Portland

The best way to describe Portland's appeal might be to start with what the City of Roses doesn't have. There are no palm trees (but no droughts either). Freeway gridlock is almost unknown, major-league baseball is something you watch on TV, and strollers have a much better chance of seeing an elk or a cougar than a movie star. Portland's easy charm rests on twin foundations: its beguiling urban amenities and its access to a wealth of recreational treasures. (It may be the only major city in the world where you can catch 30-pound chinook salmon downtown.) Within the city limits there are more than 9,400 acres of parkland—home to deer, elk, and what are probably the last urban old-growth forests in the world.

Portland became the City of Roses thanks to the efforts of Leo Samuel, a turn-of-the-century insurance mogul who planted a jungle of roses in front of his mansion and hung out shears so that passersby could help themselves to choice blooms. The idea readily took root in Portland's friendly, temperate climate. One legacy is the city's internationally renowned Rose Test Garden (in Washington Park), overlooking the downtown skyline, the Willamette River, and Mt. Hood, whose snowbound 11,235-foot summit towers 50 miles to the east.

The first settlers didn't arrive in Portland—then the highest easily navigable point on the broad Willamette—until the 1840s. In 1844 pioneers Asa Lovejoy and William Overton used an ax to mark a few boundary trees in the dense riverbank forest (near what are now Southwest Front and Washington streets), paid a 25¢ filing fee, and took possession of the 640 acres that are now downtown Portland. A year later Overton sold his share to Francis Pettygrove for $50 worth of trade goods. Pettygrove, a Maine native, and Lovejoy, a Bostonian, tossed a coin to decide who would name the town-to-be; Pettygrove won, and with homesick fondness chose Portland.

Twenty years ago the New York Times's *architecture critic described Portland's core area as a bombed-out mess. Today downtown Portland, with its award-winning mix of green public spaces, efficient mass transit, modern skyscrapers, and beautifully restored historic buildings, ranks as one of the best-planned cities in the United States. Many of the fine old structures along the waterfront, some dating from the 1850s, rest on foundations riddled with gloomy tunnels; a hundred years ago these passageways echoed with the moans of shanghaied sailors who were being carted, drugged and drunken, down to the river.*

Today the most ominous fate awaiting visitors to the area is overeating—Portland is said to have more restaurants per capita than any other West Coast city. A moribund movie house has been transformed into the glowing new Portland Center for the Performing Arts, home to the Oregon Symphony Orchestra, Shakespearean theater, and touring concerts and arts events. One of the unlovely parking lots that so offended the New York Times *is now Pioneer Courthouse Square, a broad brick piazza filled with whimsical art and equally esteemed by conservatively dressed office workers and more exotic citizenry. It's a fine place from which to begin a ramble through the heart of the city, and it's within easy walking or light-railing distance of many of the city's bed-and-breakfasts.*

Places to Go, Sights to See

Exploring Portland is easy—and you don't need a car. The city's popular six-year-old light-rail system, *MAX,* makes a loop from downtown Portland to the suburb of Gresham, 13 miles east (tel. 503/233–3511 for ticket and schedule information). Along the way, it forms a handy link between the bed-and-breakfast establishments in Northeast Portland's *Irvington* district and many of the city's most important destinations: *Memorial Coliseum* (1401 N. Wheeler St., tel. 503/235–8771), home of the National Basketball Association's *Portland Trailblazers;* the brand-new *Oregon Convention Center* (777 N.E. Martin Luther King Jr. Blvd., tel. 503/235–7575); the shops, restaurants, and historic districts of the downtown core; *Pioneer Courthouse Square* (bounded by Broadway Ave. and 6th, Morrison, and Yamhill Sts.); the *Portland Art Museum* (1219 S.W. Park, tel. 503/226–2811); and the *Portland Center for the Performing Arts* (1111 S.W. Broadway Ave., tel. 503/248–4335).

Outside the city, the *Columbia River Gorge National Scenic Area,* a remark-
ably unspoiled expanse of waterfalls, hiking trails, and mysterious fern-draped
grottoes, enfolds I–84 just 30 minutes east of downtown Portland. Mt. Hood, with
its historic *Timberline Lodge* and year-round skiing, is a half hour farther on.
Ninety minutes west of Portland, the gray-green Pacific Ocean gnaws ceaselessly
at Oregon's rock-fanged coastline. Award-winning wineries along the way help to
enliven the journey.

Parks and Gardens. Portland's *Washington and Forest parks* occupy more than
5,000 acres in the city's West Hills, forming the largest contiguous municipal park
in the United States. At its southeast end, where Washington Park meets the
tony King's Hill neighborhood, is Portland's famed *International Rose Test Garden* (400 S.W. Kingston Ave., tel. 503/796–5193), which sports more than 10,000
bushes in 400 varieties as well as gorgeous views out over the downtown skyline
to Mt. Hood and Mt. St. Helens beyond. On the opposite side of the avenue, the
serene expanse of manicured sand, boulders, trees, shrubs, rills, and ponds that
form the *Japanese Gardens* (611 S.W. Kingston Ave., tel. 503/223–4070) are a
reminder of Portland's close links with the Pacific Rim. *Hoyt Arboretum* (4000
S.W. Fairview Blvd., tel. 503/796–5193), just up the hill, contains 10 miles of near-
wilderness hiking trails and more than 700 species of trees and plants. *Washington Park Zoo* (4001 S.W. Canyon Rd., tel. 503/226–7627), founded in 1887, is one of
the world's most prolific breeding grounds for Asian elephants, and contains
major exhibits on the Alaskan tundra, the Cascade Mountains, and the African
plains.

Powell's City of Books (1005 W. Burnside St., tel. 503/228–4651) may also owe a
debt of gratitude to Portland's wet climate. With more than a million volumes, it's
one of the world's great bookstores—and a browser's haven on a gray afternoon.
Patrons can borrow a volume from the shelves and read over cups of *caffè latte* or
espresso in the commodious Ann Hughes Coffee Room.

Shopping. Powell's is midway between Portland's two main shopping districts.
In the downtown core, affluent clients browse the city's chicest shops, including
the glittering new *Pioneer Place* (700 S.W. 5th St., tel. 503/228–5800). Northwest
Portland's *Pearl District,* along N.W. 21st and 23rd streets, is home to an eclectic
array of clothing, gift, and food shops as well as art galleries, ethnic eateries, and
bookstores. Northeast Portland's Broadway district is the city's newest and
trendiest area for shopping and restaurants.

Wineries and brew pubs are another local amenity that are putting Portland on
the map. The Pinot Noir and chardonnay grown in the nearby Yamhill and
Tualatin valleys have induced several Burgundian winemakers to buy land here.
And the City of Roses is home to more microbreweries and brew pubs—tiny
breweries with attached public houses—than any other city outside Europe.
Among the most highly regarded are *Bridgeport Brewing Co.* (1313 N.W. Mar-
shall St., tel. 503/241–7179); *McMenamin Brewing* (nearly two dozen Portland
locations; call 503/223–0109 or 503/288–9498 to find the closest one); and *Portland
Brewing Co.,* with two locations (1339 N.W. Flanders St., tel. 503/222–7150; 2730
N.W. 31st Ave., tel. 503/226–7623). They all have attached pubs that serve ales
fresh from the brew house as well as hearty pub fare. The *B. Moloch Heathman
Bakery and Pub* (901 S.W. Salmon St., tel. 503/227–5700) offers a variety of local
brews and sophisticated but inexpensive nouvelle pub cuisine. McCormick &
Schmick's *Pilsner Room* at RiverPlace (0309 S.W. Montgomery St., tel.

503/220–1865) also has its own brewery, and features rarely encountered micro-brewed pilsner.

Restaurants

For a relatively small city, Portland has a surprisingly rich restaurant scene, particularly for lovers of fresh seafood and exotic ethnic cuisines. There are four contenders for the city's most elegant eatery: the Alexis Hotel's **Esplanade at RiverPlace** (1510 S.W. Harbor Way, tel. 503/295–6166), with its superb service, river views, and intensely rich Northwest cuisine; the intimate and sumptuous northern Italian elegance of **Genoa** (2832 S.E. Belmont St., tel. 503/238–1464); the impeccable country-French artistry of **L'Auberge** (2601 N.W. Vaughn St., tel. 503/223–3302), and the more exotic Mediterranean flavors and textures of **Zefiro** (500 N.W. 21st Ave., tel. 503/226–3394). But the city's best-known restaurant is undoubtedly **Jake's Famous Crawfish** (401 S.W. 12th Ave., tel. 503/226–1419). Jake's white-coated waiters serve up unimpeachably fresh Northwest seafood from a lengthy sheet of daily specials in a series of bustling wood-paneled dining rooms. **Café des Amis** (1987 N.W. Kearny St., tel. 503/295–6487) attracts an equally devoted clientele with its low-key elegance; the kitchen adds a country French spin to the superb local fish, game, and produce. For lovers of intensely flavored Thai, Vietnamese, and Chinese food, three establishments stand out: **Bangkok Kitchen** (2534 S.E. Belmont St., tel. 503/236–7349), **Yen Ha** (6820 N.E. Sandy Blvd., tel. 503/287–3698), and **Chen's Dynasty** (622 S.W. Washington St., tel. 503/248–9491).

Tourist Information

Portland/Oregon Visitors Association (26 S.W. Salmon St., Portland, OR 97204, tel. 503/275–9750).

Reservation Services

Bed & Breakfast Reservations—Oregon (2321 N.E. 28th Ave., Portland, OR 97212, tel. 503/287–4704); **Northwest Bed and Breakfast** (610 S.W. Broadway Ave., Portland, OR 97205, tel. 503/243–7616).

Heron Haus

A long flight of wooden stairs leads down from the driveway of this West Hills mansion. At the bottom is a tiny, secluded orchard of pear, apple, and cherry trees. This is just one of the many hidden charms of Heron Haus, one of the most accomplished B&Bs in the Rose City.

The house itself is a sturdy Tudor built in 1904 from stucco and Port of Portland ballast stone. It sits high in the hills above Northwest Portland, handy to the hiking trails and old-growth stands of gigantic Forest Park as well as to the shopping and restaurants of the Pearl District. Its effervescent owner, Julie Keppeler, worked in investment real estate, publishing, convention planning, and adult education before settling into the B&B business. Oh, yes—she's also a weaver, potter, and photographer.

Keppeler renovated the 7,500-square-foot house in 1986—and she did it with assurance and charm. The modern touches, such as Southwestern artwork and Scandinavian-flavor furnishings, subtly complement the house's existing features. There's a huge breakfast room with herringbone-patterned oak floors and fireplace; a warm, carpeted sunroom overlooking the backyard pool; and a sophisticated entertainment room with a big-screen TV/VCR and deep couches. Most beguiling of all is the mahogany-accented library, its leaded-glass cabinets filled with selections ranging from Isak Dinesen to Audubon, its furnishings sturdy Victorian Eastlake.

Each of the five huge guest rooms has a private bath, comfortable sitting area, phone, and a work desk—a particular convenience for business travelers. The most splendid of the five rooms is the Kulia Suite, modern and airy with a queen-size bed and a romantic, flower-shaped hot tub overlooking the downtown skyline. The Ko Room, just down the hall, is distinguished by its antique seven-headed shower, king-size brass bed, and two well-appointed sitting areas. (These two rooms can be converted into a $250-per-night suite.) At the top of the house, the Manu Room sprawls over a space so large that two average B&B rooms would easily fit into it.

Breakfast is a luxury Continental affair, with fresh fruits, croissants, pastries, and cereal.

Address: *2545 N.W. Westover Rd., Portland, OR 97210, tel. 503/274–1846, fax 503/243–1075.*
Accommodations: *5 double rooms with baths.*
Amenities: *Phone in rooms, cable TV in 3 rooms, air-conditioning; outdoor heated pool.*
Rates: *$85–$145, suite $250. MC, V.*
Restrictions: *No smoking indoors, no pets.*

The Lion and the Rose

When it was built in 1906 for Portland brewing magnate Gustave Freiwald, this startlingly ornate, Queen Anne–style mansion was one of the city's showplaces. Its grounds, occupying nearly a full city block, featured parklike gardens, a stable for Freiwald's matched team of Clydesdale horses, and, later, a garage for one of Portland's first horseless carriages, a splendid white Packard with red leather interior.

The house's current owners, Kay Peffer, Sharon Weil, and Kevin Spanier—kindred spirits, indeed—include among their possessions a unique 1955 Oldsmobile Super 88 stretch limo, whose tail-finned red-and-white contours would surely have brought a tear to old Gustave's eye. It's equally certain that he would have approved of their stewardship of his house, now restored to all its pre-Prohibition splendor.

Not to put too fine a point on it, The Lion and the Rose has quickly joined Portland's premier B&Bs since its grand opening in June 1993. From the gleaming floors of inlaid oak and scrubbed fir to the ornate period light fixtures (many original to the house), The Lion and the Rose has set a new standard of formal elegance among Portland inns.

The public areas offer an expanse of polished wood, antique silver, and delightful turn-of-the-century touches. The Freiwalds' original carved

mahogany sofas were identified from historical photographs of the house's interior and restored to their original opulence. For the musically inclined, an 18th-century Miller pump organ and a 1909-vintage Bush & Lane piano in exquisitely grained walnut face one another across a lush oriental carpet. The overall feel is substantial and ornate, but just short of florid.

The same maniacal attention to detail is evident throughout the six guest rooms, of which Lavonna is arguably the nicest; it features a round, sunny sitting area in the mansion's cupola, with a king-sized iron canopy bed and cheerful white wicker furniture.

A breakfast as opulent as the surroundings is served in the dining room from 7:30 to 9:30 AM. Location-wise, the inn is just a short saunter from Broadway Street, a newly gentrified district of fine restaurants and splendid shopping.

Address: *1810 N.E. 15th Ave., Portland, OR 97212, tel. 503/287–9245 or 800/955–1647, fax 503/287–9247.*
Accommodations: *4 double rooms with private bath; 2 double rooms share 1 bath.*
Amenities: *Writing space and phones in all rooms, TVs and VCRs available in rooms upon request, children welcome.*
Rates: *$80–$120; full breakfast. AE, MC, V.*
Restrictions: *No smoking, no pets.*

McMenamins Edgefield

I t's fair to say that you've probably never encountered an inn quite like the Edgefield complex. A sort of pastoral, self-contained English village 15 minutes east of downtown Portland and five minutes west of the magnificent Columbia River Gorge National Scenic Area, Edgefield is the brainchild of Portland brew pub moguls Mike and Brian McMenamin.

The 25-acre estate includes its own vineyard, winery, brewery, bustling village pub, bakery, meeting facilities, restaurant, movie theater, and gardens. Everywhere are signs of the McMenamins' cheerful eccentricity: in the whimsical artwork adorning the pub, theater, and brewery; in menu items with names like Jack's Stratogroover and The Vondrak (two types of French-bread pizza); and in freshly brewed house ales like Terminator Stout and Invisibility Ale.

Most of the guest rooms are in the complex's huge, four-story Colonial Revival centerpiece, Edgefield Manor, built in 1911 as the dormitory for the Multnomah County Poor Farm. When the McMenamin family bought it in 1990, it was in an advanced state of dilapidation, having stood empty for more than 10 years. A major renovation, completed in the summer of 1993, added 91 more guest rooms to the original 14, as well as dormitory space for 24 guests and a fine-dining restaurant and bar.

The quietest accommodations are in the former administrator's colonial-style house, set about 100 yards from the main building; party-animal types might opt to stay in the pub/theater building or main lodge. But all rooms are sunny and eschew Victorian opulence for a clean Old Western simplicity. They have scrubbed wood floors and are furnished with a few simple antiques and bright Native American–patterned fabrics. There are no telephones or TVs, but the lodging tariff includes admission to the on-property movie theater.

A hearty breakfast, designed to fortify guests for long hikes in the gorge or swims in the nearby Sandy River, is served in the Black Rabbit Restaurant. Choices might include omelets, crunchy French toast, corned beef hash, fresh local fruit, and, on special occasions, eggs Benedict with Dungeness crab.

Address: *2126 S.W. Halsey, Troutdale, OR 97060, tel. 503/669–8610 or 800/669–6500, fax 503/665–4209.*
Accommodations: *3 suites with baths, 24 dormitory beds, 102 rooms share 55 baths.*
Amenities: *Microbrewery, restaurant, bar, pub serving food, movie theater, winery, tasting room, meeting facilities; brewery, winery, and garden tours.*
Rates: *Single $45, double $75–$90, suites $90–$105, family room (sleeps 6; breakfast $15 extra for more than 2 guests) $180; full breakfast. Dorms, $18 per bed; no breakfast included. AE, D, MC, V.*
Restrictions: *No smoking, no pets.*

Portland Guest House

ortheast Portland's Irvington neighborhood used to be full of neatly kept working-class Victorians just like this one, with its flower-filled yard and window boxes, and its fresh coffee-with-cream paint and graceful wrought-iron fence. Most of them fell to the wrecking ball when the prosperous 'teens and '20s transformed Irvington into a neighborhood for the nouveaux riches.

This house endured decades of neglect until longtime neighborhood residents Susan and Dean Gisvold brought it back to life in 1987. Now, rebuilt from the studs outward, the house oozes a comfortable sense of place and history, from its scarred oak floors to the haunting photographs of once-resident families on the walls. It's not as grand as The Lion and the Rose *(see above)* or the nearby White House *(see below)*, but it's hardly a poor relation, and it has a fresh, sunny authenticity all its own.

Each of the seven smallish, high-ceilinged guest rooms has some special and memorable touch: an ornately carved walnut Eastlake bed or armoire, an immaculately enameled claw-foot tub, or a shady deck overlooking the back garden.

Outside the four second-floor rooms is a lace-curtained window seat that's perfect for reading or postcard writing. The tasteful mauve and gray walls of the downstairs living and dining rooms are finished with white bull's-

eye molding; a gorgeous Oriental carpet cushions the hardwood floor. The ponderous Eastlake living room suite has been reupholstered in pretty rose satin.

Fifteenth Avenue, which runs by the etched-glass front door, can be busy in the mornings and afternoons, but this is barely noticeable in the freshly soundproofed house. The conveniently central Northeast Portland neighborhood, with its broad tree-shaded avenues lined with stately old homes, offers plentiful charms of its own. The MAX light-rail line is a 10-minute walk to the south. Closer to home, the shops on Broadway Street offer Oregon wines and produce, imported cheeses, and fresh-baked breads for picnics in the landscaped yard.

The Gisvolds don't live on the premises, but they're often around, and a full-time manager occupies a downstairs apartment. Breakfast is served in front of the cheerful dining room fireplace.

Address: *1720 N.E. 15th Ave., Portland, OR 97212, tel. 503/282–1402.*
Accommodations: *5 double rooms with baths, 2 doubles share 1 bath.*
Amenities: *Phone in room.*
Rates: *$55–$85; full breakfast. AE, DC, MC, V.*
Restrictions: *No smoking indoors, no pets.*

Portland's White House

The splash of falling water provide a melodious welcome for guests at this memorable Northeast Portland B&B. Listed on the National Register of Historic Places, the house was built in 1912 in Southern Federal style. Except for the tiled roof, it bears an uncanny resemblance to its District of Columbia namesake—a resemblance indicative of the chief-executive personality of its builder, timber tycoon Robert Lytle. Its sweeping circular driveway, carriage house, and Greek columns all whisper of bygone elegance. "I always tell guests to go ahead and make a speech from the balcony if they want to," says innkeeper Mary Hough.

This White House's neighborhood, Irvington, may lack the grandeur of Pennsylvania Avenue, but its location makes it handy to downtown, Memorial Coliseum, the MAX light-rail line, and the Oregon Convention Center. Owners Larry Hough, an electrician by profession, and his Dublin-born wife, Mary, a former antiques dealer, bought the house in 1984 and have since lavished more than 8,000 hours on its restoration. The public areas gleam with hand-rubbed Honduran mahogany and ornately inlaid oak. (Even the old servants' quarters are finished with mahogany.) The sweeping hand-carved stairway is lit by exquisite Pulvey stained-glass windows. Outside, the sunny rose-hung decks make fine places for relaxing with a spot of summer tea. Downstairs is a cavernous ballroom.

The six spacious, high-ceilinged guest rooms are furnished with a tasteful mix of antiques, period pieces, and reproductions. The Canopy and Baron's rooms feature ornate canopy beds and huge claw-foot soaking tubs. In the Garden Room, French doors open onto a private veranda trellised with flowers. The Balcony Room has an ornate brass bed, tiled Art Deco bathroom, and a small balustraded balcony overlooking the courtyard fountain.

The Houghs are hardworking resident innkeepers who attack their duties with charm and zest. When Mary was a child in Ireland, her mother kept boardinghouses; Mary's blood ties to the lodging business are evident in her immaculate housekeeping and hearty breakfasts. Eggs Benedict are a morning standby. The tea kettle is always on the hob, and the pantry is well stocked with fresh-baked chocolate chip cookies and a brimming basket of local apples.

Address: *1914 N.E. 22nd Ave., Portland, OR 97212, tel. 503/287-7131.*
Accommodations: *6 double rooms with baths.*
Amenities: *Phones in rooms.*
Rates: *$99–$115; full breakfast, afternoon tea. MC, V.*
Restrictions: *Smoking in ballroom only, no pets.*

RiverPlace Hotel

The downtown Portland skyline towers above the rotunda roof and turrets of the RiverPlace Hotel on the banks of the Willamette River. A forest of sailboat masts crowds the complex's marina; the green ribbon of 2-mile-long Waterfront Park begins almost at the hotel's front door. The Alexis anchors a crescent of shops, restaurants, condominiums, and offices that went up in 1985 and breathed new life into downtown Portland's front door.

Observers disagree on the overall feel of the hotel, thoroughly modern though it is. Some say it looks vaguely Dutch; to others it has a clean Cape Cod ambience. One thing they all agree on, however, is its elegance; since the hotel opened its doors, it has become a residence of choice for visiting celebrities and CEOs.

Inside, the Alexis has the feel of an intimate European hotel. The subtle luster of teak as well as green Italian marble is everywhere, and the staff provides a level of service seldom seen in this casual western city. (The 150 employees outnumber the guest rooms nearly two to one.) The lobby, bar, and restaurant are handsome spaces, luxuriously appointed with wood-burning fireplaces, rich fabrics, and Oriental carpets.

The 84 guest rooms overlook river, skyline, and courtyard, but they lack some of the elegance of the public areas. Thick carpeting and well-sound-proofed walls are a given; the paint is a subtle pale yellow that makes the most of Portland's often wan sunlight. Furnishings are modern and comfortable, but they have a cookie-cutter uniformity. The rooms are medium in size and spare. Junior suites have huge tiled bathrooms and comfortable sitting areas. Fireplace suites are larger, with marble-top wet bars, king-size beds, small whirlpool baths, and two color TVs each.

Dinner at the Esplanade Restaurant off the lobby is an experience to savor. The nightly menu may include such delicacies as Dungeness crab with artichokes, warm-rabbit-and-wild-green salad with a star-anise vinaigrette, or medallions of elk with a savory currant-caramel sauce.

Address: *1510 S.W. Harbor Way, Portland, OR 97201, tel. 503/228–3233 or 800/227–1333, fax 503/295–6161.*
Accommodations: *39 double rooms with baths, 35 suites, 10 condominiums.*
Amenities: *Restaurant, bar, air-conditioning; cable TV and phone in rooms, voice mail, 24-hour room service; valet parking, sauna; pets by prior arrangement.*
Rates: *$150–$195, suites $180–$500, condominiums $275–$375; Continental breakfast. AE, D, DC, MC, V.*

The Clinkerbrick House

Stately chestnut trees and a facade bristling with the fancifully twisted and fused bricks that give the house its name lend personality to this countrified 1908 Dutch Colonial structure in Northeast Portland's convenient Irvington neighborhood. Innkeepers Peggie and Bob Irvine opened this small, comfortable B&B in 1987.

The house's public spaces have an American-country feel without the clutter. Beautiful old quilts spill from pine cabinets; an intriguing V-shaped corner bench invites fireside conversation. With its whimsical brickwork, unusual tin wainscoting, and lovely leaded-glass cabinetry, the house itself is a curiosity. The lovely brick patio, which gives guests a pleasant venue to enjoy the landscaped backyard, is new.

The three upstairs guest rooms have their own entrance, as well as a common area with a kitchen. In the sunny Strawberry Room, dark green carpeting, a crewel-embroidered wing chair, and a pine pencil-post bed pull the room together. The Rose Room, decorated with pink roses and white wicker, has an antique crocheted bedspread and a lace-finished daybed.

Address: *2311 N.E. Schuyler St., Portland, OR 97212, tel. 503/281–2533.*
Accommodations: *1 double room with bath, 2 doubles share 1 bath.*
Amenities: *Full kitchen.*
Rates: *$55–$65; full breakfast. MC, V.*
Restrictions: *No smoking indoors, no pets.*

General Hooker's B&B

Ebullient owner Lori Hall, a movie buff, former fashion designer, and special-ed teacher turned spinner and innkeeper, sets the cheerful tone at this Southwest Portland B&B. The house, an 1888 Queen Anne five minutes from downtown Portland, was extensively renovated in 1978; now its antique facade belies its gallerylike interior and modern furnishings.

There's a single guest room in the basement, a white-walled chamber with a loft bed: double below, twin above. On the top floor, a tree-shaded deck with views of river, skyline, and mountains provides the perfect place for sipping a beer or glass of wine from Hall's well-stocked guest refrigerator. All guests have access to it, but it communicates directly with the Rose and Iris rooms—the former a spacious

chamber with a super king-size bed and a skylighted bathroom, the latter a comfortable space with a Civil War–era armoire.

Address: *125 S.W. Hooker St., Portland, OR 97201, tel. 503/222–4435 or 800/745–4135, fax 503/222–4435.*
Accommodations: *1 double room with bath, 3 doubles share 2 baths.*
Amenities: *Air-conditioning, complimentary beer and wine in guest refrigerator, cable TV with VCR in rooms; half-price YMCA passes.*
Rates: *$70–$110; Vegetarian "expanded" Continental breakfast. AE, MC, V.*
Restrictions: *No smoking indoors, no pets.*

The Georgian House

Greek columns flank the front door of this striking red-brick Georgian Colonial, and legend has it that there are 20 $20 gold pieces in its foundation to ward off ill fortune. The house, on a quiet, tree-lined street in the historic Irvington neighborhood, was a broken-windowed wreck when the present innkeeper, Willie Ackley, bought it in 1987. It now gleams anew behind manicured lawns, flower beds, and wrought-iron fences.

Downstairs, a cheerful solarium overlooks the small formal garden, as do a broad vine-canopied deck and the gazebo. Each guest room has a personality of its own. The smallish Maid's Room feels English, from the century-old cherrywood Eastlake bed to the marble-top dresser and dark burgundy walls.

The Pettygrove Room has an out-doorsy, masculine ambience, with 150-year-old German-pine twin beds that, pushed together beneath a stunning handmade quilt, form a king-size bed. The Lovejoy Suite, the largest and sunniest of the three, has hardwood floors, a tiled fireplace, an ornate brass canopy bed, and its own TV- and chaise-equipped sitting room.

Address: *1828 N.E. Siskiyou St., Portland, OR 97212, tel. 503/281–2250.*
Accommodations: *3 double rooms share 2½ baths, 1 suite.*
Amenities: *Air-conditioning, TV/VCR.*
Rates: *$65–$85; full breakfast. MC, V.*
Restrictions: *No smoking indoors, no pets.*

MacMaster House

Don't mind the curiosity of Mac-Master House's outgoing innkeeper, Cecilia Murphy—engrossed in her duties, she says she travels vicariously through her guests. Her 1875 Colonial Revival mansion rises high in the West Hills, the 5,000-acre expanse of Washington and Forest parks beginning only two blocks from here.

The downstairs public areas are furnished in a mishmash of kinetic-sculpture modern, fertility-symbol African, bamboo-pattern Asian, and a few carved mock-Tudor chairs.

One of the charms of this vast house is its fireplaces—seven in all. Four guest rooms have one. There are thick down comforters on all the beds, and there's cable TV in every room. The best of

the lot is the MacMaster Suite, with its rattan four-poster, a 7-foot glass-fronted wardrobe filled with books, and skyline view from the balcony. The third-floor suite is almost as spacious. Skylights fill the space with light even on inclement days; a pretty wicker chaise and deep couch add to the relaxing ambience.

Address: *1041 S.W. Vista Ave., Portland, OR 97205, tel. 503/223–7362.*
Accommodations: *4 double rooms share 2 baths, 2 suites.*
Amenities: *Cable TV in rooms, air-conditioning.*
Rates: *$70–$115; full breakfast. D, MC, V.*
Restrictions: *No smoking indoors, no pets.*

North Coast

If the rest of the world had heeded the warnings of early explorers along Oregon's north coast, the area would still be a lonely, windswept wilderness of towering headlands, untracked beaches, and rivers teeming with fish. As it happens, virtually all of these descriptions still apply—except for the "lonely" part.

Four hundred years after Spanish and English adventurers wrote the area off as too stormy to be settled, the 150-mile-long north coast, stretching from Newport in the south to Astoria in the north, is sprinkled with small towns and villages. Fishing fleets leave from Newport, Garibaldi, Depoe Bay, Astoria, and, most quixotically, from tiny Pacific City. Small wineries, galleries, and antiques shops abound. U.S. Highway 101 plays tag with the rugged coastland all the way, providing easy access to an otherwise sparsely populated area.

Sir Francis Drake and Bruno Heceta, two 16th-century explorers who found the area uninhabitable, went a little overboard in their pessimism. But this is a stormy place—more than 80 inches of rain a year is the norm. The good news is that all the rain keeps the thick forests a deep, damp green. The bad news is that swimming in the North Pacific is recommended only for seals, salmon, and the odd overly ambitious surfer. Since the temperature rarely climbs above 75° F, beach walking has always been more popular than taking a dip.

Happily, long, uninterrupted public beaches are a staple of the area. In fact, Oregon has virtually no private beaches; an early 20th-century conservation law declared all land seaward from where the beach grass stops to be public. True, access is sometimes blocked, but seldom for long stretches. And more than 70 state parks—about one every other mile—ensure good access.

Places to Go, Sights to See

Antiques. Small antiques shops are as much a part of the north coast as sand and spray. The broadest selection is to be found in the 30-mile stretch between

Newport and Lincoln City. A strong association of merchants produces an up-to-date directory available at virtually every antiques shop in the area. Specialties include nautical items, Asian wood carvings, and furniture from the Civil War period.

Columbia River Maritime Museum (1792 Marine Dr., tel. 503/325–2323). Astoria's history as a seaport dates back to 1811, when it was the only American settlement west of the Rockies. This informative museum features a retired Columbia River lightship and nautical artifacts. The mainstay of the museum is a collection of U.S. Coast Guard rescue vessels once used over the last century to pluck the unlucky from a part of the ocean shoreline known as the Pacific Graveyard.

Depoe Bay. This is the world's smallest harbor, barely 40 feet across as it meets the pounding Pacific between basalt cliffs. A fishing village lies about 100 feet above the sea, but still in reach of the Spouting Horn, a hole in the cliff that allows the ocean to spray completely over Highway 101 during storms.

Ecola State Park (tel. 503/436–2844). This park lies between artsy Cannon Beach and touristy Seaside. A trail to the top of 800-foot-high Tillamook Head affords views of Tillamook Light, a 19th-century lighthouse abandoned to the storms in 1957.

Fort Clatsop National Memorial (Rte. 3, tel. 503/861–2471). In 1805, the Lewis and Clark expedition spent a miserable, stormy winter at this site in Astoria. A reproduction of the fort, with all its discomforts, has center stage. During the summer, park rangers don buckskins and demonstrate frontier skills such as making dugout canoes, smoking salmon, and fashioning clothes out of animal skins.

Fort Stevens (tel. 503/861–2000). Originally built to defend the Oregon countryside against Confederate attack during the Civil War, this former military reservation in Hammond is the only place in the continental United States attacked during World War II: A Japanese submarine lobbed a shell that landed harmlessly on the beach. A museum lodges a display exploring the fort's history. On the beach lie the remains of the *Peter Iredale*, an Irish bark that ran aground in 1906.

Galleries. Virtually every town in the area has a worthwhile gallery. One of the most interesting is *Artspace* in Bay City (9120 5th St., tel. 503/377–2782), a restaurant that features works both large and small—mostly modern, all eclectic, and all for sale. More mainstream works by Northwest artists are displayed at *Maveety Gallery* in Gleneden Beach (Market Place at Salishan, tel. 503/764–2318).

Hatfield Marine Science Center (2030 S. Marine Dr., tel. 503/867–0100). Inside the marine science center, an extension of Oregon State University just south of Newport, are displays of birds and other wildlife native to the shoreline, the skeletal remains of a whale, and numerous tanks of local marine life, including a shallow pool where visitors can touch starfish and anemones. The star of the show is the large octopus in a round, low tank near the entrance; he seems as interested in human visitors as they are in him, and he has been known to reach up and gently stroke children's hands with his suction-tipped tentacles.

Oregon Coast Aquarium (2820 S.E. Ferry Slip, tel. 503/867–3474). Close to the Hatfield Center is this delightful, family-oriented aquarium. Special exhibits allow kids and adults to view the teeming life indigenous to shallow tidal pools.

Otters, seals, and sea lions flash by in outdoor tanks whose viewing areas, cut out of natural stone, give close-up looks at these playful showmen of the sea.

Three Capes Scenic Loop. Running about 30 miles from Cape Meares in the north to Pacific City in the south, this drive embraces some of the state's most impressive coastline. The small community of Oceanside clings to a steep, forested slope overlooking offshore rocks that loom 200 feet high. *Cape Lookout State Park* includes a 1,000-foot headland, miles of trails, and 15 miles of undisturbed beaches. In the lee of *Cape Kiwanda* is a bright orange sandstone headland jutting out into the sea just north of Pacific City; here brave (some say crazy) dory fishermen run their small craft straight into the waves to reach fertile fishing areas offshore.

Tillamook Cheese Factory (4175 Hwy. 101, tel. 503/842–4481). The world's largest cheese factory, 2 miles north of town, specializes in cheddar, with tours, gift shops, and, of course, dairy delis.

Restaurants

Café de la Mer (tel. 503/436–1179) in Cannon Beach offers fresh local seafood with a French twist. **Chez Jeanette** (tel. 503/764–3434) in Gleneden Beach is unpretentious, but its food is the match of any big-city classic French restaurant. **The Dining Room at Salishan** (tel. 503/764–3635) is often rated as the state's finest. Salishan has a remarkable Continental menu plus a full retinue of Northwest specialties, such as grilled salmon, crab, and oysters. **Roseanna's** (tel. 503/842–7351) in Oceanside may be in an out of the way place, but it's worth finding. Try the delicacies proffered on the fresh board and hope they're making mussels in pesto.

Tourist Information

Astoria Area Chamber of Commerce (111 W. Marine Dr., Box 176, Astoria, OR 97103, tel. 503/325–6311); **Cannon Beach Chamber of Commerce** (207 N. Spruce St., Box 64, Cannon Beach, OR 97110, tel. 503/436–2623); **Greater Newport Chamber of Commerce** (555 S.W. Coast Hwy., Newport, OR 97365, tel. 503/265–8801); **Lincoln City Visitor Center** (801 S.W. Hwy. 101, Box 109, Lincoln City, OR 97367, tel. 503/994–8378); **Seaside Chamber of Commerce** (7 N. Roosevelt, Box 7, Seaside, OR 97138, tel. 503/738–6391); **Tillamook Chamber of Commerce** (3705 Hwy. 101 N, Tillamook, OR 97141, tel. 503/842–7525).

Reservation Services

Bed & Breakfast Reservations—Oregon (2321 N.E. 28th Ave., Portland, OR 97212, tel. 503/287–4704); **The Bed & Breakfast Register** (tel. 503/249–1997 or 800/249–1997); **Northwest Bed and Breakfast** (610 S.W. Broadway, Portland, OR 97205, tel. 503/243–7616).

Channel House

The town of Depoe Bay is perched above the sea on high black lava cliffs and wrapped around the wooded slopes of the tiny harbor. Depoe Bay's fishing fleet shoots through a 40-foot-wide aperture at full speed, heading straight into the turbulent Pacific.

Right above this meeting of waves and man is the Channel House. Here the views are everything. Whale-watching is a favorite pastime, as is watching the U.S. Coast Guard practice rescues in the rough waters just offshore. The house has some Cape Cod touches, but this is no ordinary saltbox. Indeed, the desire to have all the rooms face the sea has made for some odd interiors. Baths, often cramped, are manageable only because of the judicious use of sliding doors. In some cases, sinks are in the sleeping area. Aside from a few brass beds, furnishings are sturdy and comfortable but undistinguished. Views are best from the top-floor rooms, and the privacy is optimal. While most of the rooms have hot tubs on decks facing the ocean, on the lower floors you can't help feeling that the fishing and tour boats coming and going have as good a look at you as you do at them.

The dining area has the most distinctive look, decked out as it is with a brass wheel from an old fishing boat, rough-hewn tables, and a huge antique McCray icebox from an old restaurant. In the library you can peruse the collection of books on whales or keep a weather watch at the mini weather station, which gives continual readings of wind-speed velocity and direction as well as barometric pressure.

Depoe Bay is, after all, a fishing community—and Channel House takes full advantage. So you might awake to a breakfast of scrambled eggs, bagels and cream cheese, hash browns, and a fine piece of cod baked in a light mushroom sauce.

Innkeeper Lorena Schwabel makes you feel right at home, sometimes showing you your room with a young child in tow. Channel House is a favorite with honeymooners and those celebrating special occasions; a perusal of the entries in the guest book found in each room can be very touching.

Address: *35 Ellingson St., Box 56, Depoe Bay, OR 97341, tel. 503/765-2140 or 800/447-2140.*
Accommodations: *7 double rooms with baths, 1 suite, 2 housekeeping suites.*
Amenities: *Cable TV, radio, and binoculars in rooms, complimentary newspaper, fireplace and whirlpool bath in all rooms and suites, refrigerator in 7 rooms, kitchen in 3 rooms, deck hot tub in 7 rooms.*
Rates: *$120–$200, small room $55; full breakfast. D, MC, V.*
Restrictions: *No smoking, no pets.*

Grandview Bed & Breakfast

Seen from the quiet residential street in Astoria that it faces, the Grandview Bed & Breakfast doesn't stand out, but once you're inside the nearly 100-year-old Shingle Style house, you'll know what's special about it.

Because the Grandview rises so precipitously from a hill that falls away steeply, the views from the inn are spectacular and the sensation of floating can be intense. Innkeeper Charlene Maxwell quickly brings you back to earth, however. She has steeped herself in local lore and shares it with guests in an easygoing but authoritative manner.

The guest rooms upstairs are eccentrically decorated with a mixture of period furnishings and odd modern touches. In one room, fluffy clouds scud across sky-blue walls. In brightly painted bookcases, tiny artificial birds perch on bookends. Indeed, with unobstructed vistas of the Columbia River and the Coast Range of southern Washington and of the dozens of church steeples of Old Astoria, you'll feel as if you're in an aerie. As if this weren't enough, the Refuge Room features birdcall recordings (the real thing is right outside the window), bird-flocked wallpaper, and a bookcase filled with books on bird-watching.

For those who prefer to be earth-bound, there is a very plain two-bedroom suite in the basement with a separate entrance that's perfect for

families. Here the wallpaper is patterned with zoo animals, and some of the modern furniture is upholstered in a leopard print.

The arrangement of some of the guest rooms is flexible: Seven double rooms on the second and third floors can be divided into two suites or rented separately. Prices depend on whether you end up with a private bath.

The entrance hall is a bit cluttered with Charlene's work desk, which is only a few feet from the main door. The dining area, however, is very inviting, positioned in a light-filled turret that offers views of the river and town. For more privacy, some guests opt to dine in a smaller bullet turret on the other side of the kitchen, ideal for a twosome. Muffins, fresh fruit, and juice round out what Charlene calls a "Continental plus" breakfast.

Address: *1574 Grand Ave., Astoria, OR 97103, tel. 503/325–0000 or 800/488–3250.*
Accommodations: *3 double rooms with baths, 6 doubles share 3 baths, 1 suite.*
Amenities: *Phones available for 2 rooms, fireplace in 1 room.*
Rates: *$39–$92, suite $79–$102; Continental breakfast. D, MC, V.*
Restrictions: *No smoking, no pets, no alcohol on premises.*

Sandlake Country Inn

Sandlake Country Inn is a peaceful place, on an old cranberry farm on the road to Sandlake Park. On Christmas morning in 1890, the Norwegian schooner *Struan* was wrecked off Cape Lookout, leaving tons of heavy bridge timbers strewn on the beach. Storm-weary homesteaders with few building materials hauled the timbers off and made sturdy homes. Only a few of these are still standing, the most notable of which is the weathered-shingle Sandlake Country Inn, where innkeepers Margo and Charles Underwood preside.

Besides restoring the natural woodwork, the Underwoods removed part of the dining room's ceiling to reveal the old bridge timbers. The sitting room is a cozy creation, with velvet-covered Victorian settees, a stone fireplace, and views of flowering rosebushes outside.

From the sitting room, French doors open onto a small pink-and-white-striped guest room furnished in white wicker, set off by ecru netting that sweeps from the ceiling to the corners of the bed and a log-cabin quilt. The room overlooks another rose garden. Upstairs is the honeymoon suite, taking up the entire upper story. The plum paisley wallpaper with matching duvet and curtains and plum-colored paneling make the room a bit dark, but you can always stroll out onto the deck to survey the 2½-acre property and look out for deer and elk.

Just off the dining room is The Timbers, a new guest room styled to make any outdoors aficionado feel at home, complete with a deer's head mounted on the wall, a 1920s wicker fishing creel slung over the sturdy timber bedposts, and a stone fireplace.

Homemade apple oatmeal is a breakfast staple, as are fruit smoothies and green chili soufflés. Breakfast for guests staying in the creekside cottage, about 100 feet from the main house, is delivered to the door in a basket. Within the cottage the feeling is plush, with thick carpeting and huge throw pillows on the floor before a black marble fireplace. A large hot tub is strategically located between the bed and the deck. As in the suites, Arts and Crafts oak period pieces and reproductions predominate.

Address: *8505 Galloway Rd., Cloverdale, OR 97112, tel. 503/965–6745.*
Accommodations: *2 double rooms with baths, 1 suite, 1 housekeeping cottage.*
Amenities: *Radio/cassette players in rooms, hot tub in 1 room (wheelchair-accessible), closed-captioned TV in 1 room, TV and VCR in suite and cottage, refrigerator in suite, whirlpool tub and fireplace in cottage; bicycles.*
Rates: *$70–$115; full breakfast. MC, V.*
Restrictions: *No smoking, no pets; 2-night minimum on weekends in July and Aug., closed Christmas week.*

Sylvia Beach Hotel

For years, what is now the Sylvia Beach Hotel was known as a flophouse with a view. In Newport, once the state's honeymoon capital, the 1911 hotel overlooking the sea was for decades a low-rent residential hotel before Portland restaurateur Goody Cable and Roseburg partner Sally Ford decided to make it a kind of literary lodging—or a library that sleeps 40.

The plain green clapboard hotel takes its name not from the beach (actually, it's on a bluff on Nye Beach) but from the renowned patron Sylvia Beach, who in the 1920s and '30s ran the Shakespeare & Co. bookstore in Paris, a haven for American literati. Each room is dedicated to a famous writer, with appropriate books and decorating scheme. The Hemingway Room, for example, is all the manly Papa could have hoped for: a bed made out of tree limbs beneath a mounted antelope head, and an old Royal typewriter in the corner. The Agatha Christie Room is all green, with clues from her books lurking everywhere (the three bullets embedded in the wall are particularly menacing).

Down the hall is the Oscar Wilde Room, a smallish place resembling a Victorian gentleman's lodgings. The view, which faces a roof from the other side of the hotel, is far from awe-inspiring. But the managers are way ahead of you. Right next to the window is a framed Wilde quote: "It's altogether immaterial, a view, except to the innkeeper who, of course, charges it in the bill. A gentleman never looks out the window."

The most popular rooms are the Poe Room, a scary place in black and red, complete with raven and pendulum suspended over the bed, and the Colette Room, a sexy French suite with lace canopies, velvet window seat, and peach-colored headboard. The upper reaches of the hotel are turned over to a large library (some 1,000 books), with plenty of nooks and crannies and comfortable armchairs for book lovers.

The food at the hotel's restaurant—Tables of Content—is excellent. Breakfast is selected from a wide range of offerings on the menu, including frittatas and German-style pancakes served in the pan. But the best meal is dinner, an eight-course gourmet feast served family style.

Address: *267 N.W. Cliff St., Newport, OR 97365, tel. 503/265-5428.*
Accommodations: *20 double rooms with baths; separate dormitory with 8 bunks for women and 4 bunks for men.*
Amenities: *Restaurant, fireplace in 3 rooms.*
Rates: *$61–$129; dormitory bed $20; full breakfast, evening refreshments. AE, MC, V.*
Restrictions: *No smoking, no pets; 2-night minimum on weekends, closed first week in Dec.*

Whiskey Creek Bed & Breakfast

O n Three Capes Scenic Loop about 10 miles west of Tilla-mook, Whiskey Creek Bed & Breakfast offers quietude in rustic sur-roundings.

Built in 1900 by the operator of a cus-tom sawmill, the cedar-shingled Whiskey Creek is paneled inside with rough-hewn spruce. Originally, the mill operator made spruce oars and used the odd pieces of leftover wood for the main floor. For years, the home and the mill were powered by a small hydroelectric turbine on Whiskey Creek, about 100 feet away and the southern boundary of the property.

Innkeeper Allison Asbjornsen, an artist whose oil paintings, watercolors, collages, and sculptures adorn the downstairs suite (no spruce paneling here—just drywall), spends hours in her studio across the driveway. When she does emerge, most often barefoot, she likes to swap stories with her guests. She talks about the house as it was in the old days, of how on some evenings the lights would suddenly go dim. Realizing what was up, the men of the family would grab a lantern and a gun and head for the creek. Usually they found a bear splashing around, trying to catch a salmon and reducing the water flow, thereby cutting the power to the house.

Bear, elk, and deer still roam this area, and salmon make their way up Whiskey Creek to a state fish hatchery just across the creek from the inn.

Here you are always close to nature. (One window in the dining area over-looks Netarts Bay, Oregon's premier bay for oysters and crabs; the other, the 1,000-foot-high bulk of fir-carpeted Cape Lookout.)

Although you'll see husband Forrest Dickerson puttering around, Allison is the one who is most involved in run-ning the B&B, and she did all the deco-rating. All the rooms have queen-size futon beds and overstuffed chairs, and the two-bedroom suite, complete with kitchen, has a fabulous old wood-burn-ing stove with elaborate wrought-iron ornamentation.

Breakfasts are light, with bran muffins and fresh eggs from the inn's brood of handsome black hens. You might be lucky enough to get Swedish pancakes, a folded crepe served with powdered sugar or jam. Throughout the cathe-dral-ceilinged dining area is Allison's rabbit *objet d'art* collection.

Address: *7500 Whiskey Creek Rd., Tillamook, OR 97141, tel. 503/842–2408.*
Accommodations: *2 double rooms share 1 bath, 1 2-bedroom housekeep-ing suite.*
Amenities: *Cable TV and VCR in suite; barbecue pit.*
Rates: *$65–$85; full breakfast. MC, V.*
Restrictions: *No smoking.*

Anderson's Boarding House

Seaside is a small town with a bad case of schizophrenia. Downtown is dominated by a mile-long loop that turns back at the edge of the sea: Arcades, restaurants, candy stores, and gift shops crowd the narrow street. Yet just a few blocks away from the clamor is Old Seaside, an area of well-preserved Victorian homes now finding a second life as bed-and-breakfasts. The Boarding House, dating from 1898, when Seaside was a mere village, was the town's first B&B.

Inside you'll find tongue-and-groove walls, beamed ceilings, and a Victrola that innkeeper Barb Edwards cranks up for guests. The favored colors throughout are blue and white with rose accents. The rooms feature beds of brass and white iron, balloon curtains in floral prints, and claw-foot tubs. A restored Victorian cottage that sleeps five and has its own deck is the inn's gem. A sleeping loft allows a good look at the Necanicum River; in season, you can see the salmon moving upstream.

Address: *208 N. Holladay Dr., Seaside, OR 97138, tel. 503/738–9055.*
Accommodations: *6 double rooms with baths, 1 housekeeping cottage.*
Amenities: *Cable TV in rooms, vintage radio in 3 rooms.*
Rates: *$70–$115; full breakfast (guests in main house only). MC, V.*
Restrictions: *No pets; 2-night minimum on weekends.*

Astoria Inn

On any given night at the Astoria Inn, you might have as a fellow guest a Bulgarian folk musician or a budding rock star—or both. Here, high above the Columbia River, the views are inspiring and the musical presence constant.

John and Nola Westling have created a unique, relaxing place out of their old house on the east end of historic Astoria. John left the electronics firm he operated in San Diego in 1988 to work full-time on his hobby: harp making. All around are the tools and fruits of his craft.

The inn, a Queen Anne farmhouse with gingerbread ornament, sits atop a hill in a sedate residential area. Every effort has been made to return the look of the interior to the last century. Chair rails, imaginative use of wallpapers, decorative touches such as old fan quilts, feather boas, and wooden carousel horses, and, of course, antiques all contribute to this effect. Perhaps the inn's best feature is an airy second-floor library with wing recliners, oak moldings, and books on everything from harp making to bicycling.

Address: *3391 Irving Ave., Astoria, OR 97103, tel. 503/325–8153.*
Accommodations: *3 double rooms with baths.*
Amenities: *Cable TV and VCR in living room.*
Rates: *$75–$90; full breakfast, evening snacks. MC, V.*
Restrictions: *No smoking, no pets.*

Columbia River Inn Bed and Breakfast

Karen Nelson became an innkeeper in 1987 at the age of 71. Undaunted, she took on the renovation of the house, built in 1870, with loads of energy. The result is a luxurious bed-and-breakfast presided over by an archetypal grandma. And Karen seems to have passed along her hospitality genes: Her daughter, Renee, runs Franklin St. Station (*see below*), just five blocks away.

Fluted columns inside the living room are topped by cornices painted gold, with leaded-glass bay windows affording views of the town and the Columbia River. The rooms are large and quiet, furnished with simple brass beds and armchairs. Karen adds her personal touch in every room with cross-stitched scenes of local light-houses and roses made of ribbon that guests may take home. (She sells her crafts in a gift shop on the premises.) Somewhat more modern, a spacious room in the basement is ideal for families. Breakfast ranges from rich quiches to eggs over easy with bacon.

Address: *1681 Franklin Ave., Astoria, OR 97103, tel. 503/325–5044.*
Accommodations: *5 double rooms with baths.*
Amenities: *Refrigerators and clock radios in rooms, fireplace in 1 room.*
Rates: *$70–$85; full breakfast. MC, V.*
Restrictions: *No smoking, no pets; 2-night minimum on holiday weekends.*

Franklin St. Station

At the edge of downtown Astoria, the 91-year-old Franklin St. Station looks plain enough from the outside, but inside it is a beautifully restored home with spacious guest rooms.

The main floor is sumptuous, with high-back Victorian-style mahogany love seats covered in turquoise velvet in the living room, delicate spindle-work spandrels in the archways, and a fine old greenstone fireplace with oak mantel in the dining area.

The main-floor Lewis & Clark Room, once part of the dining room, uses a large china cupboard as a dresser. Upstairs, the Astor Suite is most impressive, with iron and brass beds, original light fixtures, large arched windows covered by hand-stitched bal-loon shades, and a deck. In the basement is a modern, functional suite with rattan furniture.

Innkeeper Renee Caldwell prepares a simple, filling breakfast of muffins, eggs, and homemade sausage. The dining area has a parquet table and a small niche displaying family china dating back to the early 1800s, one of four such displays in the house.

Address: *1140 Franklin Ave., Astoria, OR 97103, tel. 503/325–4314 or 800/448–1098.*
Accommodations: *2 double rooms with baths, 3 suites.*
Amenities: *Cable TV, VCR, stereo in 1 suite, wet bar in 2 suites.*
Rates: *$63–$115; full breakfast. MC, V.*
Restrictions: *No smoking, no pets.*

Gilbert Inn

Natural fir tongue-and-groove walls and ceilings dominate the Gilbert Inn, a block from the Seaside's busy downtown and the beach. The 1892 home reminds you why anyone bothered to settle this area in the first place: lumber.

The Gilbert is a large Queen Anne inn with eight spacious double rooms and two suites. Popularity almost swamped the Gilbert a few years ago, but innkeepers Dick and Carol Rees managed to add five rooms without disturbing the integrity of the existing house. The best part of the inn is still the original core, where the aforementioned fir creates a warm, rough-hewn atmosphere. The decor is country French, with wallpaper, down comforters, and bathrooms in matching prints, and ruffled valances and balloon shades at the windows. Some of the bedrooms have brass and ceramic bedsteads; in the Turret Room, you'll dream away on a four-poster rice bed. The newer guest rooms are attractively furnished with natural wicker, reproduction black iron and brass beds, and old wardrobes of oak and pine.

Address: *341 Beach Dr., Seaside, OR 97138, tel. 503/738–9770.*
Accommodations: *8 double rooms with baths, 2 suites.*
Amenities: *TV in rooms, large downstairs parlor available for meetings.*
Rates: *$69–$85; full breakfast. D, MC, V.*
Restrictions: *No smoking, no pets; 2-night minimum on weekends. Closed Jan.*

Hudson House

At Hudson House, in Cloverdale, the photo album tells the story. Clyde Hudson, a son of the original builder, was a pioneer photographer on the north Oregon coast. He was among the first to show the world the area's raw beauty through his postcards. The house in which he lived from the early 1900s on has been restored to its former Victorian splendor, thanks to innkeepers Anne and Steve Kuljic.

The downstairs guest room and an adjoining library have been carved out of an old mud room. Upstairs, the most popular room occupies the house's turret and features views of the Nestucca Valley, a major fishing and dairy region. Here, the fir ceiling complements the Empire oak dresser and the bed frame with pine-cone finials at the foot. Lisa's Room is a bit frilly, with pink floral wallpaper, a cherry hope chest, and a modern chair under a reading lamp.

Address: *37700 Hwy. 101 S, Cloverdale, OR 97112, tel. 503/392–3533.*
Accommodations: *2 double rooms with baths, 2 suites.*
Amenities: *Bathrobes, croquet, badminton, horseshoes.*
Rates: *$65–$75; full breakfast, evening refreshments. D, MC, V; 5% surcharge with credit cards.*
Restrictions: *No smoking, no pets; 2-night minimum on holiday weekends.*

Inn at Manzanita

Manzanita is a small, quiet town of summer homes clinging to the shoulders of Neah-Kah-Nie Mountain, a 1,700-foot cliff that towers over the Pacific between Tillamook and Cannon Beach.

Built in 1987, the Inn at Manzanita makes the most of its location in what amounts to the center of Manzanita. The feel is Scandinavian modern, with high-beamed ceilings and blond wood everywhere.

Some of the views are dramatic—Manzanita is best known for its 7-mile-long white beach—but many of the decks are closer to neighbors' rooftop picnic areas than to anything else. The inn offered a Continental breakfast for years but discontinued it recently when a café with morning hours opened in town. While the lack of an on-premises breakfast may discourage mingling with others, innkeepers Larry and Linda Martin know that more than half of their guests are either honeymooning or celebrating anniversaries, and appreciate the privacy.

Address: *67 Laneda St., Box 243, Manzanita, OR 97130, tel. 503/368–6754.*
Accommodations: *10 double rooms with baths.*
Amenities: *TV, VCR, hot tub, and wet bar in rooms; kitchens in 2 rooms; massage available.*
Rates: *$95–$140; no breakfast. MC, V.*
Restrictions: *No smoking, no pets; 2-night minimum on weekends and in July and Aug.*

K.C.'s Mansion By-the-Sea

The Pacific is a good 10 miles away, so K.C.'s Mansion By-the-Sea, in Astoria, may be a bit of a misnomer, but that's the only way in which this handsomely restored Queen Anne paradigm falls short.

The only word to describe K.C.'s is ornate. Plates that co-owner Gus Karas collected in his world travels adorn every wall. The living room has a 6-foot-high stone fireplace, baby grand piano, large velvet Victorian couches, and the original, elaborate light fixtures hanging from the 12-foot-high ceiling. Guests might start the day with seafood omelets or salmon, accompanied by muffins filled with local berries.

The ambience of luxury continues in the four guest rooms. All have wall-to-wall carpeting, couches, and brass reproduction Victorian bedsteads. The most spectacular is Monet's Suite, a purple extravaganza with Victorian velvet chairs and a settee in the large sitting area in the turret.

Address: *3652 Duane St., Astoria, OR 97103, tel. 503/325–6172 or 800/766–6482.*
Accommodations: *2 double rooms with baths, 2 suites.*
Amenities: *Sherry available, champagne or sparkling cider for guests in suites, rooms available for meetings and parties.*
Rates: *$75–$105; full breakfast. MC, V.*
Restrictions: *No smoking in rooms, no pets; 2-night minimum Apr.–Sept.*

Columbia River Gorge and Mt. Hood

The gorge, the mountain—to Portlanders, no other names are necessary. The Columbia River gorge, stretching some 70 miles east from the city, supplies the good and the bad: Dozens of waterfalls, high cliffs, mountain trails, and sweeping vistas provide an array of recreational activities.

The bad comes largely in the form of weather. The Columbia River gorge is one of the few places in the world where a river cuts through a major mountain range. That makes for unique scenery, but since the 4,000-foot-deep gash in the Cascade Range connects the high, arid Columbia Plateau with the low, moist western valleys, the collision of weather systems can spell trouble. Most frequently, the product created by this accident of nature is wind, which, in the finest Oregon tradition, the locals have latched on to. These days Hood River, a small town wedged in between Mt. Hood and the Columbia, bills itself as the windsurfing capital of the world.

Overlooking the gorge is snowcapped Mt. Hood, which at 11,235 feet above sea level is the highest point in Oregon. Its five sky areas and hundreds of miles of hiking trails are all within a 90-minute drive of downtown Portland. Sprinkled around the mountain are dozens of clear blue lakes—among them Lost Lake, Timothy Lake, and Badger Lake—each with its particular angle on the ever-changing profile of Mt. Hood. And the rivers spiral out from the glaciers of the mountain: Hood River, White River, Warm Springs River, Salmon River, Zig Zag River, Sandy River, and the Bull Run River.

Despite the area's wild appeal, it is easily reached by good roads. I–84 zips through the gorge to Hood River. Highway 35 climbs through the colorful orchard country of the Hood River valley to the icy slopes of Mt. Hood, and Highway 26 swoops down the south side of Mt. Hood back to Portland.

Each season has its pleasures. Fall brings the apple trees to full color in the Hood River valley, and the reds and golds of

*the deciduous trees blend into the deep green of the fir and pine
forests. Winters can be a skier's paradise, with most ski areas
receiving at least 8 feet of snow. But ice storms and blizzards
fueled by 100-mile-an-hour winds sometimes close the gorge
freeway for a few days each winter, leaving motorists
stranded. The spring thaw brings snowmelt to the rivers and,
once the streams clear, runs of salmon. Summer is the time for
hiking, camping, and exploring the alpine country before the
fall snows return—sometimes as early as September.*

Places to Go, Sights to See

Bonneville Dam (Cascade Locks, tel. 503/374–8820). This mammoth structure,
the first dam ever to span the river, stalls the Columbia long enough to generate
a million kilowatts of electricity (enough to supply 700,000 single-family homes).
Although the dam, opened in 1937, wiped out the most spectacular rapids on the
river, it has many wonders of its own. You can view its great turbines from
special walkways during self-guided powerhouse tours, and, at the visitor center
on Bradford Island, watch migrating salmon and steelhead as they struggle up
the fish ladders. The adjoining *Bonneville Fish Hatchery* (tel. 503/374–8393) has
ponds teeming with large salmon, rainbow trout, and sturgeon that are used to
repopulate the river.

Cascade Locks. During pioneer days boats needing to pass the rapids had to
portage around them. In 1896, the locks that gave the town its name were completed, allowing waterborne passage for the first time. Today the locks are used
by Native Americans for their traditional dip-net fishing, and Cascade Locks is
notable mainly as the home port of the 600-passenger stern-wheeler *Columbia
Gorge* (Marine Park, tel. 503/223–3928 or 503/374–8427). From June to September,
the ship churns its way upriver, then back again, on daily two-hour excursions
through some of the gorge's most awesome scenery.

Columbia River Gorge Scenic Highway (Rte. 30). Built in the early 1900s by
lumber magnate Simon Benson expressly for sightseeing, this narrow, curving
22-mile road strings along the upper reaches of the gorge from Troutdale to The
Dalles. While the journey affords some awe-inspiring views—there are a dozen
waterfalls in a single 10-mile stretch—the road itself is quite an attraction: Graceful arched bridges span moss-covered gorges, and hand-cut stone walls act as
guardrails. The route is especially lovely during the fall, but it is often impassable
during the winter.

Crown Point/Vista House (tel. 503/695–2240). Here, atop a 733-foot-high bluff,
visitors get their first full glimpse of the grandeur of the gorge. Built a few years
after the scenic Crown Point Highway on which it is located, Vista House provides a 30-mile view of the gorge and of the lights of Portland.

The Dalles. This historic town at the eastern end of the Columbia River gorge
has a fine Old Town district of brick storefronts that date from the 1840s. It was

here that Oregon Trail pioneers took a breather to decide whether the final leg of their 2,000-mile journey would be down the wild Columbia River or over the treacherous passes of Mt. Hood. The 130-year-old *Wasco County Courthouse* (404 W. 2nd St., tel. 503/296–4798) and the 1857-vintage *Ft. Dalles Surgeon's Quarters* (15th and Garrison Sts., tel. 503/296–4547) have been converted into museums; both contain outstanding displays and collections illustrating the incredible ordeal of the pioneers' journey. Today The Dalles boasts windsurfing second only to that done on Hood River.

Hood River Valley. Orchards abound in this hanging valley draped down the eastern shoulder of Mt. Hood. At its foot is the town of Hood River, which features some of the best windsurfing in the world, and its own small brewery, the *White Cap Brew Pub* (tel. 503/386–2247). There are even two wineries: *Hood River Vineyards* (4693 Westwood Dr., tel. 503/386–3772) and *Three Rivers Winery* (275 Country Club Rd., tel. 503/386–5453).

Mt. Hood National Forest (tel. 503/666–0771). Mt. Hood, reached by Highway 35 south from Hood River, is believed to be an active volcano, quiet now but capable of the same violence that decapitated nearby Mt. St. Helens in 1980. The mountain is just one feature of the 1.1 million-acre forest. You'll find 95 campgrounds and 150 lakes stocked with brown, rainbow, cutthroat, kokanee, brook, and steelhead trout. The Sandy, Salmon, and other rivers are known for their fishing, rafting, canoeing, and swimming. Both forest and mountain are crossed by an extensive trail system for hikers, cyclists, and horseback riders. The *Pacific Crest Trail*, which begins in British Columbia and ends in Mexico, crosses here at the 4,157-foot-high Barlow Pass.

Multnomah Falls (tel. 503/695–2376). At 620 feet, Multnomah Falls is the highest in the gorge, a breathtaking plunge over the lip of a high basalt cliff. A steep paved trail switchbacks to the top, but the less hearty can retire to the comfort of Multnomah Falls Lodge, an old stone structure at the foot of the falls that houses a restaurant, bar, and an inn.

Oneonta Gorge. This narrow cleft hundreds of feet deep is right off the scenic highway a few miles east of Multnomah Falls. The walls drip moisture year-round; hundreds of plant species—some of which are found nowhere else—flourish under these conditions. In late summer the intrepid can walk up the shallow creek; the gorge is so narrow that you can touch both sides.

Timberline Lodge (tel. 503/231–7979). At the 6,000-foot level of Mt. Hood's southern slope, Timberline is the mountain's oldest ski area. The lodge (*see* Restaurants, *below*), 6 miles from the intersection of Highway 26 and Timberline Road, was handmade out of mammoth timbers and stone by local craftsmen as part of a 1930s Works Progress Administration project; it's been used as a setting in many films, including *The Shining*, with Jack Nicholson. The Palmer Chair Lift takes skiers to the 8,400-foot-level for year-round skiing.

Wasson Winery (41901 Hwy. 26, Sandy, tel. 503/668–3124). Best known for its fruit-and-berry wine, this small winery in the rolling hills outside Sandy is gaining a growing reputation for its grapes.

Restaurants

The **Cascade Dining Room** at the Timberline Lodge (tel. 503/272–3311) in Timberline features Continental cuisine with a Northwest alpine twist. **Stonehedge Inn** (tel. 503/386–3940) in Hood River offers excellent European fare in a restored country house. Also in Hood River, **The Mesquitery** (tel. 503/386–2002) grills lean beef, chicken, and pork over aromatic mesquite, with the emphasis on fresh herbs and tangy marinades. **Ole's Supper Club** (tel. 503/296–6708) is a hidden place in The Dalles, but the prime rib is front and center.

Tourist Information

Cascade Locks Chamber of Commerce (Box 307, Cascade Locks, OR 97014, tel. 503/374–8619); **The Dalles Area Chamber of Commerce** (901 E. 2nd St., The Dalles, OR 97058, tel. 503/296–3385); **Hood River County Chamber of Commerce** (Port Marina Park, Hood River, OR 97031, tel. 503/386–2000); **Mt. Hood Area Chamber of Commerce** (Box 819, Welches, OR 97067, tel. 503/622–3017).

Reservation Services

Bed & Breakfast Reservations—Oregon (2321 N.E. 28th Ave., Portland, OR 97212, tel. 503/287–4704); **Northwest Bed and Breakfast** (610 S.W. Broadway, Portland, OR 97205, tel. 503/243–7616); **The Bed & Breakfast Registry** (tel. 503/249–1997 or 800/249–1997).

Auberge des Fleurs

You'll be bathed in color if you approach this inn during spring and summer. In the heart of an active nursery specializing in lilies, Auberge des Fleurs (Inn of the Flowers) is surrounded by 60 acres of flourishing bulbs.

Even if you have only a passing interest in flowers, this Dutch Colonial–style home is worth visiting. Polished walnut floors, gray marble fireplaces, bleached woodwork, and a brick patio create an elegant yet relaxing atmosphere. Just 40 minutes from Portland and 30 minutes from either windsurfing or skiing, the inn is a convenient, stylish base for exploring the Portland area and the scenery to the east.

The house was originally built by Jan de Graaf, a Dutch botanist who found the Northwest a perfect place to develop his hybridized lilies. The current owners, Molli and Don Flynn, have several nurseries along the West Coast. Although they are often at the property, day-to-day management is done by friendly local folk.

A huge living-room area has been overly modernized, but other elements—such as the original imported tile in the kitchen—are either intact or restored. Two sunny sitting rooms overlook the canyon and have excellent views of Mt. Hood's rugged northwest face. The dining room is almost too formal, with its high-back chairs and four large windows that look out on the trellised garden. Breakfasts served here are Continental, with an emphasis on fresh fruit.

It's surprising to find that this large house holds only two guest rooms, both upstairs. The larger, with views of the garden, continues the bleached-wood theme, although the spare look is tempered somewhat by modern carpeting. The second room, while a bit smaller, has a more expansive feeling because of its good light and its view of the grounds.

Perhaps the most interesting lodging available at Auberge des Fleurs is an old caretaker's cottage about 200 yards from the main house. The small house, about 300 feet directly above the confluence of the Sandy and the Bull Run rivers, is rustic and has its own kitchen and bath. The bleached-wood bed and wardrobe seem a little out of place here, but the smell of fresh air is ample compensation.

Address: *39391 S.E. Lusted Rd., Sandy, OR 97055, tel. 503/663–9449, fax 503/663–1129.*
Accommodations: *2 double rooms with private baths, 1 housekeeping cottage.*
Amenities: *Meeting facilities; horseback riding.*
Rates: *$75, cottage $115; Continental breakfast. No credit cards.*
Restrictions: *No smoking in house, no pets.*

Bridal Veil Lodge

I n 1921, Virgil Amend hauled timbers from the mill down the hill to an empty spot beside the Historic Columbia River Highway, in the tiny gorge community of Bridal Veil. There, within the sound of delicate Bridal Veil Falls, he built a lodge.

After years of functioning as a lodge, years of being a family residence, and years of being not much of anything, the old rustic Bridal Veil Lodge has reverted to its original purpose. Amend's great-granddaughter Laurel Slater and her husband have created a country-style bed-and-breakfast within 20 minutes of Portland's bustling waterfront.

But if Portland's lights are visible just to the west, it's what lies to the east that makes Bridal Veil's location special. The log structure is on the edge of the Columbia River Gorge National Scenic Area, a 90-mile-long preserve of trails, dizzying waterfalls, rock formations, high cliffs, and wilderness. Trails exploring this region can be found within a mile of the lodge.

Inside, the inn is warm and the sense of family is unmistakable. Old photos adorn the shelves in the dining area, which is dominated by a large, 1920s-vintage harvest table and a huge wrought-iron cookstove. In the main common area, a player piano holds sway beneath high, exposed fir beams.

The two rooms upstairs feature hand-tied quilts on the walls. The masculine

Grandpa's Room looks out into dense forest; knotty pine walls and a hand-carved oak headboard and matching dresser evoke the rough-hewn days when the lodge was built. Across the hall, the larger Grandma's Room is a far more feminine place, with plenty of light to keep the pine walls from dominating. A sitting area overlooks the front of the lodge: Though the view's immediate foreground is the highway and the parking lot for the state park across the road, the road isn't busy, and the lot gives way to rolling fields down to the Columbia.

Perhaps the inn's greatest asset is Laurel Slater, who grew up in the house and can answer questions about local history. Laurel's breakfasts tend to be healthy and hearty, since a good portion of her guests are either heading out to hike the gorge's notoriously steep trails or to embark on other outdoor activities, including windsurfing. German-style pancakes, fresh fruit, and plenty of sausage and bacon are regular fare.

Address: *Box 87, Bridal Veil, OR 97010, tel. 503/695–2333.*
Accommodations: *2 double rooms share 1½ baths.*
Amenities: *TV in common area.*
Rates: *$58–$65; full breakfast. No credit cards.*
Restrictions: *No smoking, no pets.*

Hood River Hotel

Although Hood River now bills itself as a kind of rustic Riviera for windsurfers, the newly restored Hood River Hotel is a reminder of the town's older character. True, Hood River's fresh identity as a recreational center is the reason the hotel was worth fixing up, but the hotel existed as a simple railroad stopover as early as 1910.

The 38-room brick-faced structure sits just off Main Street. At the front desk is Pasquale Barone, a veteran of the European hospitality industry, who came to the United States to bring a little Continental flair to Hood River. The rooms are furnished with Georgian reproductions; the beds add a much-needed touch of individuality, be they brass, four-postered, or canopy. The main appeal of the hotel is the two-story-high lobby, bar, and restaurant, which flow into one another.

You may enter past a string duo performing classical riffs before a giant hearth, the flames crackling away. To the left of the lobby, divided into several sitting areas with Chippendale and Queen Anne reproductions, is an imposing wooden bar serving local beers and wines in a classy yet laid-back atmosphere. (Remember, windsurfers are often big spenders, but they hang around in wet suits or Lycra shorts.) The bar and the dining room, which extends up to the mezzanine over the lobby, are immense, featuring the building's original pine woodwork.

The food continues the hotel's theme of being at once traditional and trendy. Dinners can get pricey, but the perfectly done seafood is worth it. Breakfasts are not included as part of the room rate, but they are worth the money with specials such as chili rellenos with spiced hash-brown potatoes.

The hotel is close to Hood River's antiques shops and also near the town's liveliest nightspots. A few blocks away is the White Cap Brew Pub (tel. 503/386–2247), home of the Hood River Brewery. Besides serving up its Full Sail Ale, one of the Northwest's most popular local ales, the pub has a panoramic view of the mile-wide Columbia as it rips through the gorge. Closer to the hotel is the Brass Rail, a hopping dance club that features bands from the Portland and Seattle club scene.

Address: *102 Oak St., Hood River, OR 97031, tel. 503/386–1900, fax 503/386–6090.*
Accommodations: *32 double rooms with baths, 6 housekeeping suites.*
Amenities: *Cable TV, phone, and ceiling fan in rooms, 2 doubles have kitchens; elevator, 24-hour room service, restaurant with sidewalk café.*
Rates: *$49–$145. AE, MC, V.*
Restrictions: *No smoking, no pets.*

Lakecliff Estate Bed & Breakfast

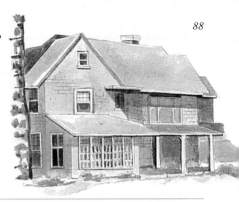

From the front room of the stately Lakecliff Estate Bed & Breakfast, the Columbia River gorge is like a three-dimensional postcard. Framed by a window that stretches the width of the large, oak-beamed room, the river view is nothing short of transfixing. The mile-wide river, about 200 feet below, with forests down to its edge and high cliffs topped by small farms, is just visible on the Washington side of the gorge. When the wind cooperates, legions of little specks with colorful sails—the gorge's latest fun seekers, windsurfers—dot the water.

While all that plays out down below, more worldly pleasures await in the Lakecliff. Sitting by the huge native stone fireplace on the west wall of the main room, even nonsmokers might feel the urge to light up the old briar pipe and tell a story of the hunt. Over the fireplace is a six-point deer, and in the hall a moose head serves as a humorous hat rack.

The estate, now on the National Register of Historic Places, was designed by A. E. Doyle, a turn-of-the-century Portland architect who also designed the Multnomah Falls Lodge and several public buildings in Portland, as well as Portland's charming downtown drinking fountains. Originally built for a Portland merchant family as a country getaway, the large home is something of a grand bed-and-breakfast by Northwest standards. Three of the four guest rooms feature rugged fireplaces made with rocks found on the property when it was built in 1908. Three also have views of the gorge, while the fourth looks back on the woods between the estate and the highway. All the rooms are done in country-French style, with oak beams and down comforters on the beds.

Innkeepers Bruce and Judy Thesenga have made an impressive place to relax while taking in the sights of the gorge. In the dining area, Judy's collection of antique milk bottles rings an upper shelf. Bruce, who runs a horse ranch in the hills across the river from the Lakecliff, often takes a turn in the kitchen, where he produces Lakecliff bacon, a sweet, crunchy bacon served cold. Other breakfast mainstays are huckleberry pancakes, frittatas, Dutch babies, and oven-baked French toast.

Address: *3820 Westcliff Dr., Box 1220, Hood River, OR 97031, tel. 503/386–7000.*
Accommodations: *2 double rooms with private bath, 2 double rooms share bath.*
Amenities: *Fireplaces in 3 rooms.*
Rates: *$80–$90; full breakfast. No credit cards.*
Restrictions: *No smoking, no pets; closed Oct.–Apr.*

Mountain Shadows Bed & Breakfast

I t takes some time and effort to get to Mountain Shadows Bed & Breakfast—about 25 miles from Sandy—but the journey up the steep mountain road is well worth it. As you climb the last pitch of the driveway, Mt. Hood looms above the huge log home tucked in among the trees.

Here, it's just you and the mountain. A wraparound deck places you within 10 miles of the summit. With binoculars, you can watch avalanches sweep down the mountain's western profile or see climbing parties traversing the spiny ridges—hopefully, not at the same time. Innkeepers Cathy and Paul Townsend, who left southern California in 1990, have found some peace and quiet on their 38 acres of woodland—and they don't mind sharing it with you.

The home is built entirely of pine logs and sits neatly on a slight incline that rolls down to the property's two creeks. Inside, the high-beamed ceilings evoke the images of both a pioneer log cabin and a grand private ski lodge. A wood-burning stove pumps heat into the public area, which is dominated by large, lodge-style couches and an 8-foot-high wardrobe of white pine. The dining area offers more close-enough-to-touch mountain views. During the summer, breakfast is served on the spacious deck, where early risers often see deer traipsing along the creek.

Breakfast is prepared tag-team style, and the results are tasty: rich German pancakes, thick local bacon, and fresh muffins.

The guest rooms are on the main floor down a long hall from the common area. The best room verges on being a suite, with its own wood-burning stove, small sitting area, and private bath. It's not particularly roomy, although the view out to the mountain lends a feeling of space. There is one cautionary note: Paul generally leaves a fire ready to go in the stove, because, even during the summer, at this elevation a solid chill is possible. The room heats up quickly, though.

The other room is less distinguished, but does possess heavy handmade quilts, exposed timbers, and that same rustic quality found throughout the rest of the house.

Address: *End of Angelsea Rd., Box 147, Welches, OR 97067, tel. 503/622–4746.*
Accommodations: *2 double rooms with private baths.*
Amenities: *Stereo in 1 room, wood-burning stove in 1 room.*
Rates: *$75–$85; full breakfast. No credit cards.*
Restrictions: *No smoking; 2-night minimum on holiday weekends.*

Old Welches Inn

During the days of the Oregon Trail, wagons frequently stopped at Welches on the Salmon River, well below the glaciers of Mt. Hood and its steep passes. Below spread the fertile Willamette Valley, the goal of the weary pioneers. By 1890 the valley had become civilized, and Welches Hotel lured the carriage trade from Portland with the promise of hiking, fishing, and relaxation.

A simple, white clapboard house is all that remains of the hotel, whose dining room once seated 120. The inn combines the atmosphere of a laid-back ski lodge and an old country estate. Bleached woodwork accentuates the sunny, airy feel of the place.

Much of that feeling comes from Judi Mondun, who operates the inn with her husband, Ted. The couple, both of whom were involved in finance in Miami, happened upon the Mt. Hood area during the late 1980s when their customary ski slopes in Colorado lacked snow. While Ted maintains his accounting practice in the Sunshine State, Judi tends to the Old Welches Inn.

A large wood-burning stove set on a base of rounded river rocks lends a rustic look to the living room, which overlooks the river through French doors. The covered patio, with a floor of hand-fitted river stones and lattice walls, boasts an 8-foot-high stone fireplace that was originally part of the old hotel.

The three upstairs rooms share two baths. The largest, which overlooks Resort at the Mountain's 27-hole golf course and has views of Hunchback Mountain, has a sleigh bed, Georgian hunting scenes on the raw silk-covered walls, and a floral upholstered rocking chair. A second room lacks a dramatic view, but the rich cedar paneling and ornate iron bedstead more than compensate. The remaining room on that level has a cannonball-style headboard and is festooned with duck decoys.

An outlying cabin is even closer to the river and the golf course—it overlooks the first hole. The 1901 structure has its own kitchen, two bedrooms, and a river-rock fireplace.

Address: *26401 East Welches Rd., Welches, OR 97067, tel. 503/622–3754.* **Accommodations:** *3 double rooms share 2 baths, 1 2-bedroom housekeeping cabin.* **Amenities:** *Fireplace in cabin.* **Rates:** *$65–$75, cabin $150; full breakfast (except for cabin). AE, MC, V.* **Restrictions:** *No smoking; 2-night minimum on holiday weekends.*

Williams House

The family of innkeeper Don Williams can be traced to The Dalles area as far back as 1862. The bed-and-breakfast he runs with his wife, Barbara, is a link to that past, when The Dalles was just a few years removed from being a simple trading post frequented by French and English trappers. A noted local historian who has been active in preserving several old buildings in The Dalles, Don is a font of information on the region.

Williams House sits halfway up a steep slope above the town's business district. Directly below is a small creek that meanders through the estate's arboretum. Built in 1899, the house is textbook Queen Anne, with spindlework porch supports and friezes, a round tower, gables aplenty, decorated verge boards, and enough gingerbread for a decade of Christmases.

The grand style continues inside with a broad, open staircase of Nicaraguan mahogany. Two sitting rooms provide ample space for lounging on Victorian settees—one with Roman heads carved on the back—and chairs while you thumb through the Williamses' eclectic book collection. The Chinese plates, bowls, and artifacts displayed throughout the main floor lend an imperial touch to the house.

A suite on the main floor features a four-poster bed and a private sitting room that face the creek. The bathroom has the original Italian marble and a 6-foot-long claw-foot tub. An unusual feature of the suite is the Victorian intercom system.

Upstairs are two guest rooms that share one modern bath. The larger room has an English canopied four-poster bed from the 1750s, a late 18th-century English Adamesque leather-top desk, an American Queen Anne maple highboy, and a private deck with views to the Klickitat Hills across the Columbia River. The other room is furnished largely with Victorian pieces from New England, but the hand-carved headboard with central walnut burl panel dates from 1775.

Breakfast—coddled eggs, cherry-tinted honey, and jam from the fruits of the Williamses' orchard—is served on Spode china. In good weather, which occurs often in this, the driest part of the gorge, breakfast is served in a gazebo on the back patio.

Address: *608 W. 6th St., The Dalles, OR 97058, tel. 503/296-2889.*
Accommodations: *2 double rooms share 1 bath, 1 suite.*
Amenities: *Air-conditioning, cable TV in rooms.*
Rates: *$65–$75; full breakfast. AE, D, MC, V.*
Restrictions: *Smoking in common areas only, no pets.*

Chamberlin House

Although it is only 30 minutes from downtown Portland, Corbett is country through and through. The old town clings to the western edge of the Columbia River gorge about 1,000 feet up the steep slopes. In the middle of Corbett is Chamberlin House, a plain brown Craftsman farmhouse that has been weathering gorge winds since 1912 and has always been in owner Nancy Wilson's family.

The house retains its hardwood interior. The rooms are small, and you are always very much aware that you're in a family home; the only public area is essentially the family living room. But those creaking stairs and upright iron beds have an undeniable appeal that harks back to the early part of the century. History is Nancy's hobby, and she serves as research historian at Vista House (*see* Places to Go, Sights to See, *above*).

Breakfast is filling and seemingly endless. Orange-baked French toast and chocolate waffles complement baked-egg dishes and plates of muffins and homemade preserves.

Address: *36817 E. Crown Point Hwy., Corbett, OR 97019, tel. 503/695–2200.*
Accommodations: *2 double rooms with private baths.*
Amenities: *Champagne splits in evening.*
Rates: *$65; full breakfast. No credit cards.*
Restrictions: *No smoking, no pets.*

Columbia Gorge Hotel

Staying at the Columbia Gorge Hotel is one of those irresistible, classic experiences. Just west of Hood River, the stuccoed hotel sits above a 200-foot waterfall that drops into the Columbia River.

Despite the hotel's size—the public rooms are huge, with plaster beams to match—the feeling is intimate, if at times intimidating. Louis XV–style armchairs surround a huge fireplace in the lounge, while such Victorian touches as round tufted velvet seats and domed lamps with hanging crystals enliven other rooms. Guest accommodations range from grand top-floor rooms that feature fireplaces and spectacular views over the falls to more pedestrian offerings on the lower floors.

As good as the dinners are, breakfast is the big production here: baked apples, apple fritters, smoked pork chops, pancakes—it goes on. And when honey is ceremoniously poured over the biscuits from on high, it's pure theater.

Address: *4000 W. Cliff Dr., Hood River, OR 97031, tel. 503/386–5566 or 800/345–1921.*
Accommodations: *46 double rooms with baths.*
Amenities: *TV and phone in rooms, fireplace in 2 rooms, restaurant, lounge, meeting rooms, catering available.*
Rates: *$150–$270; full breakfast. AE, D, MC, V.*
Restrictions: *No smoking in restaurant.*

Hackett House

Before 1989, innkeeper Sherry Pobo had never heard of Hood River. But when she decided to leave a stressful job in California's Silicon Valley, she and a partner soon found the small, windy town. They also found Hackett House, a large Dutch Colonial Revival house just a few doors down from the State Street Bed & Breakfast (*see below*).

The common areas and guest rooms of the house offer plenty of space, although the decor seems to lack inspiration. Overall, Hackett House looks like a regular-issue middle-class home—albeit a squeaky-clean one. Still, there is charm in the family snapshots on the walls. And the house's largely Victorian Anjou Pear Room features original diamond-pane leaded windows, a cherrywood Rococo Revival settee and chairs, and a sitting room.

Breakfast here is excellent, with Sherry serving up everything from eggs Lorraine to pecan waffles with homemade blueberry sauce. If the weather is favorable, you'll dine out on the deck, with Mt. Adams looking over your shoulder.

Address: *922 State St., Hood River, OR 97031, tel. 503/386–1014.*
Accommodations: *3 double rooms and 1 suite share 2½ baths.*
Amenities: *Dinner available, meeting room.*
Rates: *$65–$75; full breakfast, evening refreshments. D, MC, V.*
Restrictions: *No smoking indoors, no pets.*

State Street Bed & Breakfast

In a residential area of Hood River just west of downtown, the State Street Bed & Breakfast is a plain cedar-shake house built in 1932.

Innkeepers Amy Goodbar and Mac Lee moved from the San Diego area to Hood River in 1987 and quickly built a reputation for excellent breakfasts and advice on where to catch the wind or hike. The Massachusetts Room has Colonial reproductions; the California Room features lots of color—three shades of peach—with director's chairs and potted ferns; the Colorado Room has a Southwest look, with Old West knickknacks; and the Maryland Room conveys the graciousness of the antebellum days, with a white iron bedstead and day bed, wicker chairs, and maroon tieback curtains with white lace. The main common area affords views of the Columbia River through leaded glass windows.

Breakfast is geared to the hearty—and athletic—with such entrées as strawberry crepes and oatmeal-walnut pancakes supplemented by muffins, homemade granola, and a huge fruit bowl.

Address: *1005 State St., Hood River, OR 97031, tel. 503/386–1899.*
Accommodations: *4 double rooms share 2 baths.*
Amenities: *Game room, storage area for sports equipment.*
Rates: *$55–$75; full breakfast. MC, V.*
Restrictions: *No smoking, no pets.*

Central and Eastern Oregon
Including Bend

Drop unsuspecting travelers into the part of Oregon that's east
of the snowcapped Cascade Mountain range and they'll swear
they're someplace else—Utah, Arizona, Texas, Switzerland.

While the western third of the state is lush and green, the
eastern two-thirds is high, dry, and wild—sparsely populated,
too. The 17 counties of eastern Oregon make up an area of pine
forests, rangeland, and mountains the size of Missouri, but the
population is less than 350,000. There is only one town with
more than 20,000 people, just two commercial TV stations, and
one congressional representative, whom the vast area shares
with southern Oregon.

Central and eastern Oregon begin very visibly in the west as
soon as you reach the summit of the Cascade Mountains.
There the forests turn from fir to pine and the ground
underfoot from soggy to crunchy. The difference rests simply
in the presence of the Cascades, which drain most of the
precipitation out of the Pacific storms, dumping it on the
western slopes of the mountains. Whereas western Oregon
averages 45 inches of rain a year, the mean to the east is less
than 15 inches.

Once you're out of the mountains, the land settles down to a
broad plateau that gradually slopes down toward the
Columbia River to the north. On this high plain, much of it
more than 3,500 feet in elevation, are large mountain ranges:
the lumpy Ochocos, the stately Strawberry Range, the majestic
Wallowas, the immense, complex Blue Mountains. And in the
southern deserts, gargantuan fault-block mountains—Steens
Mountain, Hart Mountain, Abert Rim—thrust straight out of
the sagebrush.

Deer, elk, antelope, cougars, and even wild horses roam these
plains. Ranches, some running more than 10,000 head of cattle,

are sprinkled throughout the big country. Although there are few developed tourist areas outside the Bend area, the adventuresome are seldom idle in central and eastern Oregon.

The Deschutes River, a cold green stream that heads near Mt. Bachelor, shoots along the eastern edge of the Cascades, providing better than 100 miles of fishing and rafting opportunities. The John Day River winds through thousands of square miles of fossil beds in north central Oregon. Farther east, the Snake River, bordering Oregon and Idaho, dominates the terrain with Hells Canyon—apologies to the Grand Canyon—the deepest gash on the continent.

Northeastern Oregon's Wallowa Mountains, often called the American Alps because of their combination of granite peaks and hanging glacier valleys, lie just to the west of Hells Canyon, with hundreds of miles of hiking and pack trails.

Only in the southeastern corner of the state, an area about the size of South Carolina, does Oregon have a true desert environment. Here, in an area of more than 30,000 square miles, rivers from the mountains flow into the plain and evaporate in marshes and alkali flats, and birds gather from all along the western flyway.

This is lonely, self-sufficient country, so people are friendly and are likely to wave at you as you drive down the long, lonesome highways. But passersby are few and far between. Sudden snowstorms or flash floods can come out of nowhere virtually anytime of the year. It is advisable to be prepared to fend for yourself at all times.

Places to Go, Sights to See

Baker City. On the old Oregon Trail, this former mining town quickly takes you back to the Gold Rush days of northeastern Oregon. Just east of town is the *Oregon Trail Interpretive Center* (tel. 800/523-1235), an excellent museum depicting pioneer life in the 1840s.

Bend. The largest town east of the Cascades and sitting very nearly in the center of Oregon, Bend is a good fueling-up spot for the recreational activities nearby: A half hour to the east, skiers bop down the slopes of Mt. Bachelor, and the fishing and rafting of the wild Deschutes River are within easy reach. Bend is filled with decent restaurants, dance bars, pro shops, and rental places, as well as a surprising number of good hostelries. At the *High Desert Museum* (59800 S. Hwy. 97, 6 mi south of Bend, tel. 503/382–4754), you can walk through a Stone Age Indian campsite, a pioneer wagon camp, an old mine, an Old West boardwalk, and other detailed dioramas, with authentic relics, sounds, even odors. A 150-acre outdoor section features porcupines, birds of prey, and river otters at play.

Century Drive. For 100 miles this forest-highway loop beginning and ending in Bend meanders among dozens of high mountain lakes offering fishing, hiking, waterskiing, and camping. Take Route 46 for the first two-thirds of the trip and switch to U.S. 97 at LePine to return to Bend.

John Day Fossil Beds National Monument (2 mi north of the junction of U.S. 26 and Hwy. 19, tel. 503/987–2333). Millions of years ago, the arid canyons of east central Oregon were tropical forests inhabited by sloths and the prehistoric ancestors of horses. Their remains in the form of well-preserved fossils, many in lake beds of volcanic ash, are found in the valley of the John Day River.

Kah-Nee-Ta (11 mi from Warm Springs on Hwy. 3, tel. 800/831–0100). In the heart of the 600,000-acre Warm Springs Indian Reservation sits this posh resort. The hot mineral springs feeding the Warm Springs River form the focal point of Kah-Nee-Ta, which is operated by the Confederated Tribes of Warm Springs. A double Olympic-size mineral-water pool is open to nonguests for a nominal fee; golf, tennis, hiking, and fishing are also available. At the *Museum at Warm Springs* (1 mi north of Kah-Nee-Ta on U.S. 26, tel. 503/553–3331) you can see traditional dwellings and attend a real Wasco wedding. Established in 1993, the museum chronicles the pasts of the Wasco, Paiute, and Warm Springs tribes.

Owyhee River Country. The far southeastern corner of Oregon is named for the wild, thrashing river that shoots through the canyons. White-water rafting is popular here, as are fishing, hiking, and studying Indian petroglyphs. The town of Vale, at the junction of highways 20 and 26, is the best base for exploring the area.

Pendleton. Famous for its annual mid-September rodeo, this cattle town, reached by I–84, is situated on a plain between the scenic Blue Mountains and the brown Columbia Plateau. An important staging area for shipping cattle, Pendleton seems almost Texan in atmosphere.

Smith Rocks State Park (tel. 503/548–7501). The muddy Crooked River winds through these high precipices north of Redmond. A favorite with rock climbers, 300- to 500-foot-deep canyons form high spires, the most famous of which is called Monkey Face. The park, which also encompasses dense pine forest, offers excellent hiking.

Steens Mountain. Steens Mountain is one of the most unusual desert environments in the West. The 60-mile-long ridge has 5,000-foot glacial gorges carved into its sides. The summit, 9,700 feet above sea level, is reached by a passable but rugged road, and overlooks the sandy Alvord Desert. To the north, 6 miles off Route 205, lies the mammoth *Malheur National Wildlife Refuge* (tel. 503/493–2612), home to hundreds of species of migratory birds, among them sandhill cranes, snowy white egrets, and white-faced ibis.

Wallowa Mountains. Oregon's northeastern corner is a surprise to most visitors. The mountains form a giant U-shaped fortress between Hells Canyon to the east and the Blue Mountains to the west. Hundreds of alpine lakes, many more than 7,000 feet high, dot the remote hanging valleys that fall between ridges of 9,000-foot-plus peaks. The most scenic route through the area is Highway 82; take it for 80 miles, starting and finishing at either LaGrande or Joseph.

Restaurants

Pine Tavern (tel. 503/382–5581) in Bend takes its name from the two pine trees growing through the roof. But the place's reputation comes from its flawlessly prepared seafood and fresh trout served up in typically hearty Western helpings. Ask any cowpoke in the Baker Valley who serves the best steak and potatoes, and there's only one answer: **Haines Steak House** (tel. 503/856–3639). One caveat: If you order it rare, that's how you'll get it.

Tourist Information

Central Oregon Visitors Information Center (63085 N. Hwy. 97, Bend, OR 97701, tel. 503/382–3221); **Grant County Chamber of Commerce** (281 W. Main St., John Day, OR 97485, tel. 503/575–0547); **Harney County Chamber of Commerce** (18 W. D St., Burns, OR 97720, tel. 503/573–2636); **North Central Oregon Tourism Council** (25 E. Dorion, Pendleton, OR 97801, tel. 800/547–8911); **Ontario Chamber of Commerce** (173 S.W. 1st St., Ontario, OR 97914, tel. 503/889–8012).

Reservation Services

Bed and Breakfast Reservations—Oregon (2321 N.E. 28th Ave., Portland, OR 97212, tel. 503/287–4704); **Northwest Bed and Breakfast** (610 S.W. Broadway, Portland, OR 97205, tel. 503/243–7616).

Birch Leaf Farm
Bed & Breakfast

After you drive the 60-plus miles of twisty road to Halfway, your first question has to be, Halfway to what? With all that driving, surely you must be all the way somewhere. And indeed you are, smack in the middle of a wondrous green valley with glacier-gouged peaks at one end, pine forests mingled with farmland throughout, and the parched southern end of Hell's Canyon at the other.

Commercialism has yet to hit the old town, which in fact got its name by being halfway between two places that have since shuffled off into mapmaker's oblivion. But bed-and-breakfasts are something else again.

Birch Leaf, about 4 miles due north of the town, is in an 1896 farmhouse with its original orchard out back. Although the Birch Leaf is a working farm, it has a very refined feeling. Innkeepers Dave and Maryellen Olson have made the inn a haven for bird lovers and just about anyone who desires peace and quiet.

A baby grand piano beside a floor-to-ceiling bookcase in the front room gives evidence of the intellectual bent of the place. A dusty, old television reminds you that the action is outside, not on the tube. An added attraction is the wraparound deck.

The three rooms upstairs are plainly decorated but afford views down the valley; all have the original doors with frosted-glass transoms above. Also on the grounds is a bunkhouse that has four single beds on two levels and its own wood stove—ideal for families with kids or for four backpackers getting ready to hit the trail.

The 42 acres of Birch Leaf offer plenty of places to roam. Maryellen will tell about the gravity irrigation that keeps this valley green. Deer often traipse through the orchard, which hosts century-old hybrids. Maryellen will also show you the thickets where birds hide from predators. If all this activity proves too much for you, take a break in the hammock just above the two ponds that dominate the front yard and provide a home for passing ducks.

Breakfast is a tasty affair, featuring hearty eggs from the inn's free-spirited, free-roaming chickens, blueberry coffee cake, and seven-grain cereal.

Address: *Rte. 1, Box 91, Halfway, OR 97834, tel. 503/742–2990.*
Accommodations: *1 double room with bath; 3 doubles share 1 bath; bunkhouse with outhouse.*
Amenities: *Piano, deck.*
Rates: *$50–$65, bunkhouse $25 per person; full breakfast. MC, V.*
Restrictions: *No smoking; no pets.*

Elliott House

In 1908, when Elliott House was built, Prineville was a booming cattle center on the edge of the frontier. Ranching is still big in Crook County, but Prineville is now best known for rockhounding (within a few miles are huge agate beds where the curious can easily pick up "thunder eggs" and petrified wood). Despite its rough-hewn reputation, Prineville has always been the most genteel town in central Oregon. Elliott House, a Queen Anne Victorian, keeps that tradition of class in the outback alive.

To say that the innkeepers, Tuck and Carol Dunlap, have taken great pains to re-create the past is an understatement: Carol wears a Victorian costume as she welcomes guests into the sitting room for afternoon tea. When they bought Elliott House, the Dunlaps found that in their zeal to modernize, the previous owners had stripped the main floor of all its original woodwork. Luckily, some of the upstairs moldings remained, and when Tuck discovered that he couldn't find similar ones from the same period, he reproduced them himself, adding wainscoting, chair rails, and crown molding.

Tuck isn't the only craftsperson in the family—Carol has created several stained-glass hangings for the living room, sitting room, and downstairs guest room. The sitting room has an opulent look, with bright gold-frame mirrors and a curvaceous Victorian fainting couch in red velvet.

The Dunlaps are working hard to replace any reproduction furniture in the house with antiques. The conversion has not yet been made in the ground-floor room, next to the kitchen, but a bay window dressed with ecru lace adds some charm. The most romantic guest room is the Sweetheart Room, with a white iron and porcelain bedstead and a turn-of-the-century camelback settee, its top rail and arms of carved wood. The same floral print that covers the settee is used in the window swags.

The most whimsical room is the large bathroom shared by the two upstairs rooms. The velvety-looking Victorian rose-and-black wallpaper fairly jumps out at you, as does a painting of a large, sensual female nude. The sink has a marble top; the claw-foot tub's feet are painted gold. Carol unabashedly calls this her brothel bath.

Address: *305 W. 1st St., Prineville, OR 97754, tel. 503/447–7442.*
Accommodations: *1 double room with bath, 2 doubles share 1 bath.*
Amenities: *Cable TV and phones available.*
Rates: *$40–$60; full breakfast, afternoon refreshments. No credit cards.*
Restrictions: *No smoking in rooms, no pets.*

Frenchglen Hotel

It's almost impossible to miss the Frenchglen Hotel—that is, once you *find* Frenchglen, a tiny spot on the map deep in the eastern Oregon desert. The town consists of a school (most of the families live on ranches sprinkled across a 1,000-square-mile area), a store, and the hotel.

Built in 1920, still pioneer days in this remote region, the state-owned hotel resembles a simple prairie church, with a gabled roof that's visible from miles away as you approach from the north. Manager John Ross spent years as a cook on Alaskan fishing boats, so remoteness is nothing new to him. At least here, at the foot of Steens Mountain, he gets a fresh supply of faces every few days.

Inside, the hotel is simple and rustic. A huge camp-type coffeepot is always on the hob in the combination lobby/dining room. Visitors can absorb local history and whet their appetites for touring with a collection of picture books in the lobby. The dining room, really two long pine tables, serves as a gathering place for ranchers and visitors.

The food here has long been a standout. Every evening a large, hearty family-style dinner is served for overnight guests and the general public. A typical group might include a ranching couple who have driven 60 miles to celebrate their anniversary, a pair of bird-watchers, and a local mechanic. John whips up huge salads, rich casseroles, home-baked rolls, and a main meat dish. Breakfast is also bountiful, although it's served individually from a menu and isn't included in the room rate.

All the rooms are upstairs off a single hallway. The five rooms in the original part of the hotel have plain white walls and wooden bed frames handmade by John. The three rooms at the back of the hotel, added during the 1930s, have knotty pine walls. Views sweep eastward across the broad Blitzen Valley up the gradually sloping shoulders of Steens Mountain. All eight rooms share two bathrooms midway down the long hall.

Most of the people who stay at the hotel are devoted bird-watchers who are attracted by the nearby Malheur National Wildlife Refuge. In the fall, however, Steens teems with hunters. The mix of hunters, ranchers, and conservationists can make for some lively conversations over breakfast.

Address: *Frenchglen, OR 97736, tel. 503/493–2825.*
Accommodations: *8 double rooms share 2 baths.*
Amenities: *Restaurant.*
Rates: *$42–$48; breakfast not included. MC, V.*
Restrictions: *No smoking in rooms, no pets; closed Nov. 16–Mar. 1.*

Lara House

Staying at Lara House, a cross-gabled Craftsman house built in 1910, gives visitors a glimpse of what life was like in Bend when it was a four-day trip to Portland instead of the present-day three-hour drive. Beside peaceful Drake Park on the Deschutes River near downtown, Lara House stands out; it's on a huge lot with a sloping lawn atop a retaining wall of native lava rocks.

The house's original woodwork can be seen in the trim and door frames all over, and in the alderwood coffered ceiling of the living room. There a large brick fireplace dominates, to be enjoyed from two cream-and-blue patterned camelback love seats or from the ladder-back chairs about the gaming table. The walls here are heavily stuccoed. Walk through the double French doors and the atmosphere changes radically. All is soft and subtle green in the huge sunroom overlooking the 11-acre riverside park.

Visitors who enjoy the sharply pitched ceilings and nooks and crannies of an attic will appreciate the fourth-floor Summit Room, a two-bedroom suite with the best views in the house. The main bedroom has a queen-size bed, willow furniture from the 1940s, and stenciled flowers painted on the wall moldings.

One floor down are the other guest rooms, each carpeted, with seating areas and private bathrooms. The L-shaped Drake Room, furnished in dark oak, has a duck theme: wallpaper borders swimming with them, framed prints of them, a wall unit displaying knickknacks of these fine-feathered friends. The black claw-foot tub, original to the house, is big enough for a whole flock of rubber duckies.

Guests have their choice of venues for breakfast: the formal living room, sunroom, or terraced redwood deck that surrounds the house. Innkeepers Doug and Bobbye Boger will not only arrange rafting tours on the Deschutes, but Doug, a part-time ski instructor, will also lead ski tours to nearby Mt. Bachelor that include lessons.

Address: *640 N.W. Congress St., Bend, OR 97701, tel. 503/388-4064.*
Accommodations: *5 double rooms with baths, 1 2-bedroom suite.*
Amenities: *Afternoon and evening refreshments, dinner and baby-sitting available, catering; rafting and skiing tours arranged.*
Rates: *$55–$75; full breakfast. AE, D, MC, V.*
Restrictions: *No smoking indoors, no pets.*

Shaniko Hotel

Bed-and-breakfasting in a ghost town may not strike everyone as a good bet. But here on the high dusty plains south of The Dalles, the Old West feeling of the recently restored Shaniko Hotel is palpable.

Guest rooms at the hotel, which first opened in 1901, are spare and perhaps a bit too antiseptic with their period reproduction furniture. (The mock old-fashioned wooden iceboxes acting as night tables *are* clever, however.) The only special room is the pink-and-white Bridal Suite, which features a small sitting room and a two-person whirlpool tub. Still, there's plenty of atmosphere just outside; guests need only peek out of the window to see a town that's falling down around them as the wind wails through the old buildings and shutters flap eerily.

Shaniko has been a ghost town since the 1940s, when the last rail line leading to town washed out. Yet in 1900, the town's population numbered in the thousands and it was the world's biggest shipper of wool. Stagecoach lines spoked into the frontier of eastern Oregon, and Shaniko was the rail head for the only line that then penetrated the high plains.

Despite the slightly sterile feel, owner Jean Farrell, a retired plumbing contractor, does give a personal warmth to the hotel, taking a special interest in the guests. Of course, that's easy to do in this town of 19, where all except two work either in the hotel or at its adjoining restaurant. Jean is also the mayor of Shaniko, a delicate job that involves keeping the town looking run-down without allowing it to collapse completely.

Breakfasts are copious, geared to a day of shearing sheep or baling hay, and dinners are mammoth, with huge wads of sweet homemade bread complementing mashed potatoes and gravy with hunks of meat.

Those calories can be partially walked off with a stroll through Shaniko. Some of the buildings, such as the old firehouse, have been kept up to house ancient horse-drawn fire rigs. The blacksmith shop is run by a small company that makes reproduction carriages. For real culture shock, guests can tour the tiny, false-fronted Shaniko Post Office. Across the lonesome highway is the old, creaking water tower, the tallest building in town.

Address: *Shaniko, OR 97057, tel. 503/489–3441.*
Accommodations: *17 double rooms with baths, 1 suite.*
Amenities: *Restaurant, whirlpool tub in suite.*
Rates: *$56, suite $85; breakfast not included. D, MC, V.*
Restrictions: *No smoking in rooms, no pets.*

Stange Manor

When Marjorie McClure was growing up during the late 1930s in La Grande, the Stange mansion, just a few blocks away, seemed a place of unattainable glamour. Owned by lumber baron August Stange, the richest man in the county, the manse on the western edge of this small college and ranching town was an obligatory stop for any political figure and celebrity passing through.

Marjorie left La Grande in 1956 for California. It wasn't until 1992, when she and her husband Pat returned for her father's 100th birthday, that Marjorie finally got her chance to stay at the forbidding manor. Three months later, the McClures had closed the deal to buy the place that Bing Crosby and Guy Kibbe had visited during Marjorie's childhood.

Built in 1924, the imposing Georgian Revival home sits on huge grounds in an otherwise unspectacular residential neighborhood. Stange Manor's interior is full of 1920s-style class. Guests can enjoy the large carved stone fireplace in the living room from an art deco–style semicircular sectional couch upholstered in a rose-print tapestry fabric.

Throw open the French doors of the Fountain Room, complete with a working wall fountain of teal-colored Italian tiles, and the years quickly melt away. Built-in benches line the perimeter of the window-filled room, affording views of the property. White rattan furniture and an old crank-up Victrola add to the Jay Gatsby aura of the room.

As you ascend the grand staircase to the upstairs guest rooms, you'll pass a large Georgian hunting tapestry purchased by Stange and a plaster bust of Aphrodite at the top. The master suite boasts a turn-of-the-century mahogany turned four-poster bed and matching dresser with tilting mirror. The bathroom features the original "foot washer," fed with running water.

Breakfast is a lavish affair served in the dining room beneath a pewter and crystal chandelier that is original to the house. Built-in floor-to-ceiling china display cabinets, flocked wallpaper, and full-length balloon curtains contribute to the formal ambience of the room. Usually Pat and Marjorie join the guests for breakfast, which might be considered an intrusion if they weren't so cordial, informative, and easygoing.

Address: *1612 Walnut St., La Grande, OR 97850, tel. 503/963–2400.*
Accommodations: *2 double rooms with baths, 2 2-bedroom suites.*
Amenities: *Cable TV and fireplace in 1 suite, children over 9 welcome.*
Rates: *$70–$90; full breakfast. MC, V.*
Restrictions: *No smoking, no pets.*

Bed and Breakfast by the River

The Emmel Bros. Ranch sits at the foot of the stunning Strawberry Mountains near Prairie City on more than 3,000 acres of rangeland and forest, with the John Day River winding through it.

The bed-and-breakfast Helen Emmel operates here is far from fancy. The guest quarters look like the teenagers' rooms they are—or were, now that the Emmel brood is away at college. There are some interesting touches: The family room has a hand-carved oak mantel from the 1813 Georgia plantation house where the family lived until they came out west in 1969. The pie safe came from the plantation's slave quarters.

What Bed and Breakfast by the River lacks in interior design, however, is more than made up for in atmosphere.

This is a working cattle ranch, where the morning begins with biscuits, waffles, homemade bread and preserves, and meat—beef, pork, venison, or elk—all from the ranch or the family's hunting trips. The house is right by the riverbank, and guests get a great view from the breakfast table of the salmon spawning.

Address: *Rte. 2, Box 790, Prairie City, OR 97869, tel. 503/820–4470.*
Accommodations: *3 double rooms with baths.*
Amenities: *TV with VCR and pool table in game room.*
Rates: *$35–$50; full breakfast. No credit cards.*
Restrictions: *No smoking, no pets, no alcohol.*

Chandlers Bed, Bread & Trail Inn

From the small cattle town of Joseph, the pine-covered Wallowa Mountains rise some 5,000 feet. Just south of town is Wallowa Lake, nestled at the foot of northeast Oregon's dominating peaks. And just as you make the turn between Joseph and the lake is Chandlers Bed, Bread & Trail Inn.

This modern, lodge-like house is surrounded by an extensive deck. The rustic, sparely furnished rooms have high, beamed ceilings, and much of their paneling is made of old barn wood; although the deep brown carpets are a bit dark, skylights provide plenty of eastern Oregon light. The best view of the mountains is from the sunroom on the second floor.

If the name sounds a bit odd, it's because innkeeper Ethel Chandler makes her own bread, and it's a staple in the hearty breakfast she fixes up. (So are sausage casseroles and tasty hazelnut pancakes.) As for the trail part, the wild Wallowas include a wilderness area the size of Rhode Island, where hiking and backpacking either by horse or llama are popular. Both Ethel and her husband, Jim, can advise guests on the best places to go in the area.

Address: *700 S. Main St., Joseph, OR 97846, tel. 503/432–9765, 800/452–3781.*
Accommodations: *5 double rooms share 2½ baths.*
Amenities: *TV in two common areas.*
Rates: *$50–$60; full breakfast. MC, V.*
Restrictions: *No smoking, no pets.*

Clear Creek Farm Bed and Breakfast

At Clear Creek, the setting is grand, with mountains hulking behind the simple 1880s Craftsman home, but the feeling—from the abstract metal sculpture of a cow on the farm's drive to the often barefoot innkeeper—is definitely counterculture. Matt and Denise Phillips cater to the rugged sort who are about to set out on a week-long llama trek or several days of floating the wild Snake River.

While the main house—with a large, airy kitchen and plenty of blond wood—is comfortable, Clear Creek's distinction rests in its more rustic accommodations. A barn and a granary have been converted to bunkhouses with ceilings to keep out the occasional summer showers, but no windows and only thin shake walls. Of the two outbuildings, the converted barn is the best. The granary, while more enclosed, is smaller, and its views are generally blocked by the house, which offers four sparsely furnished rooms. Breakfast is up to the guests, Denise says. She specializes in lighter fare such as home-grown fruits and juices, and she seasons her meals with herbs from her own garden.

Address: *Rte. 1, Box 138, Halfway, OR 97834, tel. 503/742–2233, fax 503/742–5175.*
Accommodations: *4 double rooms share 1 bath, 2 bunkhouses share 4 baths.*
Amenities: *Outdoor hot tub.*
Rates: *$55, bunkhouses $25 per person for parties of 6 or more; full breakfast. MC, V.*
Restrictions: *Bunkhouses closed Oct.–Apr.*

Farewell Bend Bed & Breakfast

Farewell Bend Bed & Breakfast is just at the edge of downtown Bend. From the street, the Dutch Colonial–style house is common enough, but inside, innkeeper Lorene Bateman has made good use of Bend's many days of sunshine to create an airy, California-style atmosphere.

All guest rooms come with handmade quilts designed by Lorene. The largest room, predominantly mauve, has a king-size bed with a modern teak headboard and an alcove sitting area. One lavender-hued room has a king-size bed and a large English turn-of-the-century mahogany wardrobe. The old-fashioned washstand has a real sink with running water. The third room has a bathroom with a claw-foot tub and a private deck. All the rooms have ceiling fans.

Downstairs, the living room is furnished with comfortable, contemporary, floral-print love seats and wing chairs; it also has a cable TV, VCR, and large library. Breakfast—from Dutch babies to spinach-egg dishes—is served in the modern dining room. More often, guests prefer to dine on the lower backyard deck.

Address: *29 N.W. Greeley St., Bend, OR 97701, tel. 503/382–4374.*
Accommodations: *3 double rooms with baths.*
Rates: *$65–$80; full breakfast, afternoon refreshments. No credit cards.*
Restrictions: *No smoking, no pets.*

Pine Valley Lodge and Halfway Supper Club

Pine Valley Lodge, on Main Street in "downtown" Halfway, is really just another art project for owners Dale and Babette Beatty. Both have had their share of fame: Dale is a nationally recognized home and furniture builder, and Babette is *the* Babette, who graced the cover of *Sports Illustrated*'s first swimsuit issue, January 20, 1964. Both say they've had their time in the limelight, and now it's time to settle down and make an honest living.

From the outside, the large house is styled like many others that were built in eastern Oregon during the timber boom of the late 1920s. Inside, the common area is artfully cluttered with a mixture of antique Florida fishing gear, Native American artifacts, and Babette's most recent western paintings. Audubon prints from the magazine's first issue are also on view. Babette is ambitious with breakfast and dinner. She makes bread, bagels, and jam, and she raises her own chickens. She will also cook game for any hunter who brings his day's work to her kitchen. She prepares Indian, Thai, and French dishes by request.

Address: *163 N. Main St., Halfway, OR 97834, tel. 503/742-2027.*
Accommodations: *1 double room with bath, 2 doubles share 1 bath.*
Amenities: *Bicycles, restaurant.*
Rates: *$60–$65; full breakfast. No credit cards.*
Restrictions: *No smoking indoors.*

Washington

Including Idaho

Washington

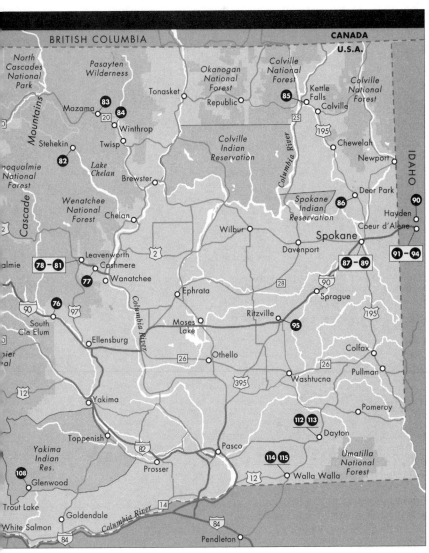

BRITISH COLUMBIA   CANADA

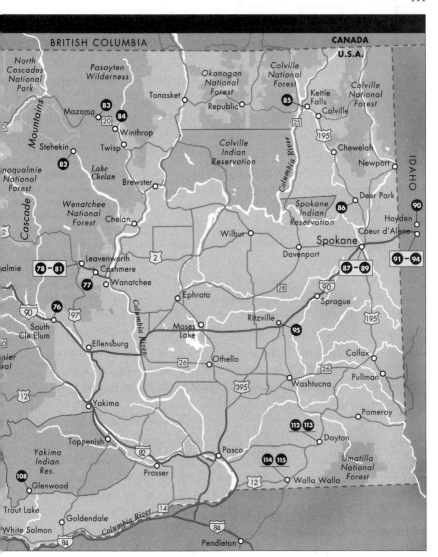

Columbia River and Long Beach Peninsula

The Columbia River Valley and Long Beach Peninsula offer a variety of outdoor experiences. Scenery in the valley is striking, with a deep gorge cutting through forested hills and rugged cliffs. Farther west, visitors flock to the peninsula for its sandy beaches, ocean swells, and migrating birds. The peninsula's reputation for fine cuisine is another big drawing card. Both areas offer many opportunities for hiking and nature walks.

The mighty Columbia River, which forms much of the Washington–Oregon border, has a rich geological, cultural, and natural history. Its bounty of salmon once fed many native tribes and later supported a thriving fishing industry. Today, in addition to providing electrical power to much of the Northwest and the West Coast, the river provides water-sports enthusiasts with one of the world's prime sailboarding sites— with winds often at 30 miles per hour or more, the 70 miles of river from Bingen to Roosevelt draws more than 200,000 windsurfers annually.

An 80-mile stretch of Highway 14 traces the wild and scenic river where it slices through a canyon between walls of basalt, designated as the Columbia River Gorge National Scenic Area. The only sea-level cut through the Cascade Mountains, the gorge divides areas of very diverse climates: The wetter western portions get up to 80 inches of rain each year, while the high-desert area on the east may get as little as 10 inches.

Just north of the mouth of the Columbia, in the southwest corner of the state, is the Long Beach Peninsula, with a chain of small fishing villages and the longest uninterrupted stretch (28 miles) of sandy ocean beach in North America. The area offers good hiking and beachcombing, but because of tremendous undertows and shifting sands, this is not a very safe place for swimming—there are several drownings each year. Driving on the beach is still a hotly disputed issue among residents, but in 1990 the state legislature closed about 40% of it to motor vehicles from April through Labor Day. A half-mile-long wooden boardwalk in Long Beach features disabled-access ramps, benches, telescopes, and great views, but no vendors. The entire peninsula is a perfect place to enjoy a winter storm, with howling winds and huge breakers crashing on the beach.

A favorite pastime in the area is birding. Migrating white trumpeter swans frequent marshes a mile or two inland, and on Long Island—an islet on the bay side of the peninsula that is home to an old-growth red cedar grove—are found the highly controversial spotted owl and the marbled murrelet.

Places to Go, Sights to See

Bingen. A number of historic sites are worth visiting here. The area's first white settler, Erastus Joslyn, arrived in 1852 and built his home and farm close to the Columbia River, just west of the present town of Bingen. The home was destroyed in a conflict with Native Americans, but Joslyn eventually built another one in town on Steuben Street; it came to be called the *Grand Old House* for its ornate Victorian architecture. On Jefferson Street, the *Theodore Suksdorf House* was the home of Bingen's founder, who originally hailed from Bingen-on-the-Rhine in Germany—thus the town's name. The *Wilhelm Suksdorf House*, built in 1905 by Theodore's son, a renowned botanist who named many native plant species, stands on Lincoln Street. Tours are offered at the *Mont Elise Winery* (315 W. Steuben St., tel. 509/493–3001), one of the oldest family-owned wineries in Washington. The 1911 Methodist Church, at the corner of Steuben and Maple streets, is now the *Gorge Heritage Museum* (tel. 509/493–3228).

Cape Disappointment. This cape at the start of the peninsula got its name from English fur trader Captain John Meares because of his unsuccessful attempt in 1788 to find the Northwest Passage here. On the bluff is one of the oldest light-houses on the West Coast, first used in 1856. Below the bluff is the *U.S. Coast Guard Station Cape Disappointment* (tel. 360/642–2384), the largest search-and-rescue station on the Northwest coast. The rough conditions of the Columbia River Bar provide intensive training for its *National Motor Lifeboat School*, the only school of its kind. Here, rescue crews from all over the world learn advanced skills in navigation, mechanics, fire fighting, and lifesaving. The observation platform on the north jetty at *Ft. Canby State Park* (tel. 360/642–3078)—site of an active military post until 1957—is a good viewing spot for watching the motor lifeboats during regular surf drills.

Cascade Locks. Before the dams were built on the Columbia River, locks were needed to allow river traffic to bypass the Columbia's dangerous rapids. At Cascade Locks, visitors can board the stern-wheeler *Columbia Gorge* (tel.

503/223–3928 or 503/374–8427), where a spirited narrator relates tales of the past to the rhythm of the giant paddle wheel. Day trips, dining cruises, and special excursions are offered. The *Cascade Locks Historical Museum* (tel. 503/374–8535) offers a look at the now obsolete locks, a steam locomotive, and other historical artifacts.

Cathlamet. The name of this river town—about an hour west of I–5, and the seat of Wahkiakum ("wa-KI-a-kum") County—comes from a Chinook word meaning "stone," so named because the tribe lived here along a stretch of rocky riverbed. Today visitors will find a pleasant marina, some 19th-century houses perched on the hill overlooking the river, and the *Wahkiakum County Historical Museum* (65 River St., no phone). From Cathlamet, one can take a bridge or a ferry—*The Wahkiakum* is the only ferry remaining on the lower Columbia—to *Puget Island*. Settled in 1884 by Scandinavians who brought herds of dairy cattle and built large barns and dikes on the low-lying island, it is popular with bicyclists for its pleasing views of boat moorages, gill-netting boats, dairy farms, and historic churches. About a mile and a half west of Cathlamet on Route 1 is the *Julia Butler Hansen National Wildlife Refuge* (tel. 360/795–3915), named for a woman who served in the U.S. House of Representatives from 1960 to 1975. In addition to protecting the endangered Columbian white-tailed deer, a small deer of the Northwest, the refuge is a wintering area for waterfowl on the Pacific flyway, and home to bald eagles, great blue herons, swans, and herds of elk.

Ft. Columbia State Park and Interpretive Center (Hwy. 101, tel. 360/777–8221). Built in 1903, this fort was one of 27 coastal defense units of the U.S. Army. Many of its 30 structures have been restored to show military life. The park is just 2 miles east of Chinook, a town named for the Native Americans who assisted Lewis and Clark—credited with "discovering" the peninsula—during their stay here in the early 1800s.

Goldendale. The *Presby Mansion* (127 W. Broadway, tel. 509/773–4303 or 509/773–5443) was built in 1902 for Winthrop Bartlett Presby, a lawyer who migrated from New Hampshire in 1888 and eventually served four years as a Washington state senator. His 20-room mansion is now a museum that illustrates pioneer life in Klickitat County and displays Native American artifacts and a collection of coffee grinders. On the northern edge of the town, the *Goldendale Observatory* (1602 Observatory Dr., tel. 509/773–3141) offers interpretive presentations concerning stars and telescopes, as well as tours and other programs; visitors are welcome to use its 24.5-inch Cassergrain reflecting telescope.

Ilwaco. This community of about 600 has a colorful past linked to the fishing industry: From 1884 to 1910, gill-net and trap fishermen were so competitive about rights to the fishing grounds that they fought each other with knives, rifles, and threats of lynchings. Since then fishermen have developed more amicable relationships, and today charters are available for salmon, crab, tuna, and sturgeon fishing. The *Ilwaco Heritage Museum* (115 S.E. Lake St., tel. 360/642–3446) presents the history of southwestern Washington through such exhibits as dioramas on Native Americans, traders, missionaries, and pioneers. It also contains a model of the "clamshell railroad," a narrow-gauge train that ran on a bed of ground clam and oyster shells to transport passengers and mail up and down the peninsula.

Leadbetter State Park (call Ft. Canby State Park for information; *see* Cape Disappointment, *above*). At the northern end of the peninsula, this wildlife refuge is a good spot for birding. The dune area at the point is closed from April to August to protect nesting snowy plovers. Biologists have identified some 100 species here, including black brants, yellowlegs, turnstones, and sanderlings.

Long Beach. Go-cart and bumper-car concessions, an amusement park, and beach activities attract tourists to this town of 1,200, which each year hosts the Washington State International Kite Festival during the third weekend in August. Other peninsula festivals include the Garlic Festival, a tasty tribute to that pungent bulb, held in mid-June, and the Water Music Festival, featuring chamber music at various locations on the third weekend in October.

Maryhill Museum of Art (35 Maryhill Museum Dr., Goldendale, tel. 509/773–3733). Built as a "ranch house" in 1914 and resembling a European château, the museum—opened in 1940—is the result of the efforts and resources of three people: Sam Hill, transportation mogul and heir to the fortune of the Great Northern Railway; his friend Loie Fuller, a pioneer of modern dance who found fame in Paris during the 1890s; and Queen Marie of Romania (Sam did war relief work in Romania after World War I; indebted, the queen came to Washington for the dedication). It includes one of the country's largest collections of Rodin sculpture; an impressive array of Native American baskets, clothing, and photographs; and royal costumes and furniture from the late queen. Nearby is Sam Hill's memorial to soldiers who died in World War I, a replica of Britain's Stonehenge.

Mt. Adams (Ranger Station, Trout Lake, tel. 509/395–2501). At 12,276 feet, Mt. Adams is the second-highest mountain in Washington, but in sheer bulk it is larger than Mt. Rainier. In the vicinity are ice caves, a self-guided-tour area formed by molten lava, and *Big Lava Bed*—12,500 acres of sculptural shapes and caves to be viewed from its edge.

Mt. Hood Scenic Railroad (110 Railroad Ave., Hood River, tel. 503/386–3556). Built in 1906, the train links the Columbia River gorge with the foothills of snow-capped Mt. Hood, at 11,235 feet the highest peak in Oregon. The route offers views of the Cascades, including Mt. Hood and Mt. Adams. Along the way, the train may pick up a carload of lumber or pears—it's still a working freight train.

Mt. St. Helens National Volcanic Monument (Rte. 1, Amboy, tel. 360/247–5473). Devastated by a great volcanic eruption in 1980, Mt. St. Helens is today a national monument. Hiking trails lead up through a regenerated evergreen forest to the mile-high crater, its lava dome, and Ape Cave, an extremely long lava tube (12,810 ft). Sporadic eruptions continue to spew steam and gases, giving lucky hikers a free show. There's a visitor center in *Castle Rock* (3029 Spirit Lake Hwy., tel. 360/274–6644).

Oysterville. This tiny community once thrived on the oyster industry but nearly turned into a ghost town when the native shellfish were fished to extinction. Tides have washed away homes and businesses, but a handful of late-19th-century structures still exist. Free maps inside the restored Oysterville Church direct you through the one-street village, now on the National Register of Historic Places.

Restaurants

Mio Amore Pensione (Trout Lake, tel. 509/395–2264) serves Northern Italian dinners nightly by reservation only. **The Ark Restaurant & Bakery** (on Willapa Bay, Nahcotta, tel. 360/665–4133) was praised by the late James Beard for its fresh local seafood. The **Shoalwater Restaurant** at the Shelburne Inn (Seaview, tel. 360/642–4142) serves nationally acclaimed Northwest cuisine—lots of seafood and local produce like edible ferns—offering vegetarian options and a children's menu. The **Sanctuary** (Chinook, tel. 360/777–8380), set in a former church, serves a varied menu, including decadent desserts.

Tourist Information

Klickitat County Tourism Committee (Box 1220, Goldendale, WA 98620, tel. 509/773–4395); **Long Beach Peninsula Visitors Bureau** (Box 562, Long Beach, WA 98631, tel. 360/642–2400 or 800/451–2542).

Reservation Services

Pacific Bed & Breakfast Agency (701 N.W. 60th St., Seattle, WA 98107, tel. 206/784–0539); **Travelers Bed & Breakfast** (Box 492, Mercer Island, WA 98040, tel. 360/232–2345); **Washington State Bed & Breakfast Guild** (2442 N.W. Market St., Seattle, WA 98107, tel. 206/548–6224).

Mio Amore
Pensione

About 20 miles north of the Columbia River in the Mt. Adams Wilderness, just outside the logger/cowboy town of Trout Lake, is Mio Amore Pensione. It has been owned since 1986 by Tom and Jill Westbrook, both retail executives. A vacation to the Trout Lake area convinced them to chuck their life in southern California and become innkeepers.

The 1904 Victorian-style farmhouse faces the creek, with expansive decks and creeping phlox-covered terraces stretching down to the river, the hot tub, and an old icehouse. Tom and Jill have renovated the inside of the house, exposing the ceiling beams and decorating it with a combination of contemporary and antique furniture and what will seem to some a heavy dose of memorabilia (including a beer stein collection) from their travels and Tom's service years. The living room is elegant, with Rococo Revival sofa and chairs and a fireplace of Mt. Adams volcanic rock. The dining room has a large sideboard where the evening's dessert usually sits late in the afternoon to tempt you, and a mirrored wall that prompts guests to dive for a spot from which they won't have to stare into the mirror during dinner.

The main house has three guest rooms, all with pastoral views. The Venus Room is really a suite, with lilac carpeting, a brass and white-painted-iron queen bed with a white quilt and eyelet flounce, and white-painted armoire.

Its sitting room, furnished in white wicker, offers views of the deck, gardens, and creek, and the large bath features a claw-foot tub. Outside is the 1890s icehouse, called the Vesta, a cozy and more rustic room with a wood-burning stove and a loft.

The Westbrooks go out of their way to make your stay memorable. Almost every night Tom cooks a four-course, Northern Italian gourmet dinner, open to guests and the public by reservation only. (While in the service, Tom was "adopted" into a restaurant family in Pisa, Italy.)

Breakfast includes an entrée—such as quiche, soufflé, or veal sausage with potatoes—and up to eight kinds of fresh-baked breads and pastries. Tom will even pack you a goody bag of leftover cakes and breads.

Address: *53 Little Mountain Rd., Box 208, Trout Lake, WA 98650, tel. 509/395–2264.*
Accommodations: *2 double rooms share 1 bath, 1 suite, 1 cottage.*
Amenities: *Restaurant, gift shop; hot tub.*
Rates: *$60–$135; full breakfast. MC, V.*
Restrictions: *No smoking indoors, pets only with prior permission.*

Scandinavian Gardens Inn

When you step into this spacious bed-and-breakfast in the heart of Long Beach, be prepared to get a taste of Scandinavian culture. Innkeepers Rod and Marilyn Dakan ran a computer business before coming to the coast. They are not Scandinavian, they say, but claim to have a friend who is half Norwegian. Before you enter, they will ask you to take off your shoes.

If this request is based on the observance of Scandinavian custom, you can immediately see a more practical reason for it—the white wool carpeting that covers the ground floor. The house is immaculate; there doesn't seem to be a single corner where even the most fastidious person wouldn't feel comfortable eating *lutefisk* off the floor.

Although the main common area, with its white carpet and blond-wood furnishings, is a bit sterile and somewhat intimidating, the colorful guest rooms easily compensate for it. On the main floor is the Icelandic Room, done in plums and greens, with an antique armoire and love seat and rosemaling on wall cabinet doors. The Danish Room, all blue and cinnamon tones, is decorated with hearts and nautical knickknacks. The Norwegian Room features greens and golds and a simple pine bed.

Upstairs, the teal and red Finnish Room offers such special touches as a skylight in the bath and an antique vanity. The main attraction here, however, is the Swedish Suite. Done in soft pinks and light blues, both rooms in the suite have dormer windows. Although the view is pedestrian—guests look out on the surrounding residential area—inside there's a hot tub for two with an overhead skylight, as well as a sitting area that includes a small refrigerator. The bedroom features a teakwood bed set, antique vanity, and a half bath of its own.

But even those who haven't booked the honeymoon suite need not go without a hot soak: The recreation room offers a large spa in addition to exercise equipment. Visitors can also enjoy the game tables in the social room, which doubles as the dining area. Rod and Marilyn serve the smorgasbord-style breakfast here wearing Scandinavian costumes. The meal features such delectables as shrimp omelets, ginger bread, and even baked Alaska.

Address: *Rte. 1, Box 36, Long Beach, WA 98631, tel. 360/642–8877.*
Accommodations: *3 double rooms with baths, 1 suite.*
Amenities: *Spa in suite, common spa, social room, recreation room.*
Rates: *$70–$120; full breakfast. MC, V.*
Restrictions: *No smoking, no pets; 2-night minimum on holiday and local festival weekends.*

Shelburne Inn

itting along the peninsula's main thoroughfare, behind a white picket fence enclosing rose and other gardens, is a green wood-frame building that is the oldest continuously run hotel in the state. Opened in 1896, the Craftsman-style inn joined to a late Victorian building is owned by Laurie Anderson and David Campiche. David was a professional potter and antiques dealer. He met Laurie—who had worked for a cruise line and traveled widely before settling here—when he helped pull her vehicle out of the sand.

The inn has a homey, country atmosphere. The lobby is somewhat cramped, with a seating area around a fireplace, a church altar as a check-in desk, a large oak breakfast table, and more. The original beaded-fir paneling, as well as large panels of Art Nouveau stained glass rescued from an old church in England, are found throughout the inn. A new section, built in 1983, is quieter than the older sections, though the latter have been soundproofed and carpeted.

Fresh flowers, original artwork, and fine art prints adorn the guest rooms, most of which have decks or balconies. Some rooms feature country pine furnishings, others mahogany or oak. Beds have either handmade quilts or hand-crocheted spreads. Some rooms are rather small, but the suites are spacious. Suite No. 9, in rose and cream, features large stained-glass panels between the bedroom, highlighted by a brass bed and a richly carved oak armoire, and a sitting room, furnished with natural wicker and an Arts and Crafts secretary. The large bathroom includes a roomy tub with gold-plated ball-and-claw feet.

The Shelburne's breakfast is one of the top three, if not *the* best, in the state. David makes use of regional produce from wild mushrooms to local seafood, and Laurie does all the baking. Guests choose from among five or six entrées, which may include an asparagus omelet or grilled oysters with salsa.

The highly regarded Shoalwater Restaurant, housed in the enclosed front porch, is owned by Tony and Ann Kischner and offers such elegant entrées as duck with dried cherry sauce. The wine list has more than 400 titles. The Heron and Beaver Pub serves light meals, along with the best concoctions of Washington's microbreweries.

Address: *4415 Pacific Way, Box 250, Seaview, WA 98644, tel. 360/642–2442, fax 360/642–8904.*
Accommodations: *13 double rooms with baths, 2 suites.*
Amenities: *Restaurant, pub.*
Rates: *$89–$160; full breakfast. AE, MC, V.*
Restrictions: *No smoking indoors, no pets; 2-night minimum on weekends and holidays.*

Sou'wester Lodge

J ust behind the sand dunes on the peninsula is this red-shingled, three-story inn. Make no mistake about it: The Sou'wester is not for everyone. Perhaps more than any other B&B in the state, it is an experience weighted as much by the unique character of the innkeepers as it is by the setting, a big old lodge built in 1892 as the country estate of Senator Henry Winslow Corbett of Oregon.

Len and Miriam Atkins left their native South Africa in the early 1950s to work in Israel, then moved to Chicago to work with the late child psychologist Bruno Bettelheim. With the idea of establishing a treatment program on the West Coast for emotionally disturbed children, in 1981 they spent six months in a camper, scouting potential sites. Instead, they opted to help adults unwind from the stresses of daily life.

The lodge is strewn with the acquisitions of a lifetime of world travels, including a hand-carved parlor set inlaid with mother-of-pearl from the Middle East. This is one of several sitting areas in the living room, which features a large fireplace, tongue-and-groove fir paneling, ceiling with massive beams, and Persian rugs.

An unusual aspect of the Sou'wester is that it bills itself not as a B&B but as a B&MYODB (make your own darn breakfast), with kitchen access provided (but not food). Second- and third-story accommodations are suites with full kitchens and views of the Pacific. Guest rooms are furnished with the occasional antique but more often Salvation Army furniture, with marbleized linoleum floors; nicer touches are the handmade quilts or chenille bedspreads and artwork done by various artists while staying in that room.

Another slightly offbeat note that adds to the Sou'wester's charm is the collection of guest cabins and trailers scattered among the firs. The cabins are a bit more rustic than the guest rooms. Trailers feature handsome blond-wood interiors with lots of 1950s rounded corners. The Disoriented Express features an exterior mural of a train full of animal passengers.

Address: *Beach Access Rd., Box 102, Seaview, WA 98644, tel. 360/642–2542.*
Accommodations: *3 double rooms share bath; 6 suites, 4 cabins, 9 trailers, all with kitchens.*
Amenities: *Cable TV available upon request in some units.*
Rates: *$35–$97; no breakfast. MC, V.*
Restrictions: *No smoking indoors, pets in outdoor units only.*

Boreas Bed and Breakfast

On Long Beach Peninsula, the north wind brings good weather. It's apt, then, that Sally Davis and Coleman White named their sunny, California-like bed-and-breakfast for Boreas, the Greek god of the north wind.

In a quiet residential area of sometimes boisterous Long Beach, Boreas is airy without putting on airs. An open kitchen in the front part of the house is a vibrant blue. The main common area in back opens up to dunes and ocean views. A downstairs suite has a private beachfront entrance, while the upstairs lodgings offer skylights.

The mix of modern and antique is handled well, perhaps because of the skills the pair brings to their new profession. Breakfasts include seafood omelets, fruit, homemade bread, quiche, and Sally's specialty—a crab and mushroom croissant.

Address: *607 N. Boulevard, Long Beach, WA 98631, tel. 360/642–8069.*
Accommodations: *1 double room with bath, 2 doubles share 1 bath, 1 suite.*
Amenities: *Bicycles, hot tub.*
Rates: *$65–$95; full breakfast. MC, V.*
Restrictions: *No smoking, no pets; 2-night minimum on weekends or $10 surcharge for 1-night weekend stays; closed Jan.–Mar.*

Coast Watch Bed & Breakfast

When Karen Johnston came to the peninsula for a weekend one spring, she saw this contemporary-style ocean-front house for sale. Partway home to Bellingham, she turned around, returned to the peninsula, signed an agreement to buy the weathered-shingle house, then rushed back home just in time for work.

Each of the two airy guest suites has a private entry and living room. Both are decorated with contemporary furnishings in earth tones and have views of the Pacific Ocean, the dunes, and the beach. One suite includes a rattan dining room set and rocker and a print by local artist Eric Wiegardt; a fishing net hangs on the wall over the bed.

Karen provides a full fruit basket in each suite and a minifridge to chill guests' wine bottles. Breakfast includes *latte* (café au lait), deadly-to-your-waistline cinnamon rolls served under glass domes, and individual platters of up to eight kinds of fresh fruit. "I start in Ocean Park and I may end up driving as far as Astoria, which is 40 miles from here, to get the fruit I want," says Karen.

Address: *Box 841, Ocean Park, WA 98640, tel. 360/665–6774.*
Accommodations: *2 suites.*
Amenities: *Kites.*
Rates: *$85; Continental breakfast. MC, V.*
Restrictions: *No smoking indoors, no pets, no phones.*

Country Keeper Bed & Breakfast Inn

Perched on a hill in Cathlamet overlooking the Columbia River is this Eastlake-style house built in 1907. Real estate appraiser Tony West and his wife, Barbara, a teacher, bought the place in 1991 after seeking a change from their San Francisco Bay area jobs.

Never remodeled, it retains the original oak floors inlaid with mahogany, and the Douglas fir staircase off the foyer. The living room features built-in bookcases, an overstuffed pink velvet sofa and chair, a pink Oriental rug from the 1930s, and the same Morris chair shown in a 1910 photo of the room.

Each guest room features comfortable, grandma's-attic-type furniture. The Monet Room is decorated in pink and white, with white-painted furniture.

The Rose Room features a king-size bed with floral canopy and spread, an Oriental rug, and a large bay window. These two front guest rooms overlook the river and the marina; the back rooms look down on gardens. Breakfast includes muffins and a hot dish such as apple pancakes, soufflés, or French toast.

Address: *61 Main St., Cathlamet, WA 98612, tel. 360/795–3030 or 800/551–1691.*
Accommodations: *2 double rooms with baths, 2 double rooms share bath.*
Rates: *$70–$85; full breakfast, afternoon refreshments. MC, V.*
Restrictions: *No smoking indoors, no pets; closed Christmas Day.*

Flying L Ranch

About 30 miles north of the Columbia, nestled in the ponderosa pines and meadows of the Glenwood Valley, is the Flying L Ranch, with spectacular views of Mt. Adams, 15 miles away. Twins Darvel (a former college instructor/administrator) and Darryl (still a ship's captain) run the 160-acre ranch where they grew up.

The look of the interior is Western ranch–style rustic, with well-worn and mismatched but comfortable furniture. The large common area has wood paneling, a beamed ceiling, Navajo rugs, a stone fireplace whose log mantel is emblazoned with the Flying L brand, and Western art. The simply furnished, almost austere guest rooms feature firm beds with comforters.

Guests can rent bikes to explore the area, or they can stroll the ranch's more than 2 miles of marked trails, pond, and picnic areas where lupine, Indian paintbrush, and other wildflowers grow. Three-night summer packages include escorted day hikes on Mt. Adams, naturalist programs, and dinners at local restaurants.

Address: *25 Flying L La., Glenwood, WA 98619, tel. 509/364–3488.*
Accommodations: *10 double rooms with baths, 4 doubles share 1 bath, 2 housekeeping cabins.*
Amenities: *Bikes, hot tub, 2 common kitchens.*
Rates: *$65–$90; full breakfast. AE, MC, V.*
Restrictions: *No smoking indoors, no pets in lodge.*

Gallery Bed & Breakfast at Little Cape Horn

Along a winding country road in Cathlamet is this contemporary Northwest-style building. Owner Carolyn Feasey opened an art and crafts gallery in 1973 in town, later moving it to the home she shares with her husband, Eric, a forestry engineer.

The interior is open and spacious, with lots of redwood, cedar, and glass. It is decorated in contemporary style with the occasional antique. Large windows in the living room and dining room overlook a multilevel redwood deck and the river.

Guest rooms are small but attractive. One room has a telescope and deck, where feeders attract hummingbirds. The elegant whirlpool in this room's bath is shared with occupants of an adjoining room and bath, so it's not always private. Another room features pieces of Carolyn's mother's English china and a 1783 survey map.

Address: *4 Little Cape Horn, Cathlamet, WA 98612, tel. 360/425–7395.*
Accommodations: *3 double rooms with baths, 1 single room with bath.*
Amenities: *Outdoor hot tub.*
Rates: *$60–$80; Continental or full breakfast. No credit cards.*
Restrictions: *No smoking indoors.*

Gumm's Bed & Breakfast

Six blocks from the ocean, on an immaculately kept lawn off the peninsula's main highway between Ilwaco and Long Beach, sits Gumm's, a yellow Craftsman house built in 1911. Owner Esther Slack ("Gumm" to her first grandson) welcomes children and has a lot of toys to amuse them, such as a collection of teddy bears and a train "for dads to play with." Still, she manages to keep the nicely decorated house neat and spotless.

The common areas include a spacious living room with beamed ceilings, a river-rock fireplace, an upright piano, two child-size rockers, and a blue-gray sofa and love seat set against raspberry carpeting. Each guest room is individually decorated: Barb's Room, for example, features a high four-poster tobacco-and-rice bed with step stool, an Eastlake chest, and a mirrored armoire.

Esther enjoys telling stories about the house, especially of when it was a hospital, during the 1930s; the formal dining room is the old operating room.

Address: *3310 Highway 101, Box 447, Seaview, WA 98644, tel. 360/642–8887.*
Accommodations: *2 double rooms with baths; 2 doubles share 1 bath.*
Amenities: *Cable TV, hot tub.*
Rates: *$65–$75; full breakfast. MC, V.*
Restrictions: *No smoking inside, no pets.*

Inn at Ilwaco

Perched on a knoll in the fishing village of Ilwaco, at the mouth of the Columbia River, is this inn, built in 1928 as a Presbyterian church. The Georgian-style building is faced in weathered shingles with white mill-work trim. Innkeeper Laurie Blancher will ring the church bell for weddings, New Year's Eve, and "little boys who behave."

The peach-and-white common area is spacious, with 10-foot ceilings, large windows, Oriental rugs, a pellet-burning stove, and eclectic furnishings, including a French Provincial sofa and chair upholstered in soft green. Guest rooms, occupying the former Sunday school on the second floor, are cozy, with country furnishings and fir floors with throw rugs. Some—like room 6, with a whitewashed pine armoire and Ralph Lauren fabrics accented by lace curtains—feature dormer windows with window seats, and some have the original board-and-bead wood paneling. The sanctuary remains in use as a wedding chapel, as well as a playhouse for regional productions. Breakfast includes such entrées as quiche or French toast with cream cheese and nuts, topped with raspberry sauce.

Address: *120 Williams St., Ilwaco, WA 98624, tel. 360/642–8686.*
Accommodations: *7 double rooms with baths, 2 doubles share 1 bath.*
Rates: *$55–$80; full breakfast. MC, V.*
Restrictions: *No smoking, no pets; 2-night minimum for summer weekends and holidays.*

Inn at White Salmon

After 30 years, Roger Holen had had enough of the computer business, so in 1990 he and his wife, Janet, a nurse, became innkeepers. From the outside, their place is short on appeal: a plain brick hotel built in 1937 and set on the main street of the small river town of White Salmon. But don't let appearances deceive you: The interior has a lot more charm.

Highlights of the lobby include beveled glass and a large brass cash register on a marble-topped mahogany desk. The parlor features an 8-foot-tall oak sideboard from the 1890s and hand-painted lithographs.

Each guest room features a few antiques, such as brass or ornate wood headboards. The bridal suite has a sitting area with a mahogany Eastlake settee upholstered in rose.

Breakfast is an extravaganza: some 20 pastries and breads, including a chocolate raspberry cheesecake, and six egg dishes.

Address: *172 W. Jewett St., White Salmon, WA 98672, tel. 509/493–2335 or 800/972–5226.*
Accommodations: *16 double rooms with baths.*
Amenities: *Air-conditioning, TV, and phone in room; outdoor hot tub.*
Rates: *$89–$115; full breakfast. AE, D, DC, MC, V.*
Restrictions: *No smoking in common rooms, no pets in most rooms.*

Kola House Bed & Breakfast

During the 1930s, Oscar Luokkala used to stay at Kola House when it was in its first incarnation—a boardinghouse in the windswept fishing community of Ilwaco. In 1980, Luokkala bought the old place just off the harbor and set about redoing it in the time left over from his busy construction business in the Portland area. Now the Kola House, bearing the name of the boat-building family that constructed it in 1919, is a sturdy bed-and-breakfast in the little town best known as a jumping-off place for deep-sea fishing off the mouth of the Columbia River.

While the decorating is very basic, two of the upstairs rooms offer harbor views. Three rooms have skylights in the bath, and the suite hosts a fireplace and a cozy Finnish sauna. Unusual features include a basement hot tub with a skylight and a small cabin that is often booked by fishermen heading out early in the morning.

The dining area is dominated by a large built-in oak cupboard featuring family china. Breakfasts also tend toward the basics, with ham, eggs, pancakes, and muffins being common fare.

Address: *211 Pearl Ave., Ilwaco, WA 98624, tel. 360/642–2819.*
Accommodations: *4 double rooms with baths, 1 suite, 1 cabin.*
Amenities: *Sauna in suite, spa.*
Rates: *$60–$75; full breakfast. MC, V.*
Restrictions: *No smoking, no pets.*

Land's End

Isolated amid the sand dunes of the peninsula and facing the Pacific Ocean, Land's End is the large, contemporary, Northwest-style home of former teacher Jackie Faas. The living room is spacious, with a marble fireplace, a grand piano, Eastlake furnishings, Oriental carpets, and 6-foot-high windows framing panoramic ocean views.

On the ground floor are the two guest rooms, done up in country style. The larger room has an ornamental Dutch enamel cookstove; its bath features a large soaking tub with a dark wood surround. A framed antique quilt that may have been made in the 1850s during the ride west in an Oregon Trail wagon train is the focal point of the smaller bedroom.

Jackie prides herself on pampering her guests, stocking each room with fresh fruit, flowers, and candy. Breakfast— typically featuring baked apples in sherry and poached eggs over smoked salmon with a white wine sauce—is presented with silver and china.

Address: *Box 1199, Long Beach, WA 98361, tel. 360/642–8268.*
Accommodations: *2 double rooms with baths.*
Amenities: *Cable TV in room, phone on request.*
Rates: *$80–$95; full breakfast. MC, V.*
Restrictions: *No smoking indoors, no pets.*

Moby Dick Hotel and Oyster Farm

On 7 acres of forest on the bay side of the peninsula is this rather plain, boxy stucco structure built in 1930 by a railroad conductor who had struck it rich mining gold in Alaska. The interior, which is fun and campy, is more interesting. The spacious dining room is done in Southwest colors, with several tables for four. Two large living rooms offer guests a fireplace, a telescope, and an upright piano; a skylit upstairs common area features Andy Warhol's *Endangered Species* prints.

Guest rooms are simply furnished; each is provided with a copy of *Moby Dick* or another Herman Melville classic, along with an artwork or a bedspread that reflects the room's theme, such as a mended heart, birds, or the sea.

The inn's owners, Fritzi and Edward Cohen, also own the Tabbard, a well-known "literary" hotel in Washington, DC. Breakfasts may include fruit cobbler, homemade shortbread and whipped cream, biscuits, zucchini bread, and such entrées as scrambled eggs with hot-pepper cheese or fried smelts.

Address: *Sandridge Rd., Box 82, Nahcotta, WA 98637, tel. 360/665–4543, fax 360/665–6887.*
Accommodations: *1 double room with bath, 9 doubles share 5 baths.*
Amenities: *TV in common area, phone available.*
Rates: *$55–$85; full breakfast. MC, V.*
Restrictions: *No smoking indoors, pets outdoors only; 2-night minimum on weekends June–Aug.*

Orchard Hill Inn

About 10 miles north of White Salmon, this 1974 Dutch Colonial sits amid fields, vineyards, apple and pear orchards, and a forest, with paths leading down to the White Salmon River.

James and Pamela Tindall opened their B&B in 1985 after three years in Germany. Now Jim teaches high school English and history, and Pam runs drug and alcohol programs while caring for their son, Zachary. Without their own private apartment, the Tindalls share the common rooms with guests. The style is casual and comfortable. The three guest rooms are furnished eclectically. The Caldwell Room has a double bed with spindle headboard and a twin four-poster and dresser that once belonged to Jim's grandmother. Both beds have hand-stitched quilts.

A German-style breakfast, served in the country-style dining room, includes a variety of cheeses and yogurts, local fresh fruit, bagels, gingerbread or huckleberry-bran muffins, and Pam's homemade jams.

Address: *199 Oak Ridge Rd., White Salmon, WA 98672, tel. 509/493–3024.*
Accommodations: *3 double rooms share 2 baths, 1 bunkhouse for groups.*
Rates: *$48–$58; Continental breakfast. MC, V.*
Restrictions: *No smoking indoors, no pets.*

Olympic Peninsula

Rugged and remote, the Olympic Peninsula, at the northwest corner of the contiguous United States, is dominated by jagged mountains and (within Olympic National Park, at least) dense, almost impenetrable forests. To the west, the Pacific Ocean rages wild. The Strait of Juan de Fuca lies to the north, and the Hood Canal, an 80-mile-long natural inlet to Puget Sound, borders the peninsula on the east. Just a bit inland, and visible from more than a hundred miles away, are the snowcapped Olympic Mountains.

These mountains trap incoming clouds, creating the rain forests of the Olympic National Park to the west and a dry "rain shadow" to the east. As a result, the peninsula has both the wettest and the driest climates on the Pacific Northwest coast.

Most of the peninsula is accessible only to backpackers, but Highway 101, in a 300-mile loop, offers glimpses of some of its spectacular wilderness. Along the ocean side of the peninsula, visitors can hike, clam, beachcomb, collect driftwood, watch tide pools, and fly kites. Olympic National Park preserves nearly a million acres of mountains, old-growth forest, and wilderness coast in their natural states. Mountain hikes are popular, especially around Hurricane Ridge, just south of Port Angeles. Fishing is a major activity throughout the peninsula. Anglers pull in trout and salmon from the rivers; charter boats out of Neah Bay take halibut and salmon, while others ply the Aberdeen and Hoquiam area for bottomfish and salmon.

A good perch for launching Olympic Peninsula excursions is Port Townsend, on Puget Sound. Here, in this picturesque little town of 6,800, a number of exquisite Victorian homes built by sea captains, bankers, and businesspeople have been turned into inviting bed-and-breakfasts.

Places to Go, Sights to See

Hurricane Ridge. Drive 30 minutes south from briny Port Angeles and you're a mile high in the craggy Olympics at Hurricane Ridge, with its spectacular views of the Olympic Mountains, the Strait of Juan de Fuca, and Vancouver Island. Despite the steep grade, the road is easily traveled. A small visitor center offers interpretive talks, ranger-led walks, and a museum, and leading off from the center are nature trails and miles of cross-country skiing trails. Herds of deer, unconcerned with human onlookers, and chubby-cheeked Olympic marmots are frequent visitors.

Neah Bay. The waters of Neah Bay offer fishermen and women an abundance of king and silver salmon, while its beaches yield treasures of driftwood, fossils, and agate. Trails lead along the shore and through surrounding deep forests to Cape Alava, an important archaeological discovery. More than 55,000 artifacts were taken from this ancient Makah village before it was covered back up, leaving nothing to see. Many are on display at the *Makah Museum* (Hwy. 112, Neah Bay, tel. 360/645–2711), where the life of the tribe is documented through relics, dioramas, and reproductions.

Olympic National Park. An information center operated by the U.S. Forest Service is along Quinault Lake on the South Shore Road. At the road's end is the trailhead to the Enchanted Valley, whose many waterfalls make it one of the peninsula's most popular hiking areas. The Hoh Rain Forest, with an average annual rainfall of 145 inches and a salmon-rich river, is one of the few old-growth ecosystems remaining in the Lower 48 states, an incredibly complex web of flora and fauna sheltering such wildlife as elk, otter, beaver, and flying squirrels. Nature trails lead off from the Hoh Visitor Center, at the campground and ranger station/information center, which also contains a small museum. There are eight other ranger stations, each with its own visitor center, scattered throughout the park; check at the stations about periodic road washouts. Port Angeles Visitors Center, just outside the park, is the most comprehensive (600 E. Park Ave., tel. 360/452–0330).

Port Gamble. This New England–style waterfront town, dating from about 1853, has been designated a National Historic Site as one of the few company-owned towns left in the United States. Along with the oldest continuously operating lumber mill in North America, visitors to this town south of Port Townsend will find an 1870 church; the *Of Sea and Shore Museum* (Rainier Ave., tel. 360/297–2426), with fishing and natural history artifacts; and a town historical museum in the General Store.

Port Townsend. This waterfront town, with its carefully restored Victorian brick buildings, was first settled in 1851, becoming a major lumber port in the late 19th century. Several of the grand Victorian homes built on the bluff during these prosperous years overlook downtown and Puget Sound. Today Port Townsend is home to a flourishing community of artists, writers, and musicians; the late Frank Herbert, author of *Dune*, lived here. The restored buildings of *Fort Worden* (tel. 360/385–2021), a former Navy base that is a National Historic Landmark, include officers' homes, barracks, a theater, and parade grounds, and was used as the location for the film *An Officer and a Gentleman*. The *Centrum Foundation* (tel. 360/385–3102), an arts organization based at the fort, presents workshops and performances throughout the summer. A jazz festival is held each July.

Poulsbo. Technically on Puget Sound's Kitsap Peninsula, but considered part of the larger Olympic Peninsula, Poulsbo was once a small Nordic fishing village. Although tourists now outnumber fisher folk, there are many reminders of its heritage, including murals on sides of buildings depicting Scandinavian life; flower-filled window boxes; rosemaling on shutters and signs; and the *Sluys Bakery* (18924 Front St., tel. 360/779–2798), known for its Scandinavian delicacies and nationally distributed whole-grain Poulsbo Bread.

Quilcene. Famous for its Canterbury oysters and the largest oyster hatchery in the world, Quilcene is about 15 miles south of Port Townsend on Highway 101. It's also the site of a fish hatchery and a ranger station for the Olympic National Park.

Sequim and Dungeness. A wide variety of animal life can be found in Sequim (pronounced "skwim") and the fertile plain at the mouth of the Dungeness (pronounced "dun-ja-*ness*") River. *Dungeness Spit*, part of the *Dungeness National Wildlife Refuge* (tel. 360/457–8451) and one of the longest natural spits in the world, is home to abundant migratory waterfowl as well as to clams, oysters, and seals. The small *Sequim-Dungeness Museum* (175 W. Cedar St., tel. 360/683–8110) displays mastodon remains discovered nearby in 1977 as well as exhibits on Captain George Vancouver, a late 18th-century English explorer of the Pacific coast, and the early Klallam Indians. *Sequim Natural History Museum* (503 N. Sequim Ave., tel. 360/683–8364) features exhibits on more than 80 varieties of birds and wildlife on the Olympic Peninsula. Dioramas show stuffed creatures in their natural habitats—saltwater beaches, marshes, and forest.

Restaurants

Port Townsend offers a number of good eating places. The **Fountain Cafe** (tel. 360/385–1364) specializes in seafood and pasta. **Lanza's Ristorante & Pizzeria** (tel. 360/385–6221) features tantalizing pasta and Continental dishes and live entertainment in a restored 19th-century brick building. The **Restaurant at Manresa Castle** (tel. 360/385–5750) offers elegant regional cuisine and fabulous Sunday brunches.

Khu Larb Thai (tel. 360/385–5023), with its explosive Thai noodles and curries, and **Cafe Piccolo** (tel. 360/385–1403), with its home-style Italian cuisine, are also esteemed by locals.

Tourist Information

North Olympic Visitor and Convention Bureau (Box 670, Port Angeles, WA 98362, tel. 360/452–8552).

Reservation Services

Pacific Bed & Breakfast Agency (701 N.W. 60th St., Seattle, WA 98107, tel. 206/784–0539); **Travelers Bed & Breakfast** (Box 492, Mercer Island, WA, 98040, tel. 206/232–2345); **Washington State Bed & Breakfast Guild** (2442 N.W. Market St., Seattle, WA 98107, tel. 206/548–6224).

Ann Starrett Mansion

This improbably ornate Queen Anne in Port Townsend, painted in cream, teal, and two shades of green, was built by George Starrett, a contractor, mortician, and sawmill owner, in 1889 at a cost of $6,000 as a wedding present for his wife, Ann. It is now on the National Register of Historic Places.

Some guests may find the almost museum quality of the Ann Starrett Mansion off-putting, but hosts Bob and Edel Sokol are low-key and friendly. Bob is a retired Air Force pilot and was navigator on *Air Force One* for President Jimmy Carter. Edel, a native of Germany, is an avid collector and baker.

The foyer—with a front desk handcrafted in Port Townsend when Washington was a territory—opens to a dramatic free-hung, three-tiered spiral staircase of Honduran and African mahogany, English walnut, oak, and cherry. At the top is the eight-sided tower dome, frescoed by George Chapman with allegorical figures of the four seasons and the four virtues. The dome was designed as a solar calendar: Sunlight coming through small dormer windows on the first days of each new season shines onto a ruby glass, causing a red beam to point toward the appropriate seasonal panel.

Other ceiling frescoes are found in the adjacent dining room and parlor, whose decor is a paean to the period. Elaborate carved moldings are featured throughout the house. An absence of fireplaces told the Starretts' observant visitors that such antiquated heating devices had been eliminated by modern central heating.

The Master Suite looks like a museum period room. Once the Starretts' master bedroom, it features Persian rugs, a Brussels tapestry tablecloth, an 1880 mahogany Eastlake bedroom suite, and a floral tapestry canopy that extends from the floor to the 12-foot ceiling. The Drawing Room has a little antique tin tub painted with cherubs, and an 1860 Renaissance Revival mahogany bed. The contemporary Gable Suite offers a view of Puget Sound and the Cascades, as well as a two-person hot tub.

Breakfast includes champagne, stuffed French toast, homemade muffins, and juice, and is served in the elegant dining room.

Address: *744 Clay St., Port Townsend, WA 98368, tel. 360/385–3205 or 800/321–0644, fax 360/385–2976.*
Accommodations: *8 double rooms with baths, 2 doubles share 1 bath, cottage with bath.*
Amenities: *Hot tub in 1 room.*
Rates: *$70–$185; full breakfast. AE, D, MC, V.*
Restrictions: *No smoking, no pets; 2-night minimum on holiday and festival weekends.*

James House

The picture-perfect location—high atop a bluff, with sweeping views of Port Townsend's waterfront, the Cascade and Olympic mountains, and Puget Sound—is only one of the many striking features of the 1889 James House.

The gray wood-frame Queen Anne house, with gables, dormers, porches, and five redbrick chimneys, is the grandest of all Port Townsend's Victorian accommodations. In an era when a large house could be built for $4,000, this one, with 8,000 square feet of living space, cost $10,000.

An atmosphere of elegance and contemplation prevails. The entrance hallway, dominated by a hand-carved cherry staircase made from logs that came around Cape Horn, is a monument to fine woodworking. Like the two front parlors, the hall features original parquet floors in elaborate patterns of oak, walnut, and cherry. Breakfast is served in the large dining room or in the homey kitchen by the Great Majestic cookstove.

Years of restoration work preceded the house's 1973 opening as one of the first Northwest bed-and-breakfasts. It is furnished with period antiques (some original to the house), Oriental rugs, an antique player piano, and many beveled- and stained-glass windows. Four of the house's nine original fireplaces remain, with carved mantels and Minton tile framing.

Guest rooms are on three floors of the house and in the cottage out back. The house's master or bridal suite offers unsurpassed views, its own balcony, a sitting parlor, a fireplace, a private bath, and the original late Victorian bed, armoire, and fainting couch. The cottage, which sleeps four, has lots of windows and a more contemporary feel.

Innkeepers Carol McGough and Anne Tiernan, both health care professionals, moved here from Boston in 1990. They enjoy tending the roses, daisies, geraniums, herbs, and other plants that spill out of the James House's gardens, as well as making potpourris for their guests from the blooms. Breakfast includes fruit, scones or muffins, and soufflés or quiches, all made from fresh ingredients.

Address: *1238 Washington St., Port Townsend, WA 98368, tel. 360/385–1238.*
Accommodations: *2 double rooms with baths, 6 doubles share 4 baths, 3 suites, 1 cottage with private baths.*
Amenities: *Fireplace in 2 rooms, parlor stove in 1 room.*
Rates: *$65–$80, suites and cottage $95–$145; full breakfast. AE, MC, V.*
Restrictions: *No smoking, no pets; 2-night minimum on holiday and festival weekends.*

The Manor Farm Inn

The silver trout rises from the dark waters of the rock-lined pool to lunge at the proffered lure. It is dusk, and the setting sun plays over the deep Oxfordshire greens of lush fields and forests. Shaggy-headed scotch cattle low softly through the gloom as the fairy-light effect from the inn's structures glows into life. The only other sound is the whistling of a sheep-dog trainer as her canine student puts a flock through its paces in an adjoining field.

Such is the dinner hour at Manor Farm Inn, an oasis of elegance and country charm just across Puget Sound from Seattle. Here, a classic 1886-vintage white clapboard farmhouse is the centerpiece of a 25-acre "gentleman's farm," complete with sheep, chickens, pigs, and other animals.

Some inns are popular because of their convenience to business districts, tourist attractions, and universities. Others, however, attract a devoted clientele because they are special places, where the pressures of modern life seem half a planet away. Manor Farm Inn, which opened in 1982 and isn't particularly convenient to anything, falls into the latter category.

Innkeeper Jill Hughes, a former teacher, provides rods, flies, even floppy fishing hats for guests who want to try their luck in the well-stocked trout pond. Bicycles, the best way to explore the inn's extensive grounds, are also available.

The interior of the Manor Farm Inn holds its own special touches. White walls, oatmeal-colored carpets, rough-hewn beams, and wide, sunny windows give the spacious guest rooms a clean and soothing simplicity. They're furnished with French and English pine armoires and writing desks and tables; eiderdown comforters warm the king-sized beds.

The kitchen is another special feature at Manor Farm. A gourmet four-course dinner is served nightly; a sonorous old brass bell summons guests to the comfortable drawing room, where a crackling wood fire and pre-dinner sherry await. The farm-style breakfast, which begins with warm scones and coffee delivered to each room, includes oatmeal, fresh eggs from the farm chickens, oven-roasted potatoes, bacon, and sausage. Be sure to save a slice or two of home-baked bread for the inn's friendly goats, Tammi and Pepe, who occupy a fenced pasture down by the trout pond.

Address: *26069 Big Valley Rd. NE, Poulsbo, WA 98370, tel. 360/779–4628.*
Accommodations: *7 double rooms with baths, 2-bedroom Farm Cottage and 2-bedroom Beach House.*
Amenities: *Restaurant, bicycles, fly fishing, croquet, horseshoes; outdoor hot tubs at cottages.*
Rates: *$95–$190; full breakfast. MC, V.*
Restrictions: *No children under 16, no pets.*

Old Consulate Inn

Another of Port Townsend's Queen Anne Victorians—like the James House (*see above*), on the bluff overlooking the water—this brick red beauty comes complete with conical turret, dormers, an unusual sloping "wedding cake" porch with a bay-view swing, well-tended gardens, and lots of white Adirondack chairs for lounging. Also known as the F. W. Hastings House, the inn was built as a private home in 1889 by the son of the town's founder and was the German consulate from 1908 to 1911.

It was a quirk of fate that brought the inn's present owners to innkeeping. Rob and Joanna Jackson had planned to celebrate their 25th anniversary with a large reception in their California home and a trip to Tahiti. Preparation for the event included refinishing their hardwood floors, but in the process, workmen set the house afire. The Jacksons changed their plans: They had a quiet dinner for 10, chucked the Tahiti trip, took a drive up Highway 101, and fell in love with Port Townsend and the Hastings House. Later that year, when they learned that the house was for sale, Rob gave up his contracting job and Joanna her post as corporate controller, and they became innkeepers.

The oak-paneled front parlor features its original chandelier, with large bunches of green glass grapes, and a fireplace framed in Italian tile.

A large sitting room is comfortable for reading and conversation, with a fireplace, Queen Anne sofas and chairs, a baby grand piano, a pump organ once owned by England's royal family, and a chinoiserie chest original to the house and inlaid with mother-of-pearl. In the evening, the Jacksons serve complimentary port and sherry by the fire. A smaller anteroom off the dining room offers cable TV, a VCR, and lots of books. The doll, beer stein, and other collections displayed throughout the house can get a bit overwhelming.

Guest rooms on the second and third floors have a Victorian ambience, with floral wallpapers, custom-made comforters, dolls placed on bureaus, and a picture hat here and there on the walls. From the Tower Room there is a sweeping view of the bay. All suites have claw-foot tubs.

Joanna is one of the friendliest innkeepers and best cooks around. Her breakfasts are leisurely seven-course affairs; Greek puffed eggs with lemon cream is a house specialty.

Address: *313 Walker St., Port Townsend, WA 98368, tel. 360/385–6753, fax 360/385–2097.*
Accommodations: *5 double rooms with baths, 3 suites.*
Amenities: *Air-conditioning, billiards, outdoor hot tub/gazebo.*
Rates: *$69–$175; full breakfast, afternoon refreshments. AE, MC, V.*
Restrictions: *No smoking indoors, no pets.*

Domaine Madeleine

Bed-and-breakfast connoisseurs have been known to travel the breadth of the continent for a stay at Domaine Madeleine, one of the Olympic Peninsula's most remarkable inns. Blessed with incomparable views of the Strait of Juan de Fuca, romantic gardens patterned after Monet's Petites Allées at Giverny, and the culinary artistry of French-born chef/owner Madeleine Chambers, the B&B has cultivated a fervently devoted return clientele.

The atmosphere is a mixture of Continental sophistication and quiet, natural charm. The rooms, public and private, are filled with European antiques, Persian carpets, and Asian artwork. In the dining area, a gigantic basalt fireplace presides over high-windowed views of the Strait.

The comfortable dining room is doubly memorable because it is here that guests encounter Madeleine's enormous five-course breakfasts. Madeleine and her husband, John, guarantee that if one of their guests eats lunch before 2 PM, they'll pay for it.

Address: *146 Wildflower La. (8 mi east of town), Port Angeles, WA 98362, tel. 360/457–4174, fax 360/457–3037.*
Accommodations: *2 double rooms with baths, 1 suite, 1 housekeeping cottage.*
Amenities: *Cable TVs, VCRs, CD players, phones; video library; air-conditioning.*
Rates: *$125–$165; full breakfast. AE, MC, V.*
Restrictions: *No smoking indoors, no children under 12, no pets.*

Heritage House

This yellow-and-white Italianate mansion was built by one of Port Townsend's founding sea captains in about 1876. From the high-wheeled Victorian velocipede leaning against the back fence to the inn's flaring mansard roof, Heritage House fairly oozes Victoriana. The house was converted to a bed-and-breakfast in 1984 after several thousand hours of intensive renovations. New owners Katherine, Gary, and Shanon Hambley took over in July 1994, and share the same meticulous attention to detail.

The Morning Glory Room features Victorian cottage furniture and a washstand hand-painted with floral bouquets and geometric designs. Highlights of the Lily Suite are a Dresden china floor lamp and a mahogany Empire-style bed. For some, the new

hot tub in the gazebo, complete with vista overlooking the bay below, will provide a distinctly sybaritic interlude.

A few guests may find the house's museum quality a bit stuffy, but certainly not the innkeepers' style. Guests are called to breakfast on an old firemen's horn.

Address: *305 Pierce St., Port Townsend, WA 98368, tel. 360/385–6800 or 800/335–4943, fax 360/379–0498.*
Accommodations: *3 double rooms with baths, 2 doubles share 1 bath, 1 suite.*
Rates: *$60–$110; full breakfast. AE, D, MC, V.*
Restrictions: *No smoking indoors, no pets; 2-night minimum on holiday and festival weekends.*

Lake Crescent Lodge

When he inspected Olympic Peninsula, a candidate for a national park, Franklin Roosevelt stayed at this 1920 lodge on the shores of Lake Crescent, 20 miles west of Port Angeles. Today it's one of two places that offer lodging inside Olympic National Park.

In the lobby, guests can relax in Arts and Crafts–style chairs and sofa before a huge stone fireplace. Accommodations include five guest rooms in the lodge with a shared hall bath, private-bath motel units, and 17 individual cottages (best bets are the four cottages with fireplaces, overlooking the lake). Not much attention has been paid to the room decor, which has a rather impersonal, motel feel. Guest rooms are paneled in red cedar and filled with nondescript contemporary pine and maple furniture. Most, however, have fine mountain and lake views.

The lakeside dining room features a selection of Northwest seafood and wines, and the gift shop offers Native American crafts.

Address: *HC 62, Box 11, Port Angeles, WA 98362, tel. 360/928–3211.*
Accommodations: *47 double rooms with baths, 5 doubles in lodge share 1 bath.*
Amenities: *Restaurant, lounge, gift shop, box lunches available; rowboat rentals.*
Rates: *$52–$89; breakfast extra. AE, D, DC, MC, V.*
Restrictions: *No pets without leash. Closed late Oct.–late Apr.*

Lake Quinault Lodge

When this old-fashioned country resort in Olympic National Park was built, men hauled the lumber, brick, glass, and plumbing fixtures over 50 miles of dirt road. They completed the large cedar-shake structure above Lake Quinault at a cost of $90,000—a very hefty sum in 1926.

The heart of the lodge is the large lobby, with Douglas fir beams, a massive brick fireplace, original wicker settees and chairs, large-burl coffee tables, Northwest art, Native American crafts, and cozy corners.

Guest rooms in the lodge are small, simple, and rustic, with country furnishings, some antique. The 36 spacious rooms in the Lakeside Wing—completed in 1990—are decorated with contemporary white wicker, a sofa, and a private balcony. The Fireplace Wing features large rooms with gas fireplaces. The eight-unit annex is quite rustic, used most often by fishermen and guests traveling with pets.

Address: *South Shore Rd., Box 7, Quinault, WA 98575, tel. 360/288–2571 or 800/562–6672, fax 800/288–2415.*
Accommodations: *89 double rooms with baths, 3 suites.*
Amenities: *Nonsmoking rooms, restaurant, gift shop, indoor pool and hot tub, sauna, pool tables; fishing, hiking, boat rentals.*
Rates: *$85–$105, suites $205; breakfast extra. AE, MC, V.*
Restrictions: *No smoking in dining rooms, pets in annex only.*

Lizzie's Victorian Bed & Breakfast

This Italianate Victorian in Port Townsend, built in 1887 by a tugboat captain and his wife, Lizzie, is owned by Bill Wickline, an optometrist, and his wife, Patti, a former interior designer. A woodworking hobbyist, Bill has built a replica of the inn in the backyard for their dog.

Lizzie's is furnished in Victorian style, with antiques in exotic woods and light Victorian-patterned wallpapers. Three cast-iron fireplaces hand-painted to look like marble, wood graining on door panels, and the Parisian wallpaper in the front parlor are all original to the house. Guests are encouraged to use the two 19th-century grand pianos in the parlors. Just off the foyer, Lizzie's Room has a half-canopied queen mahogany bed, a bay window with sitting area, a fireplace, and a claw-foot tub.

Guests gather in the country kitchen, paneled in oak and knotty pine, for breakfast. A back porch with Adirondack chairs affords views of the pear, apple, cherry, and plum trees in the orchard.

Address: *731 Pierce St., Port Townsend, WA 98368, tel. 360/385–4168.*
Accommodations: *5 double rooms with baths, 3 doubles share 2 baths.*
Amenities: *Access to health club.*
Rates: *$58–$105; full breakfast. D, MC, V.*
Restrictions: *No smoking, no pets; 2-night minimum on holiday and festival weekends.*

The Quimper Inn

With its flared, shingled second story and broad walking porch overlooking Admiralty Inlet, the Shingle-style Quimper Inn makes a nice change from most of Port Townsend's bed-and-breakfasts, which tend to be relentlessly Victorian. One of the Northwest's first B&Bs, it was originally renovated in 1972, but had reverted to a private residence when new owners Ron Ramage and Sue Cabot bought it in 1991. Now, gleaming under a fresh coat of white paint and offering a tasteful mix of antiques and modern reproductions, the Quimper lives again.

Two of the inn's five guest rooms are especially memorable. The ground-floor Library Room, just off the front entrance, is a light, charming chamber with floor-to-ceiling bookshelves, walls painted an unusual "elephant gray," and a thick down comforter on the queen bed. Upstairs, the more spacious Harry's Room (actually a two-room suite separated by sliding pocket doors) is decorated in white, teal, navy, and charcoal; triple-wide windows look out over the inlet and the Olympic Mountains beyond.

Address: *1306 Franklin St., Port Townsend, WA 98368, tel. 360/385–1060.*
Accommodations: *3 double rooms with baths, 2 doubles share 1 bath.*
Rates: *$65–$130; full breakfast. MC, V.*
Restrictions: *No smoking, no pets.*

Ravenscroft Inn

A new addition to the Port Townsend B&B scene, this mahogany-hued, clapboard, Charleston-style "shingle house"—with porches across the first and second floors and dormers on the third—was built in 1987.

Williamsburg blue, brick red, and ivory are the predominant colors at Ravenscroft Inn. The foyer leads to a comfortable library on one side and, on the other, to a "great room" with a fireplace, a grand piano, and small tables that face the open kitchen. Guest rooms feature a mix of country antiques and contemporary furnishings, including wicker; French doors that open onto balconies; fluffy comforters; and the occasional teddy bear. The gardens have been freshly landscaped, with a winding brick path leading to an outdoor seating area.

The inn is owned by Leah Hammer, who for years was a manufacturer's rep for fine crystal and china; her father, Sam Turk; and John Ranney, a professional musician for 40 years. Breakfast includes homemade breads and jams, French toast or crepes, fresh fruit, and juice, served on Leah's collection of china and crystal.

Address: *533 Quincy St., Port Townsend, WA 98368, tel. 360/385–2784, fax 360/385–6724.*
Accommodations: *8 double rooms with baths, 1 suite.*
Amenities: *Fireplace in 2 rooms.*
Rates: *$65–$135, suite $155; full breakfast. AE, D, MC, V.*
Restrictions: *No smoking indoors, no pets; 2-night minimum on holiday and festival weekends.*

Tudor Inn

S et on a knoll on a quiet residential street of Port Angeles—near Hurricane Ridge and an hour from Olympic National Park—Tudor Inn is a half-timbered home surrounded by gardens of lilies, irises, lupines, columbines, and fuschias. Built in 1910 by an English dentist, it was bought in 1983 by Texans Jane and Jerry Glass.

Guests can nestle in the sitting room on an antique Victorian Chesterfield sofa. Stained-glass windows from England, fireplaces, and hardwood floors with Oriental rugs adorn the common rooms. All guest rooms—including one with an antique brass bed and a Beaconsfield 1900 bureau—have been soundproofed and feature Roman shades that match the comforters. Several rooms have views of the water and the mountains.

Breakfast specialties include stuffed sourdough French toast and pancakes, served with homemade fruit syrup, and smoked salmon made from Jerry's catches, accompanied by an egg dish.

Address: *1108 S. Oak St., Port Angeles, WA 98362, tel. 360/452–3138.*
Accommodations: *2 double rooms with bath, 3 doubles share 2 baths.*
Amenities: *Cable TV upon request.*
Rates: *$58–$90; full breakfast. MC, V.*
Restrictions: *No smoking indoors, no pets; 2-night minimum on summer weekends and holidays.*

Seattle and Environs

Wedged between Lake Washington on the east and Elliott Bay on the west, Seattle is a city of water, parks, and heady views of the Cascade and Olympic mountains. The city's damp reputation is well deserved. The winter drizzle (which also appears during the spring, summer, and fall) keeps the city's extensive park system—designed by Frederick Law Olmsted, creator of New York City's Central Park—lush and green. The rain doesn't hamper people's enjoyment of the city's walking and bicycling paths, especially those at waterfront locations such as Lincoln Park in West Seattle; Myrtle Edwards Park downtown; Greenlake, north of downtown; Discovery Park in Magnolia; and the Burke-Gilman Trail, along the shores of Lake Washington. Clouds, fog, and long winter nights have also helped to make the city a haven for movie goers and readers.

Although its economy was once devoted exclusively to aerospace, lumber, and fishing, Seattle is now a major seaport and a vital link in Pacific Rim trade; the evidence of internationalism is everywhere. This former cultural wasteland now has all the trappings of a full-blown big city, with ad agencies and artists' co-ops, symphonies and ballet companies. There's an innovative new convention center, a covered dome for professional sports, a world-renowned theater scene, an excellent opera company, and a strong music world.

Ever since a number of national publications "discovered" Seattle's sophisticated but comfortable lifestyle, housing prices have climbed, the population has grown (some half million within the city proper, another 2 million in the surrounding Puget Sound region), and jammed freeways are no longer strictly a rush-hour phenomenon. As the city grows, so do crime, drug abuse, homelessness, and poverty. Suburban growth is rampant. But Seattleites—a diverse bunch, including Asians, Asian Americans, Scandinavians, African Americans, Native Americans, Hispanics, and other ethnic groups—are a strong political group with a great love for their city and a commitment to maintaining its reputation as one of the most livable cities in the country.

Places to Go, Sights to See

Brew Pubs. Seattle has become a hotbed of microbrews—distinctive, flavorful ales made in tiny (by national brewers' standards) batches for local consumption. Brew pubs are drinking establishments that are attached to actual breweries and serve a variety of food and nonalcoholic beverages as well. Some notable establishments include the *Pacific Northwest Brewing Co.* (322 Occidental Ave. S, tel. 206/621–7002), *Trolleyman* (3400 Phinney Ave. N, tel. 206/548–8000), *Big Time Brewery* (4133 University Way NE, tel. 206/545–4509), *Noggins* (Brooklyn Sq., 4142 Brooklyn Ave. NE, tel. 206/632–ALES), *The Red Door Alehouse* (3401 Fremont N, tel. 206/547–7521), and *Cooper's Northwest Alehouse* (8065 Lake City Way NE, tel. 206/522–2923). Perhaps the best way to tour the pubs without worrying about who's driving is to take a four-hour tour offered by *Northwest Brewery and Pub Tours* (4224 1st Ave. NE, tel. 206/547–1186), which includes free tastings and van transportation.

Festivals. The *Folklife Festival* is an annual Memorial Day weekend event, showcasing some of the region's best folk singers, bands, jugglers, and other entertainers at the Seattle Center. In late July and early August, there's *Seafair*, saluting Seattle's marine heritage with a parade in downtown and hydroplane races on Lake Washington near Seward Park. Labor Day weekend means *Bumbershoot*, four days of music that includes classical, blues, reggae, zydeco, and pop, at Seattle Center.

International District. Originally a haven for Chinese workers after they finished the Transcontinental Railroad, the "ID" is a 40-block area inhabited by Chinese, Filipinos, and other Asians. The district, which includes many Chinese, Japanese, and Korean restaurants, also houses herbalists, massage parlors, acupuncturists, and social clubs. *Uwajimaya* (519 6th Ave. S, tel. 206/624–6248), one of the largest Japanese stores on the West Coast, stocks china, gifts, fabrics, housewares, and a complete supermarket with an array of Asian foods. Also in this area is the *Nippon Kan Theater* (628 S. Washington St., tel. 206/467–6807), the site of many Asian and Asian-American performances. The *Wing Luke Museum* (4076 7th Ave. S, tel. 206/623–5124) emphasizes Oriental history and culture.

Museum of Flight (9404 E. Marginal Way S, tel. 206/764–5720). The Red Barn, the original Boeing airplane factory, houses an exhibit on the history of aviation, while the Great Gallery, a dramatic structure designed by Seattle architect Ibsen Nelson, contains 38 airplanes—suspended from the ceiling and on the ground—dating from 1916 to the present.

Pike Place Market (1st Ave. at Pike St., tel. 206/682–7453). A Seattle institution, considered by many to be the finest public market in the United States, the market began in 1907 when the city issued permits to farmers allowing them to sell produce from their wagons parked at Pike Place. Today the sprawling, rickety old market is a vibrant and highly enjoyable place to browse an afternoon away amid the shouts of fishmongers and produce sellers, the music of buskers, and a wild profusion of foods and craft items from every corner of the world.

Pioneer Square. This old section of the city boasts cobblestone streets and restored brick buildings dating from the late 19th century. Start at *Pioneer Park* (Yesler Way and 1st Ave. S), the site of Seattle's original business district, where an ornate iron-and-glass pergola now stands. In 1889, a fire destroyed many of the wood-frame buildings in the area, but residents reclaimed them with fire-resistant brick and mortar. With the Klondike Gold Rush, this area became populated with saloons and brothels; businesses gradually moved north, and the old pioneering area deteriorated. Today Pioneer Square encompasses 18 blocks, the city's largest concentration of art galleries, restaurants, bars, and shops. *The Elliott Bay Book Company* (101 S. Main St., tel. 206/624–6600) hosts lectures and readings by authors of local and international acclaim. Close by is the *Kingdome* (201 S. King St., tel. 206/296–3111), a 660-foot-diameter covered stadium that is the home of the Seattle Seahawks NFL team and the Seattle Mariners baseball team. Built in 1976, it has the world's largest self-supporting roof, which soars 250 feet above the ground. Tours are available. The *Klondike Gold Rush National Historical Park* (117 S. Main St., tel. 206/442–7220) and interpretive center explores Seattle's role in the 1897–98 Gold Rush through film presentations, exhibits, and gold-panning demonstrations.

Seattle Art Museum (100 University St., tel. 206/654–3100). The museum, which specializes in Native American, African, Oceanic, and Pre-Columbian art, has a new five-story building designed by Robert Venturi. A work of art itself, the building features a limestone exterior with large-scale vertical fluting, accented by terra-cotta, cut granite, and marble. In August 1994, the museum's exquisite collection of Asian art from Japan, China, Korea, and the Himalayas moved to the *Seattle Asian Art Museum* (1400 E. Prospect St., tel. 206/654–3100), the original Seattle Art Museum Building, in Volunteer Park, just east of downtown.

Seattle Center. This 74-acre complex built for the 1961 Seattle World's Fair includes an amusement park; the futuristic-looking *Space Needle*, with observation deck, lounge, and restaurant (tel. 206/443–2100); theaters; the Coliseum; exhibition halls; the recently renovated *Pacific Science Center* (200 2nd Ave. N, tel. 206/443–2001); and shops.

University of Washington. Some 33,500 students attend the U-Dub, as locals call the university, which was founded in 1861. On the northwestern corner of the beautifully landscaped campus is the *Thomas Burke Memorial Washington State Museum* (17th Ave. NE and N.E. 45th St., tel. 206/543–5590). Washington's natural history and anthropological museum, it features exhibits on cultures of the Pacific region and the state's 35 Native American tribes. Nearby, the *Henry Art Gallery* (15th Ave. NE and N.E. 41st St., tel. 206/543–2280) displays paintings from the 19th and 20th centuries, textiles, and traveling exhibitions. At the museum, pick up a brochure of self-guided walking tours of the *Washington Park Arboretum* (2300 Arboretum Dr. E, tel. 206/325–4510), adjacent to the museum. Rhododendron Glen and Azalea Way are in bloom from March through June; during the rest of the year, other plants and wildlife flourish. A new visitor center at the north end of the park will brief you on the species of flora and fauna you'll see here.

Waterfront. Once the center of activity in Seattle, this area stretches some 19 blocks, from Pier 70 and Myrtle Edwards Park in the north down to Pier 51 in Pioneer Square. At the base of the Pike Street Hillclimb is the *Seattle Aquarium*

(Pier 59, tel. 206/386–4320), where visitors can see otters and seals swim and dive in their pools. The "State of the Sound" exhibit explores the aquatic life and ecology of Puget Sound. Just next door is the *Omnidome Film Experience* (Pier 59, tel. 206/622–1868), where 70mm films on such subjects as the eruption of Mt. St. Helens and a study of sharks and whales are projected on a huge, curved screen.

Several guided tours of Seattle's waterfront and nearby areas are available. From Pier 55, *Seattle Harbor Tours* (Pier 55, tel. 206/623–1445) offers one-hour tours exploring Elliott Bay and the Port of Seattle. *Gray Line* (buses to the ships depart from the downtown Sheraton Hotel, 1400 6th Ave., tel. 206/626–5208) runs similar cruises. *Tillicum Village Tours* (Pier 56, tel. 206/443–1244) sails visitors from Pier 56 across Puget Sound to Blake Island for a four-hour experience of traditional Northwest Native American life, including dinner and a traditional dance performance.

Westlake Center (1601 5th Ave., tel. 206/467–1600). Controversial from the time of its inception—some residents wanted the land to be used for a park—this 27-story office tower and three-story shopping structure with enclosed walkways is the major terminus for buses and the Monorail, which goes north to Seattle Center.

Woodland Park Zoo (N. 59th St. and Fremont Ave., tel. 206/684–4800). Many of the animals are free to roam their section of the 92-acre zoo. The African savanna and new elephant house are popular features.

Restaurants

The Painted Table (Alexis Hotel, 1007 1st Ave., tel. 206/624–3646) opened in 1992 and quickly became acclaimed for a four-star kitchen featuring the freshest regional produce from the Pike Place Market. **Fuller's** (1400 6th Ave., in the Seattle Sheraton, at Pike St., tel. 206/447–5544) is favored by locals for special occasions, thanks to an innovative menu—featuring such highlights as pork loin with an apple-brandy bleu cheese sauce—and a decor enlivened with works by Northwest artists. Seattleites know their oysters, and they head for the unpretentious **Emmet Watson's Oyster Bar** (Pike Place Market, 1916 Pike Pl., tel. 206/448–7721) to find these denizens of the deep at their best. For a view to dine by—and die for—**Ray's Boathouse** (6049 Seaview Ave. NE, tel. 206/789–3770) offers picture-postcard Puget Sound outside its windows, plus impeccably fresh seafood at both its elegant restaurant and lower-priced café.

Tourist Information

The Seattle/King County Convention and Visitors Bureau (800 Convention Pl., tel. 206/461–5840).

Reservation Services

Pacific Bed & Breakfast Agency (701 N.W. 60th St., Seattle, WA 98107, tel. 206/784–0539); **The Seattle B&B Association Hotline** (Box 24244, Seattle, WA 98124, tel. 206/547–1020); **Washington State Bed & Breakfast Guild** (2442 N.W. Market St., Box 355-FD, Seattle, WA 98107, tel. 800/647–2918).

The Bacon Mansion/ Broadway Guest House

On a quiet tree-lined street in the Harvard-Belmont Historical District, only five minutes from downtown, the freshly renovated and zestfully run Bacon Mansion/ Broadway Guest House is a welcome new addition to the Seattle bed-and-breakfast scene. Owners Daryl King and Tim Avenmarg-Stiles opened the doors of this huge, imposing 1909 Edwardian-style Tudor in February 1993.

The house had been operated as an inn for several years when King and Avenmarg-Stiles bought it; they added five guest rooms to the original three, installed new bathrooms and furnishings, and in the process created an ambience of comfortable luxury. The inn's public areas are tasteful, with wool carpets in shades of rose, cream, and indigo laid over glossy hardwood floors. Headlining the decor of the main sitting room is a black concert grand piano adorned with a Liberace-style candelabra; Avenmarg-Stiles, a classically trained pianist, fills the house with music whenever his duties allow. French doors overlook the garden courtyard, complete with fountain, out back. Flowers in every room make it feel like June all year around.

One of the most inviting of the public rooms is the library, with its dark wood wainscoting, oak floor edged with a mahogany inlay, leaded-glass bookcases, carved-oak-and-tile fireplace, and rare bronze-and-alabaster chandelier. The room has a comfy sleigh couch upholstered in cream and blue, as well as several deep chairs for reading.

Guest rooms at the Bacon Mansion run the gamut from the floral motifs of the Garden Suite and Iris Room to the more masculine confines of the Clipper Room and the Capitol Suite. The latter is the largest and most impressive of the in-house accommodations, with a pine four-poster bed, carved oak fireplace, wet bar, original tiled bath (with two-person soaking tub), and a fine view of the Space Needle. There's a nice view of Mt. Rainier from the top-floor Iris Room at the opposite end of the house.

Out back, past the fountain, is the two-story Carriage House, a spacious abode with white plaster walls and forest-green carpeting, a queen-size brass bed, and a full kitchen with its charmingly passé avocado-green decor. The full-size living-room hide-a-bed makes this the best choice for families or other large groups.

Address: *959 Broadway E (corner of Broadway and Prospect), Seattle, WA 98102, tel. 206/329–1864.*
Accommodations: *5 double rooms with private baths, 2 double rooms share 1 bath, 1 carriage house with bath.*
Amenities: *Phones in rooms.*
Rates: *$64–$125; Continental breakfast. AE, MC, V.*
Restrictions: *No smoking indoors, no pets.*

Bombay House

In a quiet, rural setting just a 30-minute ferry ride from Seattle, Bombay House is a three-story Victorian mansion owned by Bunny Cameron, a former caterer, and her husband, Roger Kanchuk, who ran a business that served legal papers. The couple pulled up stakes in Anchorage, Alaska, looking for a better climate. One might question whether Puget Sound is an improvement, but in 1986, after scouring various western locations, Bunny and Roger landed on Bainbridge Island and bought the Bombay House.

The house, which has a widow's walk and wraparound porch, was built in 1907 by a master shipbuilder from Port Blakely (famous for its four-masted schooners built in the heyday of the tall ships). Today it houses comfortable country antiques with a few contemporary pieces. The entrance opens to a spacious, sunny living room with 10-foot-high ceilings, stained-glass windows from Europe, and contemporary sofa and easy chairs facing the massive brick fireplace. A century-old rock maple loom from Maine stands against one wall; a 1912 upright piano stands against another. One guest room, which has a functioning old tin bathtub in the center, is on the main floor, and an open staircase leads up to the others. The Captain's Suite is a large, airy room decorated in forest green and white, with a wood-burning parlor stove, large bird's-eye maple bed, sofa bed, and claw-foot soaking tub.

From the glass-enclosed dining area, guests can munch on Bunny's special fruit-bran muffins, quick breads, cakes, pastries, and homemade cereals while they watch the large white ferries plying the waters of Rich Passage between Bainbridge Island and the Kitsap Peninsula.

The half-acre yard contains a rough cedar gazebo and informal gardens of roses, daisies, peonies, and lilies exploding with color.

A favorite activity on the 15-mile-long island is berry picking. If you haven't immediately consumed everything you've picked, you'll have an appetite for the fresh seafood and pasta at the Pleasant Beach Grill (4738 Lynwood Center Rd., tel. 206/842–4347), an old home turned restaurant that can be very romantic.

Address: *8490 Beck Rd. NE, Bainbridge Island, WA 98110, tel. 206/842–3926 or 800/598–3926.*
Accommodations: *2 double rooms with baths, 2 doubles share 1 bath, 1 suite.*
Amenities: *Complimentary beverages, children over 5 welcome.*
Rates: *$55–$125; Continental breakfast. AE, MC, V.*
Restrictions: *No smoking indoors, no pets.*

Gaslight Inn

The three-story, teal-colored Gaslight Inn atop historic Capitol Hill was always a showplace. A developer built the Arts and Crafts foursquare-style home in 1906 to show prospective customers the kind of home they could build after they had bought their lot from him.

Owners Stephen Bennett and Trevor Logan bought the dilapidated building in 1980, and after four years of painstaking restoration, opened it as a bed-and-breakfast. Those who reject the excesses of Victorians will love the more austere aesthetic.

The inn, named for its original gaslight fixtures, also retains the original beveled and stained-glass windows on all three floors, oak millwork, graceful fluted columns, and oak-paneled wainscoting with egg and dart detailing. All the oak and the muted color schemes lend a warm feel to the inn, while large windows and unfussy furnishings—authentic Arts and Crafts, Mission, and Eastlake—give it a bright, clean look. The charcoal-gray living room to the south features a glossy green-tiled fireplace with an oak mantel, Stickley rocker, rare oak and green-glass Mission library lamps, wing chairs, an Arts and Crafts sofa, and a large console radio. The parlor, painted hunter green, contains three Arts and Crafts rocking chairs, sofa, and circa 1900 Victrola with a wooden horn. Mounted heads of elk and antelope hang in the three downstairs sitting rooms.

Each of the guest rooms is unique, with its own distinctive and well-executed decor; every one is equipped with remote-control TV and a small refrigerator. Some rooms have views of downtown, only a short bus ride away. Room 1 has a crisp, "masculine" appeal, with its ivory-and-blue mattress-ticking wallpaper and lots of wood. It features two Eastlake walnut chests and table, a walnut headboard, a hand-pieced quilt, and a bathroom with dark-stained wainscoting and a small Eastlake mirror. Despite dark taupe walls, Room 2 is warm and sunny, with white millwork, an elaborately carved golden oak bed and dresser, and an Arts and Crafts armoire. Another room is rustic, with a log bed made in the San Juan Islands and pine furniture. Five new suites, in the house next door, were added in 1992.

Address: *1727 15th Ave., Seattle, WA 98122, tel. 206/325–3654, fax 206/324–3135.*
Accommodations: *6 double rooms with baths, 3 doubles share 2 baths, 5 full suites with bath.*
Amenities: *Fireplace in 1 room and 3 suites, cable TV and refrigerator in rooms; swimming pool.*
Rates: *$66–$98; Continental breakfast. AE, MC, V.*
Restrictions: *No pets; 2-night minimum in summer (Memorial Day– Labor Day) and on weekends.*

M.V. Challenger

In a city that's defined by water, what could be more appropriate than a stay on a tugboat? Doing the improbable, owner Jerry Brown, a real-estate appraiser from the Midwest, bought the 96-foot working tug, built in 1944 for the U.S. Army, renovated it, and opened the *M.V. Challenger* as a bed-and-breakfast. It's certainly not hyperbole to call it unique.

Moored on the south end of Lake Union, a small lake 10 blocks from the heart of Seattle and filled with sailboats, cruisers, and charter boats, the *Challenger* is not for the claustrophobic. Common areas inside the vessel are open and fairly spacious, but some cabins are very snug.

Guests are asked to remove their shoes as they enter the main salon, built over the former cargo hatch, now decorated in ivory, blue, and beige with wood trim, brass candlesticks, and nautical gauges. The check-in area at the bar includes a TV, VCR, stereo, and small aquarium. Walls are covered with nautical maps, and two contemporary couches flank the granite fireplace in an adjoining carpeted conversation pit. The aft-deck solarium, which affords panoramic views of the waterfront, can be opened to the sky on sunny days and, more typically, enclosed with canvas and vinyl for Seattle's fog and drizzle.

Staterooms, some no bigger than a walk-in closet, are papered with nautical maps. Two cabins have bunks, the others double or queen-size beds. All come equipped with radios and phones. The red-striped comforter and matching pillowcases and curtains, towels, and a small painted radiator, also in red, make the Captain's Cabin cozy and bright. If you've been assigned to the Master's Cabin, you might be tempted to take to your bed, from which you can observe the busy comings and goings on the lake. A tub conveniently sits behind the bed.

Jerry, who keeps his tug especially shipshape—notice the gleaming brass—is happy to show guests around the engine room, with its 14,000-pound, 765-horsepower engine. (The tug, by the way, is still fully functional, and even changes berths from time to time.)

Address: *1001 Fairview Ave. N (park at the Yale St. Landing shopping center and marina), Seattle, WA 98109, tel. 206/340–1201, fax 206/621–9208.*
Accommodations: *3 double rooms with baths, 3 doubles share 1 bath, 1 suite.*
Amenities: *Phone, radio, and sink in rooms, TV and VCR in 4 rooms, stereo and refrigerator in some rooms; solarium.*
Rates: *$60–$135; full breakfast. AE, MC, V.*
Restrictions: *No smoking, no pets, no shoes inside.*

Roberta's Bed & Breakfast

For 24 years Roberta Barry has ruled the roost at her eponymous bed-and-breakfast in Seattle's elegant, tree-shaded Capitol Hill neighborhood, luring repeat customers with a mix of humor, energy, and genuine warmth. "People come here to have a good time," she says, explaining her innkeeping philosophy. "I just want them to be comfortable."

Roberta's freshly painted, flower-trimmed, square-frame house, built in 1903, sits in a quiet residential neighborhood across 15th Avenue from green Volunteer Park and its sumptuously restored conservatory. One small drawback is that Capitol Hill, which contains several of the city's most enjoyable B&Bs, can be a little hard for first-time Seattle visitors to find. Calling for directions will save headaches later. Note, too, that because of local zoning laws, there's no sign out front; look sharp for the address when you arrive.

Guests arriving at Roberta's make their way past a broad, covered sitting porch. Inside, the common areas are bright and sunny, personalized with a piano of antique oak, a beautifully tiled gas fireplace, and an ornate cast iron and nickel wood-burning stove. "Furniture should be comfortable," says the innkeeper. "It shouldn't break when you sit on it." There are books everywhere, because Roberta loves to read.

The five guest rooms are on the small side, with bright sunlight filtering through white lace curtains. The rugs on the hardwood floors and the comforters on the queen-size beds are modern and unpretentious. The third-floor Hideaway Suite, decorated in pale green and ivory, is the most spacious. Tongue-and-groove walls and a crazily angled ceiling enliven the space, which also includes a big claw-foot bathtub, oak chairs and tables, a queen-size brass bed, and a futon couch. Window seats in one alcove offer a view of the Cascade Mountains.

Seattle, a great restaurant town, offers a bewildering array of choices, particularly for fanciers of the Pacific Rim cuisines. Roberta is happy to make both recommendations and reservations, a thoughtful bonus for out-of-town guests. Her own tasty breakfasts are vegetarian affairs, featuring such specialties as baked eggs, Dutch babies (baked pancakes drizzled with lemon juice and powdered sugar), and fluffy omelets.

Address: *1147 16th Ave. E, Seattle, WA 98112, tel. 206/329–3326.*
Accommodations: *3 double rooms with baths, 1 double with bath in hall, 1 suite.*
Amenities: *Wood-burning stove in dining room.*
Rates: *$85–$105; full breakfast. MC, V.*
Restrictions: *No smoking, no pets.*

Shumway Mansion

East of Seattle, across Lake Washington in Kirkland, is the Shumway Mansion, a gray Shingle Style mansion with two-story bay windows, dating from 1909–10. Built by the progressive Shumways, whose daughter Carrie Holland Shumway was the first woman in the state to sit on a city council, the 10,000-square-foot house was saved from demolition by Richard and Salli Harris and their oldest daughter, Julie Blakemore. Backed by investors, the Harrises rescued the 24-room mansion, moved it 2½ miles to its present location, and renovated it to the tune of some $500,000.

A formality pervades the house, which is decorated largely with 18th- and 19th-century European pieces, Oriental rugs, lace curtains, and silk floral arrangements. The living room features the original fireplace, with two parlor sets, one a blue upholstered walnut spindle-style suite from Austria, the other French Victorian, covered in burgundy mohair. The sunroom is particularly charming, tiled in black and white with white wicker furniture, pink-and-white-striped wallpaper, and pink hanging lamps.

Guests can enjoy the grounds from two rear verandas linked by a long deck. Downstairs is a ballroom with four sets of French doors leading to a patio and gazebo. A recently opened guest room on the same level has a private garden, fireplace, and—an oddity in the bed-and-breakfast industry—a Murphy bed.

Guest rooms on the second floor share a tiny reading alcove on the same floor. Richard, a retired stockbroker, can't abide froufrou (although he does admit tolerating the odd straw hat with dried flowers here and there) and is proud of the soft easy chairs with ottomans, soundproofing, extra pillows, and good reading lights in every room. Each room mixes late-19th-century European and American furnishings with traditional-style modern pieces, old prints on the walls, Laura Ashley–style print wallpaper and bed linens, and resident stuffed animals—five or six per room.

Julie's candlelight breakfasts, served on crystal and china, include a variety of egg dishes or blueberry pancakes, as well as homemade muffins, scones, and coffee cake.

Address: *11410 99th Pl. NE, Kirkland, WA 98033, tel. 206/823–2303, fax 206/822–0421.*
Accommodations: *8 double rooms with baths, 1 suite.*
Amenities: *Soundproofing, individual heat control, and clock in rooms, TV available; free use of nearby health club; children over 12 welcome.*
Rates: *$65–$95; full buffet breakfast, afternoon refreshments. AE, MC, V.*
Restrictions: *No smoking indoors, no pets.*

Sorrento Hotel

The wings of this venerable hotel enfold its fountain courtyard like the covers of an open book. Arriving guests run a gauntlet of palm trees, valet parking, and doormen, finally winning access to the hushed interior of the ornate Sorrento Hotel, an Italianate throwback to a more gracious time, perched high on Seattle's Pill Hill.

Since 1909, visiting dignitaries ranging from President Harding and the Vanderbilt family to Debbie Gibson and David Bowie have made the Sorrento their lair while in the Emerald City. With good reason: The Sorrento provides a level of European luxury small-hotel service rarely encountered in the laid-back Northwest. Crackling fireplaces, hand-burnished Honduran mahogany, elaborate flower arrangements, and a hyperattentive staff make a memorable first impression.

In the guest rooms, the amenities and service successfully walk the line between gracious attentiveness and overkill. The home-baked butter cookies and miniatures of Dow's Port on the book-lined entertainment complex are warming touches; the Sorrento Hotel matchboxes, gold-embossed with the guest's name, are a flicker of Trumpian excess. There's plenty of space; no two rooms are exactly alike, although rose-colored carpets, cream walls, down pillows, and tasteful antique furnishings of teak, brass, oak, and walnut are consistent features. The vast, $1,000-per-night Penthouse

Suite, popular with reclusive rock and movie stars, has a deck with an outdoor soaking tub and a view of the memorable Seattle skyline, as well as a wood-burning fireplace, four-poster bed, and its own library.

Downstairs, in the octagonal, mahogany-paneled Fireside Room, cocktails are served beside a huge green-tiled fireplace. The hotel's restaurant is a hallowed temple of gastronomic excess thronged with healthy-looking Seattleites who come to smack their lips in guilty pleasure over chef Eric Leonard's richly sauced renditions of regional specialties: timbale of oyster mushroom with smoked duck and hazelnuts, for example, and sautéed filet mignon with smoked tomatoes and elephant garlic. Breakfast is on your own (the room service is excellent here).

Address: *900 Madison St., Seattle, WA 98104, tel. 206/622–6400 or 800/426–1265, fax 206/625–1059.*
Accommodations: *34 double rooms with baths, 42 suites.*
Amenities: *Cable TV, phone in rooms, air-conditioning, restaurant, bar, on-premises shiatsu masseur, concierge; access to health club, complimentary downtown limousine service.*
Rates: *$135–$165, suites $175–$355, Penthouse Suite $1,000; breakfast additional. AE, D, DC, MC, V.*
Restrictions: *No pets.*

The Chambered Nautilus

You can't miss the bright red door of this three-story Georgian Colonial Revival home near the University of Washington's campus. Called the Chambered Nautilus by personable owners Bunny and Bill Hagemeyer after an ornate seashell found in the Pacific Northwest, the house was built in 1915.

The spacious living room features Oriental rugs, large windows, and a fireplace. In one corner is a Hardman-Peck baby grand piano that was made by Bill's grandfather's company. Other interesting pieces in the room include an early English oak fire bench and a collection of rare Peruvian grave artifacts, some 2,000 years old. A 6-foot-tall carved oak headboard from the 1890s is the focal point of the Rose Room, dressed with a rose-and-

ivory striped down comforter and floral pillowcases. The Scallop Room takes advantage of the hilltop setting, with windows on three sides. Furnishings include a white iron daybed, carved chestnut armoire, and an early 19th-century commode.

Address: *5005 22nd Ave. NE, Seattle, WA 98105, tel. 206/522–2536.*
Accommodations: *4 double rooms with baths, 2 doubles share 1 bath.*
Amenities: *TV available.*
Rates: *$79–$105; full breakfast. AE, DC, MC, V.*
Restrictions: *No smoking, no pets; 2-night minimum on weekends Apr. 15–Oct. 15 and 3-night minimum on holiday weekends.*

The Inn at the Market

Ever see a 20-pound chinook salmon fly? Take a stroll through Seattle's renowned Pike Place Market, and you might—thanks to the ebullient resident fishmongers. It's all part of the show at the Inn at the Market, in the heart of Pike Place, a warren of intriguing shops, galleries, pubs, and restaurants.

Another of Seattle's ubiquitous small downtown luxury hotels, the inn is entered through a neo-Venetian courtyard; the quiet lobby is sunny and cheerful, with a cozy wood-burning fireplace and the comfortable, lived-in luxury of an old English country manor house.

The 65 rooms are large and bright, with large windows that maximize views of Elliott Bay. Furnishings are

posh and contemporary; the king-size beds are seductively comfortable. The inn has no restaurant, but a half-dozen of Seattle's best eateries lie within easy walking distance.

Address: *86 Pine St., Seattle, WA 98101, tel. 206/443–3600 or 800/446–4484, fax 206/625–1059.*
Accommodations: *56 double rooms with baths, 9 suites.*
Amenities: *Room service, rooftop deck, conference facilities, complimentary morning paper and coffee; athletic club available.*
Rates: *$125–$190, suites $220–$270; no breakfast. AE, DC, MC, V.*
Restrictions: *No pets.*

Salisbury House

On a wide, tree-lined avenue in an old residential neighborhood on Seattle's Capitol Hill sits Salisbury House. The Craftsman-style house, built in 1904, is owned by Mary Wiese, a former real-estate broker in California, and her daughter Cathryn.

The house is spacious and elegant, with maple floors, high coffered ceilings, and large leaded-glass windows. The furniture is eclectic, with few noteworthy antiques but lots of comfort. You might prefer to take a volume from the library up to the second-floor sun porch. There you can settle into the wicker chairs and make use of a refrigerator and hot pot.

Guest rooms are individually decorated in a warmly contemporary style.

The Rose Room, a large corner room with a canopy bed in rose chintz, is especially pretty. Mary's favorite room is the Lavender Room, where a country-French suite painted pale yellow combines with white wicker chairs and headboard, the lavender walls and purple floral duvet providing the chief color notes.

Address: *750 16th Ave. E, Seattle, WA 98112, tel. 206/328–8682.*
Accommodations: *4 double rooms with baths.*
Amenities: *Claw-foot tub in 1 room.*
Rates: *$70–$97; full breakfast, afternoon refreshments. AE, DC, MC, V.*
Restrictions: *No smoking indoors, no pets; 2-night minimum holiday and summer weekends.*

Villa Heidelberg

Villa Heidelberg owner Barb Thompson remembers her husband's reaction the first time they walked into the graceful, 1909 Craftsman, which had been neglected for more than 30 years. "I said, 'Wouldn't this make a great B&B?' John visibly paled." Today, seven years later, Barb's dream has become freshly painted, neatly landscaped reality.

Outside are manicured lawns and flower-filled gardens, a broad porch with views over Puget Sound, and a facade of irregular clinkerbrick and straight-grained fir. Inside, hardwood floors, heavily embossed wallpaper, lace tablecloths, a silver tea service, and a bowl of pink roses from the garden create a spare Edwardian feel, reinforced by sturdy but comfortable Arts and Crafts furniture. The four

guest rooms upstairs are named for the Thompsons' favorite German towns. The Garmish Room is bright, sunny, and floral, with a private deck. The larger Heidelberg Room, done in hardwoods and floral prints, has its own fireplace, phone, and TV.

Address: *4845 45th Ave. SW, Seattle, WA 98116, tel. 206/938–3658.*
Accommodations: *4 double rooms share 2 baths.*
Amenities: *Fireplace, TV, and phone in 1 room.*
Rates: *$65–$85; full breakfast. AE, MC, V.*
Restrictions: *No smoking indoors, no pets.*

Whidbey Island

Over the years Whidbey Island has been settled by farmers, retirees, executives who don't mind the commute, and families who want to get away from the hubbub of city life. They all grow attached to the rolling terrain of forests and meadows, to the high cliffs and sandy beaches, and to the dramatic views. Here you can tread the bluffs of Fort Ebey, marvel at the sunsets at Fort Casey or Deception Pass, bike along the many miles of wooded country roads and shoreline, or boat and fish off the same long shore.

The first white settlers included Colonel Walter Crockett and Colonel Isaac Ebey, who arrived during the early 1850s and gave their names to Crockett Lake and Ebey's Landing National Historic Reserve. Wildlife is plentiful: eagles, great blue herons, oystercatchers in the air; orcas, gray whales, dolphins, and otters in the water.

Lying 30 miles northwest of Seattle, the island ranks as the second-longest (60 miles; its width is only 8 miles) in the contiguous United States. It's easily accessible from Seattle via a ferry from Mukilteo (muck-il-TEE-oh) or a drive across Deception Pass on Highway 20.

Places to Go, Sights to See

Coupeville. Founded in 1852 by Captain Thomas Coupe, this seaport village (population 1,300) on the island's east coast passed its early years trading in timber, farm produce, and animal pelts. Much of the original town has been restored—it boasts some 54 historic landmarks. The *Island County Historical Museum* (corner of Alexander and Front Sts., tel. 360/678–3310) displays artifacts of pioneer families and the town's sea captains. Coupeville hosts an Arts and Crafts Festival in August; a Harvest Festival, with fall foods and a flea market, in October; and the "Greening of Coupeville" when it decorates for the holidays in mid-December.

Deception Pass State Park. (5175 N. State Hwy. 20, Oak Harbor, tel. 360/675–2417 or 360/293–3861). Take in the spectacular vista and stroll among the peeling, reddish-brown madrona trees. While walking across the Deception Pass Bridge, you'll have a view of the dramatic gorge below, well known for its tidal currents. The bridge links Whidbey to Fidalgo Island and the mainland; from here, it's just a short distance to Anacortes and ferries to the San Juan Islands.

Ebey's Landing National Historic Reserve (902 N.W. Alexander Rd., tel. 360/678–6084), west of Coupeville off Highway 20, encompasses more than 1,000 acres—including the areas of Keystone, Coupeville, and Penn Cove. Established by Congress in 1978, the reserve is the first and largest of its kind. It's dotted with some 91 nationally registered historical structures (mainly private homes), as well as farmland, parks, and trails with fine views.

Ft. Casey State Park (1280 S. Fort Casey Rd., tel. 360/678–4519 or 360/678–5632) lies just north of Keystone off Highway 20. The fort, built in 1890, was one of three coastal forts constructed at the entrance of Admiralty Inlet to protect Puget Sound. The park includes the fort, bunkers, and 10-inch disappearing guns, as well as a small interpretive center, campgrounds, picnic sites, fishing areas, and a boat launch.

Greenbank. The tart-sweet loganberry is grown on farms all over the island; now the 125-acre *Whidbey's Greenbank Loganberry Farm* (657 E. Wonn Rd., tel. 360/678–7700) also produces Whidbey's Loganberry Liqueur. Self-guided tours are offered daily from 10 to 5. Greenbank is also the site of the 53-acre *Meerkerk Rhododendron Gardens* (3531 S. Meerkerk La., off Resort Rd., tel. 360/321–6682), with 1,500 native and hybrid species of the flowering shrub along numerous trails and ponds. The prime time for viewing blossoms is April and May.

Langley. This quaint town on the island's southeastern shore sits atop a 50-foot-high bluff overlooking Saratoga Passage. A bluff-top sidewalk park offers spectacular views over the passage to Camano Island and the mainland beyond. Sculptor Georgia Gerber's bronze *Boy and Dog* stands sentinel over 1st Street, which is lined with restaurants and shops. The town's small-boat harbor, a 35-slip facility, is protected by a 400-foot timberpile breakwater and features a 160-foot-long fishing-pier-cum-walkway. The adjacent commercial marina offers fuel and supplies.

Restaurants

The Garibyan Brothers serve up Continental and Greek dishes, including lamb and fresh seafood, in a Mediterranean atmosphere at **Café Langley** (tel. 360/221–3090) in Langley. **Christopher's** (tel. 360/678–5480), in Coupeville, features views of the harbor as well as great stuffed island mussels and other seafood. Also in Coupeville, **Rosi's Garden Restaurant** (tel. 360/678–3989), grandly housed in a restored Victorian, offers a large menu featuring seafood and prime rib. A rustic little roadside diner called **Whidbey Fish** (tel. 360/678–3474) in Greenbank serves up great fish chowder, delicious halibut, and fabulous berry pies on picnic tables; hours and days of operation are erratic, however. Romantic European decor and fine Continental cuisine draw locals to **Kasteel Franssen** (tel. 360/675–0724) on Oak Harbor for special-occasion dinners.

Tourist Information

Central Whidbey Chamber of Commerce (5 S. Main St., Box 152, Coupeville, WA 98239, tel. 360/678–5434); **Island County Visitors Council** (Box 809, Coupeville, WA 98239, tel. 360/366–5010); **Langley Chamber of Commerce** (124½ Second St., Langley, WA 98260, tel. 360/221–6765).

Reservation Services

Pacific Bed & Breakfast Agency (701 N.W. 60th St., Seattle, WA 98107, tel. 206/784–0539); **Washington State Bed & Breakfast Guild** (2442 N.W. Market St., Box 355–FD, Seattle, WA 98107, tel. 800/647–2918); **Whidbey Island Bed & Breakfast Association** (Box 259, Langley, WA 98260, tel. 360/679–2276).

Cliff House and Sea Cliff Cottage

High on a cliff above Admiralty Strait, on 400 feet of waterfront, stand the Cliff House and the more secluded Sea Cliff Cottage. The natural beauty and tranquillity of the location led owner Peggy Moore to build her incredible home on Whidbey Island. She's proud of what she created, and rightly so, since the 1981 Cliff House—a contemporary statement in glass, wood, and stone—has brought awards to its architect, Arne Bystrom.

A large open kitchen and dining area stands on one side of a 30-foot glass atrium; a study and seating area is on the other side. The sunken living room has a fireplace and a seafoam-green sectional with a perimeter of tiny lights that make it appear to float at night. The floor-to-ceiling windows in the dining and living rooms allow glorious views of Admiralty Strait, Puget Sound, and the Olympic Mountains.

The two spacious loft bedrooms are upstairs. Because guests share living and dining facilities, Peggy will only rent the two rooms to acquainted parties; the innkeepers themselves have separate quarters. The larger room, decorated in shades of peach and ecru, opens out over the living area. Amenities that have attracted the rich and famous include a king-size feather bed, a whirlpool bath, and two upholstered chairs that swivel so guests can fully appreciate the view of the sun setting over the mountains.

The second bedroom—decorated mostly in white, with whitewashed pine furniture, Battenberg lace, pink glass lamps, and a pink chintz folding screen—overlooks the kitchen and dining area to the forest beyond. There's a skylight in the dark blue tile bathroom. Comprehensive music and video libraries keep guests entertained on chilly evenings.

Sea Cliff Cottage is as romantic and cozy as Cliff House is airy and elegant. The porch has a bit of gingerbread among the driftwood railing, and Adirondack chairs. There's a country French feel to the living room: whitewashed pine walls, pine armoire, wicker chairs and love seat with pale green and pink cushions, and a brick fireplace. The bedroom is pink, with a wicker headboard and Ralph Lauren linens on the bed, and a cushioned window seat overlooking the trees and the water. There is also a fully equipped kitchenette and a dining area, as well as a bathroom.

Address: *5440 Windmill Rd., Freeland, WA 98249, tel. 360/321–1566.*
Accommodations: *2 double rooms with baths, 1 housekeeping cottage.*
Amenities: *Fireplace in cottage; outdoor hot tub.*
Rates: *$360, cottage $165; Continental breakfast. No credit cards.*
Restrictions: *No smoking indoors, no pets; 2-night minimum most of the time.*

Colonel Crockett Farm

olonel Walter Crockett, a relative of Davy Crockett, built this house in 1855. It was derelict in 1984 when Robert and Beulah Whitlow found it; today the house is listed in the National Register of Historic Places. Robert, a former banker and personnel director, and Beulah, a retired teacher, spent 18 months and $235,000 transforming the old farmhouse into an inn which stands amid 3 acres of lawn and flower gardens.

The Victorian cross-gabled structure has Doric pilasters on pedestals, which lend an incongruous formal grandeur to an otherwise modest house. The entry hall and small solarium have stained- and leaded-glass windows and white wicker furniture. The main public room is a comfortable and well-stocked library with red oak paneling, a slate fireplace, an English brass rubbing, and a collection of bulldogs in an antique glass case. The furniture includes a mirror-back English settee and matching chairs, an upholstered Eastlake chair and matching rocker, and another rocker, this one hand-carved.

The five guest rooms have been individually decorated. The Crockett Room, the inn's bridal suite, is furnished with a draped and canopied queen-size four-poster, a marble-top washstand, and a Belgian field desk; its bathroom has an extra-long tub with lion's-head feet. The Edwardian fainting couch in the sitting area is a particularly rare piece. The Alexander Room, with a tiger maple bed and

dresser, overlooks meadows, Crockett Lake, and Admiralty Bay.

The dining room has a fireplace and a telescope for guests. The small tables are dressed up with pink and white linens, and are surrounded by the Whitlows' collections of antique porcelain plates; Royal Copenhagen, Wedgwood, and Belleek pieces; and gleaming English silver. From here guests have a view out to the iris gardens and Crockett Lake. Breakfast specialties include eggs California, generous platters of fruit, and homemade muffins with seasonal ingredients.

Address: *1012 S. Fort Casey Rd., Coupeville, WA 98239, tel. 360/678–3711.*
Accommodations: *5 double rooms with baths.*
Amenities: *Water views, gardens, fish pond.*
Rates: *$65–$95; full breakfast. MC, V.*
Restrictions: *No smoking indoors, no pets; 2-night minimum on holiday weekends.*

Inn at Langley

This contemporary structure at the edge of the Langley business district is a contemplative melding of earth, sky, water, wood, and concrete. The two cedar-shake, Mission-style buildings—inspired by Frank Lloyd Wright—are surrounded by quiet gardens of herbs, berries, flowers, and fruit trees.

An archway leads to a long, rectangular reflecting pond, which connects with the Country Kitchen, a restaurant that serves Continental breakfast to guests and opens to the public for dinner on Friday and Saturday. Behind the dining room lies a longer building with the same lines and a lot of glass and wood. This structure includes the office, 22 guest rooms, and two suites trailing down the bluff to the beach.

Lawyer/developer Paul Schell discovered Langley when he and his wife, Pam, moved from New York to Seattle during the early 1970s. After doing several redevelopments in Seattle, Paul opened the 13,000-square-foot, $1 million Inn at Langley in June 1989.

The interior, with an almost Asian sense of space and understatement, was designed to be restorative. Neutral colors—black, taupe, gray, beige—form a quiet background. The waterside wall in the common area is nearly all glass, affording guests a staggeringly beautiful view past the deck to Saratoga Passage, Camano Island, and the Cascade Mountains. The room's fireplace and its maple, fir, cherry, and pine appointments seem to meld with the outdoors.

The Country Kitchen might be a wealthy friend's dining room. You'll find no maître d' standing at an official podium, no coat check, and no cash register. A huge river-rock fireplace rises before you; tables for two line the walls unobtrusively. The restaurant, a veritable gallery of local crafts, has a locally made, Wright-inspired "great table" for 10 on the far side of the fireplace.

Steve and Sandy Nogal, the inn's managers, have seen it happen again and again: "People arrive here all aggressive," Steve says. "They're keyed up after having to wait for a ferry. Slowly, they unwind and blossom."

Address: *400 1st St., Box 835, Langley, WA 98260, tel. and fax 360/221–3033.*
Accommodations: *22 double rooms with baths, 2 suites.*
Amenities: *Fireplace, whirlpool tub, cable TV, and phone in rooms; dinner available Fri. and Sat.*
Rates: *$165–$185, suites $245; Continental breakfast. AE, MC, V.*
Restrictions: *No smoking indoors, no pets; 2-night minimum on weekends.*

Anchorage Inn

The Anchorage Inn, a reproduction Victorian home just up the hill from the shops and restaurants of Main Street in Coupeville, opened during the summer of 1991. The white-walled, red-roofed house rises three stories with such fanciful touches as gables, dormer windows, and a tower. Everything, from the hardwood floors to the reproduction furniture, is new.

The foyer has a fireplace and a large, open staircase. In Room 2 you'll find an Eastlake-style bedstead with a fluffy white comforter, a dresser, and a view of the harbor.

In "a working retirement," new owners Don and Joanne Storer moved from Boston to run the inn. They are often found chatting with guests in the crow's nest on the third floor, which the Storer's stock with cookies and drinks, reading matter, games, and an extensive video collection.

Address: *807 N. Main St., Coupeville, WA 98239, tel. 360/678–5581.*
Accommodations: *5 double rooms with baths.*
Amenities: *Air-conditioning, cable TV in rooms; guest lounge, video and book library.*
Rates: *$75–$90; full breakfast. AE, D, MC, V.*
Restrictions: *No smoking, no pets.*

Captain Whidbey Inn

The Captain Whidbey nestles along the shore of Penn Cove near Coupeville. Built in 1907 from local madrona logs, it is warm and inviting. The sitting room has smooth log walls and a double-sided beach rock and brick fireplace whose other side faces the dining room.

Guest rooms open off the hallway. They all have cozy feather beds, down comforters, and sinks. The rooms on one side have a water view, while those on the other side have a forest view. One of the suites has a four-poster bed, blue woven curtains, and a reading chair with matching upholstery. Seven cottages have fireplaces and, in some cases, kitchens. Another building contains the spacious Lagoon Rooms, all with verandas and private baths.

Candlelight dinners are available in the dining room, which looks onto Penn Cove. After dinner, guests can relax in the Chart Room, a rustic bar.

Address: *2072 W. Captain Whidbey Inn Rd., Coupeville, WA 98239, tel. 360/678–4097 or 800/366–4097, fax 360/678–4110.*
Accommodations: *12 double rooms with baths, 10 doubles and 2 suites share 2 baths, 4 cottages, 1 housekeeping cottage, 2 2-bedroom housekeeping cottages.*
Amenities: *Phone in some rooms, fireplace in cottages.*
Rates: *$85–$195; Continental breakfast. AE, D, DC, MC, V.*
Restrictions: *No pets; 2-night minimum on weekends, 3-night minimum on holiday weekends.*

Country Cottage of Langley

The Country Cottage stands two blocks from downtown Langley on 2 landscaped acres that were part of a farm until 1984. The two-story farmhouse, with dormer windows and a gabled entrance, went up in 1927. Green, in various shades, is the predominant color, and whitewashed wainscoting is used throughout. The seafoam-green dining room is done in a Laura Ashley print, and the large living room has a stone fireplace and a sunny adjoining parlor. In the TV room there's an antique slipper chair and settee. Outside, a large deck with umbrella tables and a boardwalk leads to a gazebo, and beyond, a more recent building houses two large guest rooms. Owners Mary and Bob DeCelles also converted a farmhouse creamery into a small cottage.

The upstairs guest rooms in the main house have angled ceilings, brass bedsteads, oak chests, bentwood rockers, and pilgrim-style trunks.

Breakfast, served at intimate tables in the dining room, is a gourmet buffet affair.

Address: *215 6th St., Langley, WA 98260, tel. 360/221–8709.*
Accommodations: *5 double rooms with baths.*
Amenities: *TV and fireplace in main house, TVs and refrigerators in cottage rooms; badminton, croquet, and horseshoes.*
Rates: *$95–$105; full breakfast. AE, MC, V.*
Restrictions: *No smoking, no pets; 2-night minimum on summer weekends and holidays.*

Eagles Nest Inn

The ambience of Eagles Nest Inn, just a few minute's drive from Langley, is one of comfortable elegance. This contemporary octagonal house, with views of the water and the mountains, is serenely rural.

The two-story living room has a 17-foot brick fireplace flanked by elongated octagonal windows in clear and peach-colored glass. Its peach carpet is spread with Chinese rugs on which sit dark-cherry upholstered chairs and a sofa.

Every guest room has a private bath and a view of either the woods or Saratoga Passage and the Cascade Mountains. Honeymooners love the fourth-floor peach-and-white penthouse room, which has windows on all eight walls, brass and wicker furnishings, and a deck.

Californians Jerry and Joanne Lechner took over the inn in 1994. Joanne used to teach gourmet cooking, and now puts her culinary talents to good use in preparing bountiful breakfasts.

Address: *3236 E. Saratoga Rd., Langley, WA 98260, tel. and fax 360/221–5331.*
Accommodations: *4 double rooms with baths.*
Amenities: *Cable TV and VCR in room, complimentary beverages; outdoor hot tub.*
Rates: *$95–$105; full breakfast. D, MC, V.*
Restrictions: *No smoking, no pets; 2-night minimum on holiday weekends.*

Fort Casey Inn

The Fort Casey Inn is the former officers' quarters of the old coastal defense fort, built in 1909. Gordon and Victoria Hoenig have been the owners since 1956; Gina Martin is the vivacious manager.

Victoria has renovated, one at a time, four two-story Georgian Revival duplexes. Each one has a kitchen and a living room on the lower floor and two bedrooms and a bath upstairs. The houses have been individually decorated, with painted floors and braided rag rugs; the high ceilings in the living rooms retain their original tin, and you will also come across tin chandeliers, lace curtains, folk art, hand-painted furniture, and claw-foot bathtubs.

The Doctor's House has two bedrooms and a bath, and Garrison Hall, which is used for weddings and seminars, also has a small suite.

The Hoenigs leave fixings for a Continental breakfast in each kitchen.

Address: *1124 S. Engle Rd., Coupeville, WA 98239, tel. 360/678–8792.*
Accommodations: *1 suite, 1 2-bedroom housekeeping cottage, 4 2-bedroom housekeeping suites.*
Amenities: *5 wood-burning stoves; bicycles.*
Rates: *$75–$110; Continental breakfast. AE, MC, V.*
Restrictions: *No smoking, no pets.*

Guest House Cottages

The Guest House Cottages sit at the edge of a pond in a rural area between Langley and Coupeville. Mary Jane and Don Creger first started renting their log-cabin guest house as a couples' retreat. Over the years they added more cabins and cottages on their 25 acres. There are no common areas for guests to mingle in, but the pool and small exercise room have earned the Cregers high marks.

Old scythes, a runner sled, and a lantern rest on the front porch of the Emma Jane Cottage. The living room has pine floors spread with braided rugs, knotty pine walls, a stone fireplace, a blue mohair overstuffed sofa, rocking chairs, and Pilgrim-style trunks. Potpourri and white chocolate candies are among the thoughtful touches in the cabins. Dining tables come set for breakfast, and the refrigerators are stocked with breakfast fixings.

Address: *3366 S. State Hwy. 525, Greenbank, WA 98253, tel. 360/678–3115.*
Accommodations: *6 housekeeping cottages, 1 2-bedroom housekeeping cottage.*
Amenities: *Air-conditioning in 1 cottage, whirlpool tub in rooms, exercise room; outdoor swimming pool and hot tub, video library.*
Rates: *$135–$185, 1 cottage $285; Continental breakfast. AE, MC, V.*
Restrictions: *No smoking, no pets; 2-night minimum on weekends, 3-night minimum on holiday weekends.*

Home by the Sea
Bed & Breakfast and Cottages

Two-story Nantucket-style Home by the Sea Bed & Breakfast sits on scenic Useless Bay's beach. Sharon Drew, who owns the establishment with her mother, Helen Fritts, decorated it with international treasures, such as a hand-carved screen from India and Russian samovars. Now Sharon's daughters, Laura and Linda, have joined the business.

There's a double room and a suite on the house's top floor, and attached to the house is the Sandpiper Suite. Each guest room has Ralph Lauren floral spreads, and one of the sitting rooms features a small brass bed from Afghanistan. Home by the Sea also offers visitors two romantic cottages with full kitchens.

Address: *2388 E. Sunlight Beach Rd., Clinton, WA 98236, tel. 360/221–2964.*
Accommodations: *1 double room with bath, 2 suites, 1 2-bedroom housekeeping cottage, 1 3-bedroom housekeeping cottage.*
Amenities: *Air-conditioning and sauna in B&B; wood-burning stove, phone, whirlpool tubs, and TV in suite and cottages; massage available.*
Rates: *B&B $115–$165; full breakfast. Cottages $145; breakfast delivered 2 mornings only. MC, V.*
Restrictions: *No smoking, pets in Cape Cod Cottage only; 2-night minimum on weekends in cottages.*

Inn at Penn Cove

Two side-by-side stately homes in the middle of historic Coupeville are run as an inn by first-time innkeepers Gladys and Mitchell Howard. Kineth House—a large peach-colored Victorian Italianate—was built in 1887.

Kineth House's parlor has fir floors and dusty pink-and-cream reproduction Victorian wallpaper; a cream upholstered sofa facing a faux marble fireplace has a pink frosted-glass chandelier overhead. The room also contains an antique pump organ, a Victorian music box, and two 1890s armchairs by the bay window. Guest rooms are elegant without being stuffy. Elizabeth's Room has pale pink walls, lavender carpet, a turn-of-the-century bed, and an 8-foot double-mirrored armoire.

Next door stands the 1891 Coupe-Gillespie House, which was built for the daughter of the town's sea-captain founder. This house's three guest rooms are smaller and less elaborate in their details than those of its neighbor.

Address: *702 N. Main St., Box 85, Coupeville, WA 98239, tel. 360/678–8000 or 800/688–COVE.*
Accommodations: *3 double rooms with baths, 2 doubles share 1 bath, 1 suite.*
Amenities: *Fireplaces in 3 rooms, whirlpool tub in suite; cable TV, VCR, video library, and air-conditioning in Kineth House; game room; complimentary beverages.*
Rates: *$60–$125; full breakfast. AE, D, MC, V.*
Restrictions: *No smoking, no pets.*

Log Castle Bed & Breakfast

The rustic, Northwest-style Log Castle Bed & Breakfast, owned by Norma and Jack Metcalf, sits on a secluded beach outside Langley.

Norma designed the house and Jack started building it in 1974 from local stone, driftwood, and lumber. The place has a homey, nostalgic feel: stained-glass lamps, tree-root door handles and drawer pulls, plants hanging in macramé holders, and wormwood for the stairway, doors, and kitchen cupboards. The large living/dining room has the aura of a grand old lodge: massive timbers, cathedral ceiling, large leaded-glass windows, red and tan carpets, and a table made from an ancient log slab.

The four guest rooms are named for the couple's four daughters. Ann's

Room, in the third-story tower, is decorated in white and mauve and features a 1912 wood stove, white furniture (including a metal bed), and a flowered quilt made by Norma's grandmother; it has a peaked roof and a widow's walk around the outside.

Address: *3273 E. Saratoga Rd., Langley, WA 98260, tel. 360/221–5485, fax 360/221–3822.*
Accommodations: *4 double rooms with baths.*
Amenities: *Wood stoves in 2 rooms.*
Rates: *$80–$105; full breakfast. D, MC, V.*
Restrictions: *No smoking, no pets; 2-night minimum on holiday weekends, closed 5 days during Christmas.*

Lone Lake Cottage and Breakfast

Dolores Meeks, who owns and runs the Lone Lake Cottage and Breakfast, was a restaurant manager who wanted an active retirement. Her hobby is raising birds: She keeps an aviary of over 200 rare varieties.

At Lone Lake you can stay in a cottage, a lakeside suite attached to the main house, or a houseboat. Dolores's late husband built the boat and restored its antique engine (at one time it toured the lake). The interior is decorated in shades of blue, with a queen-size loft bed and a tiny galley. The two cottages have rattan and soapstone-inlaid furniture, Oriental screens, and extra-firm queen-size beds; both have covered decks with gas barbecues and views of the lake.

Guests also have use of a mini tennis court. Dolores delivers breakfast for the first two days of your stay, but after that you're on your own.

Address: *5206 S. Bayview Rd., Langley, WA 98260, tel. 360/321–5325.*
Accommodations: *1 housekeeping houseboat with detached bath, 1 housekeeping suite, 1 housekeeping cottage, 1 2-bedroom housekeeping cottage.*
Amenities: *Fireplace, whirlpool tub, CD player, cable TV/VCR, barbeques, film library, bicycles, canoes, rowboat, paddleboat, fishing gear.*
Rates: *$110; Continental breakfast for first 2 days. No credit cards.*
Restrictions: *No smoking, no children, no pets; 2-night minimum on weekends.*

Whidbey Inn

his mauve wood-frame Craftsman-style building looks like a
collection of shops, but that's only
half the story: Two floors on the water
side hold the Whidbey Inn.

The only thing between the inn's guests
and the water is a pane of glass—and
not even that when you're sitting on
the deck. On the lower floor there are
three doubles which open onto a deck;
upstairs are three (deckless) suites.
The Wicker Suite, with a light green
and white color scheme, has a small
vestibule with a mirrored armoire; a
working fireplace; and a wicker love
seat, chairs, and a coffee table in a
pleasant corner with windows.

The inn lacks public space, but its
owner, Dick Francisco—also the owner
of Francisco's, a local Italian restaurant—has a platter of cheese and
crackers and a bottle of sherry waiting
for newly arrived guests in their
rooms. The substantial breakfast delivered to the rooms includes enough
goodies for guests to save a few for a
picnic lunch.

Address: *106 1st St., Box 156, Langley,
WA 98260, tel. 360/221–7115.*
Accommodations: *3 double rooms
with baths, 3 suites.*
Amenities: *Fireplace in suite, compli-
mentary sherry and appetizers.*
Rates: *$95–$150; full breakfast. AE,
MC, V.*
Restrictions: *No smoking, no pets.*

San Juan Islands

*The San Juan Islands offer the traveler a relaxed pace in a
setting that ranges from tranquil to wildly rain- and
windswept. There are no thoroughfares, just meandering
roads; fierce storms bring power outages; fresh water is a
precious commodity.*

*The San Juan archipelago contains 743 islands at low tide, a
number that drops to 428 at high tide. Of this total, 172 are
named, 60 are populated, and 10 are state marine parks. The
islands are home to seals, porpoises, otters, some 80 orca
whales, and more than 60 actively breeding pairs of bald
eagles. They offer an unbeatable array of outdoor activities:
bicycling, sailing, kayaking, canoeing, golfing, horseback
riding, boating, fishing, and on and on.*

*Non-native residents have moved here to escape the breakneck
pace of life elsewhere, and they become as fierce as the natives
about protecting what they find: the natural beauty, the
wildlife, the privacy. Visitors who respect the island's values
are welcome. Ferries stop at Lopez, Shaw, Orcas, and San
Juan (schedules can vary); you'll need a private plane or boat
to get to the others.*

*The first ferry stop, Lopez Island, abounds with orchards,
weathered barns, and pastures of grazing sheep and cows. The
relatively flat terrain makes it a favorite spot for bicyclists.
The Franciscan nuns who run the ferry dock at Shaw Island
wear their traditional habits; few tourists disembark here,
though, because the island is mostly residential. Orcas, the
next in line, is a mountainous, horseshoe-shaped island of 56
square miles, with 125 miles of coastline. The last stop, on San
Juan Island, is Friday Harbor, with its colorful and active
waterfront. The San Juans lie in the so-called Banana Belt,
with an annual average of 247 sunny days; compare that with
Seattle's gray weather and you'll begin to understand Friday
Harbor's holiday atmosphere.*

Places to Go, Sights to See

Moran State Park (Star Rte., tel. 360/376–5437 or 800/562–0990) lies just 10 miles from the Orcas Island Ferry landing. It offers 4,600 acres of forest and hiking trails, as well as panoramic views from a lookout tower (at the end of a 6-mile drive on paved roadway) on top of 2,400-foot Mt. Constitution. The park also has 148 campsites.

Roche Harbor (tel. 360/378–2155), at the northern end of San Juan Island, is an elegant resort complex with rose gardens, manicured lawns, a cobblestone water-front, and hanging flower baskets on the docks. It was constructed during the 1880s as a limestone mining village. A white clapboard restaurant and lounge offer great views of Roche Harbor, though the food is just average. The romantic-looking old Hotel de Haro has seen better days—the guest rooms are very worn at the heel. In addition to the harbor, the resort has a private airport. Ask for directions to Afterglow Vista, a fascinating Grecian-columned mausoleum tucked away in the woods on the property.

Rosario Spa & Resort (1 Rosario Way, tel. 360/376–2222), on Orcas Island, was built in 1905 by shipbuilding magnate Robert Moran, who had been told that he had only six months to live and wanted to do it lavishly. Moran put $1.5 million into this Mediterranean-style mansion (there are 6 tons of copper in the roof); the investment turned out to be a good one, since he lasted another 30 years. In 1960 Rosario became a resort; villas and hotel units were added (since fire codes pro-hibited rental of the mansion's rooms), but they're a far cry from the exquisite teaks and mahoganies of the original structure. The mansion itself, now listed on the National Register of Historic Places, contains the music room (where fre-quent organ concerts and 45-minute presentations are given on the history of the place), the dining room, and the spa with the original swimming pool.

San Juan Goodtime Jazz Festival (Box 98, Friday Harbor, WA 98250, tel. 360/378–5509) attracts musicians from across the country who perform at four sites in Friday Harbor for three days at the end of July.

San Juan Island National Historic Park. For a number of years, both the Americans and the British occupied San Juan Island. In 1859 a Yank killed a Brit's pig, igniting long-smoldering tempers. Both nations sent armed forces to the island, but no further gunfire was exchanged in the "Pig War" of 1859–72. The remains of this scuffle are the English Camp near the north end of the island, with a blockhouse, commissary, and barracks; and the armaments from the Amer-ican Camp on the southeastern tip of the island. The visitor center is on Spring Street one block up from the ferry terminal.

Whale Museum (62 1st St. N, tel. 360/378–4710). This modest museum in Friday Harbor focuses on the great cetaceans and doesn't attempt to woo you with expen-sive exhibits, but it does have whale models, whale skeletons, whalebone, whale recordings, and whale videos. Standing on the ferry dock, you can see it at the top of the hill—it has a whale mural painted on the wall. The museum also operates a whale sighting hot line at 800/562–8832 as part of ongoing research; they'll want to know the time of your sighting and any distinctive markings you saw.

Whale-watching. For a chance to see whales cavorting, try the first official whale-watching park in the United States, *Lime Kiln Point State Park* (6158

Lighthouse Rd., tel. 360/378–2044), 9 miles west of Friday Harbor on San Juan Island's west side. Whale-spotting season is mid-June through mid-August. For an even better chance, consider a half-day *Western Prince Cruise* (tel. 360/378–5315 or 800/757–ORCA), which offers whale-watching during the summer and bird-watching and scuba diving during the spring and fall. Cruises depart from the Main Dock at the Friday Harbor Marina.

Restaurants

Lopez Island: The **Bay Café** (tel. 360/468–3700) features innovative dishes, especially fish, in a casual, cottage-style atmosphere. **Gail's** (tel. 360/468–2150) has a natural-wood Cape Cod look and specializes in fresh seafood and local lamb; Gail grows her own herbs and vegetables. For lunch, try the old-fashioned soda fountain at the **Lopez Island Pharmacy** (tel. 360/468–2644), offering soups, salads, and sandwiches as well as phosphates, malts, floats, and other fountain treats. Orcas Island: **Christina's** (tel. 360/376–4904) provides fresh local seafood in an elegant atmosphere both inside and on the rooftop terrace. **Bilbo's Festivo** (tel. 360/376–4728), in a stucco house with a courtyard decorated with Mexican tiles, features creative renditions of burritos and enchiladas as well as mesquite-grilled specialties. Two of the island's inns, the **Orcas Hotel** (tel. 360/376–4300) and the **Deer Harbor Inn** (tel. 360/376–4110), serve casual Pacific Northwest fare utilizing the fresh produce of the islands. San Juan Island: **Duck Soup Inn** (tel. 360/378–4878) serves the island's Wescott Bay oysters and other fresh seafood prepared in its Mediterranean-inspired kitchen. The **Springtree Café** (tel. 360/378–4848), in the middle of Friday Harbor, boasts its own organically grown produce as well as fresh fish and pasta dishes. For affordable and tasty salmon fettuccine, lasagna, and other Italian fare, visit **Roberto's** (tel. 360/378–6333) on the hill above Friday Harbor's ferry loading area.

Tourist Information

San Juan Island Chamber of Commerce (Box 98, Friday Harbor, WA 98250, tel. 360/378–5240); **San Juan Islands Tourism Cooperative and Visitors Information Service** (Box 65, Lopez, WA 98261, tel. 360/468–3663).

Reservation Services

Pacific Bed & Breakfast Agency (701 N.W. 60th St., Seattle, WA 98107, tel. 206/784–0539); **San Juan Island Central Reservations** (tel. 360/378–6670); **Washington State Bed & Breakfast Guild** (2442 N.W. Market St., Box 355-FD, Seattle, WA 98107, tel. 800/647–2918).

Inn at Swifts Bay

There'll always be another boat, but there may never be another property like this," said Robert Herrman when he and Christopher Brandmeir decided to sell the sailboat they had been grooming for a round-the-world adventure and buy the 1975 mock-Tudor building, 2 miles from the Lopez Island ferry landing, that is now the Inn at Swifts Bay. The inn is surrounded by rhododendrons, madronas, and firs amid 3 acres of woods, with another acre of beach a four-minute walk away.

Robert and Chris give the inn its heart. These two California transplants have woven themselves into the island community. Robert, a former gemologist and singer, now sits on the board of the local library. Chris, who has been a university administrator and a caterer, is on the board of the San Juan Islands Tourism Co-op and Visitors Information Service.

The inn's decor is sophisticated, but the rooms feel lived-in and loved. The sunny living room has large bay windows, a fireplace, a chintz sofa and chairs on an Oriental rug, and shelves of books. The raised dining room, pale yellow with hand stenciled ivy around the ceiling, is the setting for breakfast, which might include hazelnut waffles with fresh island berries and crème fraîche, or eggs with just-caught Dungeness crabs. The den/music room behind the living room features burgundy Laura Ashley wallpaper, a large brick fireplace, two Queen Anne uphol-

stered wing chairs, a TV/VCR with more than 150 tapes, and French doors that open onto the deck and the woods.

The individually decorated guest rooms are spacious and airy. Room 2 has hunter green walls with cream accents, window swags of patterned fabric, an Arts and Crafts headboard on the queen-size bed, a gateleg desk, and a large dark-cherry mirror and chest. In the attic, a large room with a sitting area has pale peach walls, a queen-size sleigh bed, and an English armoire and chest; three long, narrow skylights have been cut into the sloping ceiling, and there's a private entrance and small deck. The adjacent attic suite has a separate sitting room and large private deck. In 1994, Chris and Robert added a private cottage on Hunter's Bay, the perfect escape for romantic private retreats.

Address: *Port Stanley Rd., Rte. 2, Box 3402, Lopez Island, WA 98261, tel. 360/468-3636.*
Accommodations: *2 double rooms with baths, 2 doubles share a bath, 1 suite, 1 housekeeping cottage.*
Amenities: *Popcorn, sherry, and mineral water; VCR and movie library; terry-cloth robes and towels, flip-flops, flashlights; outdoor hot tub.*
Rates: *$75–$85, doubles with baths $125, suite $155, housekeeping cottage $195; full breakfast. AE, D, MC, V.*
Restrictions: *No smoking indoors, no pets; 2-night minimum in housekeeping cottage.*

Orcas Hotel

On the hill overlooking the Orcas Island ferry landing sits a three-story red-roofed Victorian with a wraparound porch and a white picket fence. The Orcas Hotel was built as an inn between 1900 and 1904 by Canadian landowner William Sutherland. Today the hotel is listed on the National Register of Historic Places; even the flower gardens—drifts of daffodils, wisteria vines, irises, and roses—have been restored. The hostelry is managed by Craig and Linda Sanders, Brad Harlow, and Linda Abbott—four active young people who, when they aren't bicycling, hiking, or playing volleyball or softball, are likely to be in the kitchen cooking gourmet meals.

The hotel has a colorful past. A bullet hole through a veranda post recalls the Prohibition-era escape of a bootlegger who foiled his pursuers by leaping to freedom over the porch railing. Some islanders claim that liquor was smuggled in by small boats and stored in the woodpile and the attic. During the hotel's restoration in 1985, loose planks were discovered in the attic, with enough space underneath to store dozens of bottles of booze. The ghost of Octavia, one of the original managers, was seen as recently as 1985, by two of the workmen who were doing the restoration. (Don't worry—the building has been exorcised.)

The main floor features a bakery/espresso café, a dining room, and a private parlor for overnight guests; all three rooms have harbor views. The parlor is furnished with Queen Anne settees, marble-top tables, and Oriental rugs. The dining room (open to the public) overlooks the ferry landing as well as part of the garden. Works by Orcas artists, such as a stained-glass mermaid in the cocktail lounge, grace the building.

Two romantic rooms at the front of the inn each have French doors opening onto a wrought-iron-furnished sundeck with views of the waterfront. Both rooms feature feather beds and duvets and marble-top tables, and the Blue Heron Room has an Eastlake parlor set. Each has a large bathroom with a double whirlpool bath. The innkeepers readily admit that temperatures in the building are idiosyncratic, so they've supplied each room with a fan and a space heater.

Guests often go home with jars of the inn's tasty pickled veggies, fresh preserves, and chutneys.

Address: *Box 155, Orcas, WA 98280, tel. 360/376–4300, fax 360/376–4399.*
Accommodations: *2 double rooms with baths, 2 doubles and 1 triple with half-baths share 2 full baths, 5 doubles and 1 triple share 4 baths.*
Amenities: *Restaurant, bakery, cocktail lounge; bike rentals.*
Rates: *$69–$170; full breakfast. AE, D, MC, V.*
Restrictions: *No smoking indoors, no pets; 2-night minimum on holiday weekends.*

Turtleback Farm Inn

Bill and Susan Fletcher abandoned suburban life in the San Francisco Bay area (he was a real-estate broker, she a homemaker) for 80 acres of meadow, forest, and farmland on Orcas Island, where they now herd French geese and occasionally deliver a baby lamb by flashlight. The farmhouse was derelict when they bought it in 1984. Renovated and expanded the following year, the building preserves the original Folk National style. Forest green with white trim, it stands in the shadow of Turtleback Mountain, with Mt. Constitution to the east, a 10-minute drive from the Orcas Island ferry landing.

Don't expect to spend a lot of time chatting with the innkeepers; the Fletchers appear for breakfast but generally spend the evenings in their own home down the hill. A framed Seattle newspaper clipping by the front door—a 1933 ad for *Tarzan the Fearless*—pays homage to the movie's star and Susan's father, Buster Crabbe.

The inn itself is spacious and airy but spare. The cream-colored sitting room, with a beamed ceiling and peach-and-green accents, includes a Rumford fireplace, a pilgrim-style trunk, and a cabbage-rose upholstered sofa, and a corner game table. The salmon-colored dining room has fir wainscoting and five small oak tables.

The guest rooms are decorated with Cape May Collection wallpaper. All have reading lamps, comfortable seating, cream-colored muslin curtains, and meadow and forest views. The Meadow Room has a private deck overlooking the pasture. The light fixtures and crystal doorknobs in most rooms and the claw-foot tubs and bathroom mirrors were rescued from Seattle's old Savoy Hotel before it was razed, and the sinks and beveled-glass bathroom shelves above them come from Victoria's grand old Empress Hotel. The comforters on the beds are stuffed with wool batting from the Fletchers' own sheep.

Breakfast is served in the dining room or, in fine weather, on the deck overlooking the valley, on tables set with bone china, silver, and linen. If you want the recipes, you can buy Susan's cookbook. Full meal service is available by reservation for groups.

Address: *Crow Valley Rd., Rte. 1, Box 650, Eastsound, WA 98245, tel. 360/376-4914.*
Accommodations: *7 double rooms with baths.*
Amenities: *Sherry, fresh fruit, hot beverages, guest refrigerator.*
Rates: *$75–$155; full breakfast. MC, V.*
Restrictions: *No smoking indoors, no pets; 2-night minimum on weekends and May 1–Oct. 31, 3-night minimum on holiday weekends.*

Blair House

Just four blocks up the hill from the Friday Harbor ferry landing stands a farmhouse with a wide wraparound porch furnished in wicker. Blair House was built in 1909; Bob Pittman, who had vacationed there for years, jumped at the chance to buy the inn when it came on the market in 1992. But he has since hired an innkeeper, and so is not involved in day-to-day activities.

The large, comfortable living room has floor-to-ceiling bookshelves at one end, a wood-burning stove, cable TV, tape player, and plenty of books and tapes. The large dining room is decorated with cream wainscoting and wallpaper that matches the upholstery of the living room sofa. Simple guest rooms follow animal themes, with stenciled animals on room doors and stuffed ones inside. They feature country-print wallpapers with color-coordinated linens and comforters on the beds. A detached three-room cottage with full kitchen can sleep up to five. Breakfast is served in the dining room or, in nice weather, beside the pool. Overall, the place has something of a youth hostel atmosphere and could use some polish.

Address: *345 Blair Ave., Friday Harbor, WA 98250, tel. 360/378–5907, fax 360/378–6940.*
Accommodations: *1 double room with bath, 2 doubles with half-bath share 1 full bath, 4 doubles share 1 bath, 1 housekeeping cottage.*
Amenities: *Outdoor pool, hot tub.*
Rates: *$75–$125; full breakfast. AE, D, MC, V.*
Restrictions: *No smoking indoors, no pets in main building.*

Deer Harbor Inn

Fifteen minutes west of the Orcas Island ferry landing, the Deer Harbor Inn has two parts. The Old Norton Inn—now the restaurant—overlooks Deer Harbor; this was the original hotel. Up a hill is a two-story log cabin built in 1988, and this is the inn proper. Hosts Craig and Pam Carpenter live on the property, but their three children and Craig's post as restaurant chef keep them too busy to spend much time chatting with guests.

The new log cabin has high ceilings and light, simple country-style furnishings. Both levels have decks with views of the water off the common sitting rooms, which feature peeled-log sofas, chairs, and tables, and windows swathed in white muslin tieback curtains. The eight guest rooms are furnished with peeled-log beds with white down comforters, and peeled-log chairs and tables; four have views of the water. A Continental breakfast is delivered to the rooms in picnic baskets. The restaurant, with lace-covered tables, specializes in fresh seafood and pasta dishes; during the summer it offers deck dining at umbrella tables with splendid views of the harbor.

Address: *Deer Harbor Rd., Box 142, Deer Harbor, WA 98243, tel. 360/376–4110.*
Accommodations: *8 double rooms with baths.*
Amenities: *Restaurant.*
Rates: *$89; Continental breakfast. AE, MC, V.*
Restrictions: *No smoking indoors, no pets.*

The Duffy House

The Duffy House sits above Griffin Bay on the southeast side of San Juan Island, 2 miles south of Friday Harbor, in an isolated spot surrounded by 5 acres of orchards, flowering gardens, groomed lawn, and secluded beach, with unobstructed views of the Olympic Mountains. Owners Mary and Arthur Miller fell in love with San Juan Island when traveling through the region on their boat, and ended up buying the B&B in 1992 so that they could stay.

The Tudor-style house has a solid, Old World feel; it has the original leaded-glass windows, cove ceilings, hardwood floors, Oriental carpets, and mahogany woodwork. The Panorama Room upstairs is romantic, with lace curtains, a floral spread and pillows on the cherry wood queen-size bed, and an exceptional view of Griffin Bay and the mountains beyond. Mary serves a three-course breakfast each morning that features fruits and juices, freshly baked goods, and hot entrées.

Address: *760 Pear Point Rd., Friday Harbor, WA 98250, tel. 360/378–5604.*
Accommodations: *5 double rooms share 2 baths.*
Amenities: *Wood burning stove in living room; private beach.*
Rates: *$75–$85; full breakfast. MC, V.*
Restrictions: *No smoking indoors, no pets; 2-night minimum on weekends July–Aug. and on holidays.*

Edenwild Inn

The imposing, gray, Victorian-style farmhouse surrounded by rose gardens in tiny Lopez Village is the Edenwild Inn. Although it looks restored, it's new; owner Sue Aran, an architectural designer, built the inn in 1990.

The entrance opens onto a long hallway with oak floors, handwoven rugs, and framed oils and watercolors by Northwest artists. The muted palette—whitewashed floors, walls of grayed rose and lilac, white woodwork—lends the common areas sophistication. Each of the guest rooms have a different color scheme and individualized furnishings, with custom-made bed frames and wainscoting, botanical prints, large sprays of dried flowers and grapes (and, in season, fresh flowers), Scottish lace curtains, and leaded-glass windows. Four rooms have views of Fisherman's Bay and the San Juan Channel. The blue-gray Honeymoon Suite, overlooking the water, has a fireplace flanked by antique fireplace chairs.

Dinner (open to the public) is available six nights a week in the dining room; during the summer there is a sunny patio for alfresco meals.

Address: *Box 271, Lopez Island, WA 98261, tel. 360/468–3238.*
Accommodations: *8 double rooms with baths.*
Amenities: *Afternoon aperitif; dinner available; bicycle rentals; ferry, seaplane, and airport pickup.*
Rates: *$85–$140; full breakfast. MC, V.*
Restrictions: *No smoking indoors, no pets; 2-night minimum on holiday weekends.*

Hillside House

When Dick and Cathy Robinson left San Luis Obispo, California, they spent three years traveling in their 46-foot boat before purchasing Hillside House, which stands—yes—on a hillside a half mile from downtown Friday Harbor. Cathy loves island life, but she jokes that the population of retired professionals—attorneys, doctors, architects—are "just as competitive about the zucchini they grow for the county fair as they used to be about their careers."

The open living and dining room areas give onto a spacious and spectacularly scenic deck above the garden. The living room has a large brick fireplace, an Arts and Crafts coffee table, and overstuffed chairs. The seven sophisticated, comfortable guest rooms are furnished with king- and queen-size beds (except for one room with twins), oak chests, and window seats. In the Charlotte's Web Room there's a quilted chintz bedspread with pink cabbage roses on an ivory background, sea-green carpet, and views of the birds in the two-story flight aviary just outside.

Address: *365 Carter Ave., Friday Harbor, WA 98250, tel. 360/378–4730 or 800/232–4730.*
Accommodations: *7 double rooms with baths.*
Amenities: *Robes; aviary.*
Rates: *$65–$155; full breakfast. AE, D, MC, V.*
Restrictions: *No smoking indoors, no pets.*

Kangaroo House

Nestled on 2 acres of lawn and gardens less than a mile from the Orcas Island village of Eastsound is the 1907 Craftsman-style home known as Kangaroo House. The innkeepers are Mike and Jan Russillo; Jan has been an executive, a teacher, and the director of a crisis line, and Mike, who can be a bit gruff, was a career army officer—a combination that equips them to handle just about anything.

There's a solid, old feel to the dark hardwood floors and the Oriental rugs, but there's no need to be anxious about knocking over precious antiques. The living room is spacious, with a sitting area in front of a large stone fireplace, beamed ceilings, lace curtains, settees, and wing chairs. The Louisa Room—red, teal, and tan—has an old brass double bed and a small twin bed with a painted iron headboard, handmade quilts, and angled ceilings.

The Russillos serve a full breakfast on tables set with china, silver, and linen; they'll also pack coffee and muffins for guests who have to meet an early morning ferry.

Address: *5 N. Beach Rd., Box 334, Eastsound, WA 98245, tel. 360/376–2175.*
Accommodations: *1 double room with bath, 3 doubles share 1½ baths, 1 suite.*
Amenities: *Guest refrigerator, game room.*
Rates: *$70–$110; full breakfast. MC, V.*
Restrictions: *No smoking indoors, no pets.*

MacKaye Harbor Inn

In 1978 Mike Bergstrom retired from professional golfing so that he could be with his wife, Robin, and their young children. In 1985, inspired by family and friends who enjoyed visiting them, the Bergstroms bought a 1920s wood-frame Victorian-style sea captain's house along a quarter-mile of beach at the south end of Lopez Island, across the road from MacKaye Harbor.

The sitting room has white wicker furnishings as well as a light blue sofa and love seat in front of a brass-and-glass-doored fireplace, and a stained-glass window with roses designed by Robin. This room looks west out to the harbor, as do three of the guest rooms. One large room boasts a fireplace, a private deck, and a golden oak bedroom set from Italy.

The Bergstroms have turned management of the inn over to Sharon and Brooks Broberg, who, in addition to cleaning and maintaining the inn, serve fresh-baked pastries in the afternoon, chocolate truffles in the evening, and a hearty breakfast each morning.

Address: *Rte. 1, Box 1940, Lopez Island, WA 98261, tel. 360/468–2253, fax 360/468–9555.*
Accommodations: *2 double rooms with baths, 3 doubles share 2½ baths.*
Amenities: *Kayak tours and rental, mountain bikes.*
Rates: *$69–$130; full breakfast. MC, V.*
Restrictions: *No smoking indoors, no pets; 2-night minimum July–Sept.*

Mariella Inn & Cottages

Mariella is the only inn right on the waterfront on San Juan Island. This stately 1902 Victorian has cabins in varying styles and sizes along the waterline, and equipment for outdoor activities. It was a resort from 1926 through World War II, after which it became a private residence; it reverted to seaside retreat status in 1992.

Of the 11 rooms in the main house, Sweet Briar, in the southeast corner, is a favorite: Two walls of lace-covered windows look out on the garden and harbor, allowing sunshine to stream in on forest-green carpet, wicker and dark-wood trimmed furniture, rose print wallpapered walls, and coordinating down-filled duvet on the tall oak bed. The room has a private bath, as do the other rooms downstairs, while

most of the upstairs rooms share baths. Several of the cottages have kitchenettes and private decks that jut out over the water.

Address: *630 Turn Point Rd., Friday Harbor, WA 98250, tel. 360/378–6868, fax 360/378–6822.*
Accommodations: *4 double rooms with bath, 7 doubles share 2 baths, 6 1-, 2-, and 3-bedroom housekeeping cottages, 1 studio cottage with detached bath.*
Amenities: *Hot tub; volleyball court, boat dock, private beach, fishing pond, bike and kayak rentals.*
Rates: *$100–$160, cottages $100–$225; full breakfast for inn guests, Continental breakfast in cottages. MC, V.*
Restrictions: *No smoking, no pets; 2-night minimum on weekends July–Aug. and on holidays.*

The Moon and Sixpence

This B&B named after the Somerset Maugham novel was built as a dairy farmer's home in 1900. The restored Victorian farmhouse has an open, airy, arty feel, with stained-glass windows, white woodwork, glossy floors of local fir, a cozy parlor with a wood-burning stove, a pair of original Hepplewhite chairs, and a Pembroke table; and there's a library that contains an old upright piano. The restored water tower has been turned into a suite with a sitting loft at the top. Decorated in Early American blue-gray with red accents, it has a stenciled floor, a bed with a hand-stitched wedding-ring quilt, and a copy of *The Moon and Sixpence* on a bedside table.

Today the serenely rural 15-acre farm, 3 miles outside Friday Harbor, belongs to Charles and Evelyn Tuller. Ev's Pennsylvania Dutch background comes to the fore in such touches as bright handwoven blankets, her mother's needlepoint upholstery and rugs, and fabrics that Ev weaves herself.

Address: *3021 Beaverton Valley Rd., Friday Harbor, WA 98250, tel. 360/378–4138.*
Accommodations: *1 double room with bath, 2 suites.*
Amenities: *Guest refrigerator, lounge, game room.*
Rates: *$90, suites $105–$120; full breakfast. No credit cards.*
Restrictions: *No smoking indoors, no pets; 2-night minimum July–Aug. and on holiday weekends.*

Old Trout Inn

David and Cady Wood spent two years in Pakistan setting up a new cancer hospital before touring the West Coast in search of "the most beautiful spot in the world" to start a B&B. Having owned an inn in Maine years earlier, they come well prepared and are polished hosts, going that extra step (e.g., breakfast served in guest's choice of location).

Walls of burgundy, gray, and white serve as a palate for subtle artwork hung throughout this large, three-story contemporary. The most stunning features of this inn, situated less than 3 miles inland from the Orcas Island ferry, are the soaring windows and broad decks that look out over an idyllic 2½-acre pond surrounded by cattails and trees. Pretty guest rooms tend to stand empty because guests are frequently outside on the decks listening to the soothing trickle of a stone waterfall; watching the ducks, hummingbirds, cranes, and woodpeckers; paddling the little rowboat on the pond; hiking the nature trail to a gazebo across the pond; or soaking in the waterside hot tub on the lower deck.

Address: *Horseshoe Hwy., Rte. 1, Box 45A, Eastsound, WA 98245, tel. 360/376–4037.*
Accommodations: *2 double rooms share a bath, 2 suites, 1 housekeeping suite.*
Amenities: *Sauna in housekeeping suite, fireplace in 2 suites; hot tub, robes, ferry pickup, binoculars, bikes, nature trail, boat charters.*
Rates: *$80, suites $105–$135; full breakfast. No credit cards.*
Restrictions: *No smoking, no pets.*

Olympic Lights

In 1985 Lea and Christian Andrade took a vacation from the San Francisco Bay area and fell in love with San Juan Island—so much so that they returned a month later and discovered this 1895 farmhouse, 5½ miles south of the Friday Harbor ferry landing.

While many inns are hideaways, Olympic Lights stands out in a wind-blown field with few trees to block the view of Puget Sound and the Olympic Mountains. Guests have the run of the entire house—the hosts live in a small building behind the main house. Decorated almost exclusively in white (save for a few pale pastels), with no curtains except for white valances, the house feels expansive and open to both sunlight and starlight. The parlor has white wicker furniture with pale peach cushions; breakfast is served (on Lea's aunt's ivory, green, and pink rose-patterned china) either there or in the kitchen. Guest rooms feature brass reading lamps, wicker chairs and tables, and fluffy duvets and pillows.

Address: *4531-A Cattle Point Rd., Friday Harbor, WA 98250, tel. 360/378–3186, fax 360/378–2097.*
Accommodations: *1 double room with bath, 4 doubles share 2 baths.*
Amenities: *Croquet, boccie, horseshoes.*
Rates: *$70–$105; full breakfast. No credit cards.*
Restrictions: *No smoking on property, no pets; 2-night minimum on holiday weekends.*

Sand Dollar Inn

Follow Horseshoe Highway through Eastsound to the quiet side of Orcas Island, and you'll come to the tranquil Sand Dollar Inn. Set on an incline across the road from Buck Bay, this white-trimmed, gray farmhouse built in 1926 enjoys fine views of the San Juan Channel, Lopez Island, and the Olympic Mountains in the distance.

Opened in 1989 by Ric and Ann Sanchez, formerly of Carmel, California, the inn is striking but homey; the many Oriental antiques reflect the time Ann spent teaching English in Japan. All the guest rooms feature woodblock prints, Japanese tansu chests, and queen-size beds; the three second-floor rooms boast terrific ocean views. There are also great vistas from the sunny dining area, where such morning specialties as baked salmon on an English muffin topped with white cream sauce help you greet the day.

Down the road a bit farther is Doe Bay, a jumping-off point for kayak tours of the San Juan waterway and home to the soothing mineral baths and sauna of Doe Bay Village Resort.

Address: *Horseshoe Hwy., Box 152, Olga, WA 98279, tel. 360/376–5696.*
Accommodations: *4 double rooms with baths.*
Amenities: *Guest refrigerator and phone; 1 guest room has a balcony.*
Rates: *$88–$115; full breakfast. AE, MC, V.*
Restrictions: *No smoking on property, no pets.*

San Juan Inn

Annette and Skip Metzger began looking for an inn of their own in 1989; after a nationwide search for the right place at the right price, they settled on the San Juan Inn. Facing Friday Harbor's main street, the 1873 Victorian that once housed the town's wireless station stands a block uphill from the ferry landing.

A rose garden behind the building offers a secluded spot for a picnic or a glass of wine. Inside, the inn is clean and comfortable but not luxurious. The tiny lobby and stairway have stained-wood paneling. An upstairs sitting room features a rose Queen Anne parlor group, a wood-burning stove, a Mission oak rocker, and a harbor view.

The 10 guest rooms, all upstairs, are fitted with brass, wicker, or painted iron bedsteads. The San Juan Room has wicker chairs, flowered comforter, iron bedstead, washstand, and soft pink walls hung with framed needlework samplers. The Metzgers serve a Continental breakfast on bone china in the second-floor parlor, which, sadly, no longer has a view of the harbor because of a neighboring building that recently went up.

Address: *50 Spring St., Box 776, Friday Harbor, WA 98250, tel. 360/378–2070 or 800/742–8210, fax 360/378–6437.*
Accommodations: *4 double rooms with baths, 6 doubles share 3 baths.*
Rates: *$75–$95; Continental breakfast. AE, D, MC, V.*
Restrictions: *No smoking indoors, no large pets; closed Dec. 25–29.*

Spring Bay Inn

At the end of the trek to Spring Bay Inn, 20 miles (the last mile on a potholed dirt road) from the Orcas ferry landing, guests are rewarded by seclusion in an incredible waterfront setting. While the contemporary cedar inn, nestled on 57 acres of largely undisturbed forestland, is lovely in and of itself, its innkeepers, Carl Burger and Sandy Playa, make this place special. These retired park rangers have managed to keep their fingers in the environmental pie by purchasing the land bordering Obstruction Pass Saltwater Park to protect it from subdivision and development. They offer guests nature tours, either by kayak or on foot, as part of their visits, to impart a better understanding of the uniqueness of the San Juans' flora and fauna.

Airy, sunny guest rooms have fireplaces, claw-foot tubs, fresh flowers, and windows overlooking Spring Bay; two larger corner rooms also have private balconies and cozy feather mattresses. Following the morning nature outing, a hearty brunch is served in a room that is flanked by twin stone fireplaces and has a fir floor and 13-foot ceiling with exposed beams.

Address: *Obstruction Pass Park Rd., Box 97, Olga, WA 98279, tel. 360/376–5531, fax 360/376–2193.*
Accommodations: *4 double rooms with baths.*
Amenities: *Hot tubs, nature trails, kayak and hiking tours, binoculars, barbecue.*
Rates: *$155–$175; full breakfast and evening refreshments. MC, V.*
Restrictions: *No smoking, no pets.*

States Inn

It was a schoolhouse in the early 1900s and for a time it served as a dance hall, but now the States Inn—restored and remodeled in 1989—is a working equestrian center in addition to being a bed-and-breakfast; inn guests get discounts on guided horseback tours.

Nestled in a tranquil valley not far from British Camp and Roche Harbor, the house retains its original maple floor in the living room and a tall, stone fireplace; otherwise it's thoroughly modern, with casual, ranch-style decor and contemporary American furnishings. Each of the nine guest rooms features decorative touches reminiscent of the state for which it's named—colorful Mexican blankets in the New Mexico Room, for example, and seashells on the fireplace mantel in the Rhode Island Room. The hearty breakfasts served by charming innkeepers Kip and Linda Taylor might include no-fat waffles or French toast Foster (covered in sautéed bananas).

Address: *2039 W. Valley Rd., Friday Harbor, WA 98250, tel. 360/378–6240, fax 360/378–6241.*
Accommodations: *7 double rooms with baths, 2 doubles share 1 bath.*
Amenities: *Guest phone, bike storage rooms; horseback riding available, ferry and airport pickup/drop off.*
Rates: *$80–$110; full breakfast. MC, V.*
Restrictions: *No smoking indoors, no pets; 2-night minimum on holiday weekends.*

Wharfside Bed & Breakfast

Board the *Jacquelyn*, a 60-foot motor-sailer anchored near the Friday Harbor ferry landing, and you'll find yourself on the Wharfside, the town's only floating bed-and-breakfast. Clyde Rice and his wife, Bette, decided to combine their love of boating and their flair for hospitality in 1984, when they opened the *Jacquelyn* as a B&B.

The main salon has two sofas and a skylight, a fireplace, and lots of polished wood and brass. The head has a Japanese-style tile soaking tub as well as a shower. The two guest rooms stand at opposite ends of the boat: the aft stateroom, a romantic low-beamed captain's cabin with a queen-size bed, a small settee, and a half-bath; and the forward stateroom, furnished with a double bed and two bunks.

Bette serves a four-course, all-you-can-eat breakfast. She also provides children with nets and cans for gathering shrimp (and jellyfish and other treasures) from the harbor.

Address: *K-Dock, Slip 13, Port of Friday Harbor Marina, Box 1212, Friday Harbor, WA 98250, tel. 360/378–5661.*
Accommodations: *1 double room and 1 triple share 1 bath.*
Amenities: *Robes; rowboat.*
Rates: *$80–$85; full breakfast. MC, V.*
Restrictions: *No smoking inside, 2-night minimum in summer.*

Whatcom and Skagit Counties
Including Anacortes, Bellingham, and La Conner

About 90 minutes north of Seattle on the way to Vancouver, British Columbia, I–5 passes through Skagit and Whatcom counties, where gently rolling dairy farmland is juxtaposed with flat rectangles of brilliant color—fields of commercially grown daffodils and tulips that are a major attraction for gardeners, photographers, and city dwellers in search of a pleasant weekend drive. To the east in these two northernmost counties in coastal Washington, low foothills often wrapped in mist nestle against the snowcapped mountains of the Cascade range.

Far from being exclusively agrarian, however, the three major communities in Whatcom and Skagit counties are very much associated with the sea. La Conner, at the mouth of the Skagit River, is a fishing village with a decidedly artsy accent, a legacy of the 1940s, when modernist painters Morris Graves and Mark Tobey settled there. Ferries ply the waters of Anacortes, a fishing and logging town on Fidalgo Island that serves as the gateway to the San Juan Islands, while Bellingham, a center of fishing and lumber activity and the southern terminus of the Alaska Marine Highway System, is the site of Western Washington University, a campus that offers splendid views of Puget Sound. Nowhere are the ocean views more dramatic than from Chuckanut Drive (Highway 11), a dramatic 23-mile stretch between Bellingham and Bow along Chuckanut Bay.

Today in this pastoral area, artists and college professors coexist with farmers and fishermen. A number of the residents are descendants of the native tribes that have lived here for the past 12,000 years or offspring of relative newcomers: the Spanish, who arrived in 1774, and the English, who followed four years later.

Places to Go, Sights to See

Bellingham Waterfront. Several spots make for good dock walking, fishing, lounging, and picnicking. *Squalicum Harbor Marina* (Roeder Ave. and Coho Way, tel. 360/676–2542), the second-largest marina on Puget Sound, is home to more than 1,700 commercial and pleasure boats. An aquarium in the adjacent Harbor Center shopping mall contains examples of many of the local sea creatures; children will especially enjoy the "touch tank." *Boulevard Park* (S. State St. and Bayview Dr., tel. 360/676–6985), midway between downtown and Old Fairhaven, is a 14-acre waterfront park with a half mile of shoreline. With views of both the San Juan Islands and the Cascades, it's a logical choice for picnickers. *Marine Park* (at the foot of Harris St. in Old Fairhaven) is small, but it is popular for crabbing and watching sunsets.

Birch Bay State Park (5105 Helwig Rd., Blaine, tel. 360/371–2800). Most of this 200-acre park, 10 miles from the Canadian border, is heavily wooded, but the shore and a few of the 167 available campsites offer impressive views of the San Juan Islands. The clamming and crabbing here are excellent, and opportunities for fishing, swimming, and hiking along interpretive trails are plentiful. Campsites are open year-round but can be reserved only from Memorial Day to Labor Day.

Chuckanut Drive (Hwy. 11). You're advised to take this 23-mile drive along Chuckanut Bay heading south out of Bellingham; that way you'll have the steep and densely wooded Chuckanut Mountain on your left, with stunning views of Puget Sound and the San Juan Islands relatively unobstructed. The drive begins along Fairhaven Park in Old Fairhaven and joins I–5 in the flat farmlands near Bow in Skagit County. The full loop can be made within a few hours. Several good restaurants are toward the southern end of the drive, so you may want to plan your jaunt around lunch or dinner (*see* Restaurants, *below*). In addition to a number of lookout points, there are several other worthwhile stops along the way: *Larrabee State Park* (245 Chuckanut Dr., tel. 360/676–2093), with nearly 1,900 acres of forest and park and 3,600 feet of shoreline; the 6-mile-long *Interurban Trail*, a former train track along the water used for cycling, walking, jogging, and horseback riding; and the *Taylor United/Samish Shellfish Farm* (188 Chuckanut Dr., Bow, tel. 360/766–6002), where visitors, by appointment, can watch oysters being harvested, sorted, shucked, and packed. A store on the premises sells oysters, scallops, crabs, and mussels in season. The trailhead begins in the north near 24th Street and Old Fairhaven Parkway and in the south near Larrabee State Park.

Ferndale Parks. *Hovander Homestead Park* (5299 Nielsen Rd., Ferndale, tel. 360/384–3444) is a "farm park" complete with a Victorian-era farmhouse, farm animals, vegetable gardens, old farm equipment, a blacksmith's shop, and walking trails. *Pioneer Park* (1st and Cherry Sts., Ferndale, tel. 360/384–6461) features a handful of restored log buildings from the 1870s, including a granary, Whatcom County's first church, a hotel, and several houses. *Lake Terrell Wildlife Preserve* (5975 Lake Terrell Rd., Ferndale, tel. 360/384–4723) is an 11,000-acre spread that allows visitors to observe a wide variety of waterfowl. Hunting is permitted in season (ducks and pheasants are most prevalent), and fishing on the lake, year-round, yields trout, catfish, bass, and perch. Nearby is *Tennant Lake Natural History Interpretive Center* (5236 Nielsen Rd., Ferndale, tel. 360/384–3444), featuring an early homestead, nature walks around the lake, and an observation tower from which the 200 acres of marshy habitat, bald eagles, muskrats, otters, and other wildlife can be seen. The rich perfumes emanating from the fragrance garden there are intended for the seeing-impaired, but, naturally, sighted visitors enjoy them as well. Special events include crafts fairs and evening walks with a modern-day Henry David Thoreau in 19th-century costume.

Gaches Mansion (602 S. Second St., La Conner, tel. 360/466–4288). Ever since Morris Graves, Mark Tobey, Kenneth Callahan, and other pioneering American modernist painters settled in La Conner during the 1940s, the town has been an artists' haven. Aside from sampling the local talent at one of the village's many galleries, visitors can see the works of area artists at the Valley Museum of Northwest Art, housed on the second floor of this restored Victorian Tudor mansion. The first and third floors are especially popular because visitors are encouraged to touch and sit on the period furniture that is on display. The turret of the house offers an excellent view of La Conner.

Gardens of Art (2900 Sylvan St., Bellingham, tel. 360/671–1069). Visitors can wander through this 2½-acre garden in Bellingham that features the works of artists from the Northwest.

Maritime Heritage Center (1600 C St., Bellingham, tel. 360/676–6806). This urban park is a tribute to Bellingham's fishing industry and heritage. On self-guided tours, visitors learn about hatcheries and the life cycles of salmon, watch salmon spawn, see how rearing tanks work, watch mature salmon swim up the fish ladders, and actually fish for salmon and trout.

Padilla Bay (1043 Bay View-Edison Rd., Bay View, tel. 360/428–1558). This estuary features an interpretive center that focuses on the area's natural history, with exhibits and saltwater aquariums, a mile-long nature trail, beachwalk, a pair of resident bald eagles, and a variety of waterfowl and sea life.

Skagit Valley Tulip Festival (Box 1007, Mount Vernon, WA 98273, tel. 360/428–8547 or 800/4–TULIPS). Held during the first three weeks of April in Mount Vernon, Burlington, Anacortes, and La Conner, the festival centers around more than 1,500 acres of spring flowers—daffodils, irises, and, of course, tulips—with tours of the blossoming fields and bulb sales. Festivities include footraces, an art show featuring local talent, a community fair, horse-drawn wagon rides, a salmon barbecue, sailboat regatta, concerts, dance performances, an antiques show, a food fair, petting zoo, and sky-diving and kite-flying demonstrations.

Western Washington University (516 High St., Bellingham, tel. 360/650-3000) overlooks downtown Bellingham and Bellingham Bay. As you drive through the campus to take in the panorama, you'll be treated to a fine collection of outdoor sculpture, including works by Mark DiSuvero, Isamu Noguchi, Richard Serra, and George Rickey.

Whatcom County Museum of History and Art (121 Prospect St., Bellingham, tel. 360/676–6981). Housed in a large redbrick Victorian building in downtown Bellingham, the museum concentrates on the early coal and lumber industries, the history and culture of Native American tribes that lived in the area, and the habitat and characteristics of local waterfowl. The museum also hosts traveling exhibitions.

Restaurants

At **Boomers Landing** (tel. 360/293–5108) in Anacortes, you can dine on some of the town's best seafood while watching the sun set over Guemes Channel. The well-regarded French cuisine at **La Petite** (tel. 360/293–4644) is served in a romantic setting. If you enjoy the bustle of a marina, try Anacortes's **Slocum's** (tel. 360/293–0644), which offers fresh salmon, seafood, prime rib, and pasta. Among Bellingham's dining spots, seek out **Il Fiasco** (tel. 360/676–9136), which, despite its name, serves good Italian fare, and **La Belle Rose** (tel. 360/647–0833), a country French restaurant that specializes in seafood. The **Oyster Creek Inn** (tel. 360/766–6179), in Bow, overlooks a rushing creek on Chuckanut Drive and specializes in—what else?—oysters. The **Black Swan** (tel. 360/466–3040), in La Conner, features Mediterranean cooking. Also in La Conner, **Palmer's,** in the La Conner Country Inn (tel. 360/446–4261), prepares pasta and seafood in Pacific Northwest style.

Tourist Information

Anacortes Chamber of Commerce (819 Commercial Ave., Suite G, Anacortes, WA 98221, tel. 360/293–7911); **La Conner Chamber of Commerce** (109 S. 1st St., Box 1610, La Conner, WA 98257, tel. 360/466–4778); **Mount Vernon Chamber of Commerce** (200 E. College Way, Box 1007, Mount Vernon, WA 98273, tel. 360/428–8547); **Whatcom County Visitor & Convention Bureau** (904 Potter, Bellingham, WA 98826, tel. 360/671–3990).

Reservation Services

Anacortes Bed and Breakfasts (tel. 360/293–5773, phone rotates among members); **Bed & Breakfast Service** (Box 5025, Bellingham, WA 98227, tel. 360/733–8642); **Fidalgo Island Bed & Breakfast Guild** (1312 8th St., Anacortes, WA 98221, tel. 360/293–5773); **Pacific Bed & Breakfast Agency** (701 N.W. 60th St., Seattle, WA 98107, tel. 206/784–0539); **Washington State Bed & Breakfast Guild** (2442 N.W. Market St., Box 355-FD, Seattle, WA 98107, tel. 800/647–2918); **Whatcom County Bed & Breakfast Guild** (tel. 360/676–4560, phone rotates among members).

The Channel House

Midway between downtown Anacortes and the ferry terminal is the Channel House, a 1902 shingled Craftsman bungalow with awe-inspiring views of Guemes Channel and the ferry landing that can be seen from most rooms. Innkeepers Dennis and Patricia McIntyre, who formerly owned a restaurant, dreamed of acquiring a smaller business when their daughter went off to college, but when she turned 15, they thought, "Why wait?" An ad in the *Los Angeles Times* turned up the Channel House.

The dining room, certainly the most spectacular room in the house, features lush ferns and other potted plants that stand against dark blue and peach floral print wallpaper, white painted wainscoting, and the original glazed terra-cotta tile floor with cobalt-blue borders. A window with the original stained glass depicts lily pads in shades of green and pink. As guests dine on the house specialty—French toast stuffed with cream cheese, pineapple, and pecans—they can watch the ferries plying Rosario Strait.

Ten steps up are the living room, with exposed beams and a 10-foot-high ceiling, and a cozy study. Both rooms display porcelain dolls made by Dennis's mother from antique molds, complete with hand-painted features and hand-sewn costumes.

Each guest room has its own style, but all are spacious and light, with high ceilings, hardwood floors, and Oriental rugs. Grandma's Room is furnished with an antique brass bed, a log-cabin-style quilt, and a turn-of-the-century Eastlake-type oak dresser; children's boaters hang on the walls. The more formal Canopy Room has a canopy bed covered with the same antique lace that dresses the window and an early-19th-century fainting couch upholstered in cream-colored damask. The walls are covered with a cream and green striped paper with a floral border. In a separate cottage, the Victorian Rose Suite seems a perfect spot for reverie; its window seat is crowded with soft throw pillows, and the fireplace has cream tiles with hand-painted pink roses that are echoed in the pale-pink walls and ceiling border of roses against a black background.

Address: *2902 Oakes Ave., Anacortes, WA 98221, tel. 360/293–9382 or 800/238–4353.*
Accommodations: *4 double rooms with baths, 2 double rooms with baths in cottage.*
Amenities: *Whirlpool baths and fireplaces in cottage rooms; outdoor hot tub.*
Rates: *$69–$95; full breakfast. D, MC, V.*
Restrictions: *No smoking indoors, no pets.*

La Conner Channel Lodge

One of only a handful of water-side inns in the Puget Sound area is this shingled, Northwest contemporary structure with rose-entwined lattice fences. It is ideally located on Main Street, a short walk from the many restaurants and boutiques lining the waterfront.

Twig furniture, bark bowls, hand-woven baskets, and dried and fresh flower arrangements impart a lodge-like feeling to the lobby lounge. A towering stone fireplace and a cozy adjacent library help create a relaxed, homey atmosphere. Weekend evenings, entertainers tickle the ivories of the shiny grand piano between the lounge and library. Fir doors just behind the piano open onto a terraced stone deck leading down to the pier. There is a Native American reservation opposite the hotel; guests occasionally hear the songs and drums of a tribal meeting floating across the narrow waterway.

In the guest chambers, fish prints on the walls and shell-motif pillow shams and duvets reflect the inn's waterfront location. There are loads of extras—gas fireplaces; cushioned lounge chairs; coffeemakers; minifridges and cable TVs discreetly hidden in cabinets; chocolate truffles on the bedside table; soft terry robes; and roomy, slate-tiled bathrooms with two-person Jacuzzi tubs. Each of the rooms has a deck or balcony; those on the second and third floors offer the best views of the channel. The Captain's Suite, perfect for

families, has a small second bedroom with twin beds, porthole windows, and a nautical door. Couples seeking romance and privacy might opt for the gatehouse with a Jacuzzi in the bedroom (but no view of the channel).

A Continental breakfast buffet with trays of fruit, fresh baked goods, and bowls of yogurt and granola is served in the small second-floor dining room. Cozy tables are set up near the corner fireplace and on the open balcony across the hallway, which overlooks the lounge below and the Swinomish Channel just outside. If you prefer, the congenial staff will deliver breakfast to your room.

Address: *205 N. 1st St., Box 573, La Conner, WA 98257, tel. 360/466–3101, fax 360/466–1525.*
Accommodations: *29 double rooms with baths, 12 suites.*
Amenities: *Cable TV, phone, clock radio, coffeemaker, refrigerator, and fireplace in all rooms, double Jacuzzis in 18 rooms; moorage and charter boats available.*
Rates: *$132–$160, suites $170–$199; Continental breakfast, afternoon refreshments. AE, DC, MC, V.*
Restrictions: *No smoking indoors, no pets.*

Majestic Hotel

Many of the guests who use the Majestic Hotel merely as a stopover on the way to the nearby San Juan Islands end up wishing they could linger. Dominating the historical district of Anacortes, the Majestic is one of the Northwest's premier small hotels.

Standing in the two-story-high lobby filled with 19th-century English leather sofas and wing chairs, an elegant brass chandelier, a white marble mantelpiece flanked by engaged columns, and copious flower arrangements, it's difficult to believe that this space was part of a meat market until 1954. Happily, Jeff and Virginia Wetmore, restaurant and inn developers from northern California, recognized this diamond in the rough, which was built in 1889. Stripping away everything except the original framework, they opened the hotel in 1990 after six years of restoration. Two years later they added a charming English garden, an oasis of greenery and flowers where guests can relax over a cup of coffee or play with their children.

The Wetmores take particular pride in the Rose & Crown Pub behind the lobby, where guests can enjoy light meals and draft beers from local microbreweries amid 200-year-old English mahogany wainscoting, a backbar from a Victorian ice-cream parlor, and beveled- and stained-glass doors from a London pub. More substantial fare is served in Janot's Bistro, where cuisine such as Dungeness crab cake on seasonal greens with goat cheese vinaigrette and Northwest bouillabaisse in a saffron broth features the freshest ingredients available in the area.

Each of the hotel's 23 guest rooms is individually decorated and furnished with antiques from around the world, collected by the Wetmores. The Scottish Highland Room sports fishing rods, baskets, and old shotguns mounted on the walls, and there is a Scottish military chest from the 1880s. In the Asian Room the walls have been marbleized, and Japanese, Korean, and Chinese furniture and art are featured. An oak-paneled cupola affords a 360-degree view of Puget Sound, the marina, the San Juan Islands, and the Cascade and Olympic mountains.

Address: *419 Commercial Ave., Anacortes, WA 98221, tel. 360/293–3355, fax 360/293–5214.*
Accommodations: *23 double rooms with baths.*
Amenities: *Cable TV, phone, and coffeemaker in rooms; wet bar, refrigerator, VCR, and soaking tub in some rooms; restaurant and pub, 2 meeting rooms.*
Rates: *$89–$177; Continental breakfast. AE, D, MC, V.*
Restrictions: *Smoking on second floor only, no pets.*

Albatross

Y ou'll enjoy the warm hospitality and homey comforts of this 1927 Cape Cod–style inn. It has a wide deck overlooking the harbor at Flounder Bay and is painted—what else?—Cape Cod blue with white trim. Just a mile from the ferry terminal for the San Juans and Vancouver Island, it's a good base for exploring the islands.

The Scarlett O'Hara Room, with a view of the marina through lace curtains, is named for its authentic plantation furnishings (including an 1860s Victorian half-tester bed covered with a pink silk-moiré comforter, Lincoln rocker, and cranberry glass lamp), while another favorite room, Monet's Garden, is named for its view of the colorful backyard garden.

Guests can guess that owners Ken and Barbie Arasim are avid collectors, from the treasure trove of vintage Barbie dolls (given their names, what else) on view in the dining room and the Native American art displayed in the hallway. Getting to and from the Albatross can easily be more than half the fun, thanks to the renovated 1930 Model A delivery truck the Arasims use to transport guests to the San Juan Islands ferry.

Address: *5708 Kingsway W, Anacortes, WA 98221, tel. 360/293–0677, or 800/484–9507 (code 5840).*
Accommodations: *4 double rooms with baths.*
Amenities: *Cable TV, VCR, guest phone, library; airport and ferry pickup on request.*
Rates: *$75–$85; full breakfast. MC, V.*
Restrictions: *No smoking indoors.*

Anderson Creek Lodge

D own a quiet country lane 13 miles east of Bellingham stands a gray-stained clapboard-and-glass lodge. Built in 1986 on 65 secluded acres, it's the perfect setting for a recreational retreat: Options include soccer, baseball, basketball, and volleyball, and wilderness trails for hiking or biking (bring your own).

Inside the attractive lodge, a massive stone fireplace in a sunken den and a video library in the TV lounge offer further possibilities for relaxation. Each of the six simple but comfortable guest rooms has a theme. Nautical San Juan, done in navy blue and stark white with images of ships on the walls, lamps, and above the fireplace mantel, is the largest room; Oriental Juan de Fuca, with a futon couch, kimono wall hanging, and paper umbrella lamp shade, is the smallest.

Address: *5602 Mission Rd., Bellingham, WA 98226, tel. 360/966–2126, fax 206/734–9284.*
Accommodations: *3 double rooms with baths, 3 doubles share 2 baths.*
Amenities: *Cable TV, VCR, tape library, guest phone, sports fields, wilderness trails.*
Rates: *$75–$125; full breakfast. AE, D, MC, V.*
Restrictions: *No smoking indoors, no pets; 2-night minimum on holiday weekends.*

Anderson House

A few miles south of the Canadian border, just off I–5 in Ferndale, Anderson House sits atop a hill just west of downtown. In 1986 Dave Anderson, a pilot and former ski salesman, and his wife, Kelly, a medical technician, bought and restored the American Foursquare house—one of Frank Lloyd Wright's earliest designs—built by the town's first butcher in 1897.

The foyer and living room feature the original fir trim. The guest rooms have been decorated imaginatively, with white-iron reproduction bedsteads featuring porcelain finials, Pilgrim-style trunks that double as luggage racks, crystal reading lamps, and some of the most comfortable mattresses in the Northwest.

Breakfast is served at a large oak table in the dining room overlooking the flower gardens. Kelly designed the crystal chandelier with Bavarian swans that hangs over the table in honor of the graceful trumpeter swans that winter in the area.

Address: *2140 Main St., Box 1547, Ferndale, WA 98248, tel. and fax 360/384–3450.*
Accommodations: *3 double rooms with baths, 1 suite.*
Amenities: *Complimentary sherry.*
Rates: *$49–$79; full breakfast. AE, MC, V.*
Restrictions: *No smoking indoors, no pets; 2-night minimum on holiday weekends.*

Downey House

It is difficult to believe that Jim and Kaye Frey got their 1904 two-story Victorian-style farmhouse "free for the moving" in 1965 from a farm called Downey Place. They moved the house to a pastoral site less than 4 miles from downtown La Conner; in the dining room there's a photograph of the house mounted on wooden beams to prove it.

The house is filled with objects associated with family and friends. The parlor boasts a pump organ from Jim's home state of Nebraska. Photos, antique furniture, and other heirlooms of the Freys' pioneering ancestors are also found in the public areas, intermixed with works by local artists.

Rooms are wallpapered in small floral patterns and feature photographs and antiques from Kaye's great-grandparents. The McCormick Room features bay windows, an old brass-and-iron bed, a Pilgrim-style family trunk, and a mannequin wearing Kaye's great-grandmother's wedding nightgown.

Address: *1880 Chilberg Rd., La Conner, WA 98257, tel. 360/466–3207.*
Accommodations: *3 double rooms with baths, 2 doubles share 1 bath.*
Amenities: *Outdoor hot tub.*
Rates: *$75–$95; full breakfast. MC, V.*
Restrictions: *No smoking indoors; 2-night minimum first 3 weekends in Apr.*

Hasty Pudding House

It wasn't long after banker Mike Hasty arranged for the financing of a bed-and-breakfast for a customer that he and his wife, Melinda, began to search for a B&B of their own. Sunshine streaming through wide windows onto the distinctive fir wainscoting and built-ins of the cheery 1913 Craftsman sold them on this home, and they set to work renovating and remodeling it.

The four charming guest rooms are appointed in walnut or oak antiques (primarily Eastlake and Victorian), Waverly wallpapers, and bed linens. Generous swaths of ivory lace and an elaborately carved 7½-foot-high burled walnut headboard from the 1850s make the Queen Anne's Lace Room the romantic choice. Each room has a private bath; two feature deep clawfoot tubs, perfect for a relaxing soak.

Mounds of Melinda's hand-stitched pillows fill the home's broad window seats, and an exquisite collection of antique china and silver graces the living and dining room corners. The Hastys' smoothies and pancakes with homemade toppings help start the day off right.

Address: *1312 8th St., Anacortes, WA 98221, tel. 360/293–5773 or 800/368–5588.*
Accommodations: *4 double rooms with bath.*
Amenities: *Cable TV.*
Rates: *$60–$85; full breakfast. AE, D, MC, V.*
Restrictions: *No smoking indoors, no pets.*

Heather House

Within easy walking distance of downtown La Conner, with views of farmland, Mt. Baker, and the Cascade Mountains, Heather House is a replica of a turn-of-the-century shingled Cape Cod house. Wayne Everton and his wife, Bev, bought the house in 1982.

The Evertons live next door, an arrangement that gives guests maximum privacy. The kitchen is always stocked with coffee and an array of sodas, juices, cheeses, and cookies. The Continental breakfast, equally generous and served by Wayne, always includes fresh-baked scones and an entrée such as poached apples with sour-cream sauce, peach melba, or strawberry cobbler. Comfort is the watchword at Heather House; you won't find anything out of the pages of

Architectural Digest, but you'll probably feel very much at home. Thumbing through the short-story collections and magazines, trying your hand at the resident games and puzzles, and taking in the views from the back porch are encouraged; the Evertons take pride in not having a television.

Address: *505 Maple Ave., La Conner, WA 98257, tel. 360/466–4675.*
Accommodations: *3 double rooms share 2 baths.*
Amenities: *Off-street parking, bicycles.*
Rates: *$50–$70; Continental breakfast. MC, V.*
Restrictions: *No smoking indoors, no pets.*

Heron Inn

Co-owner Jim Gibbons is heron crazy, and this Victorian-style inn five blocks from the La Conner waterfront is just brimming with them, from stained-glass windows of herons to the heron watercolors, prints, and etchings on every wall. Even the outside is painted a heron blue-gray.

Large windows with lace curtains and a high cove ceiling contribute to the light, airy feel of the lobby/parlor, where guests can relax on the Queen Anne–style camelback couch or in wing chairs in front of the fireplace.

Guest rooms, all carpeted and featuring a blue-and-rose color scheme, mix modern reproductions, such as wing chairs and beds with oak, walnut, and brass headboards, with antique armoires. All the suites have gas fireplaces.

When guests tire of antiquing on Morris Street, they can sit on the old-fashioned cast-iron and wood park benches on the deck or soak in the outdoor hot tub.

Address: *117 Maple Ave., La Conner, WA 98257, tel. 360/466–4626.*
Accommodations: *9 double rooms with baths, 3 suites.*
Amenities: *TV, clock radio, and phone in rooms, 1 suite with 2-person whirlpool bath; outdoor hot tub.*
Rates: *$65–$83, suites $95–$117; Continental breakfast. AE, MC, V.*
Restrictions: *No smoking indoors, no pets.*

Hotel Planter

In downtown La Conner, the Hotel Planter is a masonry building that was constructed in 1907 of solid concrete blocks made on location. The hotel, whose clientele consisted of lumber-mill and fish-cannery workers, merchants, and tourists from Seattle, was modern for its day, with indoor plumbing—one bathroom for 22 rooms—electricity, and a cement sidewalk. Later the writers, artists, and craftspeople responsible for La Conner's reputation as a cultural center moved in. Today guests can enjoy that artistic heritage by stepping right out onto First Street, lined with art galleries, bookstores, crafts shops, and restaurants.

Owners Donald and Cynthia Hoskins bought the building in 1986 and opened their street-level Earthenworks Gallery, then renovated the second-story hotel. Now creamy walls, custom-made Southern pine headboards and armoires, and wicker chairs lend a country-French atmosphere. To keep the feeling of the old hotel, the original doors, window moldings, railings, trim, and many of the old light fixtures were restored.

Address: *715 1st St., La Conner, WA 98257, tel. 360/466–4710 or 800/488–5409, fax 206/466–1320.*
Accommodations: *12 double rooms with baths.*
Amenities: *Phone, TV, and clock radio in rooms; hot tub.*
Rates: *$70–$110; no breakfast. AE, MC, V.*
Restrictions: *No smoking, no pets.*

Ridgeway House

This 1928 yellow brick Dutch Colonial occupies a prime location on Skagit Valley's famous Tulip Route. In keeping with its farmstead past, the interior of the home is country comfortable, with a mixture of Early American antiques, lace curtains, and dried flowers.

Louise and John Kelly, the hospitable owners, have named the five guest rooms after their daughters and granddaughters. Cynthia, one of the two rooms with its own bath, has a claw-foot tub at the foot of the floral spread-covered bed and a commode in a side alcove (without a door to set it off from the room). The room's soft-pink-and-teal color scheme enhances the antique furnishings, which include an Eastlake cherry dresser and night table.

Bright orange Gordo Cooper the Astrocat, the Kellys' pet feline, is very chummy and enjoys entertaining guests in the living room before the Kellys serve their generous, farm-style breakfast.

Address: *1292 McLean Rd., Box 475, La Conner, WA 98257, tel. 360/428–8068 or 800/428–8068.*
Accommodations: *1 double room with bath, 3 doubles share 2 baths.*
Amenities: *Games, cable TV in guest lounge.*
Rates: *$70–$90; full breakfast, evening refreshments. AE, D, MC, V.*
Restrictions: *No smoking indoors, no pets, 2-night minimum during first 2 weeks in Apr.*

Schnauzer Crossing

On a slope above Lake Whatcom sits this contemporary cedar home that dispels the notion that B&Bs in this area mean Victorian. The three guest rooms have a Japanese feel to them: A Japanese iris print covers the down comforters and futon furniture, and the cottage suite, completely redecorated in 1994, features rattan furniture and an Oriental motif.

The unusual name of this B&B derives from innkeeper Donna McAllister's pets, a lovable pair of well-behaved standard schnauzers. Guests pretty much have the run of the main-floor great room, whose glass doors reach up to a dramatic cathedral ceiling. Breakfast, accompanied by classical music, is a special occasion—with individual quiches, rhubarb crisps, and

blueberries and raspberries fresh from the garden (guests may pick their own). The pampering extends to fruit and cheese baskets, home-baked cookies, fresh flowers, terry robes, and "schnauzer" slippers in every room.

Address: *4421 Lakeway Dr., Bellingham, WA 98226, tel. 360/733–0055 or 360/734–2808, fax 360/734–2808.*
Accommodations: *1 double room with bath, 2 suites (wheelchair-accessible).*
Amenities: *Cable TV, VCR, whirlpool tub, and fireplace in suites; microwave and wet bar in 1 suite; outdoor hot tub.*
Rates: *$100, suites $150 and $175; full breakfast. MC, V.*
Restrictions: *No smoking indoors; 2-night minimum on weekends and holidays.*

White Swan Guest House

Tucked away along a narrow country road near the Skagit River is the White Swan Guest House. In 1898, a Scandinavian farmer, who ran the ferry across the river, built the Queen Anne clapboard farmhouse with a turret from which he could watch for passengers. A few years ago, New Yorker Peter Goldfarb fell in love with the house and used his training as an interior designer to make each room colorful and airy, yet warm. Public and guest rooms feature bright pastel walls, white trim, lace curtains, handmade quilts, fresh flowers, and a collection of needlework samplers.

Guest rooms in the main house have king- or queen-size beds with brass and iron headboards and hand-hooked rugs. The Pink Room features a little sitting area in the six-sided turret. The two-story cottage has more contemporary furnishings in pine and other light woods, wicker chairs, and Pendleton Indian blankets.

Guests enjoy munching on Peter's homemade chocolate chip cookies and wandering through the 3-acre grounds.

Address: *1388 Moore Rd., Mount Vernon, WA 98273, tel. 360/445–6805.*
Accommodations: *3 double rooms share 2 baths, 1 housekeeping cottage.*
Rates: *$75–$125; Continental breakfast. MC, V.*
Restrictions: *No pets in main house.*

Cascade Mountains

The Cascades form the backbone of western Washington State, stretching from the Oregon border to Canada. This massive mountain range, dominated by Mt. Rainier, actually begins in California continuation of the Sierra Nevada. The mountains offer spectacular scenery; good skiing in winter; and hiking, camping, fishing, river rafting, and wildlife viewing in summer.

Day trips and longer excursions from Seattle, just west of the range, take visitors into the heart of the Cascades to sample the scenery, a sprinkling of mountain villages—some originally gold- or coal-mining towns from the last century, some simple ski resorts—and a wide range of inns and lodges nestled in valleys or perched on crests.

A variety of mountain experiences are available within two hours of Seattle. Interstate 90, for example, leads east to Snoqualmie Pass, with both downhill and cross-country skiing, and on to the mining towns of Roslyn and Cle Elum. Highway 2 heads northeast across Stevens Pass, another downhill skiing area, to the Bavarian-style village of Leavenworth. Not far from the Canadian border, Highway 20 (closed during the winter months) cuts through North Cascades National Park, a half-million-acre preserve studded with glaciers and mountain lakes. Heading south out of Seattle, Highways 12, 706, 165, and 410 take you to various entrances of Mt. Rainier National Park.

Drives through the Cascades take you past mountain valleys, alpine meadows, lakes, and waterfalls, but only by hiking the trails can you really experience the beauty and grandeur of the mountains. Not all the trails are rugged; in fact, some are more like alpine walks. The best time to view mountain wildflowers is from the end of July to early August.

Places to Go, Sights to See

Lake Chelan. Scenic excursions up the 55-mile-long lake aboard one of the *Lady of the Lake* boats (tel. 509/682–2224) leave from the town of Chelan on the south shore, where the sun shines 300 days a year. The boat takes you to the northern terminus town of Stehekin where passengers can disembark for a picnic lunch or a short tour in an open bus before returning to Chelan, where you'll find rentals for waterskiing, boating, fishing, and cross-country skiing.

Leavenworth. This former mining and railroading town with a population of about 1,500 is at an elevation of 1,170 feet, surrounded by mountains rising to 8,000 feet. Thirty years ago, Leavenworth was a has-been; when civic leaders turned it into an alpine village, giving every downtown building a Tyrolean-style facade, tourists flocked.

Mt. Rainier National Park (tel. 360/569–2211). Designated in 1899 as the nation's fifth national preserve, the park encompasses all of Mt. Rainier, at 14,410 feet the state's highest mountain. Among the park's 240,000-plus acres are forests, alpine meadows, and glaciers (when the weather is cooperative, hiking trails lead right up to the glaciers' edge). Major visitor centers are at Paradise, Sunrise, and Ohanapecosh; some offer slide shows, summer videos, naturalist-guided hikes, and information on hiking trails and the many breathtaking lookouts.

Mt. Rainier Scenic Railroad (tel. 206/569–2588). A vintage steam locomotive takes you on a 14-mile trip across spectacular bridges and through lush, tall forests with views of Mt. Rainier. The train departs from Elbe in season. The trip takes 90 minutes and is accompanied by live banjo and guitar music.

Northwest Trek (near Eatonville, tel. 360/832–6116). This is one of the country's most unusual parks. Through 5½ miles of forest, bog, and pasture, trams take visitors to view North American wildlife—elk, deer, bears, bison, caribou, bighorn sheep, pronghorn antelopes, mountain goats, moose, gray wolves, cougars, lynx, bobcats, birds, waterfowl—in their native habitats.

Puget Sound and Snoqualmie Valley Railroad (tel. 360/746–4025). This steam-locomotive-driven train, operated by volunteers, runs between Snoqualmie and North Bend (just east of Seattle on I–90) from May through September. Tickets can be purchased in the restored 1890 depot in downtown Snoqualmie. The ride takes about 70 minutes and offers views of mountains, forest, and meadowland—views that may already be familiar to fans of the "Twin Peaks" series, which was filmed largely in this area. (Try the cherry pie at North Bend's Mar-T Cafe—the actual setting for Agent Cooper's favorite restaurant.)

Roslyn. This old mining town, off I–90 near Cle Elum, has mostly fallen into disrepair but manages to support a handful of retail shops, two restaurants (*see* Restaurants, *below*), and a first-run movie theater (in an old mortuary). It has been described as more Alaskan than Alaska by the folks who chose to film the television series "Northern Exposure" here.

Snoqualmie Falls. These 268-foot falls just outside the town of Snoqualmie are a crashing spectacle in the spring, when the mountain snows thaw, and when fall rains come thundering down. At the top is an observation deck and a mile-long marked trail down to the base of the falls.

Winthrop. This historic town on Route 20, the North Cascades Highway, is about a four-hour drive from Seattle. Once a bustling gold-mining town, Winthrop has been returned to its colorful 1890s appearance with barn-board storefronts, hitching posts, and boardwalk-style sidewalks. You can inspect an excellent collection of Old West memorabilia at the *Schafer Historical Museum* (tel. 509/996–2712) in a 100-year-old log cabin, or rest at *Three-Fingered Jack's* (Hwy. 20 and Bridge St., tel. 509/996–2411), the state's oldest saloon.

Restaurants

Alexander's Country Inn (tel. 360/569–2300) in Ashford serves trout fresh from the pond behind the inn, plus seafood, pasta, and delicious desserts. **The Herbfarm** (tel. 360/784–2222) in Fall City allows guests to tour the farm and watch as six-course gourmet extravaganzas are prepared. **Mama Vallone's Steak House & Inn** (tel. 509/674–5174) in Cle Elum can be counted on for great pasta, steak, and service. The **Roslyn Cafe** (tel. 509/649–2763) offers a jukebox with vintage 78s and good pasta and burgers. The **Old Honey Farm Country Inn** (tel. 206/888–9399) in Snoqualmie serves country fare at reasonable prices in a room with pasture and mountain views. The **Salish Lodge** (tel. 206/888–2556 or 800/826–6124), also in Snoqualmie, serves gourmet cuisine and a very popular brunch in its dining room, with large windows overlooking Snoqualmie Falls.

Tourist Information

Leavenworth Chamber of Commerce (Hwy. 2, Leavenworth, WA 98826, tel. 509/548–5807); **North Central Washington Tourism Association** (324 S. Pioneer Way, Moses Lake, WA 98837, tel. 509/765–7888 or, in WA, 800/992–6234); **South Puget Sound Tourism Association** (Box 1754, Tacoma, WA 98401, tel. 206/627–2836).

Reservation Services

Pacific Bed & Breakfast Agency (701 N.W. 60th St., Seattle, WA 98107, tel. 206/784–0539); **Seattle Bed & Breakfast Association** (2442 N.W. Market St., Seattle, WA 98107, tel. 206/547–1020); **Travelers Bed & Breakfast** (Box 492, Mercer Island, WA 98040, tel. 206/232–2345).

Mazama Country Inn

East of the North Cascades National Park, nestled in a valley laced with cross-country skiing trails, is this serenely rural, rustic mountain lodge. Owned by Cal and Ann Merriman, the Mazama is a sprawling 6,000-square-foot, two-story wood-sided building with a front entry of stone and log posts, dormer windows, and a brick-red roof set against a backdrop of pine trees and mountains.

The spacious dining and living room features a massive Russian stone fireplace, vaulted ceiling, peeled-log furniture, and floor-to-ceiling windows that look out at the valley floor and the mountains beyond. Glass doors lead to the deck, furnished with umbrella tables for picnic lunches. Watercolor landscapes by a local artist are displayed throughout.

Most guest rooms are comfortable, but certainly not opulent. Four larger rooms connect to the lodge via covered walkway. Also available are two cabins and the original, six-bedroom ranch house (for families or groups); both cabins and house have kitchens, bathrooms, and wood-burning stoves.

The inn attracts guests who want a mountain experience. In summer, the area offers mountain biking, hiking, horseback riding, river rafting, llama trekking, and fishing. In winter, the inn itself provides ski rentals and lessons and arranges for heli-skiing and inn-to-hut ski touring. One of the hedonistic experiences enjoyed by

guests after a day of cross-country skiing is slipping into the outdoor hot tub, surrounded by snowbanks, and gazing at the stars.

Winter breakfasts include hearty oatmeal, eggs, biscuits, coffee cake, and fruit; in summer, the main dish might be a vegetarian omelet or a whole-wheat sesame-seed waffle. Makings for sandwiches are set out after breakfast for guests to fix their own brown-bag lunches. Winter dinners are served family style and include appetizer, entrée, and dessert. In summer, dinners are ordered from the restaurant menu and may include Cajun shrimp or chicken fettuccine with broccoli and artichokes; a favorite dessert is chocolate mousse cake.

Address: *42 Lost River Rd., HCR 74/Box B9, Mazama, WA 98833, tel. 509/996–2681 or, in WA, 800/843–7951.*
Accommodations: *14 double rooms with baths, 6 farmhouse rooms share 2 baths, 4 housekeeping cabins.*
Amenities: *Restaurant, sauna, outdoor hot tub.*
Rates: *Summer $60–$75, breakfast not included; winter $155–$175, including all meals; cabins (year-round) $95–$120, no meals. MC, V.*
Restrictions: *No smoking, no pets; 2-night minimum in cabins and farmhouse.*

Run of the River Inn

On the Icicle River a half mile from Leavenworth, with a bird refuge on two sides, is this bed-and-breakfast in a classic log structure. It was built in 1979 to take advantage of extraordinary views of the river, Tumwater and Icicle canyons, and the towering Cascades.

A second story with cathedral ceilings was added by innkeepers Karen and Monty Turner, who moved here in 1987 from Las Vegas, where they both taught fifth grade. Karen still teaches, while Monty runs the inn and maintains his collection of classic and antique bicycles.

Guests have the entire fireplace-warmed living area downstairs to themselves now that the Turners built a small house adjacent to the inn. The country breakfast may include yogurt with fruit or a fresh fruit plate, hash browns, cinnamon rolls, and a cheese and sausage strata.

A guest sitting room is at the top of the circular staircase; supported by hand-peeled logs fashioned by a local craftsman, the staircase is one of the inn's many hand-hewn log features custom-made for the Turners. Like the rest of the inn, the sitting room has an upscale country look, with handmade willow furniture and a stenciled pine dry sink. Beverages and fresh gingerbread cookies are set out to make guests feel at home.

Bedrooms have high cathedral ceilings of pine, hand-hewn log furniture, and locally made hand-embroidered quilts on queen-size beds. Each room has a commanding view of the natural surroundings, along with an old fly rod, ski pole, or snowshoe on one wall as a reminder of the diversions the area offers.

The inn overlooks 70 acres of wetlands, including a small island in the river. The Turners' own landscaping includes a small pond with a log bench, a wildflower meadow with a few trails, and aspen and alpine fir trees.

In the winter, the area affords guests the opportunity for sleigh rides drawn by thoroughbred Belgian draft horses, and plenty of cross-country skiing and snowmobiling. Summer activities include hiking, white-water rafting, bicycling, horseback riding, fishing, golfing, and harvesting fruit at peach, apple, and plum orchards.

Address: *9308 E. Leavenworth Rd., Box 285, Leavenworth, WA 98826, tel. 800/288–6491.*
Accommodations: *4 double rooms with baths, 2 suites.*
Amenities: *Cable TV in rooms, phones on request, hot tub; bikes.*
Rates: *$90–$95, suites $125–$140; full breakfast. AE, D, MC, V.*
Restrictions: *No smoking, no pets; 2-night minimum on weekends and during festivals.*

Salish Lodge

At the crest of Snoqualmie Falls is the lodge whose authentic Northwest look and dramatic site made it the choice for exterior shots of the Great Northern Hotel in the TV series "Twin Peaks." The lodge was rebuilt in 1988 following the style of the original roadway inn built here in 1916, with dormers, porches, and balconies.

The entire inn is decorated in a casual but elegant country theme, with warm red-hued woods, rusticated stone, and fabrics and wallpapers in rich shades of rust, blue, and cream. Northwest art and Native American crafts complement the decor.

The library is an inviting room, with a hardwood floor, hefty maple beams, and rows of maple bookshelves; coffee is always available here, and tea and cookies are set out in the afternoon. Comfortable armchairs, a sofa, and a game table are arranged around the large stone fireplace. Although the lodge is used for meetings and the restaurant is open to the public, access to this room, as well as to the open-air rooftop hot tub and the fitness center, is restricted to overnight guests.

Guest rooms have stone fireplaces, minibars, natural wicker and Shaker-style furniture, either a balcony or a window seat, and goose-down comforters. All baths feature double whirlpool tubs, with French doors that open for fireplace viewing (candles are provided); each comes with thick,

hooded terry robes. The four corner suites all offer spectacular views of the waterfalls.

Lighted paths leading to the top of the falls make for romantic evening walks. Walking trails lead to the bottom of the falls, and bike paths connect with extensive country roads. A sports court (for pickleball, volleyball, and badminton) is across the road.

The dining room serves excellent regional cuisine and a large selection of champagnes and wines, with a particularly strong Northwest collection. The country breakfast is legendary, with course upon course of oatmeal, eggs, bacon, trout, pancakes, hash browns, and fresh fruit.

Address: *37807 S.E. Snoqualmie Falls Rd., Box 1109, Snoqualmie, WA 98065, tel. 206/888–2556 or 800/826–6124, fax 206/888–2533.*
Accommodations: *91 double rooms with baths, 4 suites.*
Amenities: *Air-conditioning, sauna, exercise room; TV, whirlpool tubs, and phones in rooms; VCRs and movie rentals available, restaurant, lounge; outdoor hot tub, 3 lighted sports courts, bikes.*
Rates: *$180–$295, suites $575; breakfast extra. AE, D, DC, MC, V.*
Restrictions: *Pets on first floor only.*

Sun Mountain Lodge

erched high on a mountaintop above the former gold-mining town of Winthrop, this grand resort offers panoramic vistas of the 2,000 acres of wilderness surrounding the resort, 500,000 acres of national forest, the North Cascades, and the Methow Valley below. The lodge, built in 1968, underwent a multimillion-dollar renovation in 1990.

In keeping with its mountain setting, the lodge is constructed from massive timbers and local stone. In the lobby of the main building—a busy place, with restaurants, meeting rooms, and many other guest facilities—sitting areas include hand-hewn furniture, stone floors, and large picture windows. A huge wrought-iron chandelier dates back to the days of the Pony Express.

Guest rooms feature hand-hewn birch furniture, hand-painted bedspreads, original regional art, and, of course, fine views. The best views are from the Gardner Wing, actually a separate building adjacent to the lodge. All rooms there are equipped with lava-rock gas fireplaces, private decks, wet bars, and refrigerators. (Some main-lodge rooms also feature fireplaces and wet bars.) Housekeeping cabins, with kitchenettes, brick fireplaces, and walls of natural pine, are available on Patterson Lake, about a mile from the main lodge.

The original dining room and lounge—both with expansive views—were retained during the renovation. Dinner entrées in the main dining room may include applewood-smoked duckling, autumn-run salmon, or pork with cilantro and red chili butter.

An interpretive center offers a full program of nature activities, including slide shows and guided walks. Trail rides, riding lessons, hayrides, and cookouts are available; rowboats, sailboats, canoes, and mountain bikes are for hire. In winter, the lodge offers sleigh rides, ice skating, ski lessons, and more than 50 miles of cross-country trails.

Address: *Patterson Lake Rd., Box 1000, Winthrop, WA 98862, tel. 509/996–2211 or 800/572–0493.*
Accommodations: *74 double rooms with baths, 5 suites, 8 housekeeping cabins.*
Amenities: *Phone in lodge rooms, lounge, exercise room, 2 restaurants, gift shop, athletic shop, meeting rooms; heated outdoor pool, 2 outdoor hot tubs, 2 tennis courts, horseback riding, ice-skating rink, 2 playgrounds.*
Rates: *$85–$160, suites $150–$230; breakfast extra. AE, MC, V.*
Restrictions: *No smoking in main dining room, no pets.*

Alexander's Country Inn

This Victorian-style inn was built in 1912, 1 mile from an entrance to Mt. Rainier National Park. Today's innkeepers, Jerry Harnish and Bernadette Ronan, bought it in 1980, but the original builders' presence is still felt through the many old photographs of the family on display.

Beyond the front doors, inset with two 1890 Viennese stained-glass panels of Romeo and Juliet, is the inn's public restaurant. Upstairs is a large, open living room with a fireplace.

Many of the guest rooms have wicker headboards and handmade quilts, Art Deco stained glass, and some fine antiques, such as room 10's New England armoire with fruit-basket designs inlaid in wood and mother-of-pearl. For the Tower Suite, you'll need to be fairly agile to climb a carpeted ladder up from the white wicker sitting room to the bedroom, where you'll find a 1920s suite of fan-detailed, bird's-eye maple furniture and stained glass in a fleur-de-lis design.

Address: *37515 State Rd. 706 E, Ashford, WA 98304, tel. 360/569–2300 or 800/654–7615.*
Accommodations: *5 double rooms with baths, 4 doubles share 2 baths, 4 suites.*
Amenities: *Restaurant; outdoor hot tub.*
Rates: *$69–$115 winter, $75–$125 summer; full breakfast. MC, V.*
Restrictions: *No smoking, no pets.*

All Seasons River Inn Bed & Breakfast

Built as a bed-and-breakfast in 1992, the All Seasons River Inn in Leavenworth offers antique furnishings in a contemporary setting. Innkeepers Kathy and Jeff Falconer designed the three-story cedar structure, which rests on the terraced banks of the Wenatchee River. As its name implies, the inn affords guests fishing in the river, sunbathing, or hiking in a variety of nearby scenic areas, skiing, and golf nearby.

Each guest room has a private deck, a river view, and a spacious seating area inside. For a view of the river and the Cascade Mountains from a whirlpool tub, ask for the Enchantment Room; it also has a four-poster bed, a bay window, and a private patio on the river.

In the morning you might be served Dutch pancakes, along with such side dishes as German baked potatoes, sausage and apples, or applesauce.

Address: *8751 Icicle Rd., Leavenworth, WA 98826, tel. 509/548–1425.*
Accommodations: *5 double rooms with baths.*
Amenities: *Cable TV, air-conditioning, game room. bicycles.*
Rates: *$95–$125; full breakfast. MC, V.*
Restrictions: *No smoking on the property, no pets; 2-night minimum stay on weekends, festivals, and holidays.*

Cashmere Country Inn

Thoroughly renovated by owners Dale and Patti Swanson, this 1907 Victorian farmhouse was once the post office for the fruit-growing town of Cashmere, just 10 minutes from Leavenworth. In the dining room, French doors on three sides overlook well-manicured gardens, an outdoor pool, and an orchard.

With lots of windows and white, the whole house has a light and airy feel. The four guest rooms, on the second story, are furnished with homey pieces, creating a grandma's-attic look.

By prearrangement, Patti serves candlelight dinners in the dining room or at sunset on Battenberg lace–covered tables beside the pool.

The farm was originally on 180 acres, and Patti's dream is to buy it all back. Meanwhile, in the fall, guests can pick apples from the inn's 1 acre of orchard and use the inn's cider press.

Address: *5801 Pioneer Dr., Cashmere, WA 98815, tel. 509/782–4212.*
Accommodations: *5 double rooms with baths.*
Amenities: *Dinner by prearrangement; outdoor pool, hot tub, ski packages available.*
Rates: *$70–$90; full breakfast. AE, MC, V.*
Restrictions: *No smoking indoors, no pets; 2-night minimum on weekends Sept.–Feb. and on holiday and festival weekends.*

Hous Rohrbach Pensione

On a hillside a mile outside Leavenworth, this alpine chalet with window boxes full of red geraniums has views of the valley, the village, and the Cascades. It has been owned since 1978 by the Harrilds: Robert, a former phone company cable splicer, and Kathryn, who comes from a family of resort-motel owners.

With clean lines and dark pine wainscoting, the house has a somewhat spartan, impersonal look, softened by white eyelet curtains and the occasional dried-flower arrangement. The comfortable common room, with a large open kitchen, wood-burning stove, sofas, and game tables, looks out to the deck that runs across the front of the house. Guest rooms, some with handcrafted pine bedsteads, are decorated in cream with rose and soft blue accents.

Homemade desserts—pies, sundaes, rhubarb crisp, white chocolate mousse cake—are available for purchase in the evening. Kathryn will pack a picnic for you if you want to explore the countryside.

Address: *12882 Ranger Rd., Leavenworth, WA 98826, tel. 509/548–7024 or 800/548–4477.*
Accommodations: *5 double rooms with baths, 4 doubles share 2 baths, 3 suites.*
Amenities: *Air-conditioning, hot tub; outdoor pool.*
Rates: *$65–$160; full breakfast. AE, D, DC, MC, V.*
Restrictions: *No smoking indoors, no pets; 2-night minimum on weekends Sept.–mid-Mar. and on festival weekends.*

Maple Valley Bed & Breakfast

Turning their home into a B&B was, for the Hurlbuts, a natural progression. Jayne, who had worked in the travel industry in the San Francisco Bay area, and Clarke, a northwesterner and retired air traffic controller (now a stonemason), started by taking in Japanese exchange students. Later, the students' families visited. In 1977, they went public.

This contemporary cedar house in a wooded area 40 minutes southeast of Seattle has a rustic look—open-beam ceilings, peeled-pole railings, and cedar walls. A large room downstairs has a huge stone fireplace and couches with sheepskin throws. The upstairs sitting room offers games, books, and a field guide and binoculars for spotting wildlife in the pond it overlooks. Lace curtains and crystal lamps gracefully accent one guest room whose French doors open onto a deck. Its four-poster bed of hand-hewn logs is topped with a floral comforter and lacy pillow shams.

A fun, thoughtful touch: On cool evenings the Hurlbuts give guests a "hot baby," a bed warmer filled with heated sand.

Address: *20020 S.E. 228th St., Maple Valley, WA 98038, tel. 206/432–1409.*
Accommodations: *2 double rooms share 1 bath.*
Rates: *$50–$65; full breakfast. No credit cards.*
Restrictions: *No smoking indoors, no pets.*

Moore House Bed & Breakfast

In the town of South Cle Elum, by the old tracks of the Chicago, Milwaukee, St. Paul & Pacific Railroad, is a wood-frame building that once housed railroad employees. Built in 1909, it's now owned by Eric and Cindy Sherwood.

The inn is crammed with railroad memorabilia, including vintage photographs, model trains, and schedules. The large sitting room has a 2-foot-tall train for kids to play on. Guest rooms—decorated with calico prints, coordinating colors, and some antiques—include written descriptions of the railroad workers and their lives.

Outside are two caboose cars that have been converted to suites with oversize decks. In the red caboose, with dark green wallpaper and carpet, bleached pine wainscoting, rolltop desk, and brass reading lamps, you can climb a ladder up to the cupola to sit and read.

Address: *526 Marie Ave., Box 629, South Cle Elum, WA 98943, tel. 509/674–5939 or 800/22–TWAIN.*
Accommodations: *3 double rooms with baths, 6 double rooms share 2½ baths, 3 suites.*
Amenities: *Air-conditioning; minifridge, coffeemaker, and TV in suites, full meal service for groups by prior arrangement; outdoor hot tub.*
Rates: *$45–$105; full breakfast. AE, MC, V.*
Restrictions: *No smoking in guest rooms, no pets; 2-night minimum mid-Dec.–Feb.*

Mountain Home Lodge

T hree miles up a winding, rutted mountain road outside Leavenworth, you emerge into the lush alpine meadow that surrounds the inn. The remote location affords breathtaking views of the Cascades and soothing quiet. Winters, guests park at Duncan Orchard Fruit Stand just east of Leavenworth and the owners—Chris Clark and her husband, Charlie Brooks—transport guests in a heated Sno-Cat to the lodge.

The contemporary cedar and redwood inn has broad decks for summer barbecues and dining. A massive stone fireplace at the center of the dining room is flanked by large sofas crafted from burled redwood and covered with shaggy sheepskins. Guest rooms are clean and neat, but lack the personality of the lounge area.

Guests will find miles of hiking and cross-country ski trails, a tennis court, badminton, volleyball, and a 1,700-foot-long toboggan run.

Address: *Box 687, Leavenworth, WA 98826, tel. 509/548–7077.*
Accommodations: *9 double rooms with baths.*
Amenities: *Air-conditioning; outdoor pool, year-round hot tub, tennis court.*
Rates: *Summer $88–$168, breakfast extra; winter $$188–$258, all meals included. AE, D, MC, V.*
Restrictions: *No smoking indoors, no children, no pets; 2-night minimum Dec.–Mar.*

Mountain Meadows Inn

P igs and chickens as well as a visiting herd of elk frequent the park-like grounds of this rambling, homey inn 6 miles from the entrance to Mt. Rainier National Park. The Colonial-style wood-frame house was built in 1910 for the superintendent of what was then the largest sawmill west of the Mississippi.

Owner Chad Darrah has collected hundreds of pieces of railroad memorabilia, including model trains, displayed in the dining and living room alongside a 1909 player piano. Guest rooms include queen- and king-size beds with duvets, calico prints, and reproduction Early American furnishings.

In the summer, Chad hosts evening campfires by the trout pond; in winter, the 90 miles of nearby cross-country ski trails beckon. Guests are welcome in the kitchen while Chad and a helper prepare country breakfasts of home-raised pork, eggs, and fruit on an 1889 wood-fired cookstove.

Address: *28912 State Rte. 706 E, Ashford, WA 98304, tel. 360/569–2788.*
Accommodations: *3 double rooms with baths, 1 housekeeping double with bath, 2 single rooms share 1 bath, 1 suite.*
Amenities: *Access to sauna and hot tub.*
Rates: *$75–$95; full breakfast. MC, V.*
Restrictions: *No smoking, no pets.*

Old Honey Farm Country Inn

alfway between Seattle and Snoqualmie Pass is this Colonial-style country inn, set on a 35-acre farm with unobstructed pasture and mountain views. Built in 1989 by Conrad and Mary Jean Potter, and Conrad's sister, Marilyn, all former university professors, the inn has a simple, country flavor. The lobby is furnished with a sofa and comfortable chairs before a fireplace. The open and airy dining room is flanked by windows with views of the pasture and Mt. Si. A large backyard deck is used for outdoor dining in summer.

Most guest rooms are simply decorated, with down comforters on queen-size beds, rocking chairs, pine furnishings, and a calico-print stuffed animal to cuddle with if you didn't bring your own. The mountain-view room has a reclining love seat facing the fireplace, a king-size bed, and a whirlpool tub. The inn has a public restaurant which serves breakfast, lunch, and dinner; there are a number of other good places to eat within 10 miles.

Address: *8910 384th Ave. SE, Snoqualmie Falls, WA 98065, tel. 206/888–9399 or 800/826–9077.*
Accommodations: *9 double rooms with baths.*
Amenities: *Deck, fireplace.*
Rates: *$75–$125; full breakfast. D, MC, V.*
Restrictions: *No smoking, no pets.*

Silver Bay Lodging

ituated on 700 feet of Lake Chelan waterfront, with expansive lawns and panoramic views of 9,000-foot mountain peaks, this inn near the Stehekin terminus of the *Lady of the Lake* tour boat is nicely situated for hikers, swimmers, and nature observers.

Randall and Kathy Dinwiddie furnished their solar home and two cabins with antiques and original art. Guest rooms have down comforters and handmade quilts; the suite has two private decks and a bathroom with delicate wallpaper, paneled walls, a Persian carpet, and an Italian-tile soaking tub. Breakfast is served in a long sunroom decorated with a collection of fruit-label art, Indian baskets, and stained-glass windows.

Address: *Box 43, Stehekin, WA 98852, tel. 509/682–2212.*
Accommodations: *1 double room with bath, 1 suite, 2 housekeeping cabins.*
Amenities: *Wood-burning stove in cabins; croquet, lake swimming.*
Rates: *$75–$110, full breakfast; cabins $80–$120 for 2 people, $15 for each additional person, no breakfast. No credit cards.*
Restrictions: *No smoking, no pets; 2-night minimum in suite (closed mid-Oct.–mid-May), 5-night minimum in cabins July–mid-Sept.*

Spokane and Environs
Including Coeur d'Alene

Because of Seattle's moist climate, many think of Washington
State as being waterlogged from Idaho all the way to the
Pacific Ocean. But poised between the Rocky and Cascade
mountains is Spokane, with weather that's both dry and sunny
most of the year. Three hundred miles east of Seattle, Spokane
is Washington's second-largest city (population 182,000) and,
with a plethora of mountains, forests, and lakes in the area, a
year-round paradise for outdoors enthusiasts. At the same
time, the city's slow pace and reversals of fortune make it an
inviting place for strollers and history buffs to explore.

The fur trade first drew white men to the Spokane River
valley, and in the early 19th century they coexisted more or
less peacefully with the Spokane Indians and other tribes of
the region. By 1858, however, a fierce battle waged against the
Northwest tribes had forced the Native Americans onto
reservations, and the white settlers began to develop the area
aggressively.

The gold, silver, and lead in the nearby Coeur d'Alene
Mountains and in British Columbia drew many prospectors
who soon began to pour mining money into Spokane, officially
founded in 1871. Millionaires were created overnight, and the
city attracted gamblers, adventurers, and dance-hall girls. By
the turn of the century, the nouveaux riches were building
elaborate mansions in a neighborhood called Browne's
Addition, importing materials and furnishings from Europe
at tremendous cost in their game of one-upmanship. Spokane's
economic upswing continued as the transcontinental railroad
brought more commerce and more settlers to the city.
Spokane's fortunes have since waxed and waned with those of
the mines, the timber industry, and agriculture.

When the city entered a period of economic decline during the
1960s, civic leaders moved to rejuvenate it in a bid for an

international exposition. Expo '74 drew more than 5 million visitors. Riverfront Park, created for the event, remains a popular tourist spot in the heart of downtown. Its 100 acres feature a century-old carousel, a movie theater with a five-story-high screen, carnival rides, and ducks and swans feeding along a willow-bordered river.

Spokane maintains a gentle hustle-bustle. It has the feel of a small town, with many of its low-rise buildings dating from the early part of the century. These days, the city's livelihood is heavily based on service industries and the wholesale and retail trade, although mining, timber, and agriculture still play an important role in the region's economy. During the past decade, many transplants from California and other parts of the country have added diversity to the city. And its well-earned reputation for a hardworking labor force and good public schools has drawn such corporations as Boeing and Seafirst Bank, which have transferred some of their operations here from Seattle.

One of the biggest advantages of Spokane's compact size is the fact that the countryside can be reached within minutes. The Selkirk and Coeur d'Alene mountains, rising to the north and east, 76 lakes, and four major rivers are all within a 50-mile radius of the city, offering activities ranging from swimming, boating, rafting, hiking, and fishing to downhill and cross-country skiing and snowmobiling.

Just 35 miles from Spokane is Coeur d'Alene, Idaho, site of a postcard-perfect lake with 125 miles of shoreline, ringed by richly forested mountains. Coeur d'Alene is Spokane's most popular playground, especially during the summer, when residents and visitors flock to the sandy beach and boardwalk at the edge of the lake. The Coeur d'Alene Resort offers a breathtaking view to those who take refreshment at its restaurants or lounges. The resort has added to its list of amenities a world-class golf course, complete with a floating green in Lake Coeur d'Alene.

Places to Go, Sights to See

Browne's Addition. This was Spokane's first residential community, named for lawyer J. J. Browne, who bought its original 160 acres in 1878, when Spokane was a small settlement with fewer than 50 residents. Planned during the early 1880s, this neighborhood in southwest Spokane went on to become one of the most socially correct addresses in the city. During the 1880s, Queen Anne architecture was predominant. As mining money began to pour into the area during the next decade, mansions became more ostentatious, built in historical revival styles that included Greek, Tudor, and Colonial Revival. Today many of the buildings remain, and Browne's Addition is a mixture of trendy and down-at-the-heels. Some of the old homes are now apartments and halfway houses, while others have been lovingly restored. Architecture buffs can stop at the *Cheney Cowles Museum bookstore* (*see below*) for a booklet offering a self-guided walking tour of the neighborhood. Along the way, be sure to stop for refreshments at the *Elk* (1931 W. Pacific St., tel. 509/456–0454). A square brick-and-tile building dating from 1940, Elk's still has its original soda fountain. Now a popular restaurant, it serves breakfast, lunch, and light fare for dinner.

Cheney Cowles Memorial Museum (W. 2316 1st Ave., tel. 509/456–3931). In Browne's Addition, the Cheney Cowles Museum has exhibits that trace the history of the Northwest, including the early days of Spokane, and hosts shows featuring nationally known and regional artists. The adjacent Grace Campbell House, built in 1898, features period rooms that show visitors how a mining tycoon and his family lived during Spokane's "Age of Elegance."

Green Bluff Growers (tel. 509/238–6978). This consortium of fruit and vegetable growers can be found 16 miles north of Spokane in the foothills of Spokane between Mead and Colbert. They produce many of the apples for which Washington is famous, plus cherries, strawberries, and other seasonal bounty. Depending on the season, you can pick your own fruit in their orchards. A Cherry Festival is held mid-July, and the Apple Festival runs every weekend in October. To locate their farms, produce stands, and antiques and gift shops, which feature locally produced crafts, homemade preserves, and honey, pick up a map at Spokane Regional Convention and Visitors Bureau (*see* Tourist Information, *below*).

Manito Park (tel. 509/456–4331). South of downtown Spokane, in the midst of residential neighborhoods, Manito Park was designed in 1912 by landscape architects Frederick Law Olmsted (of New York's Central Park fame) and John Charles Olmsted. Today it is a serene, 91-acre oasis for walkers, joggers, and bicyclists. Garden aficionados will enjoy the formal Japanese garden, rose garden featuring 180 varieties, Duncan Garden, with its annuals arranged in geometric symmetry around the Davenport fountain, and a greenhouse brimming with warm-weather plants.

Mt. Spokane State Park (off Hwy. 2, tel. 509/456–4169 or, for ski information, 509/238–6281). Thirty miles northeast of downtown, Mt. Spokane State Park is a popular spot for winter recreation, with an alpine ski resort and 35 groomed trails for cross-country skiers. During warm weather it offers hikers scenic trails along mountain ridges and through cool forests.

Riverside State Park (tel. 509/456–3964). Just 3 miles northwest of downtown Spokane, Riverside State Park is minimally developed, offering a wild and natural setting on 3,000 acres. Ponderosa pines tower above the Spokane River, which is enjoyed by fishermen and rafters. Hikers can venture up Deep Creek Canyon to explore the fossil beds of a forest that existed more than 7 million years ago, or view centuries-old Indian rock paintings. You can rent a horse at *Trailtown Stables* (tel. 509/456–8249) and roam the basalt cliffs above the river. At the *Spokane House Interpretive Center* (closed mid-September–early April), site of an early trading post, visitors can view exhibits that examine the fur trade during the early 19th century.

Silverwood (Hwy. 95, Athol, ID, tel. 208/683–3444). An Old West theme park 15 miles north of Coeur d'Alene, Silverwood is a popular summer attraction. It offers rides on an old-style locomotive, an antique-airplane museum and air show, plus carnival rides and entertainment.

Skiing. Downhill skiers seeking more challenging slopes than those of Mt. Spokane can find three larger resorts within 90 minutes of Spokane: *49 Degrees North* (Chewelah, WA, tel. 509/935–6649), with eight runs, four double chair lifts, and condominium rentals; *Schweitzer* (Sandpoint, ID, tel. 208/263–9555), with 48 runs, one quad, six chair lifts, hotels, a guest lodge, and restaurants; and *Silver Mountain* (Kellogg, ID, tel. 208/783–1111), with 50 runs, one quad, two triple and two double chair lifts, and a surface lift—but no lodgings. The ski area is accessed by the world's longest single-stage gondola.

Wineries. Tours are offered at four wineries near downtown Spokane. *Arbor Crest Wine Cellars* invites visitors to tastings at their Cliff House, a national historic site that overlooks the Spokane River (4705 N. Fruithill Rd., Spokane, tel. 509/927–9463). Built in 1924, the Tuscan villa-style house is built in white stucco with a red-tile roof. Most of the house is now reserved for private parties, but its dramatic location, perched on a brink of a cliff, provides visitors with a panoramic view of the Spokane River, Spokane Valley, and Idaho as they enjoy the cool gardens surrounding the house. Visitors can also take part in tours and tastings at *Latah Creek* (E. 13030 Indiana Ave., Spokane, tel. 509/926–0164), *Worden* (off I–90 on Thorpe Rd., Spokane, tel. 509/455–7835), and *Catarina Winery* (N. 905 Washington, Spokane, tel. 509/328–5069).

Restaurants

Any list of Spokane's finest restaurants should include **Amore's** (tel. 509/838–8640), which serves up such Italian dishes as salmon and Gorgonzola fettuccine in a funky setting where religious kitsch adorns the walls. **Milford's Fish House** (tel. 509/326–7251) takes its specialty seriously, offering a daily menu with many fresh regional fish and shellfish dishes. Housed in a century-old building with a tin ceiling, the restaurant, open for dinner only, caters to a young and energetic crowd. Look for spicy Cajun crayfish pie and halibut divan on the menu. **Patsy Clark's Mansion** (tel. 509/838–8300) was the turn-of-the-century residence of Patrick Clark, who in 1895 commissioned local architect Kirtland Cutter to design and build the mansion for a reported $1 million. Its ornate rooms now offer intimate dining areas where patrons can enjoy such dishes as duck with amaretto sauce and lamb with cream of shallot sauce. **Beverly's** (tel. 208/765–4000 or

800/688–5253), on the seventh floor of the Coeur d'Alene Resort, is famous for its beautiful view of Lake Coeur d'Alene and its fine seasonal cuisine, which features traditional Northwest dishes prepared with a French influence. Its wine cellar boasts some 9,000 selections.

Tourist Information

The Greater Coeur d'Alene Convention & Visitors Bureau (Box 1088, Coeur d'Alene, ID 83814, tel. 208/664–0587); **Spokane Regional Convention and Visitors Bureau** (W. 924 Sprague, Spokane, WA 99204, tel. 509/624–1341 or 800/248–3230).

Reservation Services

Spokane Bed & Breakfast Reservation Service (E. 627 25th Ave., Spokane, WA 99203, tel. 509/624–3776).

Clark House on Hayden Lake

Visit the Clark House on Idaho's Hayden Lake, a 40-minute drive from Spokane, and you will instantly be caught up in the history and mystery surrounding the place. A reclusive mining millionaire, F. Lewis Clark had the home built as a copy of a summer palace of Kaiser Wilhelm II of Germany. With 33 rooms and 10 fireplaces, the building, whose construction began in 1895, wasn't completed until 1910. Clark and his wife, Winifred, lived in the house for four years; then he and all of his money disappeared mysteriously. Winifred waited patiently for her husband's return but was soon forced to sell off the land, furnishings, and eventually the house to pay back taxes.

Innkeeper Monty Danner and his son Mark bought and extensively restored the mansion after it had sat empty for 20 years. The result is a sumptuously comfortable hostelry on a secluded 13-acre estate. Each of the five guest rooms has a bathroom with an immense Roman tiled tub. Beds are equipped with both puffy down comforters and European-style featherbeds atop firm mattresses. Light filters through grand Palladian windows at both ends of the long gallery linking the upstairs bedrooms.

Monty has decorated Clark House in an uncluttered, eclectic way, using furniture with simple lines and the occasional spectacular decorative flourish, such as the cascading French crystal chandelier in the reception room or the intricately carved walnut buffet crafted in Connecticut during the 1870s. Oriental vases, lamps, and screens and bronze sculptures by Erté add to the elegance. Guest rooms are similarly lacking in froufrou, with neutral colors favored, whether in the white-and-gold-trimmed Louis XIV–style writing table and high chest in Mrs. Clark's Room or in the Hayden Lake Room, where natural wicker furniture and a ceiling fan give it a summery look. (This room, by the way, has the best view of the lake.) French doors are in every room, some leading outdoors to deck and terrace areas, a lush lawn overlooking Hayden Lake, and a wildflower-filled garden. Guests can swim at a sandy beach 1½ miles away or rent boats at a nearby marina.

Address: *E. 4550 S. Hayden Lake Rd., Hayden Lake, ID 83835, tel. 208/772-3470 or 800/765-4593, fax 208/772-6899.*
Accommodations: *5 double rooms with baths.*
Amenities: *Fireplace in 2 rooms, TV upon request, wine and beer available, meeting facilities.*
Rates: *$100–$165; full breakfast. AE, D, DC, MC, V.*
Restrictions: *Smoking in kitchen or outside only, no pets; 2-night minimum on holiday weekends.*

The Portico

Travelers between Spokane and Seattle can pull off the freeway and find respite at the Portico, a beautifully restored historic landmark in an unlikely place—Ritzville, a farming town 60 miles southwest of Spokane. At first glance, there seems to be little to see or do here, but this unassuming little town is home to a 1937 Art Deco movie house, a nine-hole golf course, a bowling alley, and a park, which, coupled with Ritzville's clean, safe streets, evoke a simpler time.

The Portico was originally built in 1902 as the home of Nelson H. Greene, a prominent merchant, financier, and wheat broker. When the town burned down in 1889, Greene financed its reconstruction, encouraging the use of brick; hence the Portico's unusual mating of material—buff-colored brick— and Queen Anne, Classical Revival, and Craftsman styles.

Innkeepers Bill and Mary Anne Phipps are passionate about architecture and period furnishings; their attention to detail is evident, starting with the entrance hall, whose parquet floor bears a pattern of unstained dark and light oak, bordered with serpentine work in bird's-eye maple. In the parlor the wallpaper, in rich reds and golds, is a reproduction of a turn-of-the-century design. A bearskin rug lies at one end, where the fireplace is framed by oak spindle work supported by Ionic columns. The ceiling, which resembles pressed tin, was actually produced by anaglyph, a process favored at the turn of the century for creating a design in relief.

The restoration has created two guest rooms, one very large and the other fairly small. The bigger one is decorated with rich paisley wallpaper and mid- to late-19th-century English furniture. A carved walnut bed sports a two-tailed mermaid at its head and an angel protecting a child at its foot, both symbols of good luck. A settee covered in crewelwork is shaped to allow two ladies to sit comfortably without wrinkling their gowns. The other room is bright and cheerful, with a white wrought-iron bed topped with a quilt handmade by Mary Anne.

Breakfast is fresh and generous. In season, Mary Anne serves raspberries and blackberries fresh from her garden; homemade cinnamon rolls, eggs with a cheese sauce, delicious yeasty waffles, and homemade granola are often on the menu.

Address: *502 S. Adams St., Ritzville, WA 99169, tel. 509/659–0800.*
Accommodations: *2 double rooms with baths.*
Amenities: *Air-conditioning, cable TV in rooms.*
Rates: *$59–$74; full breakfast. AE, D, MC, V.*
Restrictions: *No smoking indoors.*

Waverly Place

Waverly Place offers lodgings in a quiet old neighborhood just five minutes from downtown Spokane. The turreted Queen Anne house sits across the street from Corbin Park, whose 11½ acres encompass tennis courts, a jogging track, a baseball diamond, and a playground. Waverly Place, built in 1902, is one of several turn-of-the-century houses bordering the park; the neighborhood is listed on the state's Register of Historic Places.

Innkeepers Marge and Tammy Arndt are a mother-and-daughter team whose love for rambling Victorian houses led them to buy the building nearly a decade ago. With distinctive late Victorian pieces—many of them from Marge's mother-in-law's attic— they've created an environment in which the furnishings seem truly at home amid the graceful architecture of the house. Guests have exclusive use of two parlors, where the gleaming fir woodwork includes intricate beading around the mantelpiece and Grecian columns that separate the rooms. Most of the original lighting is intact, including the dining room chandelier in brass, cupids perching at its sides. Victorian lamps throughout the house sport fringed shades handmade by Tammy. Both women enjoy researching the house; in painting its exterior they consulted old photographs and the builder's grandson in order to remain faithful to the original look: bright white with green and red trim.

Although they both have outside jobs—Tammy is a meeting coordinator and Marge is a consultant for a church directory service—one of the women is always on hand. The guest rooms are airy and comfortable, with queen-size reproduction beds (four-poster, sleigh, and wrought iron), and braided and dhurrie rugs over shiny hardwood floors.

Breakfast is, in Tammy's words, "decadent, delicious, and high in fat and cholesterol," although Waverly Place is quick to accommodate special diets. The usual fare, served in the dining room on Haviland china, reflects the innkeepers' Swedish heritage. Menus feature puffy Swedish pancakes with huckleberry sauce and almond-flavored pastries called *kringla*, as well as egg dishes, sausage, and fresh fruit and juice.

Address: *W. 709 Waverly Pl., Spokane, WA 99205, tel. 509/328–1856.*
Accommodations: *1 double room with bath, 3 doubles share 2 baths.*
Amenities: *Air-conditioning, TV available; outdoor pool.*
Rates: *$60–$75; full breakfast. AE, D, MC, V.*
Restrictions: *No smoking, no pets; 2-night minimum first weekend in May.*

Blackwell House

Although Blackwell House sits on Coeur d'Alene's main street, the grand proportions of the house and generous garden seem to insulate it from the hustle-bustle of the town.

Owner Kathleen Sims began a two-year remodeling of this Georgian Revival home in 1984. She now promotes the house, built in 1904, not only as a bed-and-breakfast but also as a setting for weddings and dinner parties. Indeed, the house's common areas feel more like hotel banquet facilities than family rooms.

Most of the guest rooms are large, light-filled, and comfortable, and all are furnished with turn-of-the-century pieces or replicas. Three have large sitting areas. Shower lovers, beware: Many of the bathrooms are equipped only with claw-foot tubs. Breakfast is served in the cheerful morning room, where French doors open onto the garden and bright-colored stenciling decorates the doorway, ceiling, and fireplace.

Address: *820 Sherman Ave., Coeur d'Alene, ID 83814, 208/664–0656.* **Accommodations:** *6 double rooms with baths, 2 doubles share 1 bath.* **Amenities:** *Fireplace in 1 room; air-conditioning in some rooms; evening refreshments.* **Rates:** *$75–$119; full breakfast. AE, D, MC, V.* **Restrictions:** *No pets.*

Cricket on the Hearth Bed and Breakfast Inn

Those who are turned on by theme rooms will have their fantasies fueled at the Cricket on the Hearth Bed and Breakfast Inn. Hosts Al and Karen Hutson have made their theme rooms a popular feature of their 1920 stucco Craftsman cottage that's 10 minutes from downtown Coeur d'Alene. Miss Kitty from "Gunsmoke" was the inspiration for one of them, where a large claw-foot tub sits in the middle of the floor, illuminated by a brass lamp with red-fringed shade. A patchwork-quilt-covered brass bed completes the "naughty but nice" atmosphere. If your taste is more rustic, there's the Navajo Room, filled with lodgepole pine furniture, Navajo and Zuni pottery, and weaving.

Guests can relax in the game room, decorated with a tiger's head, deer antlers, and other trophies and hunting memorabilia (the former owner was a big-game hunter). The room opens onto a deck equipped for barbecuing.

Address: *1521 Lakeside Ave., Coeur d'Alene, ID 83814, tel. 208/664–6926.* **Accommodations:** *3 double rooms with baths, 2 doubles share 1 bath.* **Amenities:** *Guest refrigerator; ski packages available.* **Rates:** *$50–$80; full breakfast. No credit cards.* **Restrictions:** *No smoking indoors, no pets.*

Fotheringham House

In the heart of historic Browne's Addition in Spokane, Fotheringham House is a century-old Queen Anne home built by the city's first mayor. Among the many decorative features original to the house are tin ceilings throughout most of the building, ball-and-spindle fretwork separating the entrance hall and living room, and an intricately carved oak fireplace and open staircase. The common rooms have been furnished with period pieces, from claw-foot sofas to lawyers' bookcases and brass standing lamps. The innkeepers'—Graham and Jackie Johnson—fondness for antique furniture restoration and stained glass is evident throughout the house.

The guest rooms have romantic flowered wallpaper, chintz and lace curtains, and oak and mahogany reproduction Victorian beds. Guests breakfast in the dining room, where carved cherubs grace a china cabinet and a gilt mirror hangs above a marble-top buffet. Tennis courts are available in Coeur d'Alene Park just across the street, and architecture aficionados will enjoy strolling through this Victoriana-filled neighborhood.

Address: *2128 W. 2nd Ave., Spokane, WA 99204, tel. 509/838–1891.*
Accommodations: *1 double room with bath, 2 doubles share 1 bath.*
Amenities: *Air-conditioning.*
Rates: *$65–$70; full breakfast. MC, V.*
Restrictions: *No smoking, no children under 12, no pets.*

Gregory's McFarland House

At Gregory's McFarland House in Coeur d'Alene, a spacious 1905 Craftsman structure boasting elegant family heirlooms, old meets new, flawlessly, with modern comforts and conveniences.

Innkeepers Winifred, Stephen, and Carol Gregory share with guests a home full of family history; many of their 19th-century antiques came from Winifred's ancestral home in England. The carved claw-foot table in the dining room, which once made a journey around Cape Horn, sits on one of several Chinese rugs scattered throughout the house's gleaming bird's-eye maple floors. Guest rooms are large and bright, with rose and pink accents, hand-crocheted bedspreads, and curtains of German lace. One room features an inlaid-wood bedroom suite from the 1860s, with a marble-top table and low dresser. Several rooms have four-poster beds. On a quiet tree-lined street, Gregory's McFarland House provides a soothing atmosphere only six blocks from downtown.

Address: *601 Foster Ave., Coeur d'Alene, ID 83814, tel. 208/667–1232.*
Accommodations: *5 double rooms with baths.*
Amenities: *Air-conditioning; complimentary refreshments, high tea upon request.*
Rates: *$85–$120; full breakfast. MC, V.*
Restrictions: *No smoking indoors, no pets; 2-night minimum on summer and holiday weekends.*

Love's Victorian Bed and Breakfast

Forty-five minutes from downtown Spokane, Love's Victorian Bed and Breakfast is a salute to Victoriana. Indeed, the exterior is a veritable encyclopedia of gingerbread. Innkeepers Bill and Leslie Love built this reproduction house in 1986. Working from the plans of an 1886 Queen Anne house, Bill incorporated original Victorian decorative elements: In the sitting room, he fashioned a mantelpiece out of the remains of an 1858 piano; grill- and fretwork in the entrance hall and balusters on the stairway and porch were salvaged from turn-of-the-century houses in Spokane.

The largest guest room boasts a fireplace, balcony, and a sitting area occupying the house's turret. Chintz balloon shades, floral wallpaper, Victorian memorabilia, and breakfast by candlelight give the house an unabashedly romantic air. Amid fields, evergreen forests, and rolling hills, this house is a place where you can get away from it all. Evening walks offer encounters with deer and even moose. Guests can swim or fish at nearby lakes, and cross-country ski trails are five minutes away.

Address: *31317 N. Cedar Rd., Deer Park, WA 99006, tel. 509/276–6939.*
Accommodations: *3 double rooms with baths.*
Amenities: *Indoor hot tub, air-conditioning; bikes and cross-country skis available.*
Rates: *$75–$98; full breakfast, evening refreshments. MC, V.*
Restrictions: *No smoking indoors; closed the first weekend in Dec.*

Marianna Stoltz House

Marianna Stoltz House sits across from Gonzaga University, five minutes from downtown Spokane. Innkeepers Jim and Phyllis Maguire named the classic American Foursquare for Phyllis's mother. The decor is a strange mix: Elegant features that suit the architecture, such as the original dark fir woodwork, leaded-glass china cabinets, and Rococo Revival and Renaissance Revival settees and armchairs in the parlor and sitting room share space with lamps and fake-flower arrangements that you would expect at a chain motel. Still, the service is both friendly and unobtrusive.

Upstairs, brass and mahogany beds are covered in quilts that have been in Phyllis's family for decades. One private bathroom has a 7-foot-long clawfoot tub. The largest room is also the noisiest. It has a king-size brass bed, but faces a busy street; the smallest room has twin beds. In the evening, the Maguires offer their guests homemade liqueurs and local wines.

Address: *427 E. Indiana Ave., Spokane, WA 99207, tel. 509/483–4316.*
Accommodations: *2 double rooms with baths, 2 doubles share 1 bath.*
Amenities: *Air-conditioning, TV available.*
Rates: *$60–$69; full breakfast, evening refreshments. AE, D, DC, MC, V.*
Restrictions: *No smoking indoors, no pets; 2-night minimum on holiday weekends.*

My Parents' Estate

This inn, nestled in the Selkirk Mountains less than two hours from Spokane, has both a scenic setting and a unique history. Opened as a mission in 1873, its 47 acres were home to the Sisters of Providence and later to a convent for Dominican nuns who ran a school on the site. The main house was once the Mother Superior's quarters and office. It also contained a chapel, now the two-story-high living room reserved for guests. Reminders of the property's history abound, including religious statues once used in services and intricate linen handwork done by the nuns.

Owner Bev Parent, a professional artist, has amassed collections of handmade quilts and antique tools and kitchenware, and painted designs on several old pieces in the guest rooms.

One room has a rare hand-painted bedroom suite of so-called cottage furniture from the 1890s. All of the rooms have Laura Ashley–style bed linens and wonderful views of surrounding pastureland and mountains. Guests can enjoy the solitude in the gazebo in a new cottage garden, which also sports a fountain.

Address: *719 Hwy. 395, Kettle Falls, WA 99141, tel. 509/738–6220.*
Accommodations: *3 double rooms with baths; 1 housekeeping suite with fireplace.*
Amenities: *Hot tub in winter; air-conditioning; pool table, half basketball court in gymnasium; ice skating.*
Rates: *$65–$100; full breakfast. MC, V.*
Restrictions: *No smoking, no children under 15, no pets; closed Dec. 20–Jan. 2.*

Warwick Inn

Travelers who long to check their car keys at the door and explore an area on foot may do so at the Warwick Inn. A block from Lake Coeur d'Alene, this bed-and-breakfast is just steps away from the lake's sandy beach and boardwalk.

The 1905 Craftsman lodging was built as officers' quarters when the property was on the grounds of Ft. Sherman. Given the architectural style of the house, innkeepers James and Bonnie Warwick have taken an unorthodox approach to the decorative details, giving its exterior a "painted lady," multicolor scheme, painting the interior woodwork a glowing white, and adding Victorian gingerbread detailing. The final effect is a bright and cheerful environment, with all the ground floor curtains matching the light blue and

rose floral-and-ribbon print of the living room sofa. Pierre Deux fabrics and bone china dress the breakfast room table. Guest rooms are large, with lace curtains, antique quilts, and turn-of-the-century oak furniture.

Address: *303 Military Dr., Coeur d'Alene, ID 83814, tel. 208/765–6565.*
Accommodations: *2 double rooms share an upstairs bath (another bath available downstairs); 1 suite.*
Amenities: *Guest robes; off-street parking.*
Rates: *$85–$125; full breakfast, evening refreshments. AE, MC, V.*
Restrictions: *No smoking indoors, no children, no pets; 2-night minimum on holiday weekends.*

The Palouse

An area of gently rolling hills in southeast Washington, the Palouse—French for "waves of blowing grass"—was named by fur trappers who traveled up the Columbia River from Fort Astoria in present-day Oregon as early as 1811. The Lewis and Clark Expedition had passed through the region in 1805 on its way to the Pacific Ocean, but it was settlers looking for a new life—or, like missionary Marcus Whitman, intending to bring Christianity to the Native Americans—who brought agriculture to the region. They established communities such as Dayton and Walla Walla early in the 19th century; about 90 years later a land-grant college, now Washington State University, was started in Pullman.

Because the northern branch of the Oregon Trail passed just south of Walla Walla, many farmers, finding rich, deep soil, stayed in the Palouse rather than heading on down the raging Snake and Columbia rivers to Fort Astoria and Oregon's Willamette Valley. The farmers quickly built large houses in town, and, as a result, Dayton now boasts more Victorian-era homes than Port Townsend on Puget Sound. Walla Walla, too, has many beautifully restored homes dating from the 19th century.

Agriculture still reigns in this area, but now it's wheat, not grass, for which this farming region is best known; indeed, Whitman County produces more wheat than any other county in the United States. It also bills itself as the lentil capital of the world, and several community celebrations follow the lentil harvest each August. Walla Walla is famous for its sweet onions and throws an onion festival each year in late July. (Walla Walla's other chief industry is the state penitentiary, on a bluff above town.) Some of those not directly involved in farming are employed at the Green Giant canning and labeling plant in Dayton, which processes much of the asparagus grown locally. Dust from plowed fields and nearly constant winds combine to create stunning deep orange and red sunsets.

Although Dayton, Walla Walla, and Pullman are separated by miles of hills, the towns themselves are best seen on foot. Because the region is in a rain shadow, a pocket of land protected from clouds, its climate is less severe than that of Spokane, 158 miles north of Walla Walla. Hence, spring comes earlier in the Palouse; tulips and daffodils burst into bloom in late March. Summer daytime temperatures can reach well into the 90s, however. The best times to visit are spring, when the Palouse is carpeted in green winter wheat, and fall, when the heat has relented and the sun of Indian summer plays off the golden fields.

Places to Go, Sights to See

Dayton. On the main stage route between Walla Walla and Lewiston in northwest Idaho, Dayton profited from an 1861 gold rush in Idaho. Merchants and farmers built lavish houses during the boom years; an impressive 88 Victorian buildings in town are on the National Register of Historic Places. A brochure with two self-guided walking tours is available from the Chamber of Commerce (*see* Tourist Information, *below*). One tour encompasses the 73 homes and buildings on the original townsite platted in 1871 (Main Street was formerly the drag used by Native Americans to race horses), while the other explores the many Queen Anne, Italianate, and Gothic homes built in the late 1800s. The 1886 Italianate *Columbia County Courthouse*, the oldest in the state still in use for county government, was recently renovated. Dayton also is home to the oldest family-run hardware store in the state, *Dingle's*, as well as the state's oldest volunteer fire department and oldest rodeo. One block off Main Street and adjacent to the railroad tracks, the restored *Dayton Railroad Depot*, built in 1881, was in use until 1971.

Juniper Dunes Wilderness. The 7,140-acre Juniper Dunes Wilderness at the western edge of the Palouse includes some of the biggest sand dunes—up to 130 feet high and ¼-mile wide—and the largest natural groves of western juniper in the state; some are 150 years old. This is all that remains of an ecosystem that stretched over nearly 400 square miles south to the Snake and Columbia rivers. The most scenic portion is a 2-mile hike northeast from the parking area where all visitors must leave their cars. Getting to the parking area, 15 miles northeast of Pasco, involves driving some unmarked back roads through farmland; for directions, contact the Bureau of Land Management (tel. 509/353–2570). No camping or fires are allowed, and no drinking water is available.

Palouse Falls. Just north of the confluence with the Snake River, the Palouse River gushes over a basalt cliff higher than Niagara Falls and drops 198 feet into a steep-walled basin. Hiking trails at the 105-acre Palouse Falls State Park lead to an overlook above the falls and to streams below them. The falls are best during spring runoff, starting in late March. Just downstream at the *Marmes Rock Shelter*, remains of some of the earliest known inhabitants of North America, dating back 10,000 years, were discovered by archaeologists. The Marmes site is accessible via a 2½-mile unmaintained trail from Lyons Ferry State Park, at the point where the Snake and Palouse rivers meet, and by canoe (there's a boat launch at Lyons Ferry). Much of the actual shelter area is flooded by the backwaters of Lower Monumental Dam, but the area is still popular with canoeists.

Pullman. Although Colfax, 30 miles to the north, is the county seat, Pullman is considered the big town in Whitman County because of *Washington State University*, which anchors the community. Founded in 1890 and now boasting a campus that sprawls across several hills, the university has some 16,000 students. Tours at the university (tel. 509/335–4527) can keep visitors busy for a couple of days. National-caliber exhibits, changed monthly, are hung at the WSU Museum of Fine Art in the Fine Arts Center. For an impressive insect collection, visit the Museum of Anthropology and Maurice T. James Entomological Collection in Johnson Hall. Other campus destinations include the Marion Ownbey Herbarium in Herald Hall, the Beef, Dairy, and Swine Centers, and the Jewett Astronomical Observatory (tel. 509/335–8518 for tours). Pick up a campus map and parking pass from the visitor center adjacent to the fire station (follow the signs on Stadium Way).

Skiing. In season, head for the Blue Mountains and *Ski Bluewood* (tel. 509/382–4725), 21 miles southeast of Dayton (52 miles from Walla Walla) for cross-country and downhill skiing. The area, which gets more than 300 inches of snow a year, has two triple chair lifts and two T-bars serving 26 runs. The vertical rise is 1,125 feet, the highest base elevation in the state. Ski Bluewood's season usually runs from Thanksgiving through the first week of April. Forty miles southeast of Walla Walla, just outside Oregon's North Fork Umatilla Wilderness, *Spout Springs* (tel. 503/566–2164) ski area has two chair lifts and two T-bars, along with a cross-country skiing trail system. Some of the runs are lit for night skiing.

Steptoe Battlefield and Steptoe Butte. In the Palouse area, Highway 195 offers turnoffs that will satisfy history buffs as well as those who like panoramic views. Following this road, the Steptoe Battlefield, near Rosalia, is 40 miles north of Pullman. As with Little Bighorn later, the U.S. Cavalry lost the battle fought here in 1858 to the Native Americans. Although all you can see now is a wheat field, a marker map on the roadside offers details that help you envision it as a field of action. For a commanding view of the rolling Palouse, take the winding drive 9 miles north of Colfax on Highway 195, to the top of Steptoe Butte. There's a picnic area here, but plan for wind, which is constant.

Walla Walla. An Indian name meaning "many waters" or "small, rapid streams," Walla Walla (population 26,000) dates to 1856, when Colonel Edward Steptoe established a settlement here; Main Street was built on the Nez Perce Indian Trail. Now the streets are tree-lined and downtown Walla Walla has 25 historic buildings, many recently renovated. Information about walking and bicycling tours of town can be obtained from the Chamber of Commerce (*see* Tourist Information, *below*). *Whitman College*, a private liberal arts institution, is an excellent place for a stroll; a creek runs through the tree-filled campus. *Pioneer Park*, one of the oldest in the state, has an aviary with a fine collection of native and exotic birds. On the western outskirts of town, *Fort Walla Walla Museum* (Myra Rd., tel. 509/525–7703) houses most of the heirlooms and artifacts of the town's early families. More interesting, however, is the museum's Pioneer Village, a collection of 14 original settlers' buildings. Seven miles west of present-day Walla Walla, the *Whitman Mission* (Hwy. 12, tel. 509/529–2761) was founded in 1836 by Marcus and Narcissa Whitman. In 1847 a band of Cayuse Indians attacked the settlement and killed the Whitmans and a dozen others; they also took 50 captives, most of whom were later ransomed. The outlines of the mission building foundations are marked; an overlook on an adjacent hill affords a good sense of the vista that the settlers had of the area.

Wineries. Although not as extensive as the wine district near the Tri-Cities in central Washington, the Palouse has its own version of a winery tour. Tourists can stop at *Woodward Canyon Winery* (Hwy. 12, 10 mi east of Walla Walla, tours by appointment, tel. 509/525–4129), which has a small tasting room behind a grain elevator, or *Waterbrook* (just south of Lowden off Hwy. 12 on McDonald Rd., tel. 509/529–4770), set in a converted warehouse. Housed in the historic old Lowden schoolhouse, *L'Ecole No. 41* (tel. 509/525–0940) offers a dining area and will cater luncheons and dinners on request. In Walla Walla, *Leonetti Cellars* (41 Lowden School Rd., tel. 509/525–1428) has a tiny tasting room open just one weekend a year in September. The tasting room of *Biscuit Ridge Winery* (in Dixie, 11 mi northeast of Walla Walla on Hwy. 12, tel. 509/529–4986) is in the vineyard of a working farm; owner Jack Durham was formerly a fishing and hunting guide in Alaska.

Restaurants

Some gastronomes head to Dayton just for **Patit Creek Restaurant** (tel. 509/382–2625), named after the creek that meanders through town and in what was a service station in the 1920s. French/Continental cuisine with a Northwest bent is featured here—say, salmon with berry sauce in season or veal with sage. Call ahead; it's sometimes difficult to get in. If a burger, fries, and a milkshake are more your fancy in Dayton, stop at **Gasoline Alley** (tel. 509/382–2775), another converted service station that rolls up the old garage door and offers dining alfresco in season or in Buddy Holly's tour bus, permanently parked here, where tables have been installed. In Walla Walla, try the salads and pastas at **Jacobi's** (tel. 509/525–2677), a café partially set in a former railroad dining car connected to an old railroad depot. It's a hangout for Whitman College students, who sit and talk over espresso and beer from local microbreweries. College students in Pullman enjoy similar fare at **Swilly's** (tel. 509/334–3395), in an old brick photo studio perched on the banks of the languid Palouse River. For more formal dining, try the standard American chicken, beef, and pasta dishes at **The Seasons** (tel. 509/334–1410), set in a remodeled 1930s clapboard house on a hillside overlooking downtown Pullman.

Tourist Information

Dayton Chamber of Commerce (E. 166 Main St., Dayton, WA 99328, tel. 509/382–4825); **Pullman Chamber of Commerce** (N. 415 Grand Ave., Pullman, WA 99136, tel. 509/334–3565); **Walla Walla Chamber of Commerce** (29 E. Sumach, Walla Walla, WA 99362, tel. 509/525–0850).

Green Gables Inn

In a business where location is often everything, Green Gables Inn has everything. One block from the Whitman College campus, the Arts and Crafts–style mansion is in a picturesque historic district: Trees nearly a century old line the peaceful streets, and most of the homes in the area have been carefully restored.

Rowland H. Smith and Clarinda Green Smith, for whom the house was built in 1909, took the lead in developing the neighborhood. For nearly four decades after 1940, their place housed the nurses and offices of the Walla Walla General Hospital; it didn't return to being a private residence until 1978. Margaret Buchan and her husband, Jim, the sports editor at the local newspaper, bought the mansion in 1990 and converted it to a B&B and reception facility.

A broad porch, tucked under the overhanging eaves, sweeps across the front of the mansion and around one side, an ideal setting for relaxing on a warm afternoon, lemonade and book in hand. The Buchans filled the yard with flowering plants, bulbs, and shrubs. Inside the front vestibule, a large foyer is flanked by two sitting areas, both with fireplaces and one with a TV.

The five guest rooms, whose names are derived from the novel *Anne of Green Gables*, are on the second floor; the hallway between them is lined with floor-to-ceiling bookshelves, and a love seat tucked into a corner creates a cozy library for visitors. All of the rooms feature baths with claw-foot tubs. The only room with a fireplace, Idlewild, also has a private deck and a Jacuzzi. Dryad's Bubble is sufficiently spacious to accommodate a reading area with an overstuffed chair and ottoman, a dresser and dressing table, and a king-size bed with striped comforter; French doors open to a small private balcony. The smallest room, Mayflowers was once the maid's quarters; now the picture of Victorian femininity, with floral wallpaper, an antique quilt, and plenty of pillows with lace shams, it affords lots of privacy.

Margaret serves breakfast, which might include sausage quiche and seasonal fruit, in a formal dining room. An Arts and Crafts–style sideboard displaying her collection of china and serving pieces from the early 1900s runs the length of one wall.

Address: *922 Bonsella St., Walla Walla, WA 99362, tel. 509/525–5501.*
Accommodations: *5 double rooms with baths, 1 suite, 1 housekeeping suite in carriage house.*
Amenities: *Air-conditioning, cable TV in rooms; off-street parking; children under 12 welcome in carriage house.*
Rates: *$75–$100, carriage house $160; full breakfast. AE, D, MC, V.*
Restrictions: *No smoking, no pets.*

The Purple House
Bed and Breakfast

Although only a block off Highway 12—which is also the main street through Dayton—The Purple House Bed and Breakfast is quiet; perhaps because Dayton isn't on the way to anywhere, traffic is never oppressive here. Owner Christine Williscroft spent five years remodeling and decorating the Queen Anne–style home, built in 1882 by a pioneer physician in what is now one of Dayton's oldest neighborhoods, before opening it to guests in 1991.

A native of southern Germany, Christine brought European touches to her B&B. The main floor guest room, which she calls the master bedroom, has a bidet in the bathroom, and French doors open to the patio and swimming pool that comprise the entire backyard of the house. Christine's real passion, however, is for things Chinese. Her formal living room is filled with Chinese antiques and appointments: Oriental rugs, an antique screen, a wedding kimono, and a hutch. Two carved wooden temple dogs guard the room's grand piano, and two Shih Tzus guard the house.

Privacy was a priority in the design of the guest rooms. A studio bedroom above the garage, cozy but rather dark, has a freestanding fireplace and a kitchenette. Guests in the master bedroom have a pink sunken tub, color-coordinated with the rest of the room, which includes a rose print bedspread. Two accommodations upstairs share not only a bath with a marble shower, floor, sink, and counter, but also a small sitting area at the top of the stairs. An antique oak sleigh bed and forest-green paisley wallpaper make the smaller of the rooms feel snug. The other room, facing the front yard, lacks antiques but is cheerful and sunny.

Strudel and huckleberry pancakes often turn up at breakfast along with local bacon or sausage. Christine will pack a picnic lunch for you, and she offers afternoon pastries and tea in the parlor. Dinner, served family style, is available at $25 per person for guests (minimum six people). A typical entrée might be Hungarian goulash, pork roast, or standing rib roast.

Address: *415 E. Clay St., Dayton, WA 99328, tel. 509/382–3159.*
Accommodations: *1 double room with bath, 2 doubles share 1 bath, 1 housekeeping double.*
Amenities: *Air-conditioning, cable TV in TV room; garage storage for ski equipment and bicycles, swimming pool May–Sept.; dinner available.*
Rates: *$85–$125; full breakfast, picnic lunches, afternoon refreshments. MC, V.*
Restrictions: *No smoking indoors, small pets only.*

Stone Creek Inn

When it was built in 1883, the Moore mansion was a home in the country; now it's a 4-acre oasis in a modest residential neighborhood. The house has a distinguished history: Original owner Miles Moore was the last governor of the Washington Territories and later the mayor of Walla Walla. Stone Creek still runs through the estate and century-old trees tower over the lush lawns, punctuated by flower beds near the mansion. The pond in which Moore's three sons splashed has been replaced by a swimming pool (not available for guest use), but otherwise the estate has been carefully restored to its original splendor. Although a busy traffic artery runs by the property, a thick wall of trees and foliage is an effective sound barrier.

Greg and Gwena Petersen, owners of a Dairy Queen franchise in nearby Milton-Freewater, Oregon, bought the three-story Queen Anne structure in 1991. Little renovation was required, so the Petersens directed their energies toward decorating the first and second floors of the mansion and landscaping the grounds. They obtained a houseful of antiques at local estate auctions, and Greg, an amateur entomologist, installed his extensive collection of mounted insects and butterflies in the formal parlor and library.

Greg restores classic cars in the garage at the back of the house, and he'll happily take you for a spin in one of them. If you prefer, however, he'll give you a bicycle tour of the area; the Petersens keep five bikes for visitors.

There are only two guest rooms available now—three additional ones are being prepared—so visitors enjoy a great deal of privacy. The afternoon sun brightens the first-floor accommodation, which features a Victorian quilt on a brass bed; the bath is opulent, with a marble counter, gold-plated faucets, and crystal lighting fixtures. In winter, a fireplace warms occupants of a second-floor room that's brightened with yellow wallpaper and bedspread and lined on one wall with shuttered bay windows. Those staying in this room have a private screened porch overlooking Stone Creek and the swimming pool.

Breakfast—typically a fresh local fruit compote with Belgian waffles, French toast, Swedish pancakes, or crepes—is served in a formal dining room with a bay window.

Address: *720 Bryant St., Walla Walla, WA 99362, tel. 509/529–8120.*
Accommodations: *2 double rooms with baths.*
Amenities: *Air-conditioning, fireplace in 1 room; bicycles.*
Rates: *$75; full breakfast. No credit cards.*
Restrictions: *No smoking, no pets.*

Chez Nous

C hez Nous offers guests a rural escape just five minutes southwest of Dayton along Highway 12. French-born innkeeper Pierre-Louis Monteillet, who grows wheat on the 27-acre farm, and his wife, Joan, expanded and rebuilt the 1909 structure, which was originally used to house railroad workers. (Light sleepers note: The tracks are a stone's throw from the front gate, and a highway runs just beyond them.)

The entire house is rented rather than individual rooms, making this ideal for a family or for two couples traveling together. In addition to the one-bedroom suite with a bath, there's a 10-by-12-foot cupola with a double futon. Guests can choose from a breakfast menu that might include morel and cheese omelets (made from farm-fresh eggs) and Swedish crepes with lingonberry sauce. After this copious repast, you might want to laze the day away at the swimming hole on the river, or sit out on the deck at the front of the house.

Address: *Rte. 1, Box 61, Dayton, WA 99328, tel. 509/382–2711.*
Accommodations: *2-bedroom house; 1 suite with bath, additional bath downstairs.*
Amenities: *Air-conditioning, cable TV, whirlpool bath, sauna; tea available 4–5 PM on request; pasture available for horses.*
Rates: *$100; full breakfast. No credit cards.*
Restrictions: *No smoking indoors, no pets indoors.*

British Columbia

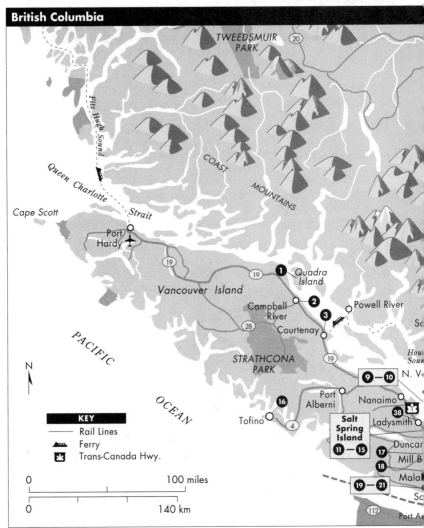

TWEEDSMUIR PARK ㉛

Fitz Hugh Sound

Queen Charlotte

Strait

Cape Scott

COAST MOUNTAINS

Port Hardy

19

19 ❶ Quadra Island

Vancouver Island

Campbell River ❷

28 ❸ Powell River

Courtenay

STRATHCONA PARK

19

PACIFIC

❾ — ❿ N. V

Port Alberni

Nanaimo

Hou Sour

Sc

OCEAN

❶❻

Tofino

4

Salt Spring Island

Ladysmith

38

KEY
— Rail Lines
🚢 Ferry
🚘 Trans-Canada Hwy.

❶❶ — ❶❺

❶❼ Duncar

Mill B

❶❽

0   100 miles
0   140 km

❶❾ — ㉑ Mala

Sc

112 Port A

Abigail's, **22**	Carberry Gardens, **27**	Edelweiss Pension, **8**	Johnson House, **41**
The Aerie, **18**	Carney's Cottage	English Bay Inn, **40**	Laburnum Cottage, **44**
April Point Lodge	B&B, **5**	Fernhill Lodge, **35**	Lacarno Beach
and Fishing Resort, **2**	Chalet Luise, **6**	Greystone Manor, **3**	B&B, **42**
Beach House	Chesterman's	Hastings House, **11**	Le Chamois, **4**
B&B, **12**	Beach B&B, **16**	Haterleigh Heritage	Malahat Farm
The Beaconsfield, **25**	Cliffside Inn, **36**	House, **23**	Guest House, **20**
The Bedford, **26**	Corbett House, **37**	Holland House Inn, **28**	Mulberry Manor, **30**
Borthwick Country	Durlacher Hof, **7**	Joan Brown's	Oak Bay Beach
Manor, **33**		B&B, **29**	Hotel, **31**

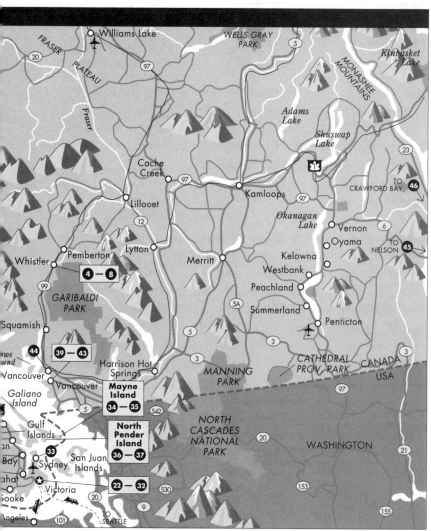

Vancouver and Environs
Including Whistler

*Bounded by the Pacific Ocean to the west and the U.S. border
to the south, the southwestern corner of British Columbia is
dramatically beautiful, with verdant forests and rocky spires
that look out majestically over fjord-like waterways. This was
long the home of the Coast Salish tribes—some of whom
remain here today—who lived for many years on the area's
abundant natural resources.*

*The face of the land began to change with the influx of miners,
trappers, loggers, fishermen, and other settlers who came in
the late 18th century, encouraged by the stories of James Cook,
George Vancouver, and other explorers. Settlements like New
Westminster and Granville (Vancouver's original townsite)
sprang up around trading posts and sawmills along the
waterfront and continued to grow and develop with the arrival
of the Canadian transcontinental railway in the 1880s.*

*With its deep natural harbor, the town of Vancouver (which
had a population of 1,000 by the time of its incorporation in
1886) was destined to become a major shipping terminus.
Today it is a dynamic, multifaceted city that comfortably
combines cosmopolitan and outdoor attractions. Tourism
joins the older shipping, fishing, logging, and mining
industries—as well as the newer banking and high-tech
businesses—as one of the major sources of revenue for the
region. The population's broad spectrum of nationalities—
British, Chinese, Japanese, Italian, French, German, Greek,
and even American—give Vancouver an exciting
international face, as well as some wonderful restaurants.*

*Many large hotel chains were attracted to Vancouver in the
past decades, but when the International Exposition came to
town in the summer of 1986, residents began to open up their
homes to accommodate the overflow of visitors. Although most
of these early B&Bs have since closed, those that remain have*

become polished, and the trend toward more intimate
hospitality continues to make inroads in town.

Whistler, 75 scenic miles northeast of Vancouver, has been a
favorite retreat for hunting and fishing since the early 1900s,
but it wasn't until the 1960s that skiing became popular here.
The multimillion-dollar European-style village built at the
base of Whistler and Blackcomb mountains in 1980 has become
one of the top-ranked ski resorts in the world. As a result, the
past decade has seen the rapid rise of alpine-style pensions in
the area—some luxurious, others bare-bones basic.

Places to Go, Sights to See

The Canadian Craft Museum (639 Hornby St., tel. 604/687–8266). One of the
newest additions to Vancouver's list of outstanding galleries, the Canadian Craft
Museum showcases traditional and contemporary works in glass, fiber, wood,
acrylics, and clay. The Museum Shop has a broad selection of one-of-a-kind,
handcrafted objects for sale.

Chinatown. Join the jostling crowds in Vancouver's Chinatown, one of the
largest in North America, with its ornate Oriental facades; dim sum restaurants;
shops selling noodles, herbs, silks, and souvenirs; and open-front produce stalls.
Look for the *Sam Kee Building,* only 6 feet wide, at the corner of Pender and
Carrall streets.

Gardens. Among the many green spots in Vancouver are two fine Oriental gardens and several flower gardens. If time permits, each of the following is worth
the trip: *Bloedel Floral Conservatory* (Queen Elizabeth Park, 33rd Ave. and
Cambie St., tel. 604/872–5513); *Dr. Sun Yat-sen Classical Chinese Garden* (578
Carrall St., tel. 604/689–7133); *Nitobe Memorial Garden* (N.W. Marine Dr., tel.
604/822–6038); *University of British Columbia Botanical Garden* (6804 S.W.
Marine Dr., tel. 604/822–4208); *Van Dusen Botanical Garden* (5251 Oak St., tel.
604/266–7194).

Gastown. Victorian gaslights and false-front shops along the cobbled streets and
narrow mews of this restored heritage area make Gastown a favorite site for
filming motion pictures. Here you'll find a statue of "Gassy" Jack Deighton,
founder of Vancouver's original townsite, and the world's first steam-powered
clock, along with antiques stores, clothing boutiques, souvenir shops, pubs, and
restaurants.

Granville Island. This revitalized industrial area across the bay from downtown
Vancouver is now home to theaters, artisans' studios, a microbrewery, an art college, waterfront restaurants, a kids-only market, a water park, and an enormous
public market. Plan to make a day of it.

Robson Street. No visit to Vancouver is complete without a stroll down Robson Street. You can browse through exclusive clothing boutiques and gift emporiums or stop for espresso at one of the many sidewalk cafés and enjoy the passing parade of people.

Sea to Sky Highway. This stretch of Highway 99, running along Howe Sound and up into the mountains en route to Whistler, takes you past some of the most beautiful scenery on the West Coast. If you're interested in copper mining, heavy machinery, and deep caverns, stop along the way at the *British Columbia Museum of Mining* (Brittania Beach, tel. 604/896–2233); this is not for the claustrophobic, however. A bit farther up, near the town of Squamish, *Shannon Falls*, a shimmering ribbon of tumbling water, and *The Chiefs*, the second-largest monolith in the world and a magnet for climbers, are both worth a quick detour.

Skiing. Three fine ski areas lie within minutes of the Vancouver city center. *Cypress Bowl* (Box 91252, West Vancouver, tel. 604/926–5612), with 23 groomed runs on two lift-serviced mountains, boasts the longest vertical run of the Vancouver resorts, along with night skiing and a variety of Nordic and backcountry skiing trails. The string of lights visible each night on the North Shore of the city mark the arc-lit runs of *Grouse Mountain* (6400 Nancy Greene Way, North Vancouver, tel. 604/984–0661), offering 13 runs and a variety of lifts. *Mt. Seymore* (1700 Indian River Rd., North Vancouver, tel. 604/986–2261) has more novice runs than the other two. The 20 downhill runs are serviced by a network of tramways, chairs, lifts, and tows that are open for night skiing; there are also cross-country trails throughout this provincial park.

One of the top ski destinations in the world, *Whistler* resort offers more than 200 marked runs and the longest lift-serviced runs in North America—with a drop of 1 vertical mile. The regular season runs from late November through May; glacier heli-skiing is available throughout the season. The Whistler Resort Association (4010 Whistler Way, Whistler, tel. 800/994–7853) can provide further information.

Stanley Park. This 1,000-acre, green oasis in the heart of Vancouver has something for everyone: the *Vancouver Public Aquarium* (tel. 604/682–1118), a zoo, tennis courts, miniature golf, a children's water park, rose gardens, totem poles, miles of sandy beaches, a 6-mile seawall promenade for bikers and joggers, and a vast network of forested trails. There are also a couple of restaurants where you can stop for tea while you catch your breath.

University of British Columbia Museum of Anthropology (6393 N.W. Marine Dr., tel. 604/822–3825). If your visit to Vancouver will be short, this museum should be on your list of must-sees in town. The incredible collections of Pacific Northwest native artifacts—totems, masks, jewelry, ceremonial costumes, canoes, even longhouses—and of contemporary art are not to be missed.

Whistler Village. The heart of the Whistler ski resort, Whistler Village is a charming European-style complex of clock towers, pedestrian avenues, shops, restaurants, and clubs. Lifts that whisk skiers from the village to the peaks of Blackcomb and Whistler mountains in winter also carry hikers and mountain bikers to flower-filled alpine meadows during the warm months.

Restaurants

The palette of international eateries in Vancouver is almost overwhelming. When the taste buds are craving Italian, **Café de Medici** (tel. 604/669–9322) and **Umberto's** (tel. 604/687–6316) are the best choices. There are numerous excellent Oriental eateries in town, but none can match the deal you'll get at the funky **Japanese Deli House** (tel. 604/681–6484), where all-you-can-eat sushi is served along with miso soup, chicken teriyaki, and tempura. Vancouverites favor the onion pie, salad with goat cheese and greens, grilled game, and other French fare at **Le Crocodile** (tel. 604/669–4298). For a special treat, take in the lavish Taste of Atlantis seafood buffet or the decadent, 20-item Chocoholic Bar available every Friday and Saturday night at **Café Fleuri** (tel. 604/682–5511); an assortment of light Continental dishes is also on the menu.

In Whistler, you can beat the crowds by dining either at **Hoz's Café & Pub** (tel. 604/932–4424), which serves reasonably priced salads, ribs, pastas, and seafood in relaxed surroundings, or at the pricey, more formal **Rimrock Cafe and Oyster Bar** (tel. 604/932–5565), offering Continental cuisine and fresh seafood. In Whistler Village (downtown Whistler), best bets are **Sushi Village** (tel. 604/932–4540) for reasonably priced Japanese food, **Araxi's** (tel. 604/932–2112) for Northern Mediterranean and Italian cuisine, **Chez Joël** (tel. 604/932–2112) for Swiss fondues, and **La Rúa** (tel. 604/932–5011) for outstanding Continental dishes.

Tourist Information

British Columbia Ministry of Tourism (865 Hornby St., Suite 802, Vancouver, B.C. V6Z 2G3, tel. 604/660–2861 or 800/663–6000); **Tourism Vancouver Travel Infocentre** (200 Burrard St., Vancouver, B.C. V6C 3L6, tel. 604/683–2000 for information, 604/683–2772 for reservations, or 800/888–8835); **Whistler Resort Association** (4010 Whistler Way, Whistler, B.C. V0N 1B4, tel. 604/932–3928 or 800/944–7853).

Reservation Services

A Home Away from Home (1441 Howard Ave., Vancouver, B.C. V5B 3S2, tel. 604/294–1760, fax 604/294–0799); **Born Free** (4390 Frances St., Vancouver, B.C. V5C 2R3, tel. 604/298–8815); **Old English Bed and Breakfast Registry** (Box 86818, North Vancouver, B.C. V7L 4L3, tel. 604/986–5069); **Town and Country Bed and Breakfast** (2803 W. 4th Ave., Box 74542, Vancouver, B.C. V6K 1K2, tel. 604/731–5942); **Whistler B&B Inns** (Box 352, Whistler, B.C. V0N 1B0, tel. 800/665–1892).

Laburnum Cottage

When you're strolling in the garden at Laburnum Cottage, set next to a quiet forest, it's hard to imagine that you're only 15 minutes from the city center on Vancouver's North Shore, near the Capilano River and various ski resorts. The Tudor influences in the architecture of this 1945 cottage are highlighted by the formal English landscaping, including a meandering creek, winding paths, and cool, serene resting areas.

Innkeeper Delphine Masterton, assisted by her daughter, Margot, and her son-in-law, Win, treats guests to tea and maple-leaf shortbread cookies after showing them around the house and garden and getting them settled in. These charming hosts are delights to chat with, but they're also happy to give you all the privacy you need. In keeping with its formal exterior, the inside of their home is appointed with fine English antiques and family heirlooms, complemented by an array of collectibles that Delphine picked up on her world travels.

The second-floor guest rooms in the main house are light and airy; they're furnished with polished antiques, brass beds, Chinese and Persian carpets, imported linens, and down comforters in white eyelet or floral duvet covers. Set amid the rhododendrons, azaleas, roses, dogwoods, willow trees, and Japanese maple in the garden, the romantic little summer house, decorated in tones of blue, mauve, and white, has heirloom wicker furniture, a large brass bed near the fireplace, and a kitchenette. In addition, a larger detached suite with a full kitchen offers two lofted sleeping areas above the master bedroom—a treat for children.

The heart of the main house is the spacious kitchen, with its yellow-and-white-striped wallpaper and shiny, green marble countertops. Breakfast, served around the big pine table or in the terra cotta–tiled breakfast room, is a real event. Margot and Delphine bustle about the English Aga stove preparing strawberry pancakes, Mexican eggs with salsa, or other tasty main dishes accompanied by cinnamon buns or scones and plates of seasonal fruit.

Address: *1388 Terrace Ave., North Vancouver, B.C. V7R 1B4, tel. 604/988–4877.*
Accommodations: *3 double rooms with baths, 2 housekeeping suites.*
Amenities: *Guest phone; German, Italian, and French spoken; children and small pets welcome.*
Rates: *$100–$150; full breakfast, afternoon refreshments. MC, V.*
Restrictions: *No smoking indoors.*

Le Chamois

The multigabled Le Chamois hotel sits across the creek from the bustling heart of Whistler Village, at the foot of the Blackcomb ski runs. This luxurious, intimate property is small enough to ensure personal service but large enough to have all the extras, and its ski-in/ski-out location can't be beat.

The mountain deer from which Le Chamois derives its name is depicted in a beautiful tapestry hung behind the front desk in the elegant marble lobby. Glass elevators whisk guests to spacious rooms outfitted with berber carpets, light oak furniture, queen-size beds, minikitchens, marble baths, and walls of picture windows overlooking mountain slopes and towering conifers. Naturally, accommodations on the upper floors have the grandest, most expansive views.

Duplex rooms with deep, oval whirlpool tubs in front of the windows and down comforter–covered beds tucked into angled alcoves are popular with those seeking a romantic setting. The one-bedroom suites with a sofa or Murphy bed in the separate living room and two full baths—slightly less expensive—are better suited to families. Elegantly appointed three- and four-bedroom suites with gas fireplaces, fully equipped kitchens, and washer/dryers are a good bet for groups on an extended stay.

For those who haven't already gotten enough exercise putting about on one of Whistler's fine golf courses, or hiking, biking, or skiing in the area, the hotel offers a heated swimming pool large enough for laps, as well as a fitness room; the outdoor Jacuzzi might help relax muscles sore from all these activities. Other amenities include a guest laundry and storage room for ski equipment and bikes in the secured basement garage. La Rúa, the Continental restaurant on the ground floor of the hotel, is the rising star of the local dining scene.

Address: *4557 Blackcomb Way, Box 1044, Whistler, B.C. V0N 1B0, tel. 604/932–8700 or 800/777–0185, fax 604/938–1888.*

Accommodations: *6 housekeeping double rooms with baths, 44 housekeeping suites, 5 3-bedroom housekeeping suites.*

Amenities: *Air-conditioning, phone, cable TV, microwave, refrigerator, coffeemaker, toaster in all rooms; soaker whirlpool tubs in some rooms; some rooms accessible to wheelchair users; restaurant, deli, limited room service, gift shop, conference facilities; children welcome; complimentary parking.*

Rates: *$230, suites $220–$950; Continental breakfast. AE, DC, MC, V.*

Restrictions: *No pets; 2-night minimum in winter, 5-night minimum over Christmas.*

West End Guest House

L attice rails with brimming baskets of flowers line the front porch of the West End Guest House, a 1906 quasi-Victorian "Painted Lady" done up in bright pink with white trim. Bay windows peer out at the small houses and apartment buildings across the street. One block south of Robson Street, the inn is within easy reach of the best shopping, dining, and entertainment Vancouver has to offer. The trails, gardens, tennis courts, aquarium, zoo, and beaches of Stanley Park are also close by, so leave the car at the inn; complimentary off-street parking—a rarity in downtown Vancouver—is available here.

Imported door frames, a grand banister, and bathrooms were added during the renovations made before the inn opened in 1986, but the period flavor of the home was preserved and the addition of many excellent Victorian and Edwardian pieces help re-create the era. The original owner was one of the first professional photographers in Vancouver; his photos chronicling life in the city from 1906 to 1925, found when the house was refurbished, now hang in stairwells and hallways.

Current owner Evan Penner, assisted by the very able and amiable Susanne Sulzberger, runs a tidy operation. Evan is an avid collector of antiques; among his recent acquisitions are the Belgian Art Deco sideboard, hutch, table, and chairs in the dining room where guests gather for multicourse breakfasts. These might include

French toast with melted Brie and fresh fruit sauces, hazelnut butter waffles with plump sausages, or poached eggs on a bed of spinach topped with tarragon hollandaise.

Guest rooms feature period appointments such as feather mattresses on shiny brass beds and antique armoires and desks, but have all the modern amenities, including phones, televisions, and ceiling fans or skylights that open to summer breezes. Other special touches include thick cotton robes, hand-knit slippers, homemade chocolates, and hors d'oeuvres and sherry served by the fire in the parlor. Number 2, the largest and most romantic room, has sponge-painted walls and a gambrel ceiling; lace curtains around double-sashed windows; a high brass bed, cozy love seat, and gas fireplace; and a long, old-fashioned slipper tub.

Address: *1362 Haro St., Vancouver, B.C. V6E 1G2, tel. 604/681–2889, fax 604/688–8812.*
Accommodations: *7 double rooms with baths.*
Amenities: *Cable TV and phone in rooms, robes and slippers; bikes.*
Rates: *$95–$180; full breakfast, evening refreshments. AE, D, MC, V.*
Restrictions: *No smoking indoors, no pets; 2-night minimum during holidays.*

Carney's Cottage Bed and Breakfast

Carney's Cottage, 2 miles outside Whistler Village (though easily accessible via the new Whistler bus system), has the most reasonable rates of all the charming pensions in Whistler. While the exterior of this two-story home is similar to the alpine chalets of the other inns in town, inside, Carney's stands alone in providing creature comforts.

Hostess Colleen Carney, a lively young woman with a knack for making guests feel right at home, keeps the room decor simple and sweet—plump comforters cover firm beds with polished wood headboards. While some rooms have in-suite baths stocked with toiletries, others share baths.

Breakfast, served in the fireside dining room, includes a cold buffet with breads, fruits, and cereals; and hot dishes such as waffles with strawberries and cream or eggs Benedict. Colleen's dogs, Winston and Kima, are always happy to take guests on walks in the adjacent park to work off meals.

Address: *8106 Cedar Springs Rd., Whistler, B.C. V0N 1B8, tel. 604/938–8007 or 800/665–1892, fax 604/938–8023.*
Accommodations: *5 double rooms with baths, 1 single and 2 doubles share 2 baths.*
Amenities: *Fireplace and balcony in one room; hot tub, sauna, guest lounge, guest phone, VCR and video library, refreshment center, ski locker, library; some dinners available.*
Rates: *$65–$149; full breakfast. MC, V.*
Restrictions: *No smoking, no children under 10 in winter, no pets.*

Chalet Luise

In 1981, Austrian-born Luise Zinsli and her Swiss husband, Eric, were the first to build an alpine-style pension in Whistler. Set in a quiet residential area close to the village, Chalet Luise is also very near the ski slopes and cross-country trails.

As traditionally alpine inside as out, the house features carved wood furnishings and a leather couch set before the fireplace in the living/dining room. The snug guest rooms have colorful furniture and very firm mattresses. Two romantic rooms with bay windows and gas fireplaces were recently added. Attention is paid to details here: A wooden crib above a staircase to the hot tub holds rolled towels, while a hallway en route to the sauna is lined with racks for ski clothing to be warmed by a wood stove.

Address: *7461 Ambassador Crescent, Box 352, Whistler, B.C. V0N 1B0, tel. 604/932–4187 or 800/665–1892, fax 604/938–1531.*
Accommodations: *8 double rooms with baths.*
Amenities: *Pay phone, sauna, hot tub, ski room, guest refrigerator; ski and summer packages; occasional dinners available; German spoken.*
Rates: *$105–$139; full breakfast, afternoon refreshments. MC, V.*
Restrictions: *No smoking indoors, no pets; 2-night minimum on summer weekends, 3-night minimum on winter weekends, 5-night minimum on holidays.*

Durlacher Hof

Enthusiastic Erika Durlacher and her husband, Peter, run the most visible château in Whistler—immediately on the main highway—and their fancy Tyrolean inn is highly praised by many, but it's the farthest from the snowy slopes of the inns reviewed here.

Custom fir woodwork and doors, exposed ceiling beams, a *kachelofen* (tiled oven), and antler chandeliers hung over fir benches and tables carry out the rustic European theme. The green and maroon bedrooms contain more fine examples of custom-crafted wooden furniture. Two upgraded rooms have such added amenities as double whirlpool tubs and minibars.

Platters of fruit salad, granola, sticky buns, French bread, imported cheeses, and Bavarian meats are set out buffet style to supplement the rich Austrian specialties served as main courses.

Address: *7055 Nesters Rd., Whistler, B.C. V0N 1B0, tel. 604/932-1924, fax 604/938-1980.*
Accommodations: *7 double rooms with baths, 1 suite.*
Amenities: *Sauna, hot tub; ski packages; afternoon tea, occasional guest-chef dinners; badminton court; shuttle to airport, German spoken.*
Rates: *$105–$150, suite $170; full breakfast. MC, V.*
Restrictions: *No smoking, no pets; 2-night minimum on weekends, 3-night minimum on holidays, closed Nov.*

Edelweiss Pension

When Jacques Morel, once a skier on the French national team, fell in love with the slopes of Whistler, he and his German wife, Ursula, decided to build a pension here in 1984. After completing the alpine chalet, with its wooden balconies, pine furniture, and *bauernmalrei* (Austrian-style painting), Jacques headed back to the slopes—he runs occasional camps for skiers—but he's around in the mornings to help with breakfast and to post ski reports.

Cheery rooms are furnished simply in authentic alpine fashion, with thick eiderdowns folded at the foot of pine bedsteads; all have bathrooms and some have telephones and balconies. In 1993, the Morels added a romantic suite with fireplace and private entrance. Ursula prepares bountiful, internationally themed breakfasts, and often has *glühwine*, a warm, spicy wine concoction, simmering on the wood stove in the evenings. A big hot tub and a sauna provide après-ski relaxation.

Address: *7126 Nancy Greene Dr., Box 850, Whistler, B.C. V0N 1B0, tel. 604/932-3641 or, in B.C., 800/665-1892; fax 604/938-1746.*
Accommodations: *8 double rooms with baths, 1 suite.*
Amenities: *Hot tub, sauna, pay phone; occasional dinners available; children welcome; ski and summer packages; French and German spoken.*
Rates: *$99–$119, suite $139; full breakfast. AE, MC, V.*
Restrictions: *No smoking, no pets; 2-night minimum on weekends, 5-night minimum on holidays.*

English Bay Inn

Bob Chapin, a former school administrator, makes innkeeping look easy. His remodeled 1939 modified Tudor is likely to become a favorite address in Vancouver because of its prime location—a quiet residential neighborhood just a block from Stanley Park and English Bay and within walking distance of Robson Street—as well as its excellent personal service.

The house, adorned throughout with fresh flowers, has floor-to-ceiling leaded-glass diamond-paned windows and cove ceilings; furnishings include a gilt Louis IV clock and candelabra, an elegant 18th-century Federal sofa in the fireside living room, and an elaborately carved Gothic dining room suite. In the equally striking bedrooms, peach or mauve walls offset the mascu-

line Victorian gentlemen's chairs, Federal mirrors, and crisply ironed Ralph Lauren bedding on reproduction Louis Philippe sleigh beds. Room 5 is a romantic choice, with a fireplace in the loft bedroom, as well as a sitting room next to the garden, and stained-glass windows and a whirlpool tub in the bathroom.

Address: *1968 Comox St., Vancouver, B.C. V6G 1R4, tel. 604/683–8002.*
Accommodations: *4 double rooms with baths, 1 suite.*
Amenities: *Phone in rooms, cable TV available, afternoon sherry.*
Rates: *$125–$145, suite $210; full breakfast. AE, V.*
Restrictions: *No smoking, no pets; 2-night minimum on weekends.*

Johnson House

This two-tone gray, 1920s Craftsman sits amid a picture-perfect rock garden overflowing with colorful azaleas and rhododendrons on a quiet, tree-lined avenue west of downtown Vancouver. Wooden Canadiana furnishings and an intriguing variety of collectibles—Gramophones and phonographs, carousel horses, barber shop poles—illustrate the antiques-dealing past of hosts Sandy and Rob Johnson.

The top-of-the-line Carousel Suite has a cathedral ceiling; big picture windows overlooking the mountains; an Indonesian iron-and-brass four-poster bed decked out in a wedding-ring quilt; and a spacious bathroom with whirlpool tub, pedestal sinks, tiled shower, bidet, and giant Toledo scale. Several of the other guest rooms also

have cathedral ceilings and antique brass beds; two share a bath with a claw-foot tub. Guests love the homemade muffins and jams, part of the hearty breakfast served in the sunny dining room with a view of the 20-foot rhododendron bush just outside.

Address: *2278 W. 34th Ave., Vancouver, B.C. V6M 1G6, tel. 604/266–4175.*
Accommodations: *1 double room with bath, 2 double rooms share bath, 1 suite.*
Amenities: *Cable TV, VCR, and fireplace in living room.*
Rates: *$65–$85, suite $105; full breakfast. No credit cards.*
Restrictions: *No smoking indoors, no pets.*

Lacarno Beach Bed & Breakfast

I f you'd rather be on the beach than in the thick of things downtown, Lacarno Beach is for you. This contemporary, cedar-and-glass home enjoys spectacular views of the downtown skyline framed by the North Shore mountains and English Bay.

Inside is a stunning collection of pottery and tribal artifacts that owner Sigrid (Billy) Whitman, an art dealer originally from Munich, Germany, either crafted or collected on her world travels. Two of the second-floor bedrooms feature Pacific Northwest native art, hand-stitched Thai quilts, modern pine furniture, and double-glazed, floor-to-ceiling windows that take full advantage of the scenery. The third is similarly furnished but lacks the ocean view, looking out on the garden instead.

The famous Museum of Anthropology at the University of British Columbia is just up the hill, and the sights of Granville Island are only minutes away by car. For views, price, and location, this one is hard to beat.

Address: *4550 N.W. Marine Dr., Vancouver, B.C. V6R 1B8, tel. 604/224–2177.*
Accommodations: *2 double rooms and 1 single room share 2 baths (private bath can be arranged).*
Amenities: *Cable TV, phone, video games, and kitchen in guest lounge; German spoken; windsurfing equipment.*
Rates: *$50–$70; full breakfast. MC, V.*
Restrictions: *No smoking indoors, no pets.*

Penny Farthing

A n antique bicycle sits in the country English garden of this 1912 Craftsman-style home, in a pretty residential area seven minutes south of downtown Vancouver. Exterior turquoise paint with raspberry trim, stained glass panes, oak floors, pillar-manteled fireplaces, and plate rails above dark-stained wainscoting give Penny Farthing lots of period charm. Folk art and dried flower arrangements abound throughout the house. The Louis XVI desk in the entryway and other Edwardian furnishings were brought over from England by innkeeper Lyn Hainstock.

Lyn's sense of humor is evident in guest rooms dubbed Abigail's Attic, Bettina's Boudoir, Lucinda's Lair, and Sophie's Salon, and her sense of romantic style in furnishings such as Victo-

rian lace curtains and big brass beds or oak four-posters. Copious breakfasts include cheese buns, Hawaiian muffins, stuffed crepes, herbed omelets, and other goodies (don't hesitate to ask for recipes). When it comes to entertaining, Lyn is always assisted by four house cats—Frisky, Fluffy, Harmony, and Melody—and occasionally by her daughters, Nikki and Wendy.

Address: *2855 W. 6th Ave., Vancouver, B.C. V6K 1X2, tel. 604/739–9002, fax 604/739–9004.*
Accommodations: *2 double rooms share 1 bath, 2 suites.*
Amenities: *Cable TV and guest phone in parlor; bikes.*
Rates: *$65–$75, suites $135–$155; full breakfast. No credit cards.*
Restrictions: *No smoking indoors, no pets.*

Wedgewood Manor

Tis board-and-batten house, built in 1910 by a retired British naval officer, is one of the finest lodgings in southeastern British Columbia. Much of the 50-acre estate remains forested, a brook babbles pleasantly beside the lodge, broad lawns blend right into the surrounding forest, and the cottage gardens draw abundant hummingbirds. Four spacious rooms upstairs all open onto a central reading/game room; both the Charles Darwin and Commander's rooms have lake views. Downstairs in the lodge is a dining room where breakfast is served beside a fire to cut the early morning mountain chill. Breakfast often incorporates wild berries (in season)—raspberries, huckleberries, strawberries, or blackberries—and hearty servings of muffins, eggs, and Canadian bacon. Afternoon tea is served in a semiformal parlor with fireplace, and in the summer, guests enjoy lemonade on the veranda or on the lawn. Several fine restaurants are within short driving distance of the lodge: Ask for a table on the terrace at the Kokanee Springs Golf Course clubhouse, just down the road, so you can watch the golfers. For those who want to play, be warned: The course is challenging, thick with water hazards.

Address: *Box 135, 16002 Crawford Creek Rd., Crawford Bay, B.C. V0B 1E0, tel. 604/227–9233.*
Accommodations: *4 double rooms with baths.*
Amenities: *Golf packages available, children over 5 welcome.*
Rates: *$69–$89; full breakfast. MC, V.*
Restrictions: *No smoking indoors; closed Oct. 16–Easter weekend.*

Willow Point Lodge

Tis two-story 1922 Victorian, rustic in appearance with cedar-shake siding, is perched on 3½ acres of a forested mountainside above Kootenay Lake. Innkeepers Sue and Alan Dodsworth landscaped and restored the stream and ponds that originally interrupted the front lawn. In summer, guests can spend afternoons lounging on the porch, which takes full advantage of the lake view. Inside, a broad stone fireplace crackles with a fire in the evening, tempting guests to linger in the living room. The Oak Room on the first floor also has a big stone fireplace, as well as a sitting area, canopy bed, and private entrance. There's a spacious, private, covered deck reached through French doors from the Green Room. All of the rooms offer generous views of the lake and Selkirk Mountains. Hiking trails begin right at the back door of the lodge and wind up the hillside, breaking out of the forest to vistas frequently. Breakfast always includes granola and homemade muffins; waffles with Okanagan raspberry syrup often follow.

Address: *2211 Taylor Dr. (R.R. 1, S-21, C31), Nelson, B.C. V1L 5P4, tel. 604/825–9411.*
Accommodations: *4 double rooms with baths, 2 suites.*
Amenities: *Hot tub, nature trails, off-street parking.*
Rates: *$65–$125; full breakfast. MC, V, local checks.*
Restrictions: *No smoking, no pets.*

Vancouver Island

Three-hundred-mile-long Vancouver Island lies stretched along the southwestern mainland of British Columbia, with Queen Charlotte Sound to the north, the Strait of Georgia to the east, the Strait of Juan de Fuca and the United States border to the southeast, and open Pacific Ocean to the west. It is an island of intense natural beauty and diversity; the Insular Mountain range runs down its spine, effectively sheltering the valleys and lowlands of the east side from the battering of Pacific rains that the rugged western coastline receives.

Surrounded by the Pacific Ocean and lapped by the warm Japan Current, the island enjoys mild temperatures in both winter and summer. Heavy winter rains feed the lush foliage that carpets its craggy peaks and rolling valleys. Though it has been logged continuously since the late 1800s, the island still hosts huge stands of old-growth Sitka spruce, western red cedar, hemlock, and Douglas fir. Its scenic wind- and water-sculpted coastline and pristine forests draw an increasing number of visitors every year.

Captain James Cook is generally credited with being the first Englishman to set foot on the island; he was met by Kwakiutl and other coastal natives eager to supply the timber, fish, and furs he sought in trade. However, it was Captain George Vancouver who named the island during later explorations of the region. The first white settlement occurred in the mid-1800s with the founding of a Hudson Bay Company post in what is now Victoria. Abundant natural resources brought in settlers who established new townsites as they slowly fanned up the island to fish, log, and mine coal.

Early mill and mining towns and fishing villages grew into such commercial centers as Campbell River (still a world-famous salmon fishing capital), Duncan, and Nanaimo. Although logging, mining, and fishing remain central to the island's economy, tourism has become increasingly important.

*Most of the 500,000 current residents live clustered around
Campbell River in the north and Victoria in the south—
sophisticated little metropolises that make the rest of the
island seem almost wild and woolly in comparison.*

Places to Go, Sights to See

British Columbia Forest Museum (R.R. 4, Trans-Canada Hwy., Duncan, tel.
604/746–1251). The highlight of a visit to this enormous indoor/outdoor showcase
of logging and milling equipment is a ride on an old steam locomotive across a
wooden trestle bridge.

Bungy Zone. If you're of a mind to swan dive off a 140-foot-high bridge over a
water-filled chasm—or perhaps just to watch others do it—follow the signs to
Bungy Zone (Nanaimo, tel. 604/753–5867), the only permanent bungy jump site in
British Columbia. Spectators are welcome to visit any day of the week; call for
reservations if you'd like to take the plunge yourself.

Cathedral Grove. Highway 4 takes you into MacMillan Provincial Park and
through Cathedral Grove, a corridor of towering old-growth Douglas fir and red
cedar. On your way to the west coast, stop to stretch your legs on the short trail
that runs along the river and through the grove.

Chemainus. When the local lumber/paper mill announced a shutdown that
spelled doom for this little town, the citizens did not sit back and bemoan their
fate. Instead they commissioned local artists to adorn buildings and walls with
more than two dozen murals depicting events of historical significance to the
area. Thus was born the "City of Murals," a worthwhile stop on any tour of the
island.

Native Heritage Centre (200 Cowichan Way, Duncan, tel. 604/746–8119). The
history and traditions of Northwest Coast natives come to life at the Native Heritage Centre through media presentations, interpretive dances, and demonstrations of basket weaving, totem carving, and spinning. You can also sample native
foods and purchase handmade Cowichan sweaters here.

Pacific Rim National Park (Box 280, Ucluelet, tel. 604/726–7721). On Vancouver
Island's far western edge and hugging the Pacific Ocean, this rain forest park is
divided into three sections: the Broken Group Islands, reached only by boat; the
West Coast Trail, accessible only to very experienced hikers; and Long Beach,
the most visited because of its network of easy trails and its fine interpretive center. Birds and wildlife are abundant in this verdant area, and the long shoreline is
lined with tidal pools and elevated areas for viewing the whale migration just offshore.

Sooke Regional Museum and Travel Information Centre (2070 Phillips Rd.,
Sooke, tel. 604/642–6351). The fascinating collection of Native Indian arts and pioneer artifacts housed in this tiny museum is worth a peek if you're in the neighborhood. A travel infocenter sharing the space provides handy maps for
exploring the area.

Strathcona Provincial Park (Hwy. 28, Campbell River, tel. 604/286–3122). The alpine meadows; thick forests; and myriad lakes, waterfalls, and marshy areas of Strathcona, British Columbia's oldest provincial park, are laced with campgrounds, hiking trails, and cross-country ski trails. Crowning all is Golden Hinde, Vancouver Island's highest peak at 7,218 feet.

Restaurants

Over the years, **Sooke Harbour House** (in Sooke, tel. 604/642–3421) has garnered international acclaim for its sophisticated cuisine, a combination of Pacific Northwest, French, and Japanese. Other choices for outstanding Northwest fare emphasizing fresh local ingredients are **Deep Cove Chalet** (tel. 604/656–3541) in Sidney, **The Old House Restaurant** (tel. 604/338–5406) in Courtenay, and **The Mahle House** (tel. 604/722–3621) in Nanaimo. Elegant Continental meals complement the stunning panoramic views at **The Aerie** (tel. 604/743–7115), perched high atop the Malahat.

Tourist Information

British Columbia Ministry of Tourism (865 Hornby St., Suite 802, Vancouver, B.C. V6Z 2G3, tel. 604/660–2861 or 800/663–6000); **Tourism Association of Vancouver Island** (302–345 Bastion Sq., Victoria, B.C. V8W 1J1, tel. 604/382–3551, fax 604/382–3523).

Reservation Services

AA Accommodations West Bed and Breakfast Reservations Service (660 Jones Terr., Victoria, B.C. V8Z 2L7, tel. 604/479–1986); **All Seasons Bed and Breakfast Agency** (Box 5511, Station B, Victoria, B.C. V8R 6S4, tel. 604/655–7173); **Town and Country Bed and Breakfast** (2803 W. 4th Ave., Box 74542, Vancouver, B.C. V6K 1K2, tel. 604/731–5942).

The Aerie

The beauty of the location convinced Austrians Leo and Maria Schuster to build a sprawling, Mediterranean-style villa high atop the Malahat overlooking the Gulf Islands. Together they created a luxurious, romantic retreat, small enough to afford plenty of personal attention but replete with every modern convenience—from the stunning dining room and inviting sauna and whirlpool lounge to a helipad for their high-flying guests.

Flower-bordered decks overlooking a waterfall, fish ponds, and reflecting pools are idyllic spots from which to soak in the sun and scenery. Resident mountain deer visit regularly to munch on the inn's tender new landscaping. Plans for a new highway will eventually cut the travel time to The Aerie from Victoria, but the drive along the Malahat Highway is very scenic and worth the extra time.

The Schusters brought a great deal of experience to their innkeeping venture: She formerly owned an exclusive resort in Eleuthera, and he was a master chef at a number of top international properties. Maria's refined tastes are reflected in the decor, which features billowing taffeta window coverings, lavish Chinese carpets, and Italian antiques. Her pale peach, green, and gray color scheme echoes the Mediterranean-style building that Leo designed.

Each of the guest rooms is different in layout and amenities, but all are graciously appointed, with custom-crafted furnishings and Dior bed linens. In addition, all have superb views. Some feature whirlpool tubs set before picture windows; others offer vaulted ceilings, fireplaces, or large balconies. A wing added in 1994 has plush, multilevel master suites, each at least 900 square feet.

Leo's well-honed culinary talents are showcased in the gold leaf–ceilinged dining room, where European-influenced dishes such as pheasant consommé, rack of lamb in raspberry port sauce, and crème brûlée vie with a million-dollar view for guests' attention. The dining room is open to the public for prix-fixe and à la carte meals each evening.

Address: *600 Ebadora La., Box 108, Malahat, B.C. V0R 2L0, tel. 604/743-7115 or 604/743-4055, fax 604/743-4766.*
Accommodations: *8 double rooms with baths, 14 suites.*
Amenities: *Restaurant, sauna, whirlpools, spa, indoor pool, tennis court, exercise room, library, conference room; chapel.*
Rates: *$150–$160, suites $200–$340; full breakfast. AE, MC, V.*
Restrictions: *Smoking in lounge or outside only, no pets; closed Jan.*

Sooke Harbour House

Highest accolades go to Fredrica and Sinclair Philip's Sooke Harbour House, arguably one of the top 10 country inns in North America. In the quiet village of Sooke, 23 winding miles west of Victoria, this unassuming 1929 Craftsman inn rests amid lovingly landscaped grounds on an oceanfront bluff that looks out over the Strait of Juan de Fuca and the Olympic Mountains in the distance.

All the guest rooms have fireplaces, handcrafted light-wood furniture, ocean views from decks or balconies, decanters of port, plates of home-baked cookies, and a profusion of fresh and dried flowers. Of the rooms in the inn, the split-level Blue Heron Room enjoys the best vistas. An oval Jacuzzi tub sits in the living room across from a stone fireplace and tall picture windows overlooking the sea.

In the 1986 white clapboard addition, the Victor Newman Longhouse Room boasts a grand collection of Northwest native art, including masks, paintings, and a chieftain's bench, along with a cedar pencil-post bed, two-sided fireplace, and ocean-view Jacuzzi. The Kingfisher Room has a deck, a greenhouse room with a hot tub, and a clawfoot tub in the spacious bathroom.

Pebbled paths lead through the vegetable, herb, and edible flower gardens used in meals that have garnered international acclaim for this inn's restaurant—an imaginative blend of Pacific Northwest, French, and

Japanese cuisine. Dinner is an elegant, leisurely affair, enhanced by accompanying wines. The menu, which changes frequently, might include miso seaweed broth with geoduck, crab-crusted rockfish with trout roe and stinging nettle sauce, and pear-lemon-thyme tart with caramel ice.

Mornings start with a huge breakfast tray of elegant gourmet goodies. After polishing this off, you might consider taking a long walk on the beach, because lunch (also included in the tariff) soon follows.

Address: *1528 Whiffen Spit Rd., R.R. 4, Sooke, B.C. V0S 1N0, tel. 604/642–3421 or 604/642–4944, fax 604/642–6988.*
Accommodations: *8 double rooms with baths, 5 suites.*
Amenities: *Fireplaces, decanters of port, coffeemakers, phones, balconies or patios in all rooms; double Jacuzzi baths, wet bars, or hot tubs in some rooms; restaurant, limited room service, gift shop; fishing and scuba-diving charters, nature tours.*
Rates: *$195–$225, suites $275; full breakfast and lunch. AE, MC, V.*
Restrictions: *No smoking indoors.*

Borthwick Country Manor

Flower boxes and awnings grace this Tudor-style home built in 1979 on Vancouver Island's Saanich Peninsula. It is ideally located in the quiet countryside within minutes of Victoria, Butchart Gardens, the airport, and the Washington and British Columbia ferries.

Pretty flower arrangements with coordinated floral bedspreads, piles of fluffy pillows, and a mixture of Canadian, Victorian, and Edwardian antiques create a bright, cheery tone in guest rooms. One room has a half canopy bed with a rose and violet spread and an Edwardian dresser, while the largest room is dominated by an eye-catching Canadiana four-poster bedstead.

The large fireplace in the formal living room is a cozy spot to chat, read, or get acquainted with the friendly house cat, Smokey. Just beyond are French doors that open onto gardens and a hot tub in the backyard. Hosts Ann and Brian Reid, originally from England, serve guests English repasts: a breakfast of eggs, sausages, bacon, fried tomatoes, and muffins with homemade jam, and afternoon tea.

Address: *9750 Ardmore Dr., R.R. 2, Sidney, B.C. V8L 3S1, tel. 604/656–9498.*
Accommodations: *1 double room with bath, 3 doubles share 1 bath, 1 2-bedroom room with bath.*
Amenities: *Cable TV, guest phone, hot tub, afternoon tea, fishing charters, children welcome.*
Rates: *$65–$130; full breakfast. MC, V.*
Restrictions: *No smoking indoors, no pets.*

Chesterman's Beach Bed and Breakfast

When Joan Dublanko visited the breathtaking southern coast of Vancouver Island in the early 1970s, she knew immediately that she never wanted to leave. She bought and learned to operate a salmon trawler until she'd saved enough money to purchase oceanfront property and build a home.

She and her young daughter live on the second floor of the West Coast contemporary Joan designed and built in 1984. The main floor of the home is given over to a two-bedroom suite with sauna, full kitchen, and fireplace. A charming garden cottage also has a kitchen, but no view of the ocean. The cozy room above the garage enjoys peekaboo views through the trees.

Just outside, tidal pools, little islands, sea caves, and rocky crevices punctuate the sandy beach. There are no signs directing tourists to this romantic retreat just beyond Pacific Rim National Park, so the peaceful atmosphere remains undisturbed.

Address: *1345 Chesterman's Beach Rd., Box 72, Tofino, B.C. V0R 2Z0, tel. 604/725–3726.*
Accommodations: *1 double room with bath, 1 2-bedroom housekeeping suite, 1 housekeeping cottage.*
Amenities: *Bikes, boogie boards.*
Rates: *$95–$150; Continental breakfast. MC, V.*
Restrictions: *No smoking indoors; 2-night minimum June–Sept.*

Greystone Manor

This 1918 cross-gabled house, one of the oldest in the Comox Valley, sits snugly amid an acre and a half of landscaped gardens overlooking the Coast Mountains across quiet Comox Bay. The lovely stained-fir paneling in the living and dining rooms is the backdrop to a mixture of Victorian and modern furniture brought from England by owners Mike and Mo Shipton when they emigrated to British Columbia.

Upstairs, the four plain, sunny bedrooms have queen, double, or twin beds, ruffled curtains on tall windows, and antique or white wicker furnishings. Most popular is a corner room with grand views through windows on three sides. There are two shared bathrooms, one with a claw-foot tub, the other with a shower.

Leisure options include meandering through the gardens; hiking to the pebble beach to watch sea lions playing in the bay; sipping coffee or tea on the veranda; or curling up with a book in the living room, next to the fire in the wood-burning stove. Hot muffins, scones, pancakes, and eggs are among the breakfast choices.

Address: *4014 Haas Rd., R.R. 6, Site 684–C2, Courtenay, B.C. V9N 8H9, tel. 604/338–1422.*
Accommodations: *4 double rooms share 2 baths.*
Amenities: *Piano, nature paths.*
Rates: *$58; full breakfast. MC, V.*
Restrictions: *No smoking, no pets.*

Malahat Farm Guest House

A handsome Edwardian farmhouse set in a quiet meadow surrounded by orchards and livestock pastures, Malahat Farm was one of the earliest homesteads in Sooke. In 1979, Diana and George Clare lovingly restored the 1910 structure and named each of the guest rooms after members of the Anderson family, the original homesteaders.

Bedrooms are country cozy, with down comforters, reproduction four-poster "beehive" beds, ruffled curtains, and claw-foot tubs. The two larger rooms on the main floor have fireplaces with wood mantles.

Guests often rise early to gather eggs and pick blackberries for Diana's generous farm-style breakfast, and usually spend time walking the meadows or visiting with the animals (the sheep, cows, peacocks, geese, chickens, cats, and dog are friendly; the large Black Angus bull is not). The hot tub in the gazebo next to the farmhouse is the best spot to soak in the serenity of the setting.

Address: *Anderson Rd., R.R. 2, Sooke, B.C. V0S 1N0, tel. and fax 604/642–6868.*
Accommodations: *4 double rooms with baths.*
Amenities: *Robes and slippers, guest phone; galoshes, mountain bikes, hot tub.*
Rates: *$90–$115; full breakfast, refreshments. No credit cards.*
Restrictions: *No smoking indoors, no pets; closed Dec. 20–28.*

Ocean Wilderness

This large, 1940s log cabin sits on 5 forested, beachfront acres 8 miles west of Sooke. In 1990, owner Marion Ralston built seven guest rooms in a rough cedar addition, and added two more during a 1993 renovation. An auction buff, she's furnished her home with a fine collection of Victorian antiques.

High beds with canopies and ruffled bed linens dominate the spacious guest rooms. For romantics, the best room choices are Captain's Quarter's and Pacific Panorama which both have soaker tubs set before windows with views of the Strait of Juan de Fuca and the Olympic Mountains.

In the dining room, a chandelier hangs over a long table set with crystal, china, and silver for Marion's elegant breakfasts. Outside, stepping-stones lead to a hot tub housed in a gazebo, and a path descends to the beach cove where Marion often hosts seafood feasts on summer evenings.

Address: *109 W. Coast Rd., R.R. 2, Sooke, B.C. V0S 1N0, tel. and fax 604/646–2116.*
Accommodations: *9 double rooms with baths.*
Amenities: *Minirefrigerators, private decks or patios, picnic lunches and dinners available; hot tub, hiking trails.*
Rates: *$85–$175, suites $185; full breakfast. MC, V.*
Restrictions: *No smoking indoors.*

Pine Lodge Farm

Avid collectors of antiques, Clifford and Barbara Clark needed a place large enough to store all their treasures; thus evolved the Pine Lodge Farm, the roomy board-and-batten "wilderness-style" home that they built. Completed in 1983, the house incorporates an amazing variety of antiques, including panes of stained glass, wooden doors, a graceful balustrade and banister, and refitted light fixtures.

Fine-grained woods (hemlock and fir) complement rather than compete with their furniture collection. Mounted animal heads, a polished hardwood floor (logged from the acreage), and a towering fieldstone-and-slate fireplace give the enormous living room a rustic tone, but an Eastlake organ, Tiffany-style lamps, and English and Welsh sideboards lend it Old World polish. The tidy second-floor rooms feature four-posters or brass beds and armoires.

Views of Satellite Channel and Salt Spring Island are an additional draw, as are the hearty, farm-style breakfasts featuring fresh eggs and fruits produced on the property.

Address: *3191 Mutter Rd., Mill Bay, B.C. V0R 2P0, tel. 604/743–4083, fax 604/743–7134.*
Accommodations: *7 doubles with baths.*
Amenities: *Nature trails.*
Rates: *$65–$85; full breakfast. MC, V.*
Restrictions: *No smoking indoors, no pets.*

Yellow Point Lodge

A kind of summer camp for adults (though it's open year-round), Yellow Point Lodge was built in the early 1900s by Gerry Hill. His son, Richard, carries on his simple philosophy of providing a relaxing retreat and satisfying meals at affordable rates. There are no phones or TVs here—just a lot of trails through 180 acres of thick, mossy forest; a huge saltwater pool; and toys galore (bikes, boats, and kayaks, to name a few).

Rooms in the main lodge are plain but comfortable, with tree-trunk beds and private decks; the water-heated towel racks are a nice touch. There is also an array of rustic cabins and cottages to choose from.

Address: *Yellow Point Rd., R.R. 3, Ladysmith, B.C. V0R 2E0, tel. 604/245–7422.*

Accommodations: *14 double rooms with baths, 25 cabins and 1 10-person barracks share 2 communal baths, 7 cottages.*

Amenities: *Sauna, hot tub, outdoor swimming pool, jogging trails, tennis, volleyball and badminton courts, mountain bikes, canoes, and rowboats; twice-weekly cutter tours in summer.*

Rates: *$97–$164; all meals included. MC, V.*

Restrictions: *No smoking in dining and living rooms, no pets; 2-night minimum on weekends, 3-night minimum on holiday weekends.*

Victoria

Fort Victoria was the first European settlement on Vancouver Island. The Hudson Bay Company, drawn by the rich fur trade, chose the sheltered southern tip of the island to establish a post in 1843 and named it for the reigning British monarch. British settlers slowly trickled in, but it wasn't until the Cariboo Gold Strike north of Vancouver in the 1850s that the town began to flourish. A steady stream of miners began filtering through to purchase supplies before heading out to the goldfields, and a booming frontier town developed as shops, saloons, and bordellos sprang up around the harbor to meet their demands.

The rough-and-tumble Barbary Coast atmosphere of the inner city was tempered by the more genteel society of British naval men, government officials, and gentlemen farmers who were also attracted to the growing community. By the time the gold supply ran out, Victoria had developed a strong economic and military foothold as a crown colony, and the established political framework stayed in place when British Columbia joined the Canadian Confederation in 1871.

This onetime English outpost clings tenaciously to its British heritage: Double-decker buses and horse-drawn carriages cruise harborside avenues lined with Edwardian lampposts draped in flower baskets; the Union Jack flutters from windows; British pubs abound; shops sell Harris tweeds, bone china, and tea cozies; and every respectable restaurant serves afternoon tea and crumpets.

However, lovely Victoria is more than just "a bit of merry Olde England"; to the many tourists who fuel the city's economy, it also offers cosmopolitan luxury resorts and shopping centers, a kaleidoscope of international restaurants, breathtaking parks and gardens, award-winning museums, and a fine opera company.

Places to Go, Sights to See

Antique Row. Stretched between Blanshard and Cook streets on Fort Street are shop upon shop selling furniture, artwork, jewelry, china, crystal, books, and nearly any other collectible one might imagine.

Bastion Square. Fine boutiques and small restaurants line this gas-lamp-lit, cobbled courtyard, which was the site of the original Fort Victoria and of the Hudson Bay Company's trading post. The *Maritime Museum of British Columbia* (28 Bastion Sq., tel. 604/385–4222), housed in the turreted former courthouse building, chronicles the extensive nautical history of the region.

Beacon Hill Park. A walk through this pretty, 184-acre park east of the Inner Harbour will lead you past abundant gardens, sandy beaches, and scenic views of the Olympic Mountains across the Strait of Juan de Fuca.

Butchart Gardens (800 Benvenuto Dr., tel. 604/652–5256). This world-famous complex on the 130-acre Butcher estate (13 mi north of downtown Victoria) offers more than 700 varieties of flowers and includes 50 acres of Japanese, Italian, and English gardens connected by winding paths. There's also a concert lawn, as well as restaurants, a gift shop, and a tearoom on the grounds.

Chinatown. The towering red Gate of Harmonious Interest on Fisgard Street marks the entrance to Chinatown, crammed with restaurants and exotic crafts and wicker shops. Narrow Fan Tan Alley was once the gambling center of the area.

Craigdarroch Castle (1050 Joan Crescent, tel. 604/592–5323). This turreted mansion on a hill overlooking Victoria was built for coal magnate Robert Dunsmuir, British Columbia's first millionaire, who died before the completion of his lavish home. Stained-glass windows, golden-oak paneling and staircase, intricate tile work, period furnishings (including an original Steinway grand piano), and numerous paintings are among the eye-catchers in this lovingly restored, fairytale castle, a must-see in Victoria.

Craigflower Manor Farm and Schoolhouse (110 Island Hwy., tel. 604/387–4697). One of four farms established by the Hudson Bay Company in its effort to colonize Vancouver Island, this Georgian farmhouse dates from 1856 and contains many of the furnishings brought from Scotland by the original overseer. The nearby schoolhouse is also worth a look.

Crystal Gardens (713 Douglas St., tel. 604/381–1213). This glass-roofed structure once housed the largest saltwater swimming pool in the British Empire and now encloses a large tropical garden and aviary. Wallabies, lemurs, and colorful toucans, flamingos, and macaws are among its residents.

Empress Hotel Tea Lobby (721 Government St., tel. 604/384–8111). No visit to Victoria is complete without afternoon tea in the lobby of the stylish Empress Hotel. Guests linger over fresh fruit, crumpets, scones, tea sandwiches, hazelnut cake, and multiple cups of tea as they gaze out the windows at the Inner Harbour and bustling Government Street. Reservations for daily sittings are a must during the busy summer months; a dress code rules out blue jeans, shorts, T-shirts, and athletic wear.

Greater Victoria Art Gallery (1040 Moss St., tel. 604/384–4101). Housed in a turn-of-the century mansion, this gallery holds one of the finest collections of Asian art in Canada, along with contemporary Canadian pieces and an array of traveling exhibitions. Don't miss the Shinto shrine in the Japanese garden outside.

Inner Harbour. This picturesque natural harbor is bordered by interesting boutiques and galleries, fine examples of 19th-century industrial architecture, and some of Victoria's kitschier tourist sights, including the *Royal London Wax Museum* (470 Belleville St., tel. 604/388–4461) and the *Pacific Undersea Garden* (490 Belleville St., tel. 604/382–5717).

Market Square (Johnson St. and Pandora Ave.). Over 40 boutiques and specialty shops now fill the restored turn-of-the-century buildings that surround a square bustling with sidewalk vendors and street entertainers.

Parliament Buildings (501 Belleville St., tel. 604/387–3046). A tour of the marbled interior of Victoria's Parliament Buildings provides a good introduction to the provincial legislative process and the history of British Columbia. The buildings are open to the public throughout the year; free guided tours are available during the summer. They are a particularly splendid sight at night, outlined in white lights that dance on the harbor.

Royal British Columbia Museum (675 Belleville St., tel. 604/387–3014). Give yourself at least half a day to take in the 12,000 years of British Columbia's history showcased in this incredible museum, considered one of the best of its kind in the world. Here you can smell the pines in the prehistoric section, walk through the streets of Old Town, explore a coal mine, poke around a replica of Captain Vancouver's ship, the *Discovery*, and sit in a native longhouse listening to potlatch songs and stories. This one should be at the top of your list.

Restaurants

Of the numerous seafood restaurants scattered around the city, **Chandler's** (1250 Wharf St., tel. 604/385–3474) never fails to please. Local fish, game, and produce are the core of the menu at the **Empress Room** (Empress Hotel, 721 Government St., tel. 604/384–8111), which features such specialties as veal sweetbreads with wild mushrooms or venison medallions with spätzle and juniper red currant sauce. Another spot for innovative, super-fresh Northwest cuisine—grilled marlin in citrus vinaigrette, crab with drawn butter and Indonesian hot-and-sour sauce, roasted chicken breast basted with a balsamic glaze—is the **Marina Restaurant** (1327 Beach Dr., tel. 604/598–8555); save room for the chocolate fetish, a feast for two that includes crème brûlée, white chocolate and Cointreau parfait, truffle torte with white chocolate sauce, warm milk chocolate soufflé, and mousse. Ask locals for dining recommendations, and the **Herald Street Cafe** (546 Herald St., tel. 604/381–1441) is bound to turn up in the conversation; the lemon veal, homemade pastas, breads, and desserts, and large selection of West Coast wines keep the customers happy. Fun and funky **Pagliacci's** (1011 Broad St., tel. 604/386–1662) is usually packed to the rafters; the Italian cuisine is all right, but the cheesecake is the primary reason to brave the crowds. The souvlaki, moussaka, and other Mediterranean specialties are good at **Periklis** (531 Yates St., tel. 604/386–3313), one of Victoria's oldest Greek restaurants. There's a fine sushi bar at **Tomoe** (726 Johnson St., tel. 604/381–0223), along with a broad selection of seafood, buckwheat noodle dishes, and Japanese standards such as tempura and teriyaki.

Tourist Information

British Columbia Ministry of Tourism (865 Hornby St., Suite 802, Vancouver, B.C. V6Z 2G3, tel. 604/660–2861 or 800/663–6000); **Tourism Victoria** (812 Wharf St., Victoria, B.C. V8W 1T3, tel. 604/382–2127, fax 604/382–6539).

Reservation Services

AA Accommodations West Bed and Breakfast Reservations Service (660 Jones Terr., Victoria, B.C. V8Z 2L7, tel. 604/479–1986); **All Seasons Bed and Breakfast Agency** (Box 5511, Station B, Victoria, B.C. V8R 6S4, tel. 604/655–7173); **Town and Country Bed and Breakfast** (2803 W. 4th Ave., Box 74542, Vancouver, B.C. V6K 1K2, tel. 604/731–5942).

Abigail's

S et in a quiet cul-de-sac just blocks from bustling Inner Harbour and within walking distance of Market Square, Antique Row, and Beacon Hill Park, this 1930s Tudor-style structure was formerly an apartment building. When he renovated Abigail's in 1985, multitalented owner Bill McKechnie (a builder, lawyer, and architect) turned it into the most romantic hotel in town.

Fanciful palm fronds, trailing ivy, and other greenery add to the charm of airy rooms done in shades of soft teal, rose, and ivory. Such touches as dimmer switches on the crystal chandeliers, two-person soaker or whirlpool tubs, vases of fresh flowers, fluffy goose-down comforters, and cozy sitting areas in front of fireplaces help create an amorous atmosphere. Bill has also eliminated such distractions as TVs or phones.

The best rooms in the house are Canterbury Bell and Orchid, named for the triangular stained-glass windows that reach up toward the peaked roof. Each has a chaise lounge beneath the colorful windows, half-canopied bed tucked into a dormer, wing chairs, Italian marble fireplace, wet bar, and hidden minirefrigerator; the roomy baths boast whirlpool tubs, wicker lounge chairs, and bidets. A canopied four-poster and leather love seat set before the fireplace in the bedroom, as well as a double whirlpool tub and bidet in the bath, make Foxglove another favorite. Tiffany and Abbey Rose on the top floor have double fireplaces that open onto both the bedroom and the bath.

In the early evening, guests gather in the well-stocked library to relax with a good book on one of the leather couches, take up a game of cards, or chat over hors d'oeuvres and sherry before the fire. The helpful concierge can make dinner arrangements or offer recommendations on the many things to see and do in Victoria.

The cheerful breakfast room has an open kitchen, so it's possible to peer over the counter and watch the chef baking fresh muffins or coffee cakes and whipping up morning specialties like eggs Abigail with smoked salmon. An able and accommodating staff are happy to arrange for cozy breakfasts in bed, splits of champagne, and Belgian truffles.

Address: *906 McClure St., Victoria, B.C. V8V 3E7, tel. 604/388–5363, fax 604/361–1905.*
Accommodations: *16 double rooms with baths.*
Amenities: *Library, pay phone, concierge service; fireplaces, whirlpool tubs, and wet bars in several rooms.*
Rates: *$112–$215; full breakfast, evening refreshments. MC, V.*
Restrictions: *No smoking indoors, no pets.*

Haterleigh Heritage House

Haterleigh Heritage House, a 1901 modified Queen Anne just blocks from the Inner Harbour, is a comfortable base for touring Victoria. After arduous restorations, the 4,400-square-foot home was opened as a bed-and-breakfast in 1990. Folks who stay here enjoy the warmth and openness of hosts Paul and Elizabeth Kelly—as well as the company of their sociable young son, Robert.

Leaded- and stained-glass windows, intricate moldings, and ornate plasterwork on 11-foot ceilings transport you to a more gracious time as you pass through the entry and into the living room of this registered historic home. This large common room hosts bookshelves, an organ, a mantled fireplace, Victorian settees, and a modern couch: The hodgepodge of simple antiques and contemporary pieces, along with the absence of Victorian clutter, helps put visitors at ease.

The guest rooms were carefully decorated: Rose-colored carpets are coordinated with floral wallpaper, rose-and-plum duvet covers, and creamy lace curtains and valances. Mounds of pillows and plump down comforters dress the beds, and tall armoires provide ample storage space. Most of the roomy bathrooms have whirlpool tubs or their original clawfoot tubs.

In the mornings, guests gather together around big dining room tables to chat over hearty family-style breakfasts of fresh juice and fruits, cereals, warm muffins and jam, and hot entrées such as eggs Benedict or mushroom quiche. A leisurely walk to the nearby Parliament Buildings or the Royal British Columbia Museum will help you work off the large morning meal.

Address: *243 Kingston St., Victoria, B.C. V8V 1V5, tel. 604/384–9995, fax 604/384–1935.*
Accommodations: *5 double rooms with baths, 1 2-bedroom room with bath, 1 suite.*
Amenities: *Whirlpool tubs in several rooms, cable TV and guest phone in living room; children welcome; transportation to and from downtown ferries and bus terminal.*
Rates: *$80–$165; full breakfast, evening sherry. MC, V.*
Restrictions: *No smoking indoors, no pets.*

Prior House

dward Gauler Prior, one of only two men to serve as both premier and lieutenant governor of British Columbia, built his Tudor Revival mansion in the prestigious Rocklands neighborhood near Government House. Constructed in 1912, this 8,500-square-foot home has 23 rooms, among them a large dining room for entertaining. Graceful innkeeper Candis Cooperrider is a font of information about Edward, who started Victoria's first theater—and was involved in a fair share of the town's scandals.

The Admiralty owned the home for many years, and it was a boarding house for an exclusive girls' school before Candis and her husband, Ted, purchased it in the 1980s. The couple continue to work hard to restore the quartersawn oak paneling and moldings, hardwood floors, and large mantled fireplaces.

The decor is posh without being stuffy, with Venetian glass chandeliers and a mixture of Victorian and Edwardian antiques. The lovely sitting room where afternoon tea and treats are served features a Victorian settee and cushioned couch. Guest chambers have a feminine appeal, with pastel walls, romantic canopied beds, and flowing, flowery drapes and table and bed covers.

The Lieutenant Governor's Suite is opulent, with a fascinating 1860s "Swedish mother-in-law" bed and other European antiques in the large bedroom; its 400-square-foot bathroom boasts a crystal chandelier, gold fixtures, green marble whirlpool tub and shower, bidet, and sitting area. The boudoir, which makes lavish use of draped Austrian floral fabrics, is the most intimate room. Darker Italian prints in the Victorian bedroom suite with Eastlake overtones give the Arbutus Room a more masculine feel. A narrow, winding servant's staircase leads to the two-bedroom Windsor Suite, which is positioned under the gables. The new, two-bedroom Garden Suite, which took over the original ballroom, features hardwood floors, a fireplace, living room, kitchen, and private entrance.

Address: *620 St. Charles St., Victoria, B.C. V8S 3N7, tel. 604/592–8847, fax 604/592–8223.*
Accommodations: *2 double rooms with baths, 2 suites, 2 housekeeping suites.*
Amenities: *Cable TV and fireplaces in 2 rooms and 2 suites, whirlpool baths in 2 suites, wet bars in 2 suites, play area.*
Rates: *$95–$150, suites $135–$250; full breakfast, afternoon tea. MC, V.*
Restrictions: *No smoking indoors, no pets; 2-night minimum on weekends and holidays.*

The Beaconsfield

S et in a 1905 Edwardian mansion, The Beaconsfield has a masculine air, its decor coordinated to its powerful architecture. Polished mahogany floors, rich paneling, stained glass, and numerous fireplaces—as well as shelves lined with old medical texts and journals—create a gentlemen's club atmosphere.

Guest rooms are furnished with down-filled chairs and love seats, velvet canopied beds, crystal chandeliers, and other Edwardian period pieces. Spacious bathrooms are outfitted with modern whirlpool baths or period claw-foot soaking tubs. The Garden Suite opens onto a small garden patio and has a bed with an arched trellis, a whirlpool tub, and a fireplace in the sitting room.

Owners Con and Judi Sollid dropped out of orthodontics and law, respectively, to combine their business acumen in managing the inn. They specialize in creative breakfast entrées such as apple French toast with amaretto yogurt topping.

Address: *998 Humboldt St., Victoria, B.C. V8V 2Z8, tel. 604/384–4044, fax 604/721–2442.*
Accommodations: *9 double rooms with baths, 2 suites.*
Amenities: *Fireplace and whirlpool tub in many rooms; library, guest phone, concierge service.*
Rates: *$110–$215, suites $235; full breakfast, afternoon tea. MC, V.*
Restrictions: *No smoking indoors, no pets.*

The Bedford

I f you like to be right in the heart of things, The Bedford on busy Government Street is a good bet. This rectangular brick structure, originally built in 1890 as a feed store, now houses a fine little hotel with an eye for personal service: During summer months, an official greeter in a uniform waves guests into the sunny, ficus-filled lobby.

Spacious guest rooms have thick, dark green carpets, mauve trim around large windows topped by balloon curtains, broad writing desks, stark white European-style bedding on painted oak frames, and tiled bathrooms. Four rooms on the west side enjoy views of the harbor and are much quieter than those facing the traffic on Government Street; there are also a few quiet interior rooms, but they seem much

smaller because they don't have large picture windows. Nice extra touches include plush bath sheets, morning coffee or tea and paper delivery, shoeshine service, and a buffet breakfast served in the L-shaped library/dining area.

Address: *1140 Government St., Victoria, B.C. V8W 1Y2, tel. 604/384–6835 or 800/665–6500, fax 604/386–8930.*
Accommodations: *36 doubles with baths, 4 suites.*
Amenities: *Cable TVs, phones in rooms; whirlpool tubs and fireplaces in some rooms; restaurant, pub; children under 6 stay free.*
Rates: *$135–$185; Continental breakfast. AE, MC, V.*
Restrictions: *No pets.*

Carberry Gardens

A 1907 gambrel-roofed, board-and-shingle home in the historic Rocklands neighborhood, Carberry Gardens is just blocks from Craigdarroch Castle, Antique Row, and the art museum. In preparation for opening their bed-and-breakfast, Lionel Usher restored the house and built reproduction furniture, while his wife, Julie, sewed quilts and robes.

The original fir floors, moldings, and staircase in the 30-foot-long entryway are eye-catching, as is the fine collection of Welsh, Scottish, and American antiques found throughout. In the three spacious second-floor rooms, the sun filters through lace curtains onto fluffy down comforters on antique bedsteads. One of the two shared bathrooms is huge, with French doors that open to a small balcony.

In the morning, guests feast on hot dishes such as croissant French toast in fresh berry sauce. The affable dog, Max, is more than happy to get acquainted with all who might give him a rub after breakfast.

Address: *1008 Carberry Gardens, Victoria, B.C. V8S 3R7, tel. 604/595–8906.*
Accommodations: *3 double rooms share 2 baths.*
Amenities: *Fireplace in 1 room, 1 room with balcony; terry robes, cable TV, piano.*
Rates: *$80; full breakfast. MC, V.*
Restrictions: *No smoking indoors, no pets.*

Holland House Inn

A wisteria-and-clematis-covered Italian Renaissance–style structure, Holland House is the unlikely showcase for an eclectic, ultramodern collection of sculpture, ceramics, charcoals, oils, and pen-and-ink works by Pacific Northwest artists—including owner Lance Olsen.

A conspicuous lack of color on the stark walls, hardwood floors, and window blinds puts more focus on the artwork, even in the spacious guest rooms with their creamy white duvet and pillow covers. The furnishings in the sitting and sleeping areas are a mixture of antiques and contemporary pieces (among them Lance's fascinating art-deco-style headboards).

Holland House is a refreshing antidote to the many Olde English–type bed-and-breakfasts in Victoria, and its James Bay location, just two blocks south of the Inner Harbour, can't be beat. However, the property is currently on the market, and it's impossible to know what changes new owners might bring.

Address: *595 Michigan St., Victoria, B.C. V8V 1S7, tel. 604/384–6644, fax 604/384–6117.*
Accommodations: *10 double rooms with baths.*
Amenities: *Cable TV and phone in rooms; 2 rooms have fireplaces, most have private entrances and balconies.*
Rates: *$115–$210; full breakfast. AE, DC, MC, V.*
Restrictions: *Smoking on balconies only, no pets.*

Joan Brown's Bed and Breakfast

In the heart of the quiet Rocklands Historic District, this stately Georgian Revival house was built in 1883 for a provincial lieutenant governor. Guests are greeted by a portico beneath a soaring stained-glass window as they make their way to the house through an arched entryway.

Owner Joan Brown has decorated the interior in light shades to soften the masculine lines of the structure. Bedrooms with Laura Ashley wallpapers and coordinating comforters have large bay windows and Oriental carpets on hardwood floors. In the largest room on the ground floor, a chandelier hangs from the 14-foot gold-leaf-trimmed ceiling above a lovely Italian sleigh daybed and comfortable king-size bed across from the fireplace.

Afternoon sherry is offered in the library. Breakfast, served in the adjoining dining room, features homemade marmalades and muffins along with baked eggs with creamed mushrooms.

Address: *729 Pemberton Rd., Victoria, B.C. V8S 3R3, tel. 604/592–5929.*
Accommodations: *1 double room with bath, 5 doubles share 3 baths, 2 2-bedroom suites.*
Amenities: *Fireplace in 2 rooms, library.*
Rates: *$80–$120; full breakfast. No credit cards.*
Restrictions: *No smoking indoors, no pets; 2-night minimum.*

Mulberry Manor

This 1924 Tudor heritage home, in a quiet neighborhood west of downtown Victoria, was the last building renowned Victorian architect Simon McClure designed; its lush grounds are the work of a gardener from the world-famous Butchart Gardens. The elegant manor has been restored and decorated to magazine-cover perfection with period antiques, crisp linens, and tiled baths.

The Angel Room, named for the cherubs on its wallpaper and in a gilt-framed oil painting, has a sunny balcony overlooking the enormous gardens that wrap around the manor. Jasmine, in country-French yellow and blue, has a wrought-iron bed facing a fireplace, a sitting room, a large bathroom with a deep soaker tub, and a balcony overlooking a pond.

Delightful hosts Susan and Tony Temple (originally from York, England) serve gourmet breakfasts at the large Georgian mahogany table, set with silver candelabra and fine china, in their stunning red dining room. The morning repast might include croissants or scones with homemade jam, fresh fruit, Swiss muesli, or eggs Benedict with smoked salmon.

Address: *611 Foul Bay Rd., Victoria, B.C. V8S 1H2, tel. 604/370–1918.*
Accommodations: *3 double rooms with baths, 1 suite.*
Amenities: *Fireplace in 1 room, balconies in 2 rooms; billiards room.*
Rates: *$95–$135, suite $150; full breakfast. MC, V.*
Restrictions: *No smoking, no pets.*

Oak Bay Beach Hotel

The first vacationers to visit Oak Bay Beach Hotel, an appealing mock Tudor–style seaside resort built in 1927, arrived by horse and buggy. Set in a very quiet, very British neighborhood not far from the sights of Victoria, the hotel enjoys a prime waterfront location (though the beach is little more than a rocky outcropping). Floral carpets, creaky floors, well-worn antiques, and afternoon high tea add to the Old World ambience.

General manager Kevin Walker takes pride in his family-run operation and makes an effort to provide extra value. For example, rates include a choice of high tea or a scenic lunch cruise on one of the hotel's small yachts.

Most of the highly individual guest rooms are appointed in antiques (lots of slipper chairs and high brass or canopy beds), though a 1992 renovation brought contemporary styling, furniture, and fixtures to some.

Address: *1175 Beach Dr., Victoria, B.C. V8S 2N2, tel. and fax 604/598–4556.*
Accommodations: *33 double rooms with baths, 18 suites.*
Amenities: *Limited room service, cable TV, phones, children under 12 stay free, no-smoking rooms available; restaurant, pub, bike rental, lunch cruises, fishing charters.*
Rates: *$98–$236, suites $370–$406; full breakfast. AE, DC, MC, V.*
Restrictions: *No pets.*

Swans

When English-born shepherd Michael Williams bought supplies for his kennel at the Buckerfield Company Feed Store in the 1950s, he never dreamed he would one day own the building and turn it into a fashionable waterfront hotel. Extensive renovations in 1988 gave the 1913 warehouse a new look, with pretty, flower-filled window grates brightening the brick exterior; a brewery, bistro, and pub on the first floor; and 25 large, apartment-like guest rooms filling the upper floors.

The high-ceilinged rooms have skylights, kitchens, oak furniture, down comforters, fresh flowers, and original Pacific Northwest art; the loft units offer sofa beds. Rooms 305 and 307 enjoy the best views of the harbor. Swans is probably the top choice for families, though on weekends you'll want to reserve rooms on the highest floors to avoid noise from the pub, one of the city's most popular watering holes.

Address: *506 Pandora Ave., Victoria, B.C. V8W 1N6, tel. 604/361–3310 or 800/668–7926, fax 604/361–3491.*
Accommodations: *9 housekeeping double rooms, 3 housekeeping studios, 13 2-bedroom housekeeping suites.*
Amenities: *In-room phone, cable TV, and fan; restaurant, pub, limited room service, laundry; free brewery tours and tastings.*
Rates: *$145–$165; breakfast not included. AE, DC, MC, V.*
Restrictions: *No pets.*

The Gulf Islands

When Captain George Vancouver traveled up the eastern coastline of Vancouver Island in the late 1790s, he dubbed the expansive body of water on which he sailed the Gulf of Georgia, thinking it led out into the open sea. After further exploration revealed that the British Columbia mainland sat to the east, the name of the waterway was changed to the Strait of Georgia, but the islands dotting it continued to be called the Gulf Islands.

Of the hundreds of islands that lie in this strait, the most popular are Galiano, Mayne, North and South Pender, Quadra, and Salt Spring. A temperate Mediterranean climate, scenic beaches, towering promontories, rolling pasturelands, and virgin forests are common to all, but each has its unique flavor.

Long, skinny Galiano, named for Spanish explorer Dionysio Galiano, was home to Coast Salish natives for centuries before the Spanish, English, and other nonaboriginal settlers arrived to stake claims. The population here is still very small (under 1,000), and the white shell beaches and thick forests remain unspoiled. Activities are generally clustered around the small commercial center of Sturdies Bay.

Middens of clam and oyster shells give evidence that tiny (15-square-mile) Mayne Island was inhabited as early as 5,000 years ago. It later became the stopover point for miners headed from Victoria to the goldfields of Fraser River and Barkersville; by the mid-1800s it had developed into the communal center of the inhabited Gulf Islands, with the first school, post office, police lockup, church, and hotel. Farm tracts and orchards established by early settlers continue to thrive today, and a bustling farmer's market is open each Saturday during harvest season. Many artists now call the island home, and several small galleries here display their work.

Salish natives were probably also the first occupants of Pender, actually two islands divided by a narrow canal dug in 1903 to allow for easier boat passage as more settlers arrived. Largely pastoral in nature, North and South Pender are the southernmost of the Gulf Islands, stretching toward the United States border. And as with many of the other islands, they are populated by artisans, farmers, and fisher folk; the lack of traffic on the network of winding, hilly roads makes it hard to believe that almost 2,000 people call Pender home.

When Captain Vancouver landed on Quadra Island in 1792, he visited an aboriginal village at Cape Mudge. The Cape Mudge band of the Kwakiutl tribe is very much in existence today, and its members still make a living fishing for herring and salmon. Quadra hosted canneries and mills by the late 19th century and heavy logging changed much of its face, but several lush wilderness areas remain, hosting such fauna as black-tailed deer, wolves, snowy owls, and the seldom-seen peregrine falcon.

Named for the saltwater springs at its north end, Salt Spring is the largest and most developed of the Gulf Islands. Among its first nonnative settlers were black Americans who came here to escape slavery in the 1850s. The agrarian tradition they established, along with Portuguese, English, German, and Japanese immigrants, remains strong, but tourism and art now support the local economy. A government wharf, two marinas, and a waterfront shopping complex at Ganges serve a community of 7,000. Ferry service into Fulford Harbour at the south end and Long Harbour at the east end connect Salt Spring with Victoria, Vancouver, and the lower Gulf Islands.

Places to Go, Sights to See

Galiano Island. The activities on Galiano are almost exclusively of the outdoor type. The long, unbroken eastern shoreline is perfect for leisurely beach walks, while the numerous coves and inlets along the western coast make it a prime area for kayaking. The best spots to view Active Pass and surrounding islands are Bluffs Park, Bellhouse Park, and Centennial Park; these are also good areas for picnicking and bird-watching. Acala Point, Porlier Pass, and Active Pass are top locations for scuba diving and fishing.

Mayne Island. Among several noteworthy vintage structures in Miners Bay are *St. Mary Magdalene Church* (ca. 1898) and the *Plumper Pass Lockup* (ca. 1896), which now houses a small museum chronicling the island's history (open July–August only). The *Active Pass Lighthouse* on Georgina Point, originally built in 1855, still signals ships into the busy waterway (open daily 1–3). In addition to scenic views of Navy Channel and Active Pass, you're bound to see soaring eagles at *Diner Bay Park*, a first-rate, community-built facility south of the ferry dock at Village Bay.

Pender Islands. Bald Cone on North Pender and Mount Norman on South Pender are the best scenic lookouts. There are over a dozen swimming beaches to explore and a Salish native archaeological site at Mortimer Spit near the one-lane trestle bridge that connects the two islands. The mild current and rich kelp beds off Tilley Point on North Pender make it a favorite dive site, and broken coastlines of coves and inlets around both islands make for fine kayaking here. A nine-hole golf course and the world's first wilderness disk (Frisbee) course on North Pender are also recreational options.

Quadra Island. Topping the list of things to see on Quadra is the *Kwakiutl Museum* (tel. 604/285–3407), an attractive modern facility that houses a collection of Kwakiutl potlatch regalia including ceremonial masks, utensils, and headdresses, along with photos of early native villages. There are petroglyphs in the park across from the museum. Pretty Cape Mudge Lighthouse, erected in 1898, stands near the point where Captain Vancouver landed. Of the nine hiking trails on Quadra, the one leading to the summit of China Mountain affords the most rewarding views of the island's lakes and coastline. For swimming and beachcombing, head to Rebecca Spit Provincial Park, north of the ferry landing at Quathiaski Cove.

Salt Spring Island. Ganges, the cultural and commercial center of Salt Spring, is the site of ArtCraft, a summer-long art, crafts, theater, music, and dance festival. There are bargains aplenty to be had at the Saturday market based in nearby Centennial Park. St. Mary Lake, Cusheon Lake, and Vesuvius Bay have the best warm-water swimming, and a hike to the summit of Mt. Maxwell affords the best views of the island and surrounding ocean. A walk through the church graveyards at St. Paul's and St. Mark's gives visitors a feel for the island's history. *Mouat's Trading Company* (Fulford-Ganges Rd.), built in 1912, is still functioning as a community store.

Restaurants

The best dining in the islands is found at the many fine country inns, which by and large offer innovative Pacific Northwest cuisine featuring local produce, seafood, and lamb. Those that have developed strong reputations include **April Point Lodge** (Quadra Island, tel. 604/285–2222), **Hastings House** (Salt Spring Island, tel. 604/537–2362), **Oceanwood Country Inn** (Mayne Island, tel. 604/539–5074), and **Woodstone Country Inn** (Galiano Island, tel. 604/539–2022). For something really different, try the historical theme dinners at **Fernhill Lodge** (Mayne Island, tel. 604/539–2544).

Tourist Information

British Columbia Ministry of Tourism (865 Hornby St., Suite 802, Victoria, B.C. V6Z 2G3, tel. 604/660–2861 or 800/663–6000); **Galiano Island Travel Infocentre** (Box 73, Galiano, B.C. V0N 1P0, tel. 604/539–2233); **Mayne Island Chamber of Commerce** (General Delivery, Mayne Island, B.C. V0N 2J0); **Salt Spring Island Travel Infocentre** (121 Lower Ganges Rd., Box 111, Ganges, B.C. V0S 1E0, tel. 604/537–5252, fax 604/537–4276); **Tourism Association of Vancouver Island** (Dept. 001, Suite 302–45 Bastion Sq., Victoria, B.C. V8W 1J1, tel. 604/382–3551, fax 604/382–3523). Ferry schedules are available from **B.C. Ferries** (tel. 604/656–0757 [Victoria] or 604/685–1021 [Vancouver]).

Reservation Services

AA Accommodations West Bed and Breakfast Reservations Service (660 Jones Terr., Victoria, B.C. V8Z 2L7, tel. 604/479–1986, fax 604/479–9999); **All Seasons Bed and Breakfast Agency** (Box 5511, Station B, Victoria, B.C. V8R 6S4, tel. 604/595–2337); **Canadian Gulf Islands Bed and Breakfast Reservation Service** (Southwind Dr., Montague Harbour, Galiano Island, B.C. V0N 1P0, tel. 604/539–5390); **Town and Country Bed and Breakfast** (2803 W. 4th Ave., Box 74542, Vancouver, B.C. V6K 1K2, tel. 604/731–5942).

Hastings House

One of the finest country inns in North America and a member of the prestigious Relais et Châteaux group, Hastings House knows how to pamper its guests. The centerpiece of this luxurious 30-acre seaside resort is a Tudor-style manor built by the Hastings family in 1940 to resemble their home in England. It comes replete with exposed cedar beams and a cowled fireplace constructed from 21 tons of stone quarried on the property.

A broad assortment of accommodations is offered here: rooms in the manor or the farmhouse; cliffside or garden cottages; and suites in the reconstructed barn. All are plushly furnished with fine antiques (primarily English) and follow an English country theme, with such extras as eiderdowns, fireplaces, stocked bars, covered porches or decks, and idyllic views of gardens, pastures, or the harbor. Laura Ashley, Sanderson, and Les Olivades fabrics feature prominently in the individually decorated suites: One sunny chamber is done in shades of French-country yellow and blue; another cooler, more intimate one has a Wedgwood blue and cream color scheme.

Individual service and attention to detail are of prime importance to innkeeper Ian Cowley. He provides many wonderful touches—bountiful flower arrangements, little gifts left on pillows at evening turndown, thermoses of early morning coffee and juice.

Guests can choose to have a deluxe Continental tray delivered to their rooms in the morning or visit the dining room for a multicourse breakfast.

Elegant dinners in the manor house are a major part of the Hastings House experience, with formal, five-course meals created by Mr. Cowley himself, who is an outstanding chef. The menu might include roasted garlic and marjoram soup, pan-fried Digby scallops in a sweet yellow pepper sauce, and *mille-feuille* of raspberries with framboise cream.

Address: *160 Upper Ganges Rd., Box 1110, Ganges, Salt Spring Island, B.C. V0S 1E0, tel. 604/537-2362 or 800/661-9255, fax 604/537-5333.*
Accommodations: *3 double rooms with baths, 6 suites, 2 2-bedroom suites, 1 2-bedroom housekeeping suite.*
Amenities: *Phone in rooms, TVs available, restaurant, limited room service; croquet, nature trails, mountain bikes.*
Rates: *$310, suites $370–$440; full breakfast. AE, MC, V.*
Restrictions: *No pets; 2-night minimum on weekends, 3-night minimum on holiday weekends, closed Thanksgiving–mid-Mar.*

Oceanwood Country Inn

The Oceanwood Country Inn on Mayne Island has developed a strong following—no doubt due in large part to its lovely waterfront location overlooking Navy Channel and several Gulf Islands. Originally constructed in 1979, this Tudor-style home on 10 quiet, forested acres was renovated and expanded in 1990 by Marilyn and Jonathan Chilvers. At press time, plans were afoot to move the dining room so that it overlooks the water, and to increase the number of guest rooms to 12. Work should be completed in time for the inn's March 1995 opening.

The stylish English country decor helps transport guests to a quieter era. Spacious, airy guest rooms are inviting rather than formal or fussy; all have cozy down comforters on comfortable beds, cushioned chairs in brightly lit reading areas, and grand ocean views from balconies or patios. Some are outfitted with broad French doors, romantic fireplaces, and raised whirlpool tubs. Pastel wall stencils matching the upholstery and curtains framing the balcony doors and whirlpool tub in the bedroom make the Rose Room a particular favorite, while a handsome Victorian mahogany bedroom suite makes the Geranium Room another popular choice.

The numerous common areas include a game room as well as a spacious living room and cozy library, both with fireplaces. Other activities include leisurely strolls with Kelly, the golden Lab; biking along the rural roads of Mayne Island; and soaking in the hot tub on the expansive terrace by the ocean.

The dining room, open to the public for dinner, features fresh regional cuisine—some of the best you'll find anywhere in the islands—emphasizing local ingredients. Tomato and Dungeness crab soup, wild mushroom and goat cheese ravioli, herb and garlic pork loin with rhubarb and lemon *confit*, and chocolate-almond cake with raspberry *coulis* are some of the selections you might find on the four-course prix-fixe menu. Overnight guests return to this room in the morning for breakfasts of fresh juices, home-mixed granola, yogurt with fruit puree, and hot entrées such as omelets or orange French toast.

Address: *630 Dinner Bay Rd., Mayne Island, B.C. V0N 2J0, tel. 604/539–5074, fax 604/539–3002.*
Accommodations: *8 doubles with baths.*
Amenities: *Restaurant, sauna, hot tub, library, VCR/video library, game room, conference room, guest pay phone; bicycles.*
Rates: *$110–$200; full breakfast, afternoon tea. MC, V.*
Restrictions: *Smoking in library and outside only, no pets; 2-night minimum on weekends, 3-night minimum on holiday weekends, closed Jan.–Feb.*

April Point Lodge and Fishing Resort

Operated for almost 50 years by the friendly Peterson family, April Point Lodge has garnered a whopping amount of repeat business. Spread across a point of Quadra Island stretching into Discovery Passage, the 1944 cedar lodge is surrounded by cabins and guest houses. The spacious accommodations are comfortably homey rather than luxurious; most rooms have kitchen facilities, fireplaces, and sundecks, and a few are equipped with Jacuzzi baths and outdoor hot tubs.

The dining room and lounge in the main lodge host an amazing collection of Kwakiutl and Haida art. On warm summer nights, native feasts are held on the beach: Salmon roasted over an open fire, steamed scallops, prawns, and clams are accompanied by wines from the lodge's extensive cellar.

Address: *1000 April Point Rd., Box 1, Campbell River, B.C. V9W 4Z9, tel. 604/285-2222, fax 604/285-2411.*
Accommodations: *16 double rooms with baths, 4 2- to 3-bedroom suites, 1 3-bedroom housekeeping suite, 12 housekeeping guest houses and lodges with 1–6 bedrooms.*
Amenities: *Cable TV, phones in rooms; restaurant, lounge, gift shop, gym, limited room service; swimming pool, trails, bikes, marina, seaplane dock, salmon charters and nature tours available.*
Rates: *$189; suites, cabins, and guest houses $99–$395; Continental breakfast. AE, D, DC, MC, V.*
Restrictions: *Some units closed Nov.–Mar.*

Beach House Bed & Breakfast

Jon and Maureen De West's dream of operating a bed-and-breakfast came to fruition when they purchased this West Coast contemporary house on a sloping beach on Salt Spring Island. From here, the sunsets over Stuart Channel and Vancouver Island are stunning.

Curved archways give the interior a vaguely Spanish Colonial feel, but the furnishings and decor are all American. Two upstairs rooms have private entrances and balconies; a romantic, cedar-lined cottage sits over the boathouse at water's edge. Extras include eiderdown comforters, thick terry robes, slippers, fruit platters, decanters of sherry, and fresh flowers.

Maureen, a Cordon Bleu–trained chef, serves a bountiful breakfast; there are often fresh baked goods with homemade preserves and jams, sliced seasonal fruits, and hot entrées such as seafood crepes.

Address: *930 Sunset Dr., Salt Spring Island, B.C. V8K 1E6, tel. 604/537-2879, fax 604/537-4747.*
Accommodations: *2 doubles with baths, 1 housekeeping cottage.*
Amenities: *Robes and slippers, sherry and fruit or chocolates; boat charters and kayak tours available.*
Rates: *$165–$195; full breakfast, afternoon refreshments. MC, V.*
Restrictions: *No smoking indoors, no pets; closed last 2 weeks in Dec.*

Cliffside Inn

Innkeeper Penny Tomlin is the third generation of her family to live on this scenic North Pender Island property. Her charming oceanfront inn, a Wedgwood blue board-and-batten contemporary with flowering window boxes under white bay windows, was constructed in 1985. Its outstanding features are a glass solarium dining room and a cliff-hanger deck with hot tub overlooking Navy Channel.

The Channel View Suite has chintz-covered wing chairs near a fireplace, a bay window with ocean views, and a terrazzo patio opening onto a fire pit and the seaside lawn. For more privacy, there's a small, homey cottage on the property.

Following a breakfast that might feature baked stuffed apples with honey and pecans, rhubarb and raspberry compote, homemade muffins, and eggs Florentine with smoked salmon, guests gather on the deck to watch Penny feed the resident eagles.

Address: *4230 Armadale Rd., Box 50, North Pender Island, B.C. V0N 2M0, tel. 604/629–6691.*
Accommodations: *2 suites, 1 2-bedroom housekeeping cottage.*
Amenities: *Cable TV available in 2 rooms; hot tub, massage, reflexology, kayak platform; dinner packages, seasonal nature cruises and kayak tours available.*
Rates: *$100–$185; full breakfast. MC, V.*
Restrictions: *No smoking indoors, no children under 16; 2-night minimum on weekends, 3-night minimum on holiday weekends.*

Corbett House

When convivial innkeepers Linda and John Eckfeldt came to Pender Island to go bicycling, they never dreamed they would end up buying the bed-and-breakfast they visited. Their creamy yellow 1902 farmhouse is named for the Corbetts, a pioneer family who built the general store and started the island's post office.

The interior is a hodgepodge of country-style antiques, John's handcrafted furniture, and locally produced artwork, much of it for sale. The upstairs Red, Blue, and Yellow rooms are simply but comfortably furnished with a mixture of Early American and contemporary pieces. Red and Blue have private half-baths and share a shower; Yellow has a full bath and a sundeck.

Edible flowers add a lovely touch to the four-course breakfast served in a dining room that overlooks the orchard. There are hiking, biking, fishing, sailing, and tennis nearby; the less active can gaze at ducks on the summer pond, sheep in the yard, and deer in the meadow.

Address: *Corbett Rd., R.R. 1, North Pender Island, B.C. V0N 2M0, tel. 604/629–6305.*
Accommodations: *1 double room with bath, 2 doubles with half-baths share 1 shower.*
Amenities: *Boots and binoculars for hikes, ferry pickup service.*
Rates: *$85–$95; full breakfast. No credit cards.*
Restrictions: *No smoking indoors, no pets; 2-night minimum on weekends.*

Fernhill Lodge

Constructed of wood from the property, this 1983 West Coast cedar contemporary is host to fantastical theme rooms—Moroccan, East Indian, Edwardian, Japanese, Colonial, Jacobean, and French. An authentic 17th-century yeoman's bed and chest in the Jacobean Room and the handwrought canopy bed and wood carvings in the Moroccan Room are examples of the attention given to detail here.

To complete the experience, Englishman Brian Crumblehulme and his wife, Mary, offer extraordinary historical dinners several nights a week. Breakfasts are rather less exotic.

Felines Tippy, Muffin, Cassie, and Champers will happily occupy a lap when you're relaxing in the sunroom or soaking in the view of Pender Island and Navy Channel from the deck; if you prefer, they'll accompany you on explorations of the Elizabethan knot garden and the medieval "garden of physic" on the 5-acre grounds.

Address: *Fernhill Rd., R.R. 1 C–4, Mayne Island, B.C. V0N 2J0, tel. 604/539–2544.*
Accommodations: *7 double rooms with baths.*
Amenities: *Hot tubs in 2 rooms; sauna, library; dinner and bikes available.*
Rates: *$90–$135; full breakfast. MC, V.*
Restrictions: *No smoking indoors, no pets; 2-night minimum on holiday weekends.*

Old Farmhouse Bed and Breakfast

Formerly the manager of the popular Umberto's Il Giardino in Vancouver, German-born Gerti Fuss now operates this delightful bed-and-breakfast with the assistance of her husband, Karl (also from Germany). Their gray-and-white saltbox farmhouse is set in a quiet Salt Spring Island meadow edged by towering trees. The architectural style of the main house, a registered historic property built in 1895, is echoed in the four-room wing with private entrance constructed by Karl in 1989.

Sunlight filters through lace curtains in country-comfortable guest rooms with pine bedsteads, down comforters, floral chintz fabrics, and wicker chairs. The two upstairs rooms have cathedral ceilings and private balconies. The bed in one of the downstairs rooms is tucked into an alcove beneath stained-glass windows. Breakfast in the dining room begins with Gerti's fresh-daily baked goods, followed by an entrée such as smoked salmon soufflé.

Address: *1077 Northend Rd., Salt Spring Island, B.C. V8K 1L9, tel. 604/537–4113, fax 604/537–4969.*
Accommodations: *4 double rooms with baths.*
Amenities: *Ferry pickup service, canoe; mystery weekends available.*
Rates: *$125; full breakfast, refreshments on arrival. MC, V.*
Restrictions: *No smoking indoors, no pets; 2-night minimum on holiday weekends.*

Sky Valley Place

Perched on 11 mountain-hugging, forested acres of Salt Spring Island, the aptly named Sky Valley Place enjoys spectacular views of the Gulf Islands and of Vancouver's North Shore mountains across the Strait of Georgia. This L-shaped West Coast contemporary cedar home has ivy-covered beams and a 20-by-40-foot heated outdoor swimming pool.

Proprietors Pauline and Florian Baumstark, originally from Germany, have created a romantic, sunny hideaway. Handcrafted pine furniture fills living and dining rooms that seem to have more windows than walls. Clean-lined bedrooms are country elegant, with floral print curtains and coordinated comforters and pillows on cozy wicker chairs. One room has a high, balloon-canopied bed as well.

Fresh berries and herbs from Pauline's gardens are served at breakfast; her mushroom and herb crepes are delicious. After eating, guests can meander through the forest or just admire panoramic scenery from the living room.

Address: *421 Sky Valley Rd., Salt Spring Island, B.C. V0S 1E0, tel. 604/537–4210, fax 604/537–4220.*
Accommodations: *4 double rooms with baths.*
Amenities: *Robes, Jacuzzi in 1 room; swimming pool.*
Rates: *$110; full breakfast. MC, V.*
Restrictions: *No smoking indoors, no children, no pets; closed Oct.–Feb.*

Suitl Lodge

Tom and Ann own this 1927 British Colonial bungalow on 20 wooded acres on picturesque Montague Bay. Family photos from the 1920s and heavy Art Deco furnishings re-create a sense of lodge life in an earlier era. The simple guest rooms have throw rugs on dark hardwood floors and beds tucked into window nooks; the shared bathrooms have antique ball-foot tubs and small corner sinks.

Out in the bay, a sleek catamaran waits to take skipper Tom and his guests on nature-watching trips. Canoes and kayaks are also available to paddle to secluded beaches nearby. Fuel for the day's activities comes from Ann's breakfasts of fresh fruit, home-baked muffins, cereals, and egg dishes.

Address: *637 Southwind Rd., Montague Harbour, Galiano Island, B.C. V0N 1P0, tel. 604/539–2930, fax 604/539–5390.*
Accommodations: *7 double rooms share 3 baths.*
Amenities: *Badminton, nature trails; nature-watching and picnic cruises, kayak and canoe rentals, tours.*
Rates: *$65–$75; full breakfast. MC, V.*
Restrictions: *No smoking indoors, no pets; 2-night minimum on holiday weekends, closed mid-Dec.–mid-Jan.*

Tsa-Kwa-Luten Lodge

Owned and operated by the Cape Mudge band of the Kwakiutl tribe, Tsa-Kwa-Luten Lodge is set on a high bluff amid 1,100 acres of forest on Quadra Island; it's a 10-minute ferry ride from Campbell River on Vancouver Island. Authentic Pacific Coast native food and cultural activities are featured here: Guests are invited to take part in ceremonial dances held occasionally in the resort's longhouse-style lounge and to visit nearby petroglyphs to make rubbings.

Resembling a modern hotel, the lodge has guest rooms that are uniform in design and decor; all have contemporary oak furnishings, mauve bedspreads, Kwakiutl artwork, large windows, and porches or balconies; several have fireplaces or lofts. Four beachfront cabins offer fireplaces, whirlpool tubs, kitchen facilities, and private verandas.

Address: *Lighthouse Rd., Box 460, Quathiaski Cove, Quadra Island, B.C. V0P 1N0, tel. 604/285–2042 or 800/665–7745, fax 604/285–2532.*
Accommodations: *14 double rooms with baths, 8 lofts (sleep 6) with baths, 4 2-bedroom suites, 3 2-bedroom housekeeping cabins, 1 4-bedroom housekeeping cabin.*
Amenities: *Phone in all rooms, fireplace in some rooms; restaurant, lounge, sauna, outdoor hot tub, fitness room; rental bikes, guided salmon-fishing charters.*
Rates: *$115–$170, suites and cabins $195–$460; breakfast not included. AE, DC, MC, V.*
Restrictions: *No pets.*

Weston Lake Inn

Amiable Susan Evans and her partner, Ted Harrison, were drawn to the Gulf Islands for years before they decided to purchase 10 pastoral acres and a contemporary English cottage–style cedar home on a hillside on Salt Spring Island. Their delightful bed-and-breakfast is also a working farm, producing fresh eggs, vegetables, beef, and flowers for island residents. Among the many attractions here are gardens, nearby Weston Lake, a hot tub, and plenty of surrogate pets to keep you company.

Canadian art, photos of sailboats, and Ted's fine petit point embroidery adorn the walls of the guest rooms, which are country cheerful with ruffled curtains, floral bedspreads, and fresh flowers; windows and skylights brighten the small bathrooms. On a formal Jacobean-style dining table, Susan serves breakfasts of homemade granola, garden-grown tomatoes, herb scrambled eggs, and other tempting dishes featuring the farm's produce.

Address: *813 Beaver Point Rd., Salt Spring Island, B.C. V8K 1X9, tel. 604/653–4311.*
Accommodations: *3 double rooms with baths.*
Amenities: *Cable TV, VCR, movie library, guest phone, library lounge, hot tub, nature trails; sailing charters available.*
Rates: *$85–$105; full breakfast. AE, MC, V.*
Restrictions: *No smoking indoors, no pets; 2-night minimum on holiday weekends.*

Woodstone Country Inn

The Woodstone Country Inn sits on the edge of a forest overlooking a meadow. Innkeepers Gail and Andrew Nielsen-Pich will loan guests gear to scout out birds in the glade just outside.

Stenciled walls and tall windows bring the pastoral setting into spacious bedrooms furnished in a mixture of wicker, antiques, and English country prints. Most of the rooms have fireplaces and patios; several feature oversize tubs.

Works by local artists decorate the walls of the living room, where wing chairs and a couch are grouped around the fireplace. Breakfasts, served in the dining room, often feature Eggs Montague (an egg baked in a croissant with salmon) or waffles with fresh blueberry sauce. Guests can also take four-course dinners here.

Address: *Georgeson Bay Rd., R.R. 1, Galiano Island, B.C. V0N 1P0, tel. 604/539–2022.*
Accommodations: *12 double rooms with baths.*
Amenities: *Fireplace; dinner available; ferry pickup service, nature trails, bird-watching platform.*
Rates: *$75–$125; full breakfast, afternoon tea. AE, MC, V.*
Restrictions: *No smoking indoors, no pets; 2-night minimum on holiday and summer weekends.*

Directory 1
Alphabetical

Directory 2
Geographical

Notes

Notes

Notes

Notes

Notes

Fodor's Travel Guides

Available at bookstores everywhere, or call 1–800–533–6478, 24 hours a day.

U.S. Guides

Alaska

Arizona

Boston

California

Cape Cod, Martha's Vineyard, Nantucket

The Carolinas & the Georgia Coast

Chicago

Colorado

Florida

Hawaii

Las Vegas, Reno, Tahoe

Los Angeles

Maine, Vermont, New Hampshire

Maui

Miami & the Keys

New England

New Orleans

New York City

Pacific North Coast

Philadelphia & the Pennsylvania Dutch Country

The Rockies

San Diego

San Francisco

Santa Fe, Taos, Albuquerque

Seattle & Vancouver

The South

The U.S. & British Virgin Islands

USA

The Upper Great Lakes Region

Virginia & Maryland

Waikiki

Walt Disney World and the Orlando Area

Washington, D.C.

Foreign Guides

Acapulco, Ixtapa, Zihuatanejo

Australia & New Zealand

Austria

The Bahamas

Baja & Mexico's Pacific Coast Resorts

Barbados

Berlin

Bermuda

Brittany & Normandy

Budapest

Canada

Cancún, Cozumel, Yucatán Peninsula

Caribbean

China

Costa Rica, Belize, Guatemala

The Czech Republic & Slovakia

Eastern Europe

Egypt

Euro Disney

Europe

Florence, Tuscany & Umbria

France

Germany

Great Britain

Greece

Hong Kong

India

Ireland

Israel

Italy

Japan

Kenya & Tanzania

Korea

London

Madrid & Barcelona

Mexico

Montréal & Québec City

Morocco

Moscow & St. Petersburg

The Netherlands, Belgium & Luxembourg

New Zealand

Norway

Nova Scotia, Prince Edward Island & New Brunswick

Paris

Portugal

Provence & the Riviera

Rome

Russia & the Baltic Countries

Scandinavia

Scotland

Singapore

South America

Southeast Asia

Spain

Sweden

Switzerland

Thailand

Tokyo

Toronto

Turkey

Vienna & the Danube Valley

Special Series

Fodor's Affordables

Caribbean

Europe

Florida

France

Germany

Great Britain

Italy

London

Paris

**Fodor's Bed &
Breakfast and
Country Inns Guides**

America's Best B&Bs

California

Canada's Great
Country Inns

Cottages, B&Bs and
Country Inns of
England and Wales

Mid-Atlantic Region

New England

The Pacific
Northwest

The South

The Southwest

The Upper Great
Lakes Region

The Berkeley Guides

California

Central America

Eastern Europe

Europe

France

Germany & Austria

Great Britain &
Ireland

Italy

London

Mexico

Pacific Northwest &
Alaska

Paris

San Francisco

**Fodor's Exploring
Guides**

Australia

Boston &
New England

Britain

California

The Caribbean

Florence & Tuscany

Florida

France

Germany

Ireland

Italy

London

Mexico

New York City

Paris

Prague

Rome

Scotland

Singapore & Malaysia

Spain

Thailand

Turkey

Fodor's Flashmaps

Boston

New York

Washington, D.C.

Fodor's Pocket Guides

Acapulco

Bahamas

Barbados

Jamaica

London

New York City

Paris

Puerto Rico

San Francisco

Washington, D.C.

Fodor's Sports

Cycling

Golf Digest's Best
Places to Play

Hiking

The Insider's Guide
to the Best Canadian
Skiing

Running

Sailing

Skiing in the USA &
Canada

USA Today's Complete
Four Sports Stadium
Guide

**Fodor's Three-In-Ones
(guidebook, language
cassette, and phrase
book)**

France

Germany

Italy

Mexico

Spain

**Fodor's
Special-Interest
Guides**

Complete Guide to
America's National
Parks

Condé Nast Traveler
Caribbean Resort and
Cruise Ship Finder

Cruises and Ports
of Call

Euro Disney

France by Train

Halliday's New
England Food
Explorer

Healthy Escapes

Italy by Train

London Companion

Shadow Traffic's New
York Shortcuts and
Traffic Tips

Sunday in New York

Sunday in San
Francisco

Touring Europe

Touring USA:
Eastern Edition

Walt Disney World and
the Orlando Area

Walt Disney World
for Adults

**Fodor's Vacation
Planners**

Great American
Learning Vacations

Great American
Sports & Adventure
Vacations

Great American
Vacations

Great American
Vacations for Travelers
with Disabilities

National Parks and
Seashores of the East

National Parks
of the West

**The Wall Street
Journal Guides to
Business Travel**

Join us in updating the next edition of your Fodor's guide

Title of Guide:

---

1 Hotel ☐ Restaurant ☐ *(check one)*

Name

Number/Street

City/State/Country

Comments

---

2 Hotel ☐ Restaurant ☐ *(check one)*

Name

Number/Street

City/State/Country

Comments

---

3 Hotel ☐ Restaurant ☐ *(check one)*

Name

Number/Street

City/State/Country

Comments

Your Name *(optional)*

Address

General Comments